WORLD HISTORY

IN

DOCUMENTS

WORLD HISTORY
IN
DOCUMENTS

•

A COMPARATIVE READER
SECOND EDITION

•

Edited by Peter N. Stearns

NEW YORK UNIVERSITY PRESS
New York and London

NEW YORK UNIVERSITY PRESS
New York and London
www.nyupress.org

Library of Congress Cataloging-in-Publication Data

World history in documents : a comparative reader / edited by Peter N. Stearns. — 2nd. ed.
　　p. cm.
　Includes bibliographical references and index.
　ISBN-13:　978-0-8147-4047-7 (cloth : alk. paper)
　ISBN-10:　0-8147-4047-2 (cloth : alk. paper)
　ISBN-13:　978-0-8147-4048-4 (pbk. : alk. paper)
　ISBN-10:　0-8147-4048-0 (pbk. : alk. paper)
　1. World history—Sources.　I. Stearns, Peter N.
　D5.W67 2007
　909—dc22　　　　2007025223

New York University Press books are printed on acid-free paper
and their binding materials are chosen for strength and durability.

Manufactured in the United States of America
c 10 9 8 7 6 5 4 3 2 1
p 10 9 8 7 6 5 4 3 2 1

CONTENTS

v

PART IV: The Long Nineteenth Century   219

ACKNOWLEDGMENTS

Assistance from Steven Beaudoin and Carl Zimring, both experienced world history teachers, was invaluable. Clio Stearns provided additional service for the new edition. Karen Callas and Alicia Smallbrock assured vital clerical support. Several colleagues, including Andrew Barnes, Erick Langer, Michael Adas, Donald Sutton and Abraham Marcus, provided very useful suggestions. I wish to thank also what is now several generations of world history students at George Mason University, whose interest and good ideas continue to motivate and educate me.

INTRODUCTION

Comparative World History

This book advances an understanding of world history and develops two of the essential skills the study of world history should promote: the ability to deal with primary sources and the ability to compare important aspects of major societies.

Primary sources—documents and other materials prepared at various times and places in the world's history—offer a distinctive means of understanding the nature of the past. They invite readers to put themselves in other people's shoes— to consider patterns of thinking and behavior different from our own. They also teach skills in assessment, interpretation, and the construction of arguments from data that can be applied to contemporary materials as well. Figuring out the meaning of diverse materials indeed connects history directly to contemporary analysis.

Comparison is also vital. World historians are eager to discuss contact among major societies and the operation of global forces such as trade or migration. But they also must provide the means of improving our understanding of these partially separate patterns, as well as diverse reactions to common forces. Comparison forces decisions about what is really distinctive about a society and what is shared—perhaps beneath the surface of superficial differences.

Unlike textbooks, this collection does not seek fully comprehensive coverage. It deals with various aspects of the human experience, from government to gender systems, but it does not treat each aspect of every major society. The book does work to establish a sense of change over time, along with document assessment and comparison. Materials are organized according to key periods in world history so that readers can use sources and comparisons to discuss changing world frameworks. Major societies initially operated in considerable isolation, and this pattern requires comparison around similar functions but separate origins. Traces of this separateness persist to this day. The reasons why twentieth-century China embraced Communism but the Middle East did not go back, in part, to distinctions in cultures and political systems established 1,500–2,500 years ago, when these regions formed their own identities. With the passage of time—and particularly from about 500 C.E.* onward—major societies accelerated mutual contacts and exchanges. By the fifteenth and sixteenth centuries contacts intensified still further. Even in the twentieth century, however, reactions to global contacts varied in the major civilizations, making comparison a vital analytical method in ongoing world history.

Primary Sources

The first emphasis is on primary sources, that is, documents written for the time and not intended, like a textbook, to explicitly inform current college students of world history. These primary sources, drawn from religious treatises, government pronouncements, economic regulations, and the like, require careful interpretation in order to figure out their historical significance. The sources must be not only read; they must also be assessed and recombined so that they can be used to answer historical questions that go beyond merely repeating what the document said. Thus, a religious passage intended to define morality might be used to ask questions about gender—basic views concerning men and women—that the author was not fully aware of. Or a company record listing the daily obligations of factory workers might be expected to reveal fundamental assumptions about the nature of work. Through sources of this sort, the volume deals with various facets of modern civilizations in Asia, Africa, Europe, and the Americas, ranging from the growth of governments and the impact of new science to the formation of novel work systems and the development of intense loyalties such as nationalism.

Reading a primary source requires some creative imagination because the thinking behind it will almost never be just like your own. Words that appear to be the same as ours may have different meanings. It's useful to ask of each source, What are the key assumptions here, and which ones require the biggest stretch from current habits of thought? Different kinds of sources involve different interpretive tasks. Some are accounts of events; they need to be assessed for possible bias. Others are documents in action, such as a declaration of war or a treaty. These can be evaluated for assumptions, but a bias test is less relevant. In every case there is some subtlety of meaning to be discovered, with the aid of the contexts provided in the introductory notes to each chapter. The results can

---

*The designation C.E. means "of the common era"; B.C.E means "before the common era." B.C.E. technically starts from the beginning of time and moves to the conventional date for the birth of Christ. Many world historians prefer this term to the Christian B.C. ("before Christ"), but it covers the same time period, as do C.E. and the Christian A.D. (*anno domini* or "in the year of the Lord"). The first century B.C.E. (100–1 B.C.E.) comes right before the first century C.E. (1–100); there was no year zero.

reach more deeply into the notions of past societies than any other type of reading.

Grouping the materials in comparative settings actually helps focus the task of analyzing their meaning. Documents can be read to determine what two or more societies had in common, in an area such as religion or slave-holding, and what differentiated them. They also reveal how differently major societies can operate and still be "successful." The documents themselves do not do the task of comparing, for with rare exceptions they were not written with another society in the mind. But comparison can guide the task of deriving meaning. Documents on Mexican and Russian revolution, for example, invite interpretations that will produce a sense of what some of the central features of modern revolution were—and also a sense of how the two movements differed around the common dynamic.

World History and Civilizations

Studying world history involves examining the evolution of major individual societies or civilizations. Major civilizations include those such as China or Western Europe that generated certain shared cultural values and political forms and that were usually organized around strong internal trading networks. Each civilization, in other words, established some coherence that gave its members a certain sense of identity—an ability to determine that other societies were different, that members of other civilizations were "outsiders"—and that created more intense internal than external contacts, for example, in commercial exchanges. A major civilization did not necessarily have a single government—it might be composed of many separate kingdoms or nations—but its regions or nations, even when rivalrous, nevertheless shared certain values. Thus, Western Europe has almost always been politically divided, often convulsed in internal wars, yet it has gained some common features through its participation in Christianity and more modern shared cultures like science and mutual trade.

The evolution of major societies is not the only subject of world history. Important international developments, such as sweeping contagious diseases, migrations, missionary religions, and world trade, affect individual societies powerfully, and these developments demand careful attention in their own right. Yet international factors are usually handled through the institutions and beliefs of the individual civilizations. An epidemic disease thus may be interpreted quite differently by two separate societies, even though objectively it is the same disease, with approximately the same physical consequences. International trade opportunities may affect all societies, but some, because of prior culture, will attempt to limit the impact of such trade while others will embrace the opportunity to gain new contacts. Global factors, in other words, need to be understood as they filtered through partially separate civilizations—even when they reduced the distinctiveness and isolation of those civilizations.

The list of major civilizations in world history, defined in terms of what a civilization is (a form of human organization having economic surplus, formal government, and so on) and in terms of special size and importance, contains some standard entries. China, India, and the Muslim Middle East/North Africa are on any list. So is Western Europe. Many centers of civilization formed in Africa south of the Sahara, a vast territory; they had some features in common, and so references to sub-Saharan African civilization are standard in world history, even though the category embraces a great deal of diversity. The Asian, European, and African civilizations were established well before 1450, but their separate trajectories continued to exercise a powerful influence on world history thereafter. Latin American civilization, emerging from the mixture of Spanish/Portuguese, American Indian, and African elements, created a distinct identity, building in part on earlier American Indian civilizations such as the Mayans, the Aztecs, and the Incas. The basic list of major civilizations, by the sixteenth century, thus includes at least six entries, most of them already quite old, with one, Latin America, just taking shape.

Inevitably issues of definition emerge. Same regions reflect influence from large civilizations but retain distinctive features of their own: should Japan or Korea be seen as separate societies, or as part of a larger East Asian civilization strongly touched by China? Are the United States or Australia new civilizations or part of a larger Western complex? Eastern Europe and Southeast Asia also raise key definitional questions, as they blend their own experiences with outside influence. Finally, key areas were not embraced by a single civilization at all, at least until modern times. The vast nomadic territories of central Asia form a particularly important case in point. Comparison helps shape our understanding of many key issues in defining societies and regions.

Comparing Societies

Comparison is a standard form of human thought. We often try to understand individual entities better by comparing them with something else we know. To take a very simple example, person X gains identity and recognizability when we see that she is taller than person Y. The same gains accrue from comparing societies. The United States, to take another fairly simple example, is often called a violent society. By itself, that statement is hard to assess. It acquires meaning only if we compare rates of violence—murders per capita, for example—with those of other societies. And in fact, compared to Western Europe, the United States is a violent society. But—and here comparison obviously becomes more complex, for it entails questions about what comparisons are most revealing and relevant—compared with Latin America the United States is fairly violent but not extremely so.

Virtually every characteristic we use to identify societies assumes some comparative standard. China is usually portrayed in world history as having a relatively centralized government and a tendency to scorn outside cultures. These features can be traced by charting the evolution of Chinese history all by itself, but they gain real meaning only if we compare Chinese politics and cultural receptivity to another case, such as that of India (which comparison reveals that the characterizations are accurate on the whole).

Without comparison, world history risks becoming a list of developments in one place, followed by a list of developments in another, and on and on without much meaning. Comparison, actively juxtaposing major civilizations, helps us know what particularly to look for and appreciate about each case. It also sets up other analytical tasks. Causation is one: if China is more centralized politically than India, in most periods of world history, including today, then why—what other factors in the two societies help explain the initial difference and then explain why it was perpetuated? Impact is the second: what difference does it make, in family life or beliefs, for example, that China is usually more centralized politically than India? (One twentieth-century answer is birthrate: because China has frequently used government to regulate society in the past, its policies toward birthrate limitations have been far more rigorous and successful than those of India.) Comparing major civilizations stands at the core of making sense of world history, by relating the identities of the civilizations and clarifying questions of causation and impact.

Comparison even helps chart the real results of that other principal strand of world history: international crosscutting. Why does one civilization respond differently to the arrival of religious missionaries, or a new military technology, or a major epidemic, than does another? In modern history, comparing differences between African and Indian reactions to Western influences is an obvious way to deal with one of the major international forces of modern times, as soon as we realize that although Western influence has some common components, its actual impact varies considerably from case to case across the world.

Comparison generates better understanding. But it is not always an easy analytical assignment. Using the readings in each section of this book requires some vital analytical habits, and questions in each chapter will apply these habits to the materials presented. The comparer faces several key issues:

1. *Comparison must be active.* There is sometimes an impulse to describe one society, and then describe another, and assume that the comparison has been

made. Not so. Comparison requires that the two cases be brought together, so that the comparer makes direct statements about how Muslim family structure, for example, compares to Christian. If a facet of one society is discussed, it must be discussed for the other as well, for otherwise comparison is impossible. Comparison may require some separate descriptions of each case by way of background, but ultimately, at the heart of the presentation, direct juxtaposition is essential. In comparing documentary sources of the sort presented in this book, this means that it is not enough simply to summarize one document and then another; they must be explicitly brought together.

2. *Comparison must allow for similarities as well as differences.* This is obvious, but sometimes it is tempting to stress differences above all. Major civilizations often had a lot in common, in part because they experienced similar global influences. The trick in comparison is to figure out what the balance between similarity and difference is, and not to overdraw contrasts.

3. *Comparison involves a sensible choice of cases.* Comparing the importance of palm trees in Jamaica and in northern Ontario is possible but silly—the contexts are too different to provide any useful meaning. Comparing Russian and American concerns about dieting in the mid-twentieth century is also silly, beyond an initial finding that Russians, worried mainly about finding enough food, did not develop a systematic diet culture during the decades in which Americans worried about the subject incessantly. The most revealing comparisons involve societies that have enough in common that exploring differences really gets to the heart of some major distinctions between the two cases.

In the chapters of this book, that test has been imposed: total disparities are not presented, because they are not very informative. This is one reason why, societies are compared in the same time period. Comparing industrial Japan with early Mesopotamian civilizations would quickly reveal huge differences, starting with technology, but it would not be as useful as comparing Mesopotamia with its early civilization neighbor Egypt, or the Japanese version of industrial society with that of Germany. Even with relatively precise comparative choices, there is always room for debate. In the violence example presented above, which comparison is more useful if the goal is to understand the United States? Europe is Americans' standard historical reference, because a (shrinking) majority of Americans are of European origin and because many Americans think of Europe as the measure of all things civilized. But perhaps choosing Latin America, another society with a strong and recent frontier tradition, is actually more revealing. Here, selection of the cases is complex and invites open discussion. It will be well to keep in mind, while studying the chapters of this book, what other comparative sets might have been useful in dealing with the phenomenon in question.

4. Comparison involves a decision about how many cases to compare. Comparing two cases, Christianity and Islam, is easier than adding a third, Buddhism. Sometimes a three-way comparison may be helpful, for example, in showing that two cases, which look rather different when compared with each other, actually have some striking similarities when an even more distinctive case is brought into the picture. Christianity and Islam, for example, are quite similar religions (and for good historical reason), compared with Buddhism, even though Christians and Muslims often like to emphasize their mutual differences and dislikes. (Disliking another society is not proof of difference; often the societies that are most similar particularly dislike each other because they need to establish separate identities.)

5. Comparison involves flexibility and imagination. In comparing, be alert for revealing, if unfamiliar, subjects, and don't be surprised when comparisons don't produce the results that a preliminary comparative sense might lead one to anticipate. Take an unexpected comparative finding as a challenge to explore further. Compared to all other societies in the world today, the United States has more people in jail per capita. How and why has the nation generated this distinctive feature? The answer, even though the category is not a very standard component of our assessment of American history, could be very revealing. Another comparative topic: France has a rich history of fascination with fancy cooking and foods. Butter-based cooking entered French dining as early as the seventeenth century. The United States historically has been much more conscious of nutritional aspects of food (reformers were discussing this as early as the 1830s, hence new products like the graham cracker and Kellogg's cereals). So which society produces the lower percentage of overweight people? The answer: France, hands down. The average French person has lost an average of about two pounds between 1940 and 1990 while the average American has gained eight, height held constant. This is on the surface an unexpected comparative finding, which should then dictate a search for the reasons, given a comparative food history that perhaps ought to have produced the opposite results.

Using Documents and Comparisons in Teaching and Learning World History

Many world history courses already use documents and comparisons, which was one reason the first edition of this book proved useful. The standards of the new

Advanced Placement program in world history, which emphasize both primary source analysis and comparison, also testify to the importance of the skills this collection promotes.

It is also true, however, that introducing comparative analysis of sources into some world history programs remains challenging. The topics in this collection are designed to fit, and enhance, much standard coverage. Each chapter is introduced in ways that help connect the material to fundamental themes in the world history course—to discussions of the nature of government in the classical period, for example, or of the evolution of labor systems in Latin America. Emphasis on the major societies of Asia, Africa, Europe, and the Americas, and organization in terms of the standard world history time periods, additionally facilitates integration with other reading and classroom work. Materials in the final section, on the contemporary period in world history, invite assessment in terms of earlier patterns and traditions, where world history past actively conditions world history present.

Using the Book

Each section of this book opens with an introduction to the main characteristics of the time period in world history. The introductions explain how the ensuing chapter topics relate to basic patterns and why the comparative selections make sense in terms of the activities emphasized—trade, or religion, or gender—and in terms of the specific civilizations included.

Each chapter also has an introduction, identifying the comparative topic and the societies involved and placing both in world history context. This introduction also explains how the civilizations selected are significant for the topic—why classical China and Greece, for example, should be compared politically, or why Indian religions should be compared with religions that arose in the Middle East.

After the introduction to each chapter, a set of questions raises some of the specific comparative issues that can be found in the documents that follow. A final set of questions, "For Further Discussion," presents wider comparative issues that can be handled partially from the documents but that need further comparative information—from textbooks or other historical studies or, sometimes, from other chapters in this book.

Questions in the first segment, before "For Further Discussion," can be answered from the documents. Looking at the questions first can help guide the reading of the documents, and then the questions should be reexamined after the documents have been read. The questions apply to a particular topic—the conditions of women in Africa and Latin America, for example, using the comparative approaches discussed above. They thus ask about similarities as well as differences and about causes and impacts of comparative features (calling for imaginative extensions). And they promote direct comparison rather than a mere sequencing of data from one civilization to the next.

Finally, each document or document set has a brief heading that gives details about the time, the place, and the authorship of the document or documents. The context supplied by this information should be included in assessing the document's meanings and in preparing for the comparisons.

River Valley Civilizations, 3500–1000 B.C.E., and the Classical Period, 1000 B.C.E.–450 C.E.

THE EARLY RIVER VALLEY civilizations formed in the Middle East, North Africa, India, and China. (Later, the expansive classical civilizations developed both in these regions and beyond.) Early civilizations and their classical successors set up important cultural and institutional characteristics that had enduring influence, providing vital topics for comparative analysis.

Early Cultures and the Early Civilization Period

The early civilization period began around 3500 B.C.E. in the Tigris-Euphrates valley in the northern Middle East. Early civilization periods in other regions, also for the most part based in river valleys exploited for irrigation as well as transportation, had somewhat different dates. Egypt developed from about 3000 B.C.E. onward, China from 1500, and the first civilizations in Central America (the Olmecs) from about 800 B.C.E. No civilization could emerge without the prior development of agriculture.

For historians studying early cultures and civilizations, a key problem is the lack of abundant sources. Many important cultures, with well-defined belief systems and elaborate rules for behavior, never generated writing. Furthermore, much writing has been destroyed over time, and writing on stone tablets or bones was so laborious that it was not very widespread in any event.

The first chapter, as a result, deals with only a few topics, but those are fundamental to early societies. The writings of early civilizations must be asked questions that they were not explicitly designed to answer. Law codes, for example, provide our only real evidence about family patterns and social structures, even though these topics were not formally laid out. Only after the nature of the evidence is assessed can comparison among belief systems or civilization forms be attempted.

The Classical Period, 1000 B.C.E.–450 C.E.

Between 1000 and 500 B.C.E., several civilization centers began to transcend the patterns of river valley societies. Using iron tools and weapons, governments conquered new territories and economies generated new opportunities for regional trade and specialization. The twin themes in this period were civilization expansion, from river valley origins to much larger regions, and territorial integration. As societies grew geographically, they had to find ways to form a region into a coherent trade area; into a roughly common cultural zone where elites, at least, would share some basic ideas and art forms; and—at times—into a single political unit. Major classical civilizations arose in India, China, and the Mediterranean, with a fourth center in Persia. All of these regions created political empires that sought considerable political unity as part of the integration— though the durability of the empires varied considerably. Everywhere, a series of new invasions, occurring between the third and the sixth centuries C.E., introduced disruptions that ended the classical period.

With the classical period opportunities for comparison among the civilizations increase. Developments in this period—the emergence of Confucianism in China and the religious emphases of classical India, for example—set an enduring framework for the areas involved, which makes comparison all the more significant. Some of the differences between India and China today go back to contrasts that first became apparent in the classical centuries.

The major classical civilizations built on the precedents of the river valley centers, but their territories were larger and their cultural systems were more formal. They used some earlier ideas, including those of the polytheistic religions, but they shaped more systematic statements. Thus, in India a priestly, polytheistic religion evolved into Hinduism. China produced Confucianism as a unifying cultural approach, at least for much of the upper class. Political institutions expanded. All the major centers formed huge empires, at least during key portions of the classical period. In China the imperial form became the standard political framework. Commercial exchange increased. Social structures perpetuated inequalities that had undoubtedly started earlier but were now more formalized, more fully integrated with beliefs and political practices. Thus, India developed its caste system, and the Mediterranean region relied considerably on slavery. The same formalization applies to gender relations, where the assumptions of patriarchy were spelled out more fully.

In politics, in diverse cultural expressions, and in social forms, the classical civilizations shared important characteristics. They were all rooted in agricultural economies in which trade was expanding. They all faced the task of integrating larger territories into a common civilization orbit, and this required innovation in political institutions and ideas and in cultural forms. The classical civilizations even had some mutual contacts—more, on the whole, than the more isolated river valley civilizations had maintained. Greek and Indian civilizations encountered each other in the fourth century B.C.E. through the conquests of Alexander the Great; the result was some mutual imitation of ethical ideas, artistic forms, and mathematics. Later in the classical period, Chinese trade with India brought knowledge of Buddhism, and Chinese pilgrims journeyed to India to learn more. Trade routes took Chinese silk as far west as the Roman Empire.

On the whole, however, the key developments of the classical period took place separately, with each civilization putting a distinctive stamp on its social, political, and cultural forms. Rome received Chinese silk, but it knew almost nothing about China, and the converse was true as well. Separateness was compounded by a heightened sense of identity. As the Greeks or the Chinese developed their societies, they became proudly aware of how different (and, usually, inferior) other peoples were. Separate historical patterns and a concern for identity add up to an obvious comparative challenge. As in the early civilization period, comparison most obviously focuses on how key civilizations differed, even as they addressed common themes such as the presumed inferiority of women. Explaining why the differences arose and what impact they had extends this comparative analysis. Comparison highlights the distinctive traditions and identities that were taking shape in the classical period and that would echo later on. But comparison can also tease out some of the common features, even when the leaders of the principal civilizations were unaware of them.

CHAPTER 1

CREATION STORIES

Many societies—probably the vast majority—generate explanations of how the world began, or at least how humans began. Such explanations are often part of a larger religious outlook.

Comparing creation stories raises key issues about beneath-the-surface similarities, including, of course, why so many otherwise distinctive societies felt a similar need to account for origins.

The variations among the stories are significant too, suggesting different specific religious beliefs and different ideas about the relationship between humans and other aspects of nature.

The following stories come from the Americas, from Africa, and from the Middle East. Three—Babylonian, Egyptian, and Mayan—derive from early civilizations. Two are from hunting and gathering groups, recently recorded though of much older origin. In addition to one-to-one comparisons, the collection may suggest different kinds of groupings that will assist further comparative analysis.

Questions

1. What are the most important differences among the stories? Are the differences significant or superficial?
2. What do the stories have in common? Is it possible to identify similar elements in the origins beliefs of early human societies?
3. Do the stories group together in meaningful ways? Do the stories from early civilizations share elements that differentiate them from the hunting and gathering stories? Are there common elements in terms of geography?

For Further Discussion

1. What might have caused significant differences among the stories?
2. How do the stories compare to those of major religions, like Christianity and Islam? Are they very different, and if so why?
3. In addition to comparing features and causes, is it historically useful to

evaluate comparatively? Are some of the stories better or more satisfying than others? On what basis can you judge?

4. **Is it possible to infer significant characteristics of a society from a creation story? Does a story suggest distinctive religious beliefs or attitudes toward nature?**

A Kabyl Story

This story comes from the Kabyl peoples of the Sahara; a nomadic group, they live in what is now Morocco and Algeria. It is not known when this oral legend first developed, or what other influences it reflected (the Kabyl are now Muslims).

• • •

In the beginning there were only one man and one woman and they lived not on the earth but beneath it. They were the first people in the world and neither knew that the other was of another sex. One day they both came to the well to drink. The man said: "Let me drink." The woman said: "No, I'll drink first. I was here first." The man tried to push the woman aside. She struck him. They fought. The man smote the woman so that she dropped to the ground. Her clothing fell to one side. Her thighs were naked.

The man saw the woman lying strange and naked before him. He saw that she had a vagina. He felt that he had a penis. He looked at the vagina and asked: "What is that for?" The woman said: "That is good." The man lay upon the woman. He lay with the woman eight days.

After nine months the woman bore four daughters. Again, after nine months, she bore four sons. And again four daughters and again four sons. So at last the man and the woman had fifty daughters and fifty sons. The father and mother did not know what to do with so many children. So they sent them away.

The fifty maidens went off together towards the north. The fifty young men went off together towards the east. After the maidens had been on their way northwards under the earth for a year, they saw a light above them. There was a hole in the earth. The maidens saw the sky above them and cried: "Why stay under the earth when we can climb to the surface where we can see the sky?" The maidens climbed up through the hole and onto the earth.

The fifty youths likewise continued in their own direction under the earth for a year until they, too, came to a place where there was a hole in the crust and they could see the sky above them. The youths looked at the sky and cried: "Why remain under the earth when there is a place from which one can see the sky?" So they climbed through their hole to the surface.

Thereafter the fifty maidens went their way over the earth's surface and the youths went their way and none knew aught of the others.

At the time all trees and plants and stones could speak. The fifty maidens saw the plants and asked them: "Who made you?" And the plants replied: "The earth." The maidens asked the earth, "Who made you?" And the earth replied, "I was already here." During the night the maidens saw the moon and the stars and they cried: "Who made you that you stand so high over us and over the trees? Is it you who give us light? Who are you, great and little stars? Who created you? Or are you, perhaps, the ones who have made everything else?" . . .

A North American Version

the haida story[1]

The Haida are a Native American people in the Canadian Northwest, along the Pacific coast of what is now British Columbia.

• • •

Then one day the water began to fall, and at last even the thin spit of sand now known as Rose Spit lay dry. The Raven flew there and found it covered by clams, cockles, rock oysters, crabs, scallops, sea cucumbers, abalone, red turbans, sea urchins, mussels in their dark blue mantle, and fish of all kinds left behind by the falling water. For a long time, he did nothing but eat, gorging himself on these delic acies. But at last even his gluttony was satisfied and he began to think of the other things he liked doing, playing tricks, changing things so the world would not settle down to a boring routine.

There certainly was not much to play with or change on this deserted beach, with no companions except the rapidly expiring sea creatures left stranded there. The Raven walked along getting more bored and restless by the minute.

He had almost decided to fly away to some more interesting spot even if it meant leaving all this lovely ripe food behind, but decided there must be something more on this beach. So he continued his stroll, calling out in frustration now and then.

"This is a fine place for food," he said, and "I must say that the big bright ball, the Sun I stole from the old man and hung up there in the sky is a big improvement. But there certainly is not much to do here." He threw back his head and called to the empty sky in his loudest voice, "Isn't there anybody anywhere?" Almost immediately he heard an answering cry which seemed to come from far beneath him. At first he saw nothing, except a remarkably large clamshell half buried in the sand.

"I have seen lot of clams in my time," he said, "but the most noise they have been able to make was a sort of squishy sound. So this is at least a different kind of clam." He leaned closer and saw that the shell was an old one and that its original

---

[1] From Leo Frobenius and Douglas Fox, *African Genesis* (New York: Benjamin Blair, 1966), 49–50.

occupant had long since departed. It was now filled with a mass of squirming creatures all trying to hide from the enormous black shape that seemed intent on destroying them.

If the Raven had not eaten so much so recently, the little creatures might have become part of his dinner, and the world would have been a much different place. But his curiosity at the moment was much stronger than his appetite. So instead of picking up the shell and dropping it on a rock to break it open, he very gently, using his most charming and seductive voice, a lovely bell-like croon, certainly one of the most beautiful sounds in the world, which seems to come from the roots of the mountains, from the wellsprings of the sea, from the caves where the winds are born, he coaxed the little creatures to come out of their shell. He told them of the land that waited for them, covered the great red cedar trees from which they could build their big houses and seagoing canoes, and in time tall totem poles to commemorate their great deeds. He sang of the restless seas, which every year would bring the salmon to the rivers and are the home of the great whales, the porpoises, the seals and sea lions, the sea otters and all the fish, which would feed them through their time on earth.

So with much hesitation, afraid but unable to resist, they finally came out.

Very strange creatures they were: two legs like the Raven, but no shiny feathers on their bodies or wings. In fact no wings at all, just long thin appendages which moved constantly. Except for their shiny black hair on their round heads, they were naked, quite the strangest creatures the Raven had ever seen—these first people—who were to become Haida.

For a long time the Raven amused himself with his new playthings, teaching the men and women all kinds of clever tricks: how to build the beautiful Haida canoes which took them on fishing and sea hunting trips, and, as they grew in numbers, to visit and trade or go to war with their neighbors.

He watched the children grow up and have children of their own, and the old people die. He watched some of them become chiefs and some slaves, and he saw the chiefs prove how great they were by building great houses, beautifully decorated with carvings telling of their heraldic pasts, and filled with exquisite ceremonial works of art to be used at the great winter feasts. He watched them dance and listened to them sing, and enjoyed the stories they told, particularly those about him.

It was a fine game he played with the little people from the clamshell, and it lasted for many centuries.

A Babylonian Story

This story comes from a tablet found in the ruins of the city of Ashur, dating back to approximately 800 B.C.E. It was a version of an older Sumerian story. It

provided names for the first humans, Ulligarra and Zalgarra, and implied that they were divine to some degree—created from divine blood possibly mixed with clay.

• • •

Another Account of the Creation of Man[2]

A tablet discovered among the ruins of the city of Ashur and dating back to approximately 800 B.C. gives us still another version of the creation of man. This text consists of three columns. The first contains signs which are held by some to be musical notes but which are most likely symbols of some kind of secret writing; the second contains the Sumerian version of the story of man's creation; and the third offers the Babylonian translation of it. On this tablet mention is made for the first time in Babylonian-Assyrian literature of the first two human beings and their names, Ulligarra and Zalgarra. Before each one's name is placed the sign for "deity," which means that the first ancestors of mankind were regarded as being divine at least to some degree. The reason for this conception lies, of course, in the fact that they were thought to have been created with divine blood, which, according to other sources, was mixed with clay.

Obverse

  1. When heaven had been separated from the earth, the distant trusty twin,
  2. [And] the mother of the goddesses had been brought into being;
  3. When the earth had been brought forth [and] the earth had been fashioned;
  4. When the destinies of heaven and earth had been fixed;
  5. [When] trench and canal had been given [their] right courses,
  6. [And] the banks of the Tigris and the Euphrates had been established,
  7. [Then]
  8. The great gods,
  9. [And] the Anunnaki, the great gods,
10. Seated themselves in the exalted sanctuary
11. And recounted among themselves what had been created.
12. "Now that the destinies of heaven and earth have been fixed,
13. Trench and canal have been given their right courses,
14. The banks of the Tigris and the Euphrates
15. Have been established,
16. What [else] shall we do?

---

[2]From Alexander Heidel, *The Babylonian Genesis* (2nd ed., Chicago: University of Chicago Press, 1951), 69–71. Reprinted with permission of the publisher.

17. What [else] shall we create?
18. O Anunnaki, ye great gods,
19. What [else] shall we do?
20. What [else] shall we create?
21. The great gods who were present,
22. The Anunnaki, who fix the destinies,
23. Both [groups] of them, made answer
24. "In Unumua [a saved city], the bond of heaven and earth,
25. Let us slay [two] Lamga gods.
26. With their blood let us create mankind.
27. The service of the gods be their portion,
28. For all times
29. To maintain the boundary ditch,
30. To place the hoe and the basket
31. Into their hands
32. For the dwelling of the great gods,
33. Which is fit to be an exalted sanctuary,
34. To mark off field from field,
35. For all times
36. To maintain the boundary ditch,
37. To give the trench [its] right course,
38. To maintain the boundary stone [?],
39. To water the four regions of the earth [?],
40. To raise plants in abundance, . . .

Reverse

1. To make field of the Anunnaki [earth] produce plentifully,
2. To increase the abundance in the land,
3. To celebrate the festivals of the gods, . . .
4. To pour out cold water
5. That they should increase ox, sheep, cattle, fish, and fowl,
6. The abundance in the land,
7. Enul [and] Ninul [god and goddess of abundance]
8. Decreed with their holy mouths.
9. Aruru, the lady of the gods, who is fit for rulership,
10. Ordained for them great destinies:
11. Skilled worker to produce for skilled worker [and] unskilled worker for unskilled worker,
12. [Springing up] by themselves like grain from the ground,

13. A thing which, [like] the stars of heaven, shall not be changed forever.
14. Day and night
15. To celebrate the festivals of the gods
16. The great gods, decree [for them].
17. In the place where mankind was created,
18. There Nisaba [goddess of grain and wisdom] was firmly established.
19. Let the wise teach the mystery to the wise.

An Egyptian Story

The story was preserved in a document written around 310 B.C.E., but it undoubtedly refers to much older materials.

• • •

The Book of Knowing the Genesis of the Sun-God[3]

"The Master of Everything saith after his forming:
'When I had formed, then [only] the forms were formed.
All the forms were formed after my forming.
Numerous are the forms from that which proceeded from my
      mouth.

The heaven had not been formed,
The earth had not been formed,
The ground had not been created
[For?] the reptiles in that place.

I raised [myself] among them in the abyss, out of [its] inertness.
When I did not find a place where I could stand,
I thought wisely [?] in my heart,
I founded in my soul [?].
I made all forms, I alone.

I had not yet ejected [other gods],
None else had arisen who had worked [?] with me.
[Then] I founded in my own heart;

[3]From Louis Gray, ed., *The Mythology of All Races*, vol. 12 (New York: Cooper Square Publishers, 1964), 68–69. Reprinted by permission of the publisher.

There were formed many [forms?]
The forms of the forms in the forms of the children,
(And) in the forms of their children.

What I ejected was Shu,
What I spat out was Tefenet.
My father, the abyss, sent them.
My eye followed them through ages of ages [?]
As [they] separated from me. After I was formed as the only [god],
Three gods were [separated] from me [since?] I was on this earth.
Shu and Tefenet rejoiced in the abyss in which they were.
They brought me my eye [back] [following] after them.
After I had united my members, I wept over them.
The origin of men was [thus] from my tears which came from my eye.
It became angry against me after it had come [back],
When it found that I had made me another [eye] in its place
[And] I had replaced it by a resplendent eye;
I had advanced its place in my face afterward,
[So that] it ruled this whole land.
Now [?] at its [?] time were there [?] plants [?].
I replaced what she had taken therefrom.
I came forth from the plants [?].
I created all reptiles and all that was in [?] them.
Shu and Tefenet begat [Qeb] and Nut.
Qeb and Nut begat Osiris, Horus,
One of them after the other;
Their children are many on this earth.' "

THE MAYAN STORY, FROM POPOL VUH

Popol Vuh was a Council Book used as a source of advice for Mayan leaders in Quiche, a center in present-day Guatemala, around 1000 c.e. (The only existing document was written in the sixteenth century after the Spanish conquest.) The book was used to guide decisions and interpret omens. The book included a creation story dealing with the origins of the planets, animals, even ball games—as well as humans.

• • •

The Mayan Story of Human Creation from Popol Vuh[4]

And here is the beginning of the conception of humans, and of the search for the ingredients of the human body. So they spoke, the Bearer, Begetter, the Makers, Modelers named Sovereign Plumed Serpent:

"The dawn has approached, preparations have been made, and morning has come for the provider, nurturer, born in the light, begotten in the light. Morning has come for humankind, for the people of the face of the earth," they said. It all came together as they went on thinking in the darkness in the night, as they searched and they sifted, they thought and they wondered.

And here their thoughts came out in clear light. They sought and discovered what was needed for human flesh. It was only a short while before the sun, moon, and stars were to appear above the Makers and Modelers. Broken Place, Bitter Water Place is the name: the yellow corn, white corn came from there.

And these are the names of the animals who brought the food: fox, coyote, parrot, crow. There were four animals who brought the news of the ears of yellow corn and white corn. They were coming from over there at Broken Place, they showed the way to the break.

And this was when they found the staple foods.

And these were the ingredients for the flesh of the human work, the human design, and the water was for the blood. It became human blood, and corn was also used by the Bearer, Begetter.

And so they were happy over the provisions of the good mountain, filled with sweet things, thick with yellow corn, white corn, and thick with pataxte and cacao, countless zapotes, anonas, jocotes, nances, matasanos, sweets the rich foods filling up the citadel named Broken Place, Bitter Water Place. All the edible fruits were there: small staples, great staples, small plants, great plants. The way was shown by the animals.

And then the yellow corn and white corn were ground, and Xmucane did the grinding nine times. Corn was used, along with the water she rinsed her hands with, for the creation of grease; it became human fat when it was worked by the Bearer, Begetter, Sovereign Plumed Serpent, as they are called.

After that, they put it into words:

> the making, the modeling of our first mother-father,
> with yellow corn, white corn along for the flesh,
> food alone for the human legs and arms,
> for our first fathers, the four human works.
> It was staples alone that made up their flesh.

[4]From Dennis Tedlock, *Popol Vuh: The Mayan Book of the Dawn of Life* (New York: Simon and Schuster, 1996). Reprinted with the permission of Simon and Schuster Adult Publishing Group. Copyright 1985, 1996 by Dennis Tedlock.

. . .

These are the names of the first people who were made and
    modeled.
This is the first person: Jaguar Quitze.
And now the second: Jaguar Night.
And now the third: Mahucutah.
And the fourth: True Jaguar.

And these are the names of our first mother-fathers. They were simply made and
modeled, it is said; they had no mother and no father. We have named the men by
themselves. No woman gave birth to them, nor were they begotten by the builder,
sculptor, Bearer, Begetter. By sacrifice alone, by genius alone they were made, they
were modeled by the Maker, Modeler, Bearer, Begetter, Sovereign Plumed Serpent.
And when they came to fruition, they came out human:

They talked and they made words.
They looked and they listened.
They walked, and worked.

They were good people, handsome, with looks of the male kind. Thoughts came
into existence and they gazed; their vision came all at once. Perfectly they saw, perfectly they knew everything under the sky, whenever they looked. The moment they
turned around and looked around in the sky, whenever they looked. The moment
they turned around and looked around in the sky, on the earth, everything was seen
without any obstruction. They didn't have to walk around before they could see what
was under the sky; they just stayed where they were.

As they looked, their knowledge became intense. Their sight passed through trees,
through rocks, through lakes, through seas, through mountains, through plains.
Jaguar Quitze, Jaguar Night, Mahucutah, and True Jaguar were truly gifted people.

And then they were asked by the builder and mason:

"What do you know about your being? Don't you look, don't you listen? Isn't
your speech good, and your walk? So you must look, to see out under the sky. Don't
you see the mountain-plain clearly? So try it," they were told.

And then they saw everything under the sky perfectly. After that, they thanked
the Maker, Modeler:

"Truly now,
double thanks, triple thanks
that we've been formed, we've been given
our mouths, our faces,
we speak, we listen,
we wonder, we move,

our knowledge is good, we've understood
what is far and near,
and we've seen what is great and small
under the sky, on the earth.
Thanks to you we've been formed,
we've come to be made and modeled,
our grandmother, our grandfather,"

they said when they gave thanks for having been made and modeled. They understood everything perfectly, they sighted the four sides, the four corners in the sky, on
the earth, and this didn't sound good to the builder and sculptor:

"What our works and designs have said is no good:

'We have understood everything, great and small,' they say." And so the Bearer,
Begetter took back their knowledge:

"What should we do with them now? Their vision should at least reach nearby,
they should see at least a small part of the face of the earth, but what they're saying
isn't good. Aren't they merely 'works' and 'designs' in their very names? Yet they'll become as great as gods, unless they procreate, proliferate at the sowing, the dawning,
unless they increase."

"Let it be this way: now we'll take them apart just a little, that's what we need.
What we've found out isn't good. Their deeds would become equal to ours, just because their knowledge reaches so far. They see everything," so said

the Heart of Sky, Hurricane,
Newborn Thunderbolt, Raw Thunderbolt,
Sovereign Plumed Serpent,
Bearer, Begetter,
Xpiyacoc, Xmucane,
Maker, Modeler,

as they are called. And when they changed the nature of their works, their designs, it
was enough that the eyes be marred by the Heart of Sky. They were blinded as the
face of a mirror is breathed upon. Their eyes were weakened. Now it was only when
they looked nearby that things were clear.

And such was the loss of the means of understanding, along with the means of
knowing everything, by the four humans. The root was implanted.

As such was the making, modeling of our first grandfather, our father, by the
Heart of Sky, Heart of Earth.

CHAPTER 2

COMPARING LAWS

The Importance of the State

Codes of law were a common product of relatively early civilizations. The following two selections reflect the development of written laws, associated with the operations of organized government. The first known code is that of the Babylonian emperor Hammurabi, issued around 1700 B.C.E. Jewish law, ultimately written as part of the Bible, particularly in the book of Deuteronomy, developed later, beginning about 950 B.C.E.

Law codes do much more than simply define crimes and punishments. They reveal beliefs about religion, the family and the nature of the state. Comparing codes can indicate deep-seated contrasts and commonalities between societies, though they must be interpreted beyond literal meanings. Comparison is a vital means of getting at some of the key characteristics of early civilizations.

Law codes in early civilizations shared many features—indeed, in defining crimes such as murder, they share features with modern codes as well. Codes worked toward replacing private feuds and violence with government-sponsored justice, for example—though early states often failed to enforce such edicts. Mesopotamian law surely influenced Jewish codes, for the Jewish state was often under Mesopotamian control. A surprising array of laws dealing with gender and regulating sexual behavior, particularly for women, characterized both systems, though in Judaism the rules were slightly harsher and the concern for limited protective rights slightly less well developed. Law in both societies reflected the small bureaucracies of the early states—hence a concern for punishing false testimony, in the absence of extensive investigatory police forces, and an emphasis on harsh punishments designed to deter crime. Provisions in both societies also expressed some interest in protecting general social welfare, for example, in trying to assure wages for work or (in the Mesopotamian case) reimbursing for loss in crime—a notion still being debated in the United States.

The two codes displayed crucial differences as well, reflecting different religious cultures and political institutions. Mesopotamian law stressed the power of the state, though sanctioned by gods such the creator Marduk and a polytheistic religion. In contrast, Jewish law was seen as emanating from Jehovah, in the world's first real monotheistic religion. Did this difference in framework show up in the laws themselves and in efforts to assure obedience?

Questions

1. How did Babylonian law try to reconcile the needs of the state with the fact that it could not afford a large, professional bureaucracy? How did the state use "volunteers"? How did it arrange for public works?
2. What protections did women have in Babylonian law? How do these compare with the stipulations for women in Jewish law? How can we tell that both societies were patriarchal?
3. How many social classes did Babylonia have? Was Jewish law different in its approach to the poorer classes?
4. What were the key differences between Babylonian and Jewish religions?
5. What are the sources claimed for the law in the two societies? How did the differences in these claims relate to differences in the roles of priests and government officials?
6. What are the main similarities between the two law codes?

For Further Discussion

1. How did both law codes differ from modern ideas of law?
2. What might have caused the key differences between Jewish and Babylonian law?

MESOPOTAMIA: HAMMURABI'S CODE

The Babylonians were an invading people who reunited the city states of Mesopotamia by conquest. The victorious king, Hammurabi, reigned for forty-three years, earning a reputation for justice and efficiency. His law code, from around 1700 B.C.E., consisted of 282 case laws written on a stone slab; it was discovered in 1901 in Iran. The code does not represent a carefully articulated philosophy of law or the state, but rather highlights selected decisions the king and his officials rendered for the purpose of providing precedents for just rulings.

• • •

When the lofty Anu, king of the Anunnaki, and Bel, lord of heaven and earth, he who determines the destiny of the land, committed the rule of all mankind to Marduk, the

From *The Code of Hammurabi, King of Babylon,* trans. Robert Francis Harper (Chicago: University of Chicago Press, 1904), 3, 9, 11, 17, 19, 29, 45, 51, 73, 75, 89, 99, 101, 103, 105. Reprinted by permission of the publisher.

chief son of Ea; when they pronounced the lofty name of Babylon: when they made it famous among the quarters of the world and in its midst established an everlasting kingdom whose foundations were firm as heaven and earth—at that time, Anu and Bel called me, Hummurabi, the exalted prince, the worshiper of the gods, to cause justice to prevail in the land, to destroy the wicked and the evil, to prevent the strong from oppressing the weak . . . to enlighten the land and to further the welfare of the people. Hammurabi, the governor named by Bel, am I, who brought about plenty and abundance; . . .

. . . who caused the four quarters of the world to render obedience. When Marduk sent me to rule the people and to bring help to the country, I established law and justice in the land and promoted the welfare of the people.

§1.

❡ If a man bring an accusation against a man, and charge him with a [capital] crime, but cannot prove it, he, the accuser, shall be put to death.

§2.

❡ If a man charge a man with sorcery, and cannot prove it, he who is charged with sorcery shall go to the river, into the river he shall throw himself and if the river overcome him, his accuser shall take to himself his house [estate]. If the river show that man to be innocent and he come forth unharmed, he who charged him with sorcery shall be put to death. He who threw himself into the river shall take to himself the house of his accuser.
❡ If a man has come forward to bear witness to a felony and then has not proved the statement he has made, if that case [is] a capital one, that man shall be put to death.
❡ If a man aid a male or female slave of the palace, or a male or female slave of a freeman to escape from the city gate, he shall be put to death.
❡ If a man seize a male or female slave, a fugitive, in the field and bring that [slave] back to his owner, the owner of the slave shall pay him two shekels of silver.

§23.

❡ If the brigand be not captured, the man who has been robbed, shall, in the presence of god, make an itemized statement of his loss, and the city and the governor, in whose province and jurisdiction the robbery was committed, shall compensate him for whatever was lost.

§24.

❡ If it be a life [that is lost], the city and governor shall pay one mana of silver to his heirs.

§26.

¶ If either an officer or a constable, who is ordered to go on an errand of the king, do not go but hire a substitute and despatch him in his stead, that officer or constable shall be put to death; his hired substitute shall take to himself his [the officer's] house.

§53.

¶ If a man neglect to strengthen his dyke and do not strengthen it, and a break be made in his dyke and the water carry away the farm-land, the man in whose dyke the break has been made shall restore the grain which he has damaged.

§127.

¶ If a man point the finger at a priestess or the wife of another and cannot justify it, they shall drag that man before the judges and they shall brand his forehead.

§129.

¶ If the wife of a man be taken in lying with another man, they shall bind them and throw them into the water. If the husband of the woman would save his wife, or if the king would save his male servant [he may].

§130.

¶ If a man force the [betrothed] wife of another who has not known a male and is living in her father's house, and he lie in her bosom and they take him, that man shall be put to death and that woman shall go free.

§131.

¶ If a man accuse his wife and she has not been taken in lying with another man, she shall take an oath in the name of god and she shall return to her house.

§132.

¶ If the finger have been pointed at the wife of a man because of another man, and she have not been taken in lying with another man, for her husband's sake she shall throw herself into the river.

§142.

❡ If a woman hate her husband, and say: "Thou shalt not have me," they shall inquire into her antecedents for her defects; and if she have been a careful mistress and be without reproach and her husband have been going about and greatly belittling her, that woman has no blame. She shall receive her dowry and shall go to her father's house.

§143.

❡ If she have not been a careful mistress, have gadded about, have neglected her house and have belittled her husband, they shall throw that woman into the water.

§145.

❡ If a man take a wife and she do not present him with children and he set his face to take a concubine, that man may take a concubine and bring her into his house. That concubine shall not rank with his wife.

§196.

❡ If a man destroy the eye of another freeman [i.e., a man in the upper class], they shall destroy his eye.

§197.

❡ If one break a man's bone, they shall break his bone.

§198.

❡ If one destroy the eye of a villein [a dependent laborer] or break the bone of a freeman, he shall pay one mana of silver.

§199.

❡ If one destroy the eye of a man's slave or break a bone of a man's slave he shall pay one-half his price.

§200.

❡ If a man knock out a tooth of a man of his own rank, they shall knock out his tooth.

§201.

¶ If one knock out a tooth of a villein, he shall pay one-third mana of silver.

§203.

¶ If a man strike another man of his own rank, he shall pay one mana of silver.

§204.

¶ If a villein strike a villein, he shall pay ten shekels of silver.

§205.

¶ If a man's slave strike a man's son, they shall cut off his ear.

§253.

¶ If a man hire a man to oversee his farm and furnish him the seed-grain and intrust him with oxen and contract with him to cultivate the field, and that man steal either the seed or the crop and it be found in his possession, they shall cut off his fingers.

§254.

¶ If he take the seed-grain and overwork the oxen, he shall restore the quantity of grain which he has hoed.

The righteous laws, which Hammurabi, the wise king, established and [by which] he gave the land stable support and pure government. Hammurabi, the *perfect king, am I*. . . .

The great gods proclaimed me and I am the guardian governor, whose scepter is righteous and whose beneficent protection is spread over my city. . . .

The king, who is pre-eminent among city kings, am I. My words are precious, my wisdom is unrivaled. . . .

If that man do not pay attention to my words which I have written upon my monument: if he forget my curse and do not fear the curse of god: if he abolish the judgments which I have formulated, overrule my words, alter my statues, efface my name written thereon and write his own name: on account of these curses, commission another to do so—as for that man, be he king or lord, or priest-king or commoner, whoever he may be, may the great god, the father of the gods, who has ordained my reign, take from him the glory of his sovereignty, may be break his scepter, and curse his fate! . . .

JEWISH LAW

Jewish settlers established a small kingdom along the eastern Mediterranean between 1200 and 1100 B.C.E. The people may have developed elements of their religion and culture earlier—this is what is claimed in the initial stories of the Old Testament, particularly the book of Exodus. Jewish culture was marked by its elaborate, intense religion, which featured the first durable articulation of monotheistic beliefs but also laws and religious rules of behavior. Most of the book of Deuteronomy, from which the following passages come, was written in the seventh century B.C.E., though elements of the laws themselves had undoubtedly developed earlier.

• • •

You must be entirely faithful to Yahweh your God. . . . [A]nd Yahweh said to me. . . . "The man who does not listen to my words that he speaks in my name, shall be held answerable to me for it. But the prophet who presumes to say in my name a thing I have not commanded him to say, or who speaks in the name of other gods, that prophet shall die."

You may say in your heart, "How are we to know what word was not spoken by Yahweh?" When a prophet speaks in the name of Yahweh and the thing does not happen and the word is not fulfilled, then it has not been spoken by Yahweh.

If anyone has struck his fellow accidentally, not having any previous feud with him (for example, he goes with his fellow into the forest to cut wood; his arm swings the axe to fell a tree; the head slips off the handle and strikes his companion dead), that man may take refuge in one of these cities and save his life. It must not be allowed that the avenger of blood, in the heat of his anger, should pursue the killer . . . for the man has not deserved to die, having had no previous feud with his companion. . . .

But if it happens that a man has a feud with his fellow and lies in wait for him and falls on him and wounds him fatally and he dies, and the man takes refuge in one of these cities, the elders of his own town shall send to have him seized and hand him over to the avenger of blood to die. You are to show him no pity. You must banish the shedding of innocent blood from Israel, and then you will prosper.

Boundaries

You must not displace your neighbour's boundary mark, set by your forbears, in the inheritance you receive in the land Yahweh is giving into your possession.

Witnesses

A single witness cannot suffice to convict a man of a crime or offence of any kind; whatever the misdemeanour, the evidence of two witnesses or three is required to sustain the charge.

If a malicious witness appears against a man to accuse him of rebellion, both parties to this dispute before Yahweh must be brought before the priests and judges then in office. •The judges must make a careful inquiry, and if it turns out that the witness who accused his brother is a lying witness, •you must deal with him as he would have dealt with his brother. You must banish this evil from your midst. •Others will hear of it and be afraid and never again do such an evil thing among you. •You are to show no pity.

The "Lex Talionis"

Life for life, eye for eye, tooth for tooth, hand for hand, foot for foot.

Captured Towns

When you advance to the attack on any town, first offer it terms of peace. If it accepts these and opens its gates to you, all the people to be found in it shall do forced labour for you and be subject to you. . . .

When you go to war against your enemies and Yahweh your God delivers them into your power and you take prisoners, •if you see a beautiful woman among the prisoners and find her desirable, you may make her your wife •and bring her to your home. She is to shave her head and cut her nails •and take off her prisoner's garb; she is to stay inside your house and must mourn her father and mother for a full month. Then you may go to her and be a husband to her, and she shall be your wife. •Should she cease to please you, you will let her go where she wishes, not selling her for money: you are not to make any profit out of her, since you have had the use of her. . . .

If a man has a stubborn and rebellious son who will not listen to the voice of his father or the voice of his mother, and even when they punish him still will not pay attention to them, •his father and mother shall take hold of him and bring him out to the elders of the town at the gate of that place. •And they shall say to the elders of his town, "This son of ours is stubborn and rebellious and will not listen to us; he is a wastrel and a drunkard." •Then all his fellow citizens shall stone him to death. You must banish this evil from your midst. All Israel will hear of it and be afraid. . . .

If a man marries a wife, and sleeps with her and then turns against her, and taxes her with misconduct and publicly defames her by saying, "I married this woman and when I slept with her I did not find the evidence of her virginity," the girl's father and mother must take her and produce the evidence of her virginity before the elders of the town at the gate. •The girl's father shall then declare to the elders, "I gave this man my daughter for a wife and he has turned against her, •and now he taxes her with misconduct: I found no evidence of virginity in your daughter, he says. But the evidence of my daughter's virginity is here." And they shall spread the cloth out before the elders of the town. •Then the elders of the town shall take the man and flog him •and fine him one hundred silver shekels for publicly defaming a virgin of Israel, and give this money to the girl's father. She shall remain his wife and as long as he lives he may not repudiate her.

But if the accusation that the girl cannot show the evidence of virginity is substantiated, •they shall take her to the door of her father's house and her fellow citizens shall stone her to death for having committed an infamy in Israel by disgracing her father's House. You must banish this evil from your midst. . . .

You must not allow a master to imprison a slave who has escaped from him and come to you. •He shall live with you, among you, wherever he pleases in any one of your towns he chooses; you are not to molest him. . . .

You are not to exploit the hired servant who is poor and destitute, whether he is one of your brothers or a stranger who lives in your towns. •You must pay him his wage each day, not allowing the sun to set before you do, for he is poor and is anxious for it; otherwise he may appeal to Yahweh against you, and it would be a sin for you. . . .

When reaping the harvest in your field, if you have overlooked a sheaf in that field, do not go back for it. Leave it for the stranger, the orphan and the widow, so that Yahweh your God may bless you in all your undertakings. . . .

When two men are fighting together, if the wife of one intervenes to protect her husband from the other's blows by putting out her hand and seizing the other by the private parts, •you shall cut her hand off and show no pity. . . .

If you do not keep and observe all the words of this Law that are written in this book, in the fear of this name of glory and awe: Yahweh your God, •Yahweh will strike you down with monstrous plagues, you and your descendants: with plagues grievous and lasting, diseases pernicious and enduring. •Once more he will bring on you the diseases of Egypt that you dreaded, and they will infect you. Further, Yahweh will bring on you every sickness, every plague, not mentioned in the Book of this Law, until you perish. •There will be only a handful of you left, you who were as many as the stars of heaven.

CHAPTER 3

POLITICAL IDEALS IN CHINA AND GREECE

Political life and the state were basic features of both Chinese and Mediterranean civilization in the classical period. Both civilizations had a strong secular emphasis, with provision of appropriate political order a vital component of successful societies and with appropriate service to the state a vital component of the good life. But the forms of government and the specific political ideals differed greatly.

Political institutions and values are central topics for the classical period, when governments expanded and key civilizations established durable characteristics. Comparison highlights both similarities and differences in this core feature of classical societies. Precisely because the classical societies developed largely separately, comparison provides vital analytical links while calling attention to basic issues in the period as a whole.

Confucianism was the most important single political philosophy developed in classical China; it has enduring influence on Chinese thought and politics even to the present day. Confucius (551–476 B.C.E.) developed his emphases on the state, stable social hierarchy, and social and personal order at a time of disunity and strife in China. He claimed to be restoring traditional Chinese values, and a concept of balance may well have permeated Chinese culture from an earlier period, supporting the Confucian emphasis on personal restraint. By the time of the Han dynasty (202 B.C.E.–220 C.E.), however, emperors understood the importance of Confucian thinking in supporting the government and providing guidelines for the training of a growing bureaucracy.

In contrast to classical China under the Han dynasty, Athens was not a great empire, though it gained colonies. Rather, it was a Greek city-state. Like other city-states in the divided, mountainous peninsula, Athens generated an aristocratic government early on, after 800 B.C.E. But then it went through other political phases, some of which entailed greater involvement of ordinary citizens. By the fifth century, Athens had developed an extensive participatory democracy for those who did have full rights. It also became a leading commercial center and was the site of one of the most vibrant outpourings of art, literature, and philosophy the world has ever known. Pericles, the principal leader of Athens after the mid-fifth century, was an aristocrat who usually operated behind the scenes of the bustling democracy. He was well aware of his city's diverse strengths. Pericles'

Funeral Oration, issued by Athens's main democratic leader (though of aristocratic origin) during the early stages of the Peloponnesian War (between Athens and Sparta, 431–404 B.C.E.), sought to lay out the chief qualities of Athenian democracy.

Confucianism and Athenian democracy demonstrate the great diversity possible in the development of classical societies. Confucianism served a strong, durable empire, with the world's first explicitly educated, centralizing bureaucracy. Not surprisingly, Confucian values and China's government forms were repeatedly revived and, in East Asia, widely imitated, for they provided the most successful political formula devised by any civilization until modern times. Periclean Athens, in contrast, failed after exhaustion and defeat in the war with Sparta. Later societies in the Mediterranean retained a democratic element and certainly a high esteem for cultural achievements, but aristocratic or authoritarian rule became more common. Yet the Periclean ideal, because it was so vividly stated in Thucydides' history and because it was associated with such unusual achievements in art and philosophy, did not die. It became part of a complex Greek legacy to later societies, including those of Western Europe and North America much later, when conditions ripened for a different kind of political democracy.

Questions

1. What political values do Pericles and Confucius share? Would they agree at all on the features of a good government, a good family, or a good servant of the state?

2. What are their main differences, and how would these show up in the way the two societies organized their governments and in what individuals expected from the state? How would Confucius react to the idea of a democracy? What kind of personality training does each passage suggest?

3. Both Pericles and Confucius discuss social inequality, directly or indirectly, along with gender and the role and use of wealth. What are the main differences in social views, and how do these relate to the larger political styles? How would Pericles and Confucius debate the role of merchants in a well-arranged society? How would they defend social and economic inequality?

For Further Discussion

1. Does the comparison between these two great classical leaders suggest any reason why Confucianism had much greater importance in Chinese history than Pericles and his ideas gained in the larger history of the classical Mediterranean civilization and its successors?

2. How did Confucian and Greek ideas about proper human behavior and the importance of political goals compare with the emerging ideas of Hinduism?
3. What changes had occurred in Greek politics by Pericles' time? What were the continuities in political and social values?
4. Why did some early Chinese leaders dislike Confucianism?

CONFUCIANISM: CHINESE POLITICAL VALUES

The following Confucian passage is entitled "The Great Learning." Its origin is uncertain. It may have been written by Confucius himself, but possibly some early followers devised it in the Confucian spirit. The passage was certainly completed by 200 B.C.E. It gained further importance from the attention given to it by a later, neo-Confucian philosopher, Chu Hsi (1120–1200 C.E.), and by the fourteenth century C.E. it had become a standard part of China's civil service examination.

. . .

The Way of learning to be great (or adult education) consists in manifesting the clear character, loving the people, and abiding (*chih*) in the highest good.

Only after knowing what to abide in can one be calm. Only after having been calm can one be tranquil. Only after having achieved tranquillity can one have peaceful repose. Only after having peaceful repose can one begin to deliberate. Only after deliberation can the end be attained. Things have their roots and branches. Affairs have their beginnings and their ends. To know what is first and what is last will lead one near the Way.

The ancients who wished to manifest their clear character to the world would first regulate their families. Those who wished to bring order to their states would first regulate their families. Those who wished to regulate their families would first cultivate their personal lives. Those who wished to rectify their minds would first make their wills sincere. Those who wished to make their wills sincere would first extend their knowledge. . . . when the mind is rectified, the personal life is cultivated; when the personal life is cultivated, the family will be regulated; when the family is regulated, the state will be in order; and when the state is in order, there will be peace throughout the world. From the Son of Heaven [the Emperor] down to the common people, all must regard cultivation of the personal life as the root or foundation. There is never a case when the root is in disorder and yet the branches are in order. . . .

From Wing Tsit Chan, ed., *A Source Book in Chinese Philosophy*, (Princeton, N.J.: Princeton University Press, 1963), 86–92, 94. © 1963 Princeton University Press, 1991 renewed PUP. Reprinted by permission of the publisher.

The *Book of Odes* says, "How profound was King Wen! How he maintained his brilliant virtue without interruption and regarded with reverence that which he abided (chih)." As a ruler, he abided in humanity. As a minister, he abided in reverence. As a son, he abided in filial piety. As a father, he abided in deep love. And in dealing with the people of the country, he abided in faithfulness.

The *Book of Odes* says, . . . "How grave and how dignified" indicates precaution. "How majestic and distinguished" expresses awe-inspiring appearance. "Here is our elegant and accomplished prince. We can never forget him" means that the people cannot forget his eminent character and perfect virtue. The *Book of Odes* says, "Ah! the ancient kings are not forgotten." [Future] rulers deemed worthy what they deemed worthy and loved what they loved, while the common people enjoyed what they enjoyed and benefited from their beneficial arrangements. That was why they are not forgotten even after they passed away. . . .

Confucius said, "In hearing litigations, I am as good as anyone. What is necessary is to enable people not to have litigations at all." Those who would not tell the truth will not dare to finish their words, and a great awe would be struck into people's minds. This is called knowing the root. . . .

What is meant by "making the will sincere" is allowing no self-deception, as when we hate a bad smell or love a beautiful color. This is called satisfying oneself. Therefore the superior man will always be watchful over himself when alone. When the inferior man is alone and leisurely, there is no limit to which he does not go in his evil deeds. Only when he sees a superior man does he then try to disguise himself, concealing the evil and showing off the good in him. But what is the use? For other people see him as if they see his very heart. That is what is meant by saying that what is true in a man's heart will be shown in his outward appearance. Therefore the superior man will always be watchful over himself when alone. . . .

What is meant by saying that in order to govern the state it is necessary first to regulate the family is this: There is no one who cannot teach his own family and yet can teach others. Therefore the superior man (ruler) without going beyond his family, can bring education into completion in the whole state. Filial piety is that with which one serves his ruler. Brotherly respect is that with which one serves his elders, and deep love is that with which one treats the multitude. . . . Therefore the superior man must have the good qualities in himself before he may require them in other people. He must not have the bad qualities in himself before he may require others not to have them. There has never been a man who does not cherish altruism (*shu*) in himself and yet can teach other people. Therefore the order of the state depends on the regulation of the family. . . .

What is meant by saying that peace of the world depends on the order of the state is this: When the ruler treats the elders with respect, then the people will be aroused toward filial piety. When the ruler treats the aged with respect, then the people will be aroused toward brotherly respect. When the ruler treats compassionately the young and the helpless, then the common people will not follow the opposite course. Therefore the ruler has a principle with which, as with a measuring square, he may regulate his conduct. . . .

Therefore the ruler will first be watchful over his own virtue. If he has virtue, he will have the people with him. If he has the people with him, he will have the territory. If he has the territory, he will have wealth. And if he has wealth, he will have its use. Virtue is the root, while wealth is the branch. . . .

There is a great principle for the production of wealth. If there are many producers and few consumers, and if people who produce wealth do so quickly and those who spend it do so slowly, then wealth will always be sufficient. A man of humanity develops his personality by means of his wealth, while the inhumane person develops wealth at the sacrifice of his personality. There has never been a case of a ruler who loved humanity and whose people did not love righteousness. There has never been a case where the people loved righteousness and yet the affairs of the state have not been carried to completion. And there has never been a case where in such a state the wealth collected in the national treasury did not continue in the possession of the ruler.

ATHENIAN DEMOCRACY: PERICLES' FUNERAL ORATION

Pericles was born about 495 B.C.E. An aristocrat who lived a polished life, his oratory could stir the masses of Athenian citizens. He led the city, with few interruptions, from 461 until his death in 429 and was active in advancing its empire as a source of funds. His Funeral Oration was delivered in the winter of 431–430 to honor early Athenian victims of the war with Sparta. A version of the speech was featured in the *History of the Peloponnesian War* by the historian Thucydides, who admired Pericles but who preferred outright aristocratic rule to what he saw as the whims of the masses in democracy.

• • •

I shall speak first of our ancestors, for it is right and at the same time fitting, on an occasion like this, to give them this place of honour in recalling what they did. For this land of ours, in which the same people have never ceased to dwell in an unbroken line of successive generations, they by their valour transmitted to our times a free state.

From Thucydides, *History of the Peloponnesian War*, Vol. 1 Loeb Classical Library®. Vol. 108, trans. Charles Smith (Cambridge, Mass.: Harvard University Press, 1919–1923), 321, 323, 325, 327, 329, 335, 337, 339, 341. Copyright 1928 by the President and Fellows of Harvard College. The Loeb Classical Library ® is a registered trademark of the President and Fellows of Harvard College. Reprinted by permission of the publisher and the Loeb Classical Library.

And not only are they worthy of our praise, but our fathers still more; for they, adding to the inheritance which they received, acquired the empire we now possess and bequeathed it, not without toil, to us who are alive to-day. And we ourselves here assembled, who are now for the most part still in the prime of life, have further strengthened the empire in most respects, and have provided our city with all resources, so that it is sufficient for itself both in peace and in war. . . .

We live under a form of government which does not emulate the institutions of our neighbours; on the contrary, we are ourselves a model which some follow, rather than the imitators of other peoples. It is true that our government is called a democracy, because its administration is in the hands, not of the few, but of the many; yet while as regards the law all men are on an equality for the settlement of their private disputes, as regards the value set on them it is as each man is in any way distinguished that he is preferred to public honours, not because he belongs to a particular class, but because of personal merits; nor, again, on the ground of poverty is a man barred from a public career by obscurity of rank if he but has it in him to do the state a service. And not only in our public life are we liberal, but also as regards our freedom from suspicion of one another in the pursuits of every-day life; for we do not feel resentment at our neighbour if he does as he likes, nor yet do we put on sour looks which, though harmless, are painful to behold. But while we thus avoid giving offence in our private intercourse, in our public life we are restrained from lawlessness chiefly through reverent fear, for we render obedience to those in authority and to the laws, and especially to those laws which are ordained for the succour of the oppressed and those which, though unwritten, bring upon the transgressor a disgrace which all men recognize.

Moreover, we have provided for the spirit many relaxations from toil: we have games and sacrifices regularly throughout the year and homes fitted out with good taste and elegance; and the delight we each day find in these things drives away sadness. And our city is so great that all the products of all the earth flow in upon us, and ours is the happy lot to gather in the good fruits of our own soil with no more homefelt security of enjoyment than we do those of other lands. . . .

For we are lovers of beauty yet with no extravagance and lovers of wisdom yet without weakness. Wealth we employ rather as an opportunity for action than as a subject for boasting; and with us it is not a shame for a man to acknowledge poverty, but the greater shame is for him not to do his best to avoid it. And you will find united in the same persons an interest at once in private and in public affairs, and in others of us who give attention chiefly to business, you will find no lack of insight into political matters. For we alone regard the man who takes no part in public affairs, not as one who minds his own business, but as good for nothing; and we Athenians decide public questions for ourselves or at least endeavour to arrive at a sound understanding of them, in the belief that it is not debate that is a hindrance to action, but rather not to be instructed by debate before the time comes for action. For in truth we have this point also of superiority over other men, to be most daring in action and yet at the same time most given to reflection upon the ventures we mean to undertake; with other men, on the contrary, boldness means ignorance and reflection brings hesitation. . . .

You must daily fix your gaze upon the power of Athens and become lovers of her, and when the vision of her greatness has inspired you, reflect that all this has been acquired by men of courage who knew their duty and in the hour of conflict were moved by a high sense of honour, who, if ever they failed in any enterprise, were resolved that at least their country should not find herself deserted by their valour, but freely sacrificed to her the fairest offering it was in their power to give. For they gave their lives for the common weal, and in so doing won for themselves the praise which grows not old. . . . Do you, therefore, now make these men your examples, and judging freedom to be happiness and courage to be freedom, be not too anxious about the dangers of war. For it is not those that are in evil plight who have the best excuse for being unsparing of their lives, for they have no hope of better days, but rather those who run the risk, if they continue to live, of the opposite reversal of fortune, and those to whom it makes the greatest difference if they suffer a disaster. For to a manly spirit more bitter is humiliation associated with cowardice than death when it comes unperceived in close company with stalwart deeds and public hopes. . . .

If I am to speak also of womanly virtues, referring to those of you who will henceforth be in widowhood, I will sum up all in a brief admonition: Great is your glory if you fall not below the standard which nature has set for your sex, and great also is hers of whom there is least talk among men whether in praise or in blame.

CHAPTER 4

SOCIAL INEQUALITY

All the classical civilizations paid considerable attention to organizing and justifying extensive social inequality. But the systems of hierarchy, and the thinking behind them, varied greatly. The two passages below discuss India's caste system and Roman slavery. Both documents lay out some of the fundamental features of the two systems (in the case of the Roman legal document, the key statement comes at the end). But both also grapple with gray areas in the systems. In the Roman case, lawyers focused on cases in which slaves might be freed (manumitted) and what their status would be as a result. In India, the caste system invited consideration of what would happen if people in a given caste did work outside normal caste boundaries, or even intermarried with another caste. Neither of these situations was normal. That is, although manumission was common in Rome, most slaves were never freed; and most people in India stayed within their caste boundaries. But unusual problems can bring out underlying assumptions. How did Roman and Indian jurists compare in their views of what social inequality was all about, how rigid it should be, how people came to be in the lower orders (slaves or servants or untouchables), and how inequality could be enforced? Comparison contributes to understanding the role of social structure in the classical world.

There is much omitted from the documents. Roman law, most obviously, said nothing about the tasks slaves did. These in fact could vary widely, from dreadful labor in mines to household service or even tutoring upper-class children. Indian law shows how different kinds of jobs were associated with key castes. Neither document uncovers trends: slavery spread in Rome, undermining free labor and reducing the motivation to improve production technology; India's caste system, though it became more complex and moved into additional parts of the subcontinent, was fairly stable in essence. An omission in the Roman document even suggests one of the tricky features of using the existence of a law as evidence of how it affected people's lives: the document describes an improvement in the legal protection of slaves, which did occur as far as the law itself was concerned; what the document does not reveal is that the treatment of slaves deteriorated as the Roman economy came to depend more heavily on slave labor. After all, few slaves could easily invoke the law on their own behalf.

One other complication: Roman thinking about slavery influenced later Western slave systems, but Roman slave law obviously differed from laws in the subsequent slaveholding societies in the Americas. Notably, there was no particular racial element in Rome, though foreignness was a factor. Roman slavery more directly influenced slavery in the Middle East, including the Byzantine Empire, after Rome itself fell.

India's castes seem to have originated when the Indo-Europeans overran previous inhabitants of the subcontinent. Various epics (vedas) refer to the formation of castes. The caste system was unusual in slotting people to certain social levels by birth and regulating contact among castes as well as jobs. People could move within castes, acquiring more or less money; but the system was fundamentally static, justified by a religion that argued that living up to caste duties in one life prepared a person for advancement, through reincarnation, in the next existence. The caste system solidified over time, gradually spreading through more of India and becoming more intricate, with scores of specific castes. The caste system persisted in India into the twentieth century. Now outlawed, the system has left its mark: caste origins still define considerable social barriers in Indian society. This system, in sum, is a basic feature of Indian history.

Questions

1. What was manumission in the Roman slave system; why would it have no applicability in India's caste system?
2. What kind of religious arguments supported the caste system? How did Roman law argue that slavery was compatible with justice? How is it clear, from Roman law, that slaves did not constitute a caste?
3. Were lower castes in India more or less free than Roman slaves? How might an Indian apologist argue that the caste system was a relatively beneficent form of social inequality?

For Further Discussion

1. Why did classical societies uniformly develop radical social inequality, and why were almost all major religious and political leaders comfortable in justifying it?
2. How do the Roman and Indian systems of inequality compare with systems of inequality (and their justifications) in modern industrial societies?
3. Which would be better, in terms of quality of life: to be a Roman slave or a lower-caste Indian?

INDIA'S CASTE SYSTEM: *THE LAWS OF MANU*

The Laws of Manu was written between the first century B.C.E. and the second or third century C.E., constituting the first systematic compilation of Indian law. Early legal statements had been extracted from the Indian epics. *The Laws of Manu* maintained a close relationship with Hinduism, and indeed Manu, the creator god, gave divine sanction to the social system. Other religious elements, such as the idea of pollution inherent in farming because of the need to kill even small creatures, were used to justify the laws' social prescriptions. *The Laws of Manu* provided the basic classification of the caste system, though the original four castes later expanded greatly. Note the relationship also to views of gender and the inferiority of women, and the low valuation of manual labor.

. . .

[*87*] But to protect this whole creation, the lustrous one made separate innate activities for those born of his mouth, arms, thighs, and feet. [88] For priests, he ordained teaching and learning, sacrificing for themselves and sacrificing for others, giving, and receiving. [*89*] Protecting his subjects, giving, having sacrifices performed, studying and remaining unaddicted to the sensory objects are . . . for a ruler. Protecting his livestock . . . trading, lending money, and farming the land are for a commoner. The Lord assigned only one activity to a servant; serving these [other] classes without resentment.

[*95*] A ruler in adversity may also make a living by all of these (means); but he should never be so proud as to assume the livelihood of his betters. [*96*] If a man of the lowest caste should, through greed, make his living by the innate activities of his superiors, the king should confiscate his wealth and banish him immediately. [*97*] One's own duty, (even) without any good qualities, is better than someone else's duty well done; for a man who makes his living by someone else's duty immediately falls from (his own) caste. [*98*] A commoner who cannot make a living by his own duty may also subsist by the livelihood of a servant; but he must not commit actions that (he) should not do, and he should stop when he can. [*99*] If a servant is unable to engage in the service of the twice-born and is on the brink of losing his sons and wife, he may make a living by the innate activities of a manual labourer, [*100*] practising those activities of a manual labourer and those various handicrafts by which the twice-born are served.

[*101*] A priest who remains on his own path and does not engage in the commoner's livelihood, even when he is fainting and starving for lack of a livelihood,

From *The Laws of Manu*, trans. with an introduction and notes by Wendy Doniger and with Brian K. Smith (Harmondsworth, Eng.: Penguin Books, 1991), 12–33, 242–50. Copyright © Wendy Doniger and Brian K. Smith, 1991. Reprinted by permission of the publisher.

should act in keeping with the following law: [*102*] a priest in adversity may accept gifts from anyone, for the assertion that 'What is purifying can be defiled' is not established by law. [*103*] Accepting gifts from despicable people or teaching them or sacrificing for them is not a fault in priests, for they are the equals of fire or water. [*104*] A man who eats the food of anyone, no matter who, when he is on the brink of losing his life is not smeared with evil, just as the sky is not smeared with mud. . . .

[*112*] A priest who cannot make a living should even glean (ears of corn) and gather (single grains) from any (field) whatsoever; gleaning is better than accepting gifts, and gathering is preferable even to that. . . .

[*117*] Neither a priest nor a ruler should lend money at interest, but (either) may, if he really wishes, and for religious purposes, lend at very low interest to a very evil man.

[*118*] A ruler in extremity who takes even a quarter (of the crop) is free from offence if he protects his subjects to his utmost ability. [*119*] His own duty is conquest, and he must not turn his back on a challenge; when he has protected the commoner with his sword, he may collect the just tax from him: [*120*] the tax on grain from the commoners is one eighth, (or) one twentieth, (or) at least one 'scratch-penny.' Servants, artisans, and craftsmen should give him the service of their innate activities. . . .

[*123*] Serving priests alone is recommended as the best innate activity of a servant; for whatever he does other than this bears no fruit for him. [*124*] They should assign him a livelihood out of their own family property according to his deserts, taking into account his ability, his skill, and the number of his dependants. [*125*] They should give him the leftovers of their food, their old clothes, the spoiled parts of their grain, and their worn-out household utensils.

[*126*] A servant cannot commit any crime that causes him to fall, nor does he deserve any transformative ritual; he has no authority to carry out duties, nor is he forbidden to carry out duties. [*127*] But servants who want to carry out duties, who know duty, and who emulate the duties of good men, without reciting Vedic verses, are not defiled but praised. [*128*] For the more a servant undertakes the behavior of good men, without resentment, the more he gains this world and the next, blameless. [*129*] A servant should not amass wealth, even if he has the ability, for a servant who has amassed wealth annoys priests.

ROMAN SLAVERY

The Roman slave law evolved gradually, from the republic onward. The passage below is from a textbook written in the second century C.E. by a jurist named Gaius. It pulled together a great deal of prior legislation, particularly the *Lex* [law] *Aelia Sentia* of 4 C.E., early in the empire. The text claims, of course, that

wise emperors had steadily improved the treatment of slaves. The law also reflects Roman belief in natural laws—laws that follow from the inherent order of nature—from which man-made law derived. Finally, the code reflected the importance, and the limits, of the status of citizen, an area in which Rome was like Athens in imposing strict definitions. Along with the belief that slaves were property, citizenship status helped mark off the boundaries of slave life—though, in contrast to the caste system of India, the boundaries were not impenetrable.

• • •

(1) Every community that is governed by laws and customs uses partly its own particular law and partly the law common to all mankind. For whatever system of justice each community establishes for itself, that is its own particular law and is called 'civil law' as the law particular to that community (*civitas*), while that which natural reason has established among all human beings is observed equally by all peoples, and is called 'law of nations' (*ius gentium*) since it is the standard of justice which all mankind observes. Thus the Roman People in part follows its own particular system of justice and in part the common law of all mankind. We shall note what this distinction implies in particular instances at the relevant point. . . .

(9) The principal distinction made by the law of persons is this, that all human beings are either free men or slaves.

(10) Next, some free men are free-born (*ingenui*), others freedmen (*libertini*).

(11) The free-born are those who were free when they were born; freedmen are those who have been released from a state of slavery. . . .

Subjects

(13) The *Lex Aelia Sentia* requires that any slaves who had been put in chains as a punishment by their masters or had been branded or interrogated under torture about some crime of which they were found to be guilty; and any who had been handed over to fight as gladiators or with wild beasts, or had belonged to a troupe of gladiators or had been imprisoned; should, if the same owner or any subsequent owner manumits them, become free men of the same status as subject foreigners. . . .

(14) 'Subject foreigners' is the name given to those who had once fought a regular war against the Roman People, were defeated, and gave themselves up.

(15) We will never accept that slaves who have suffered a disgrace of this kind can become either Roman citizens or Latins (whatever the procedure of manumission and whatever their age at the time, even if they were in their masters' full ownership); we consider that they should always be held to have the status of subjects.

Citizens

(16) But if a slave has suffered no such disgrace, he sometimes becomes a Roman citizen when he is manumitted, and sometimes a Latin. . . .

(19) A just reason for manumission exists when, for example, a man manumits in the presence of a council a natural son, daughter, brother or sister; or a child he has brought up, or his *paedagogus* [the slave whose job it had been to look after him as a child], or a slave whom he wants to employ as his manager (*procurator*), or a slave girl whom he intends to marry.

(20) . . . Slaves over thirty can in fact be manumitted at any time; so that manumissions can even take place when the Praetor or Proconsul is passing by on his way to the baths or theatre, for instance.

(21) Furthermore, a slave under thirty can become a Roman citizen by manumission if he has been declared free in the Will of an insolvent master and appointed as his heir [i.e. to take over the liabilities: the *heres necessarius*], provided that he is not excluded by another heir. . . .

Digression—Subjects

(25) But those who have the status of subjects cannot receive anything at all by Will, no more than any foreigner can, and according to the general opinion, they cannot make a Will themselves.

(26) The lowest kind of freedom is therefore that of those whose status is that of subjects; and no statute, Senate Recommendation or Imperial Constitution gives them access to Roman citizenship.

(27) They are even banned from the city of Rome or anywhere within the hundredth milestone from Rome, and any who break this law have to be sold publicly together with their property, subject to the condition that they must never serve as slaves in the city of Rome or within a hundred miles of Rome, and that they must never be manumitted; if they are manumitted, the law stipulates that they become slaves of the Roman People. . . .

(39) Just reasons for manumission exist where, for instance, someone manumits his father or mother, or his *paedagogus,* or someone who has been brought up with him. . . .

(43) Those who own more than two and not more than ten slaves are allowed to manumit up to half the number; those who own more than ten and not more than thirty are allowed to manumit up to a third; but those who own more than thirty and not more than a hundred have the right to manumit up to a quarter; and finally, those who own more than a hundred and not more than five hundred are allowed to manumit not more than a fifth; those who own more than five hundred are not given the right to manumit any more—the law forbids anyone to manumit more than a hundred. But if you only own one or two slaves, you are not covered by this law, and there are no restrictions upon your freedom to manumit. . . .

(52) Slaves are in the power of their owners. This power is derived from the common law of nations, for we can see that among all nations alike owners have the power of life and death over their slaves, and whatever is acquired by a slave is acquired on behalf of his owner.

(53) But nowadays neither Roman citizens nor any other people who are subject to the sovereignty of the Roman People have the right to treat their slaves with excessive and unreasonable brutality. For a Constitution of the Divine Emperor Antoninus orders anyone who kills his own slave without due reason to be brought to justice in exactly the same way as one who kills another's slave. Excessively harsh treatment on the part of owners is also limited by a Constitution of the same Emperor; for when certain provincial governors asked him for a ruling regarding slaves who had taken refuge at the temples of gods or statues of emperors, he declared that owners were to be forced to sell their slaves if the cruelty of their behaviour appeared to be unbearable.

CHAPTER 5

CONDITIONS OF WOMEN IN THE CLASSICAL CIVILIZATIONS

China and India

Like the early civilizations, all the classical centers of civilization were patriarchal societies, in which women were treated as inferiors to men and, in some respects, as their property. Materials from China and India abundantly illustrate women's inferiority. They also obviously contrast with predominant modern values, where inequality is at least more contested. Yet, it is important not to oversimplify classical patriarchy. Women were not absolutely powerless. By observing certain behaviors and by using various private or even public recourses available to them, they might gain partial control over their condition. This important complexity in patriarchy also emerges from presentations of women in the laws and literature of classical societies. Of course, these materials offer only partial insight into women's real lives; they suggest standards for women more than real behaviors, and their relevance varied with social class. Even the cultural discussions of women, however, suggest how some women might use existing standards to their benefit or, by force of personality, might even defy the standards to some degree. The discussions also demonstrate important disagreements within classical societies, even among dominant men, over exactly how women should be treated. Here, it is particularly important to assess the extent to which defenders of women really offered different evaluations of women's rights and qualities—a particularly interesting issue in Rome.

Paying attention to women in world history presents some challenges, in part because of lack of sources, in part because women's inferior conditions hinder an understanding of their potential range of activity. Comparison helps show differences as well as similarities in patterns of inferiority, opening the topic for more sophisticated analysis.

Each of the classical societies offered a somewhat different version of patriarchal inequality. Chinese materials reflect the Confucian emphasis on hierarchy and on order, while also illustrating certain opportunities for informal expression for women within this system. In India women's conditions were more commonly portrayed in terms of religion and intense emotion, with an emphasis on moral duty but also more frequent reference to attachments through love and beauty.

The selections that follow constitute cultural evidence—beliefs held by men and at least some women—of women's inferiority and separate roles. Culture is very powerful, and that helps explain why women, taught ideas of these sorts from girlhood, might accept their distinct conditions. But culture is not the only story of women and gender relations. Societies also have birthrates, specific work assignments, and educational systems, all of which may be influenced by beliefs but which also may vary or change for other reasons. These parts of the picture also affect women powerfully. We lack details in many of these areas for the classical period, which is one reason for relying on cultural documentation. Furthermore, cultures not only helped shape actual conditions but also tended to persist, which explains why ideas formed in classical civilizations lasted so long. One of the Chinese documents cited below, from a manual by the upper-class woman author Ban Zhao, was still being used to educate women in China as late as the nineteenth century.

Questions

1. Did any of the classical cultures authorize men to think they could treat women any way they saw fit?
2. How do Chinese ideas about women reflect larger Confucian values? How do Indian ideas mirror larger religious and social beliefs? (Note: Indian thinkers disagreed about whether women would need to be reincarnated as men to reach a higher spiritual plane.)
3. What would Chinese and Indian thinkers agree about, where women are concerned? Where would they disagree? Did their ideal women embody the same characteristics? Which society produced greater emphasis on factors such as emotion and love in describing relations between men and otherwise inferior women?
4. Standards for women produced measurements of inadequacy. How do the Indian and Chinese materials differ in suggesting why a husband might want to reject a wife?
5. What hints do the following materials give about how women could survive in classical, patriarchal societies? What kinds of women had the most power? (Answering this question provides an important clue to the lives of many real women in patriarchal families.) Could women make any claims to fair treatment in any of the societies? How could a Chinese woman make a case, within the cultural system, that she was not getting what she needed to fulfill her obligations as a woman? Could Roman or Indian women make such a case, and would it resemble China's?

For Further Discussion

1. Why did patriarchal conditions develop so widely? Why didn't women rebel against them?
2. Why was there less gender inequality in the lower classes than in the upper classes in the classical period?
3. Judging by the cultural standards, were women better off in classical India or classical China.
4. What other kinds of evidence, besides stories and prescriptions, is essential to evaluating women's conditions in the past?

CHINA: "MOTHER OF MENCIUS" AND BAN ZHAO

Chinese authors paid considerable attention to women during the Han dynasty. The following three selections show various facets of patriarchal beliefs: the devoted mother, a bad wife, and a standard statement of women's characteristics and duties. Do they fit together consistently? The first selection is from *Biographies of Heroic Women* written by the eminent scholar Liu Xiang in about 79–78 B.C.E. Mencius was a Confucian philosopher who lived from about 372 to 289 B.C.E. and who was widely revered. Because he was left fatherless, his mother played a great role in raising him, and the stories about her provided standard examples of maternal ideals. The second selection is from the most famous Han text on women's virtue, by Ban Zhao (ca. 45–116 C.E.); she was a prominent woman scholar whose own life would seem to contradict the values she preached.

• • •

THE MOTHER OF MENCIUS

The mother of Mencius lived in Zou in a house near a cemetery. When Mencius was a little boy he liked to play burial rituals in the cemetery, happily building tombs and grave mounds. His mother said to herself, "This is no place to bring up my son."

She moved near the marketplace in town. Mencius then played merchant games of buying and selling. His mother again said, "This is no place to bring up my son."

So once again she moved, this time next to a school house. Mencius then played games of ancestor sacrifices and practiced the common courtesies between students

From Patricia Buckley Ebrey, ed., *Chinese Civilization: A Sourcebook* (2nd ed., New York: Free Press, 1993), 72–74. Copyright © 1993 by Patricia Buckley Ebrey. Reprinted by permission of The Free Press, a Division of Simon & Schuster Adult Publishing Group.

and teachers. His mother said, "At last, this is the right place for my son!" There they remained.

When Mencius grew up he studied the six arts of propriety, music, archery, charioteering, writing, and mathematics. Later he became a famous Confucian scholar. Superior men commented that Mencius's mother knew the right influences for her sons. The *Book of Songs* says, "That admirable lady, what will she do for them!"

When Mencius was young, he came home from school one day and found his mother was weaving at the loom. She asked him, "Is school out already?"

He replied, "I left because I felt like it."

His mother took her knife and cut the finished cloth on her loom. Mencius was startled and asked why. She replied, "Your neglecting your studies is very much like my cutting the cloth. The superior person studies to establish a reputation and gain wide knowledge. He is calm and poised and tries to do no wrong. If you do not study now, you will surely end up as a menial servant and will never be free from troubles. It would be just like a woman who supports herself by weaving to give it up. How long could such a person depend on her husband and son to stave off hunger? If a woman neglects her work or a man gives up the cultivation of his character, they may end up as common thieves if not slaves!"

Shaken, from then on Mencius studied hard from morning to night. He studied the philosophy of the master and eventually became a famous Confucian scholar. Superior men observed that Mencius's mother understood the way of motherhood. The *Book of Songs* says, "That admirable lady, what will she tell them!"

After Mencius was married, one day as he was going into his private quarters, he encountered his wife not fully dressed. Displeased, Mencius stopped going into his wife's room. She then went to his mother, begged to be sent home, and said, "I have heard that the etiquette between a man and a woman does not apply in their private room. But lately I have been too causal, and when my husband saw me improperly dressed, he was displeased. He is treating me like a stranger. It is not right for a woman to live as a guest; therefore, please send me back to my parents."

Mencius's mother called him to her and said, "It is polite to inquire before you enter a room. You should make some loud noise to warn anyone inside, and as you enter, you should keep your eyes low so that you will not embarrass anyone. Now, you have not behaved properly, yet you are quick to blame others for their impropriety. Isn't that going a little too far?"

Mencius apologized and took back his wife. Superior men said that his mother understood the way to be a mother-in-law.

When Mencius was living in Qi, he was feeling very depressed. His mother saw this and asked him, "Why are you looking so low?" . . .

Mencius answered, "I have heard that the superior man judges his capabilities and then accepts a position. . . . Today my ideas are not being used in Qi, so I wish to go somewhere else. But I am worried because you are getting too old to travel about the country."

His mother answered, "A woman's duties are to cook the five grains, heat the wine, look after her parents-in-law, make clothes, and that is all! Therefore, she cultivates the skills required in the women's quarters and has no ambition to manage affairs outside of the house. The *Book of Changes* says, 'In her central place, she attends to the preparation of the food.' The *Book of Songs* says, 'It will be theirs neither to do wrong nor to do good, / Only about the spirits and the food will they have to think.' This means that a woman's duty is not to control or to take charge. Instead she must follow the 'three submissions.' When she is young, she must submit to her parents. After her marriage, she must submit to her husband. When she is widowed, she must submit to her son. These are the rules of propriety. Now you are an adult and I am old; therefore, whether you go depends on what you consider right, whether I follow depends on the rules of propriety."

Superior men observed that Mencius's mother knew the proper course for women. The *Book of Songs* says, "Serenely she looks and smiles, / Without any impatience she delivers her instructions."

BAN ZHAO'S *ADMONITIONS FOR WOMEN*

Humility

In ancient times, on the third day after a girl was born, people placed her at the base of the bed, gave her a pot shard to play with, and made a sacrifice to announce her birth. She was put below the bed to show that she was lowly and weak and should concentrate on humbling herself before others. Playing with a shard showed that she should get accustomed to hard work and concentrate on being diligent. Announcing her birth to the ancestors showed that she should focus on continuing the sacrifices. These three customs convey the unchanging path for women and the ritual traditions.

Humility means yielding and acting respectful, putting others first and oneself last, never mentioning one's own good deeds or denying one's own faults, enduring insults and bearing with mistreatment, all with due trepidation. Industriousness means going to bed late, getting up early, never shirking work morning or night, never refusing to take on domestic work, and completing everything that needs to be done neatly and carefully. Continuing the sacrifices means serving one's husband-master with appropriate demeanor, keeping oneself clean and pure, never joking or laughing, and preparing pure wine and food to offer to the ancestors.

There has never been a woman who had these three traits and yet ruined her reputation or fell into disgrace. If a woman loses these three traits, she will have no name to preserve and will not be able to avoid shame.

Devotion

According to the rites, a man is obligated to take a second wife but nothing is written about a woman marrying twice. Hence the saying, "A husband is one's Heaven: one cannot flee Heaven; one cannot leave a husband." Heaven punishes those whose actions offend the spirits; a husband looks down on a wife who violates the rites and proprieties. Thus the *Model for Women says*, "To please one man is her goal; to displease one man ends her goal." It follows from this that a woman must seek her husband's love—not through such means as flattery, flirting, or false intimacy, but rather through devotion. . . .

If a husband be unworthy then he possesses nothing by which to control his wife. If a wife be unworthy, then she possesses nothing with which to serve her husband. If a husband does not control his wife, then the rules of conduct manifesting his authority are abandoned and broken. If a wife does not serve her husband, then the proper relationship (between men and women) and the natural order of things are neglected and destroyed. As a matter of fact the purpose of these two (the controlling of women by men, and the serving of men by women) is the same.

Now examine the gentlemen of the present age. They only know that wives must be controlled, and that the husband's rules of conduct manifesting his authority must be established. They therefore teach their boys to read books and (study) histories. But they do not in the least understand that husbands and masters must (also) be served, and that the proper relationship and the rites should be maintained.

Yet only to teach men and not to teach women,—is that not ignoring the essential relation between them? According to the "Rites," it is the rule to begin to teach children to read at the age of eight years, and by the age of fifteen years they ought then to be ready for cultural training. Only why should it not be (that girls' education as well as boys' be) according to this principle? . . . As *Yin* and *Yang* are not of the same nature, so man and woman have different characteristics. The distinctive quality of the *Yang* is rigidity; the function of the *Yin* is yielding. Man is honored for strength; a woman is beautiful on account of her gentleness. Hence there arose the common saying: "A man though born like a wolf may, it is feared, become a weak monstrosity; a woman though born like a mouse may, it is feared, become a tiger."

Now for self-culture nothing equals respect for others. To counteract firmness nothing equals compliance. Consequently it can be said that the Way of respect and acquiescence is woman's most important principle of conduct. So respect may be defined as nothing other than holding on to that which is permanent; and acquiescence nothing other than being liberal and generous. Those who are steadfast in devotion

From Nancy Lee Swan, *Panchao : Foremost Woman Scholar of China* (New York: Century Company, 1932), 82–87.

know that they should stay in their proper places; those who are liberal and generous esteem others, and honor and serve (them).

If husband and wife have the habit of staying together, never leaving one another, and following each other around within the limited space of their own rooms, then they will lust after and take liberties with one another. From such action improper language will arise between the two. This kind of discussion may lead to licentiousness. Out of licentiousness will be born a heart of disrespect to the husband. Such a result comes from not knowing that one should stay in one's proper place.

Furthermore, affairs may be either crooked or straight; words may be either right or wrong. Straightforwardness cannot but lead to quarreling; crookedness cannot but lead to accusation. If there are really accusations and quarrels, then undoubtedly there will be angry affairs. Such a result comes from not esteeming others, and not honoring and serving (them).

(If wives) suppress not contempt for husbands, then it follows (that such wives) rebuke and scold (their husbands). (If husbands) stop not short of anger, then they are certain to beat (their wives). The correct relationship between husband and wife is based upon harmony and intimacy, and (conjugal) love is grounded in proper union. Should actual blows be dealt, how could matrimonial relationship be preserved? Should sharp words be spoken, how could (conjugal) love exist? If love and proper relationship both be destroyed, then husband and wife are divided.

India: *The Ramayana*

The following excerpts are from a great Indian epic, the *Ramayana*, attributed to an author named Valmiki. It was written in Sanskrit during the third century B.C.E., but a more definitive version was compiled around 200 C.E. The story deals with the turbulent life of a god-king, Rama, and his wife, Sita. Rama is driven into exile, and his wife insists on accompanying him. Sita is abducted and Rama battles successfully to win her back. The story provides a host of complex clues about marriage ideals in India's version of a patriarchal society. One reference, to an ordeal by burning, foreshadows a custom (suttee) introduced in a later period of Indian history, according to which some women were expected to throw themselves on their husbands' funeral pyres, based on the assumption that with her husband dead, a woman's life was over.

• • •

From Valmiki, *The Ramayana*, trans. Hari Prasad Shastri (London, 1957), 1: 221, 227; 3: 103–4, 287–89, 310–16, 334–38, 341–42.

The sweet-speaking Sita, worthy of Rama's love, thus being instructed to remain in Ayodhya, though filled with affection, indignantly replied: "O Offspring of a great king, O Rama, how canst thou speak in such wise? O Prince, thy words evoke laughter. O Chief of Men, father, mother, son and daughter-in-law live according to their merit and are dependent on it, but a wife enjoys the fortune of her husband since she is a part of himself. I am therefore entitled to share thy father's command and also go into exile.

"The happiness of a woman depends on her husband, neither father, mother, son, relative or companion avail her at death; in this world and in the other world, the husband alone is her all-in-all. If thou to-day depart for the forest, I will precede thee on foot, clearing the thorns and kusha grass from thy path. O Hero, relinquishing anger and pride, take me with thee without hesitation. There is no fault in me that merits my remaining here, without thee. The joy experienced by lords of men whether dwelling in a palace or transported in an aerial chariot through the heavens or possessing the eightfold psychic powers, is far inferior to the joy of the wife in the service of her lord. My royal father has instructed me fully in the duties of a wife and, therefore, I have no need of further instruction in the matter. Assuredly I shall accompany thee to the forest, uninhabited by men, filled with savage beasts, such as bears and bulls. O My Hero, I will dwell in the forest as happily as in the palace of my father, having no anxiety in the three worlds save the service of my spouse. O Hero, I will wander with thee in the forest according to the ancient spiritual ordinance, free from desire for pleasure, traversing the honey-scented woodland. O Lord of my Life, since thou canst protect and support innumerable people, canst thou not more easily protect me? Without doubt to-day I shall enter the forest with thee, O Fortunate Prince, none can break my resolve. . . .

Thus Sita, lamenting and embracing . . . Rama, wept aloud. From her eyes, like a she elephant wounded by poisoned arrows, long-restrained tears issued, as fire is kindled by the friction of wood. Crystal drops fell from her eyes as water slips from the petals of the lotus flowers. The face of the princess resembling the full moon, withered by the fire of intense grief, looked like a lotus withdrawn from water.

Shri Ramachandra, taking Sita, afflicted and fainting, in his arms, spoke to her in the following wise: "O goddess I do not desire even to enter heaven if it causes thee pain! Nought do I fear! Like Brahma [the creator God], I am wholly fearless! Though able to protect thee in every way, yet not fully knowing thy mind, I declined to let thee share my exile. Seeing thou art destined to share my exile, I do not desire to abandon thee, as a man of virtuous conduct determines not to sacrifice his good name. . . .

This is eternal righteousness—to obey the command of thy parents, fixed in the practice of truth. O Sita, not knowing thy mind, I advised thee not to accompany me, but now seeing thy fixed resolve I desire to take thee with me. . . . [During the exile Sita is seized by a king, Ravana, aided by a demon. Rama ultimately defeats Ravana.]

Rama Repudiates Sita

Beholding Sita standing humbly beside him, Rama gave expression to the feelings he had concealed in his heart, saying:—

"O Illustrious Princess, I have re-won thee and mine enemy has been defeated on the battlefield; I have accomplished all that fortitude could do; my wrath is appeased; the insult and the one who offered it have both been obliterated by me. To-day my prowess has been manifested, to-day mine exertions have been crowned with success, to-day I have fulfilled my vow and am free. As ordained by destiny the stain of thy separation and thine abduction by that fickle-minded titan has been expunged by me, a mortal. Of what use is great strength to the vacillating, who do not with resolution avenge the insult offered to them? . . .

When Sita heard Rama speak in this wise, her large doe-like eyes filled with tears and, beholding the beloved of his heart standing close to him, Rama, who was apprehensive of public rumour, was torn within himself. Then, in the presence of the monkeys and the titans, he said to Sita, whose eyes were as large as lotus petals, her dark hair plaited, and who was endowed with faultless limbs:—

"What a man should do in order to wipe out an insult, I have done by slaying Ravana for I guard mine honour jealously! . . . Be happy and let it be known that this arduous campaign, so gloriously terminated through the support of my friends, was not undertaken wholly for thy sake. I was careful to wipe out the affront paid to me completely and to avenge the insult offered to mine illustrious House.

"A suspicion has arisen, however, with regard to thy conduct, and thy presence is as painful to me as a lamp to one whose eye is diseased! Henceforth go where it best pleaseth thee, I give thee leave, O Daughter of Janaka. O Lovely One, the ten regions are at thy disposal; I can have nothing more to do with thee! What man of honour would give rein to his passion so far as to permit himself to take back a woman who has dwelt in the house of another? Thou hast been taken into Ravana's lap and he has cast lustful glances on thee; how can I reclaim thee, I who boast of belonging to an illustrious House? The end which I sought in re-conquering thee has been gained; I no longer have any attachment for thee; go where thou desirest! . . . Assuredly Ravana, beholding thy ravishing and celestial beauty, will not have respected thy person during the time that thou didst dwell in his abode."

On this, that noble lady, worthy of being addressed in sweet words, hearing that harsh speech from her beloved lord, who for long had surrounded her with every homage, wept bitterly, and she resembled a creeper that has been torn away by the trunk of a great elephant.

"Why dost thou address such words to me, O Hero, as a common man addresses an ordinary woman? I swear to thee, O Long-armed Warrior, that my conduct is worthy of thy respect! It is the behavior of other women that has filled thee with distrust! Relinquish thy doubts since I am known to thee! If my limbs came in contact with

another's, it was against my will, O Lord, and not through any inclination on my part; it was brought about by fate. [Sita enters a burning pyre to demonstrate her innocence.] Thereafter the Witness of the whole world, the god of fire, addressed Rama, saying:—

"Here is Vaidehi, O Rama, there is no sin in her! Neither by word, feeling or glance has thy lovely consort shown herself to be unworthy of thy noble qualities. Separated from thee, that unfortunate one was borne away against her will in the lonely forest by Ravana, who had grown proud on account of his power. Though imprisoned and closely guarded by titan women in the inner apartments, thou wast ever the focus of her thoughts and her supreme hope. Surrounded by hideous and sinister women, though tempted and threatened, Maithili never gave place in her heart to a single thought for that titan and was solely absorbed in thee. She is pure and without taint, do thou receive Maithili; it is my command that she should not suffer reproach in any way."

These words filled Rama's heart with delight and he, the most eloquent of men, that loyal soul, reflected an instant within himself, his glance full of joy. Then the illustrious, steadfast and exceedingly valiant Rama, the first of virtuous men, hearing those words addressed to him, said to the Chief of the Gods:—

"On account of the people, it was imperative that Sita should pass through this trial by fire; this lovely woman had dwelt in Ravana's inner apartments for a long time. Had I not put the innocence of Janaki to the test, the people would have said:— 'Rama, the son of Dasaratha is governed by lust!' It was well known to me that Sita had never given her heart to another and that [she], was ever devoted to me. . . . That virtuous woman could never belong to any other than myself for she is to me what the light is to the sun. [A later chapter was added, responding to the belief that even innocent cohabitation with another man is unacceptable and detailing Rama's renewed exile of Sita and her death.]

CHAPTER 6

MILITARY ROLES IN CHINA AND ROME

The great empires that culminated in the Han dynasty in China and the Roman Empire around the Mediterranean invite comparison in many ways. They both ruled huge territories (not too dissimilar in total size) and populations (about 56 million people at the height of Han China, about 54 million in the Roman Empire). They created monuments and institutions long remembered, indeed long influential, and they both ultimately declined, though at slightly different times and with markedly different long-range outcomes. The Chinese Empire began to form earlier than its Roman counterpart, and it defined elements that persist in China to the present day, including core geography. The Roman achievement later became more fragmented.

Both empires, of course, depended greatly on military conquest and sustained military organization. The great Roman legions formed one of the most famous and effective fighting forces in world history, with rigorous training and comradeship among the soldiers, under the leadership of powerful generals. Chinese generals lacked the power of their Roman counterparts, for there was more bureaucratic control. They too stressed discipline, but they also delved more deeply into issues of strategy and even basic philosophy. Sun-Tzu, in the fifth century B.C.E. (under the still-fragmented Zhou dynasty), wrote one of the great theoretical works of all time, *The Art of War*, still widely studied and indeed revived by Mao Zedong and used to promote doctrines of guerrilla warfare in the century.

The following documents come from very different stages of empire: Sun Tzu was writing to promote better military organization when Chinese imperial unity had yet fully to form. Vegetius wrote at the end of empire, intending to advise one of the later Roman emperors (either Theodosius I or Valentian III) and to correct contemporary failings in recruitment and training. Vegetius did borrow from earlier writings, dating back to the Republican period, but his work may certainly have been colored by the increasing problems Rome was facing with the Germanic invasions.

Questions

1. How do Sun-Tzu and Vegetius approach the subject of military success? Do both works suggest the reasons China and Rome achieved such great military power in the classical period? Are the reasons entirely different in the two cases?
2. To what extent do the two works reflect very different stages in the imperial process? Can Sun-Tzu be interpreted as an author writing before the full development of empire, and Vegetius as an author writing when the empire is on the defensive?
3. What do the two works imply about the importance of the military in the larger society, in China and in Rome, respectively?

For Further Discussion

1. Is it valid to suggest that these two documents imply significant differences in the military role in the Chinese and Roman empires, respectively? What else would you need to know to deal with this question more fully?
2. Why has Sun-Tzu survived as a military treatise worth reading, and no comparable Roman treatise exists?

SUN-TZU, *THE ART OF WAR*

This is probably one of the two most famous military books ever written. (The other would be the much more modern work by Clausewitz, written in the 1820s.)

• • •

Strategic Offense

Master Sun said:

In War,
    Better take
    A State
    Intact
    Than destroy it

Better take
    An army
    A regiment,
    A detachment,
    A company,
    Intact
    Than destroy them.

Ultimate excellence lies
    Not in winning
    Every battle
    But in defeating the enemy
    Without ever fighting.
    The highest form of warfare
    Is to attack
    Strategy itself;

The next,
    To attack
    Alliances;

    The next,
    To attack
    Armies

The lowest form of war is
    To attack
    Cities.
    Siege warfare
    Is a last resort.

In a siege,
    Three months are needed
    To assemble
    Protective shields,
    Armored wagons,
    And sundry
    Siege weapons and equipment;
    Another three months
    To pile
    Earthen ramps.

The general who cannot
    Master his anger
    Orders his troops out
    Like ants,
    Sending one in three
    To their deaths,
    Without taking the city.
    This is the calamity
    Of siege warfare.

The Skillful Strategist
    Defeats the enemy
    Without doing battle,
    Captures the city
    Without laying siege,
    Overthrows the enemy state
    Without protracted war.

He strives for supremacy
    Under heaven
    Intact,
    Intact,
    His men and weapons
    Still keen,
    His gain
    Complete.
    This is the method of
    Strategic attack.

In War,
    With forces ten
    To the enemy's one,
    Surround him;
    With two,
    Split in half.
    If equally matched,
    Fight it out;
    If fewer in number,
    Lie low;
    If weaker,
    Escape.

A small force
    Obstinately fighting
    Will be captured
    By a larger force.

The general is the prop
    Of the nation.

When the prop is solid,
    The nation is strong.
When the prop is flawed,
    The nation is weak.

A ruler can bring misfortune
    Upon his troops
    In three ways:

    Ordering them
    To advance
    Or to retreat
    When they should not
    Is called
    Hobbling the army;

    Ignorant interference
    In military decisions
    Confuses
    Officers and men;

    Ignorant meddling
    In military appointments
    Perplexes
    Officers and men.

When an army is confused and perplexed,
    The feudal princes
    Will cause trouble;
        This creates
    Chaos in the ranks
    And gives away
    Victory

There are five essentials
    For victory:

    Know when to fight
    And when not to fight;

    Understand how to deploy
    Large and small
    Numbers;

    Have officers and men who
    Share a single will;
    Be ready
    For the unexpected;

    Have a capable general,
    Unhampered by his sovereign.

These five
    Point the way to
    Victory.

Hence the saying
    "Know the enemy,
    Know yourself,
    And victory
    Is never in doubt,
    Not in a hundred battles."

    He who knows self
    But not the enemy
    Will suffer one defeat
    For every victory.
    He who knows
    Neither self
    Nor enemy
    Will fail
    In every battle

The Making of Plans

The Way
  Causes men
  To be of one mind
  With their rulers,
  To live or die with them,
  And never to waver. . . .

On which side
Is discipline
More effective?

Which army
Is the stronger?
Whose officers and men
Are better trained?

In which army are rewards and punishments
Clearest?

From these
  Can be known
  Victory and defeat.

The Way of War is
  A Way of Deception

  When able,
  Feign inability;

  When deploying troops,
  Appear not to be.

  When near,
  Appear far;
  When far,
  Appear near.

Lure with bait;

Strike with chaos.

If the enemy is full,
Be prepared.
If strong
Avoid him.

VEGETIUS, *EPITOME OF MILITARY SCIENCE*

Little is known about Publius Flavius Vegetius Renatus. He was a Christian and a prominent horse breeder who probably lived either in Spain or in France (Gaul) and served a high position in the Roman imperial bureaucracy. He also wrote a book on curing diseases in mules.

•   •   •

(1.3) Whether recruits from the country or from the city are more useful.

The next question is to consider whether a recruit from the country or from the city is more useful. On this subject, I think it could never have been doubted that the rural populace is better suited for arms. They are nurtured under the open sky in a life of work, enduring the sun, careless of shade, unacquainted with bathhouses, ignorant of luxury, simple-souled, content with a little, with limbs toughened to endure every kind of toil, and for whom wielding iron, digging a fosse, and carrying a burden is what they are used to from the country. . . .

(1.6) That the potentially better recruits are recognized at selection from the face and physical posture.

He who is charged with carrying out the levy procedure should take great pains to choose those able to fill the part of soldiers from the face, from the eyes, from the whole conformation of the limbs. For quality is indicated not only in men, but even in horses and dogs, by many points. . . . So let the adolescent who is to be selected for material activity have alert eyes, straight neck, broad chest, muscular shoulders, strong arms, long fingers; let him be small in the stomach, slender in the buttocks, and have calves and feet that are not swollen by surplus fat, but firm with hard muscle. When

From N. P. Milner, *Vegetius: Epitome of Military Science* (2nd ed., Liverpool, 1996), 4–13. Used by permission of Liverpool University Press.

you see these points in a recruit, you need not greatly regret the absence of tall stature. It is more useful that soldiers be strong than big.

(1.8) When recruits should be marked.

The recruit should not be tattooed with the pin-pricks of the official mark as soon as he has been selected, but first be thoroughly tested in exercises so that it may be established whether he is truly fitted for so much effort. Both mobility and strength are thought to be required of him, and whether he is able to learn the discipline of arms, whether he has the self-confidence of a soldier. For very many, though they seem not unacceptable in appearance, are yet found unsuitable in training. Therefore, the less useful ones should be rejected, and in their place the most energetic should be substituted. For in any conflict it is not so much numbers as bravery that pays off. So once the recruits have been tattooed, the science of arms should be shown them in daily training. . . .

(1.9) Recruits should be trained in the military step, in running, and in jumping.

So, at the very start of the training, recruits should be taught the military step. For nothing should be maintained more on the march or in battle than that all soldiers should keep ranks as they move. The only way that this can be done is by learning through constant training to maneuver quickly and evenly. For a divided and disordered army experiences danger from the enemy which is always most serious. So at the military step, twenty miles should be covered in five hours, at least in summer time. At the full step, which is faster, twenty-four miles should be covered in the same time. If you add anything to this, it now becomes running, for which a distance cannot be defined. . . . The soldier should also be trained at jumping, whereby ditches are vaulted, and hurdles of a certain height surmounted, so that when obstacles of this kind are encountered, he can cross them without effort. Furthermore, in actual conflict and clash of arms, the soldier coming on by a running jump makes the adversary's eyes flinch, frightens his mind, and plants a blow before the other can properly prepare himself. . . .

(1.10) Recruits should be trained in the art of swimming

Every recruit without exception should, in the summer months, learn the art of swimming, for rivers are not always crossed by bridges, and armies both when advancing and retreating are frequently forced to swim. Torrents often tend to flood after sudden falls of rain or snow, and ignorance of swimming incurs risk not only from the enemy but the water also. Therefore, the ancient Romans, who were trained in the whole art of warfare through so many wars and continual crises, selected the Campus Martius next to the Tiber in which the youth might wash off sweat and dust after training in arms, and lose their fatigue from running by the exercise of swimming. . . .

(1.11) How the ancients trained recruits with wicker shields and with posts.

The ancients, as one finds in books, trained recruits in this manner. They wove shields from withies, of hurdle-like construction, and circular, such that the hurcle had twice the weight that a government shield normally has. They also gave recruits wooden foils, likewise of double weight, instead of swords. So equipped, they were trained not only in the morning but even after noon against posts. Indeed, the use of posts is of very great benefit to gladiators as well as soldiers. Neither the arena nor the [practice]-field ever proved a man invincible in armed combat, unless he was judged to have been thoroughly trained at the post. Each recruit would plant a single post in the ground so that it could not move, and protruded six feet. Against the post, as if against an adversary, the recruit trained himself using the foil and hurdle like a sword and shield, so that now he aimed at, as it were, the head and face, now threatened the flanks, then tried to cut the hamstrings and legs, backed off, came on, sprang, and aimed at the post with every method of attack and art of combat, as though it were an actual opponent. In this traning, care was taken that the recruit drew himself up to inflict wounds without exposing any part of himself to a blow.

(1.19) Recruits should be trained in carrying a burden.

Recruits should very frequently be made to carry a burden of up to sixty pounds, and route-march at the military step, since on arduous campaigns they have necessarily to carry their rations together with their ams. This should not be thought hard, once the habit has been gained, for there is nothing that continual practice does not render very easy. We know that the ancient soldiers used to do this exercise from the evidence of Vergil himself, who says: "Just as the bold Roman in his national arms cruelly laden takes the road, and before the enemy expects it, stands in formation, having pitched camp."

CHAPTER 7

BUDDHISM AND CHRISTIANITY

The origin and early development of two of the great world religions lie in the classical period. Both Buddhism and Christianity arose where important religious developments had already occurred, but partially in protest against established formulas. Both sought to dispense with what their leaders viewed as excessive ceremonies and religious officialdom, in favor of a focus on spiritual values. Both, unquestionably, spurred new interest in otherworldly goals.

Buddhism originated in India, with Prince Gautama (563–483 B.C.E.), who later took the name "Buddha," or "Enlightened One." Protesting key features of Hinduism, including the great role of priests and ritual and the caste system, Buddhism maintained and extended Hindu disdain for earthly life, looking to an ultimate union with the divine essence, which the new religion called *nirvana*. Buddha transmitted his thoughts to disciples orally, and they were only gradually written down. From a small movement concentrated around its holy founder, Buddhism spread widely in India during the classical period, rivaling but also coexisting with Hinduism. By the end of the classical period, Buddhism was shrinking in India itself, as Hinduism consolidated its majority hold. But it was gaining new converts in Sri Lanka, in other parts of southeastern Asia, and in China.

Christianity originated later, in the other great center of religious origins in world history, the Middle East. Inspired by Jesus Christ, who was crucified in 30 C.E., Christianity developed quickly as various disciples and early converts spelled out their story of Jesus' life and doctrines and began to form religious communities. For a brief time, Christian leaders emphasized reform within the Jewish religion, but soon other converts were sought as the religion linked to the wider Greco-Roman world. By 300 C.E. probably about 10 percent of all the people in the empire were Christian, drawn to the message of hope for the poor and an intellectual and spiritual structure that added important elements to existing Greco-Roman culture. A strong church organization, with religious officials such as priests and bishops, arose in many regions, paralleling the organization of the empire itself.

Christianity and Buddhism shared many features, which helps explain their similar success in converting masses of people in various regions and of various cultural backgrounds. They both offered hope for religious advancement, mainly after this life but to a limited extent during it. They both expressed suspicion of worldly things and offered an ethic designed to help religious people avoid giving in to snares and temptations. Both, not surprisingly, sponsored monastic movements where small groups of people could seek holiness apart from normal worldly cares.

The two religions also differed greatly. Their attitude toward the world and its doings diverged; a careful comparison might begin by trying to define this difference. Buddhists emphasized miseries, whereas Christian leaders such as Paul stressed sin. How would Christian and Buddhist attitudes toward government or human achievement compare? A second difference lies in the teachings about how to deal with misery or sin: what is the good religious life, and how much control does an individual have over it? Buddhists and Christians differed greatly in their views on how to lead a holy life and also on the intervention of divine forces. This difference relates to the strong organizational contrast between the two religions, with Christianity being far more focused on church institutions as the embodiment of faith.

Questions

1. What aspects of Christianity and Buddhism—whether similar or different— help explain their great appeal?
2. How did Buddhist and Christian leaders define the main goals of life? What are the concepts of nirvana and Christian salvation? How did the two religions view the human body and its needs?
3. How did Buddhist and Christian leaders define divinity? What were the roles of Buddha and of Christ in religious life?
4. In what respects did Buddhist and Christian leaders agree, and in what respects did they disagree, about how to lead a holy life? How would the two religions view the state? How would they view acts of charity in relation to a holy life?
5. Why did Buddhism develop less of a formal church structure than Christianity? Does the difference relate to differences in the ideals of the two religions? How would the two religions, as they matured, approach problems of truth and error? What was the Christian approach, by the fourth century, to what it called heresy? Which religion would be more tolerant, and why?

For Further Discussion

1. How did Buddhism and Christianity reflect the earlier traditions of their cultures—Hinduism and the Indian epics, for Buddhism; Greek philosophy and Roman law, for Christianity?

2. **How did Buddhism resemble Hinduism? How did it differ?**

3. **How would Buddhist monasticism compare with Christian, in institutions devoted to the holiest possible life?**

4. **Why did Christianity and Buddhism both have such wide appeal during the late classical centuries and beyond? How did the spread of both religions relate to the decline of Classical Chinese and Roman Civilizations?**

BUDDHISM

The first Buddhist selection below, entitled "The Four Noble Truths," lies at the core of Buddha's quest for understanding after he had renounced worldly things. It suggests a central definition of Buddhist goals. The second passage, which more explicitly explains what an individual should do to live a holy life, comes from the *Dhammapada*, or *Footsteps of the Law*. This was probably written down toward the end of the period, when Buddhist doctrines had been fully established, at about 70 B.C.E. Later Buddhism also reflected some belief in the holiness of Buddha himself, which had not been part of Gautama's original vision but which helped spread the religion as people sought to attach their otherworldly aspirations to the merits of saintly leaders.

• • •

THE FOUR NOBLE TRUTHS

1. The Truth Concerning Misery

And how, O priests, does a priest live, as respects the elements of being, observant of the elements of being in the four noble truths?

Whenever, O priest, a priest knows the truth concerning misery, knows the truth concerning the origin of misery, knows the truth concerning the cessation of misery, knows the truth concerning the path leading to the cessation of misery.

And what, O priests, is the noble truth of misery?

Birth is misery; old age is misery; disease is misery; death is misery; sorrow, lamentation, misery, grief, and despair are misery; to wish for what one cannot have is misery; in short, all the five attachment-groups are misery.

This, O priests, is called the noble truth of misery.

From Henry Clarke Warren, *Buddhism in Translations: Passages Selected from the Buddhist Sacred Books and Translated from the Original Pali into English*, Student's Edition Harvard Oriental Series. (Cambridge, Mass.: Harvard University Press, 1953), 365–74. Copyright © 1953 by the President and Fellows of Harvard College. Reprinted by permission of the publisher.

2. The Truth of the Origin of Misery

And what, O priests, is the noble truth of the origin of misery?

It is desire leading to rebirth, joining itself to pleasure and passion, and finding delight in every existence,—desire, namely, for sensual pleasure, desire for permanent existence, desire for transitory existence.

But where, O priests, does this desire spring up and grow? where does it settle and take root?

Where anything is delightful and agreeable to men, there desire springs up and grows, there it settles and takes root.

And what is delightful and agreeable to men, where desire springs up and grows, where it settles and takes root?

The eye is delightful and agreeable to men; there desire springs up and grows, there it settles and takes root.

The ear . . . the nose . . . the tongue . . . the body . . . the mind is delightful and agreeable to men; there desire springs up and grows, there it settles and takes root.

The Six Organs of Sense.

Forms . . . sounds . . . odors . . . tastes . . . things tangible . . . ideas are delightful and agreeable to men; there desire springs up and grows, there it settles and takes root.

The Six Objects of Sense.

Eye-consciousness . . . ear-consciousness . . . nose-consciousness . . . tongue-consciousness . . . body-consciousness . . . mind-consciousness is delightful and agreeable to men; there desire springs up and grows, there it settles and takes root. . . .

The Six Sensations.

Perception of forms . . . sounds . . . odors . . . tastes . . . things tangible . . . ideas is delightful and agreeable to men; there desire springs up and grows, there it settles and takes root. . . .

The Six Reasonings.

Reflection on forms . . . sounds . . . odors . . . tastes . . . things tangible . . . ideas is delightful and agreeable to men; there desire springs up and grows, there it settles and takes root.

The Six Reflections.

This, O priests, is called the noble truth of the origin of misery.

3. The Truth of the Cessation of Misery

And what, O priests, is the noble truth of the cessation of misery?

It is the complete fading out and cessation of this desire, a giving up, a losing hold, a relinquishment, and a nonadhesion.

But where, O priests, does this desire wane and disappear? where is it broken up and destroyed?

71

Where anything is delightful and agreeable to men; there desire wanes and disappears, there it is broken up and destroyed.

And what is delightful and agreeable to men, where desire wanes and disappears, where it is broken up and destroyed?

The eye is delightful and agreeable to men; there desire wanes and disappears, there it is broken up and destroyed. . . .

This, O priests, is called the noble truth of the cessation of misery.

4. The Truth of the Path Leading to the Cessation of Misery

And what, O priests, is the noble truth of the path leading to the cessation of misery?

It is this noble eightfold path, to wit, right belief, right resolve, right speech, right behavior, right occupation, . . . , right contemplation, right concentration.

And what, O priests, is right belief?

The knowledge of misery, O priests, the knowledge of the origin of misery, the knowledge of the cessation of misery, and the knowledge of the path leading to the cessation of misery, this, O priests, is called "right belief."

And what, O priests, is right resolve?

The resolve to renounce sensual pleasures, the resolve to have malice towards none, and the resolve to harm no living creature, this, O priests, is called "right resolve."

And what, O priests, is right speech?

To abstain from falsehood, to abstain from backbiting, to abstain from harsh language, and to abstain from frivolous talk, this, O priests, is called "right speech."

And what, O priests, is right behavior?

To abstain from destroying life, to abstain from taking that which is not given one, and to abstain from immorality, this, O priests, is called "right behavior."

And what, O priests, is right occupation?

Whenever, O priests, a noble disciple, quitting a wrong occupation, gets his livelihood by a right occupation, this, O priests, is called "right occupation." . . .

And what, O priests, is right contemplation?

Whenever, O priests, a priest lives, as respects the body, observant of the body, strenuous, conscious, contemplative, and has rid himself of lust and grief; as respects sensations, observant of sensations, strenuous, conscious, contemplative, and has rid himself of lust and grief; as respects the mind, observant of the mind, strenuous, conscious, contemplative, and has rid himself of lust and grief; as respects the elements of being, observant of the elements of being, strenuous, conscious, contemplative, and has rid himself of lust and grief, this, O priests, is called "right contemplation."

And what, O priests, is right concentration?

Whenever, O priests, a priest, having isolated himself from sensual pleasures, having isolated himself from demeritorious traits, and still exercising reasoning, still exercising reflection, enters upon the first trance which is produced by isolation and characterized by joy and happiness; when, through the subsidence of reasoning and reflection, and still retaining joy and happiness, he enters upon the second trance, which is an interior tranquilization and intentness of the thoughts, and is produced by concentration; when, through the paling of joy, indifferent, contemplative, conscious, and in the experience of bodily happiness—that state which eminent men describe when they say, "Indifferent, contemplative, and living happily"—he enters upon the third trance; when, through the abandonment of happiness, through the abandonment of misery, through the disappearance of all antecedent gladness and grief, he enters upon the fourth trance, which has neither misery nor happiness, but is contemplation as refined by indifference, this, O priests, is called "right concentration."

This, O priests, is called the noble truth of the path leading to the cessation of misery.

THE WAY, FROM THE *DHAMMAPADA*

The best of ways is the eightfold; the best of truths the four words; the best of virtues passionlessness; the best of men he who has eyes to see.

This is the way, there is no other that leads to the purifying of intelligence. Go on this path! This is the confusion of Mâra, the tempter.

If you go on this way, you will make an end of pain! The way preached by me, when I had understood the removal of the thorns in the flesh.

You yourself must make an effort. The Tathâgatas (Buddhas) are only preachers. The thoughtful who enter the way are freed from the bondage of Mâra.

"All created things perish," he who knows and sees this becomes passive in pain; this is the way to purity.

"All created things are grief and pain," he who knows and sees this becomes passive in pain; this is the way that leads to purity.

"All forms are unreal," he who knows and sees this becomes passive in pain; this is the way that leads to purity.

He who does not rouse himself when it is time to rise, who, though young and strong, is full of sloth, whose will and thought are weak, that lazy and idle man never finds the way to knowledge.

Watching his speech, well restrained in mind, let a man never commit any wrong with his body! Let a man but keep these three roads of action clear, and he will achieve the way which is taught by the wise.

Through zeal knowledge is gained, through lack of zeal knowledge is lost; let a man who knows this double path of gain and loss thus place himself that knowledge may grow.

From *The Sacred Books of the East*, trans. Epiphanus Wilson (New York: Colonial Press, 1900), 138–39.

Cut down the whole forest of desires, not a tree only! Danger comes out of the forest of desires. When you have cut down both the forest of desires and its undergrowth, then . . . you will be rid of the forest and of desires!

So long as the desire of man towards women, even the smallest, is not destroyed, so long is his mind in bondage, as the calf that drinks milk is to its mother.

Cut out the love of self, like an autumn lotus, with thy hand! Cherish the road of peace. Nirvâna has been shown by Sugata (Buddha).

"Here I shall dwell in the rain, here in winter and summer," thus the fool meditates, and does not think of death.

Death comes and carries off that man, honored for his children and flocks, his mind distracted, as a flood carries off a sleeping village.

Sons are no help, nor a father, nor relations; there is no help from kinsfolk for one whom death has seized.

A wise and well-behaved man who knows the meaning of this should quickly clear the way that leads to Nirvâna.

CHRISTIANITY

The two Christian passages below come from different stages of the religion's development. Paul's Letter to the Romans was written at the height of his career as Christian missionary and formulator of doctrine, between 54 and 58 C.E. It became part of the New Testament of the Christian Bible. The letter reflects an effort to appeal to all peoples with the message of Christian truth, Christ's redemption from sin, and potential salvation. The second document was written by a monk, Vincent of Lerins, in 434, as Christianity became established and began to deal systematically with quarrels over doctrine. Vincent grappled with the problem of knowing religious truth from falsehood, in a work that became known as the Vincentian Canon. His approach obviously reflected the role the institutional church had gained in defining Christian beliefs.

• • •

LETTER FROM PAUL TO THE ROMANS

So sin must no longer reign in your mortal body, exacting obedience to the body's desires. You must no longer put its several parts at sin's disposal, as implements for doing wrong. No: put yourselves at the disposal of God, as dead men raised to life; yield

From *The New English Bible* (New York: Cambridge University Press, 1922), 182–85, 189–91. Copyright © Oxford University Press and Cambridge University Press 1961, 1970. Reprinted by permission of the publisher.

your bodies to him as implements for doing right; for sin shall no longer be your master, because you are no longer under law, but under the grace of God.

What then? Are we to sin, because we are not under law but under grace? Of course not. You know well enough that if you put yourselves at the disposal of a master, to obey him, you are slaves of the master whom you obey; and this is true whether you serve sin, with death as its result; or obedience, with righteousness as its result. But God be thanked, you, who once were slaves of sin, have yielded wholehearted obedience to the pattern of teaching to which you were made subject, and, emancipated from sin, have become slaves of righteousness (to use words that suit your human weakness)—I mean, as you once yielded your bodies to the service of impurity and lawlessness, making for moral anarchy, so now you must yield them to the service of righteousness, making for a holy life.

When you were slaves of sin, you were free from the control of righteousness; and what was the gain? Nothing but what now makes you ashamed, for the end of that is death. But now, freed from the commands of sin, and bound to the service of God, your gains are such as make for holiness, and the end is eternal life. For sin pays a wage, and the wage is death, but God gives freely, and his gift is eternal life, in union with Christ Jesus our Lord.

You cannot be unaware, my friends—I am speaking to those who have some knowledge of law—that a person is subject to the law so long as he is alive, and no longer. . . . So you, my friends, have died to the law by becoming identified with the body of Christ, and accordingly you have found another husband in him who rose from the dead, so that we may bear fruit for God. While we lived on the level of our lower nature, the sinful passions evoked by the law worked in our bodies, to bear fruit for death. But now, having died to that which held us bound, we are discharged from the law, to serve God in a new way, the way of the spirit, in contrast to the old way, the way of a written code.

What follows? Is the law identical with sin? Of course not. But except through law I should never have become acquainted with sin. For example, I should never have known what it was to covet, if the law had not said, 'Thou shalt not covet.' Through that commandment sin found its opportunity, and produced in me all kinds of wrong desires. In the absence of law, sin is a dead thing. There was a time when, in the absence of law, I was fully alive; but when the commandment came, sin sprang to life and I died. The commandment which should have led to life proved in my experience to lead to death, because sin found its opportunity in the commandment, seduced me, and through the commandment killed me.

Therefore the law is in itself holy, and the commandment is holy and just and good. Are we to say then that this good thing was the death of me? By no means. It was sin that killed me, and thereby sin exposed its true character: it used a good thing to bring about my death, and so, through the commandment, sin became more sinful than ever.

We know that the law is spiritual; but I am not: I am unspiritual, the purchased slave of sin. I do not even acknowledge my own actions as mine, for what I do is not what I want to do, but what I detest. But if what I do is against my will, it means that I agree with the law and hold it to be admirable. But as things are, it is no longer I who perform the action, but sin that lodges in me. For I know that nothing good lodges in me—in my unspiritual nature, I mean—for though the will to do good is there, the deed is not. The good which I want to do, I fail to do; but what I do is the wrong which is against my will; and if what I do is against my will, clearly it is no longer I who am the agent, but sin that has its lodging in me.

I discover this principle, then: that when I want to do the right, only the wrong is within my reach. In my inmost self I delight in the law of God, but I perceive that there is in my bodily members a different law, fighting against the law that my reason approves and making me a prisoner under the law that is in my members, the law of sin. Miserable creature that I am, who is there to rescue me out of this body doomed to death? God alone, through Jesus Christ our Lord! Thanks be to God! In a word then, I myself, subject to God's law as a rational being, am yet, in my unspiritual nature, a slave to the law of sin.

The conclusion of the matter is this: there is no condemnation for those who are united with Christ Jesus, because in Christ Jesus the life-giving law of the Spirit has set you free from the law of sin and death. What the law could never do, because our lower nature robbed it of all potency, God has done: by sending his own Son in a form like that of our own sinful nature, and as a sacrifice for sin, he has passed judgement against sin within that very nature, so that the commandment of the law may find fulfilment in us, whose conduct, no longer under the control of our lower nature, is directed by the Spirit.

Those who live on the level of our lower nature have their outlook formed by it, and that spells death; but those who live on the level of the spirit have the spiritual outlook, and that is life and peace. For the outlook of the lower nature is enmity with God; it is not subject to the law of God; indeed it cannot be: those who live on such a level cannot possibly please God.

But that is not how you live. You are on the spiritual level, if only God's Spirit dwells within you; and if a man does not possess the Spirit of Christ, he is no Christian. But if Christ is dwelling within you, then although the body is a dead thing because you sinned, yet the spirit is life itself because you have been justified. Moreover, if the Spirit of him who raised Jesus from the dead dwells within you, then the God who raised Christ Jesus from the dead will also give new life to your mortal bodies through his indwelling Spirit.

It follows, my friends, that our lower nature has no claim upon us; we are not obliged to live on that level. If you do so, you must die. But if by the Spirit you put to death all the base pursuits of the body, then you will live.

For all who are moved by the Spirit of God are sons of God. The Spirit you have received is not a spirit of slavery leading you back into a life of fear, but a Spirit that makes us sons, enabling us to cry 'Abba! Father!' In that cry the Spirit of God joins with our spirit in testifying that we are God's children; and if children, then heirs. We are God's heirs and Christ's fellow-heirs, if we share his sufferings now in order to share his splendour hereafter.

For I reckon that the sufferings we now endure bear no comparison with the splendour, as yet unrevealed, which is in store for us. . . .

Therefore, my brothers, I implore you by God's mercy to offer your very selves to him: a living sacrifice, dedicated and fit for his acceptance, the worship offered by mind and heart. Adapt yourselves no longer to the pattern of this present world, but let your minds be remade and your whole nature thus transformed. Then you will be able to discern the will of God, and to know what is good, acceptable, and perfect. . . .

The gifts we possess differ as they are allotted to us by God's grace, and must be exercised accordingly: the gift of inspired utterance, for example, in proportion to a man's faith; or the gift of administration, in administration. A teacher should employ his gift in teaching, and one who has the gift of stirring speech should use it to stir his hearers. If you give to charity, give with all your heart; if you are a leader, exert yourself to lead; if you are helping others in distress, do it cheerfully. . . .

Never pay back evil for evil. Let your aims be such as all men count honourable. If possible, so far as it lies with you, live at peace with all men. My dear friends, do not seek revenge, but leave a place for divine retribution; for there is a text which reads, 'Justice is mine, says the Lord, I will repay.' But there is another text: 'If your enemy is hungry, feed him; if he is thirsty, give him a drink; by doing this you will heap live coals on his head.' Do not let evil conquer you, but use good to defeat evil.

Every person must submit to the supreme authorities. There is no authority but by act of God, and the existing authorities are instituted by him; consequently anyone who rebels against authority is resisting a divine institution, and those who so resist have themselves to thank for the punishment they will receive. For government, a terror to crime, has no terrors for good behaviour. You wish to have no fear of the authorities? Then continue to do right and you will have their approval, for they are God's agents working for your good. But if you are doing wrong, then you will have cause to fear them; it is not for nothing that they hold the power of the sword, for they are God's agents of punishment, for retribution on the offender. That is why you are obliged to submit. It is an obligation imposed not merely by fear of retribution but by conscience. That is also why you pay taxes. The authorities are in God's service and to these duties they devote their energies.

Discharge your obligations to all men; pay tax and toll, reverence and respect, to those to whom they are due. Leave no claim outstanding against you, except that of mutual love. He who loves his neighbour has satisfied every claim of the law. For the commandments, 'Thou shalt not commit adultery, thou shalt not kill, thou shalt not steal, thou shalt not covet', and any other commandment there may be, are all summed up in the one rule, 'Love your neighbour as yourself.' Love cannot wrong a neighbour; therefore the whole law is summed up in love. . . .

VINCENT OF LERINS

I have therefore continually given the greatest pains and diligence to enquiring, from the greatest possible number of men outstanding in holiness and in doctrine, how I can secure a kind of fixed and, as it were, general and guiding principle for distinguishing the true Catholic Faith from the degraded falsehoods of heresy. And the answer that I receive is always to this effect; that if I wish, or indeed if any one wishes, to detect the deceits of heretics that arise and to avoid their snares and to keep healthy and sound in a healthy faith, we ought, with the Lord's help, to fortify our faith in a twofold manner, firstly, that is, by the authority of God's Law, then by the tradition of the Catholic Church.

(2) Here, it may be, some one will ask, Since the canon of Scripture is complete, and is in itself abundantly sufficient, what need is there to join to it the interpretation of the Church? The answer is that because of the very depth of Scripture all men do not place one identical interpretation upon it. The statements of the same writer are explained by different men in different ways, so much so that it seems almost possible to extract from it as many opinions as there are men. . . .

. . . Therefore, because of the intricacies of error, which is so multiform, there is great need for the laying down of a rule for the exposition of Prophets and Apostles in accordance with the standard of the interpretation of the Church Catholic.

(3) Now in the Catholic Church itself we take the greatest care to hold THAT WHICH HAS BEEN BELIEVED EVERYWHERE, ALWAYS, AND BY ALL.

That is truly and properly 'Catholic,' as is shown by the very force and meaning of the word, which comprehends everything almost universally. We shall hold to this rule if we follow universality [i.e. œcumenicity], antiquity, and consent. We shall follow universality if we acknowledge that one Faith to be true which the whole Church throughout the world confesses; antiquity, if we in no wise depart from those interpretations which it is clear that our ancestors and fathers proclaimed; consent, if in antiquity itself we keep following the definitions and opinions of all, or certainly nearly all, bishops and doctors alike.

From Henry Bettenson, ed., *Documents of the Christian Church* (2d ed., New York: Oxford University Press, 1963), 83–84. Reprinted by permission of Oxford University Press.

PART II

The Postclassical Period, 450–1450

A MAJOR PHASE OF world history opened with the decline or collapse of the great empires of Rome, Han China, and Gupta India by the fifth and sixth centuries C.E. New forces were set in motion that persisted until the thirteenth century, followed by a two-century transition lasting until about 1450.

During the classical period, the key developments in world history had been the construction of large regional civilizations and their integration. This theme did not disappear. Chinese history, for example, resumed many of its earlier patterns after three centuries of real confusion. Indian civilization retained its basic integrity also, though without the capacity to generate large, internally directed empires. The Mediterranean was hopelessly divided, however, with Greco-Roman traditions persisting only in the Byzantine Empire in the northeastern corner of the region. This empire combined the use of the Greek language and culture with Roman imperial institutions, Orthodox Christianity, and a lively trade. But overall, the formation of empires loomed less large in this new period; other, looser political structures were emphasized.

Several new trends emerged. First, major world religions, defined in terms of their ability to convert peoples in various civilization areas, began to gain a greater hold. The collapse of the classical empires prompted many people to turn to more otherworldly goals; in some cases, such as Western Europe, the new religions also provided the clearest shared beliefs and even institutional structures. Buddhism was not new, but during this period it spread far more widely in eastern and southeastern Asia. Christianity had already gained strength in the Mediterranean and in a few parts of the Middle East and sub-Saharan Africa. Now it spread vigorously northward, in two main strands (Catholic and Orthodox), ultimately reaching Scandinavia in the west and Russia in the east. The third religion was new and by far the most dynamic of all. Islam arose in the Middle East early in the seventh century. It spread rapidly with Arab conquests in the Middle East and North Africa, where a new government, the Caliphate, controlled vast territories. Islam also soon won massive conversions in Central Asia, India (as a minority religion), parts of sub-Saharan Africa, Spain, and Southeast Asia.

The sheer spread of civilization was the second major development of the postclassical period, in some cases related to the impact of Arab influence or the consequences of the various missionary religions. Although the most sophisticated cities and trade still were in the Middle East and North Africa, the Byzantine Empire, India, and China, civilization also developed in additional parts of sub-Saharan Africa (particularly a series of great kingdoms in present-day West Africa, known as the Sudanic kingdoms); in Western Europe, under the influence of Catholic Christianity; in Japan; in Southeast Asia; and in Russia and Eastern Europe. These new civilization areas traded with the leading centers and were able to imitate important aspects of culture (often including writing itself) and some political forms. Finally, though quite separately, larger civilization zones spread in Central America, culminating in the great Aztec Empire, and in the Andes region, with the Inca Empire taking shape toward the end of the postclassical period.

By 1000 C.E. the major societies of Afro-Eurasia were in regular contact. Here was the third main theme of the postclassical centuries. Trade levels, cultural exchanges, and some military clashes created a new regional network. Inventions developed in one center, such as China's introduction of paper, began to spread more rapidly to other areas. Not only religious ideas but also some artistic forms began to affect numerous different civilizations. Heightened international contact also sped the dissemination of diseases, for example, the great bubonic plague (Black Death) of the fourteenth century, which began in China and within decades reached both the Arab world and Europe, with deadly effects. An increasingly important component of world history involves understanding the different reactions by the major civilizations to their wider contacts. Muslim traders organized the interregional network during much of the period, but Mongol conquests and, briefly, Chinese initiative played major roles in the final postclassical centuries.

Two kinds of comparison focus attention on the major developments of the postclassical period: comparison of separate patterns and comparison of reactions to common forces.

First, the distinct characteristics of individual civilizations continue to command attention. Particular world religions provided new contrasts among regions. Thus, the impacts of religion on government forms created some common themes but also some new differentiation between the Middle East and Christian Europe. Conditions of women were affected by the different cultures of Islam and the major strands of Christianity, whereas China, less affected by new cultural influences, displayed more continuity. Comparison is vital to determine the characteristics of the new civilization centers and their relationship to the older civilizations.

The second type of comparison is possible because of the intensification of interactions among civilizations in Asia, Africa, and Europe. Still distinctive, many civilizations had to respond to common influences and events. Increasing interaction thus organizes a new set of comparative issues, which had not existed in the previous world history periods: comparison around a common development or contact. Europeans and Muslims encountered each other in Christian crusades to conquer the Holy Land. These conflicts provided important new influences on Europe but also allow analysis of differences and hostilities between the two societies that were sharpened by contact. Merchant activity increased in the postclassical centuries, through both internal and external trade. Despite new commercial contacts, different societies maintained different ideas about merchants and their contributions. Near the end of the period, the Mongol conquests in China, Russia, and elsewhere created new channels of international exchange—but again, reactions to this episode varied, showing how civilizations could change as a result of common impacts but retain their distinctive patterns.

CHAPTER 8

RELIGION AND STATE IN ISLAM AND CHRISTIANITY

Relationship with secular government is a problem for any religion and its leaders (and vice versa). Governments normally concentrate at least in part on issues of war and earthly justice, and perhaps some economic issues such as provisioning cities or helping the poor. What connection do these functions and the people responsible for them have with the purposes of life as defined by religion? What if a government does not attend properly to religion or even is hostile to it? Or, from a government standpoint, what if religious officials seem to be falling down on the job or interfering with obviously secular concerns? The Chinese government ultimately turned against Buddhism in the ninth century, because it felt it must protect the primacy of loyalties to the state. Issues of this sort were different from leading political ideals in the classical period, when except in India religion was less prominent. One change was clear: no Christian or Muslim ruler could claim he was god, unlike some Romans and as opposed to the Chinese Son of Heaven concept.

Early on Christian leaders had faced the issue of what to do about the state. As he tried to spread the new religion to a wide audience, Paul stressed the importance of obeying government authorities even though the chief interests of the good Christian centered on divine power (see chapter 6). As the Christian church developed in Western Europe, with officials and institutions independent of the state, questions of mutual relations became more pressing. The adoption of Christianity by the Roman Empire, and then later by governments in Western Europe, complicated the issue still further: Christian political leaders thought they had a religious role to play (and might want to use religion to bolster their power); church leaders might welcome political support but would often fear secular control.

The rapid rise of Islam, following Muhammad's formulation of the religion early in the seventh century, raised broadly similar concerns. Here was another religion devoted to the power and glory of God; purely political purposes would pale by comparison. Yet, even more than Christianity, Islam developed a highly legalistic impulse. The Koran, which Muhammad presented as the word of Allah, contained a host of rules for family and business behavior. Further religious codes developed, particularly in the Hadith. But if religion regulated so many aspects of human affairs, was there a separate place for government? The situation was further complicated by the fact that although Islam had religious officials—including scholars who interpreted Muslim law—there was no institutional church of the sort that developed in Western Europe, with a clear leadership hierarchy. And Muhammad, like Paul, had explicitly urged the faithful to obey even a bad ruler—religious people should not be distracted by political concerns.

The following passages present some of the Christian and Muslim views as they took shape in the postclassical period, and suggest on balance that they are different. The differences reflected variations in the two religions, but they also had huge implications concerning the power of the state—at the time and subsequently.

Questions

1. What were the main differences in the ways Christian and Muslim thinkers defined the state in its relationship to religion? What state functions would both religions agree on? How does the existence of a separate church differentiate the Christian from the Muslim approach?
2. Might Muslims disagree about the state's relation to religion in ways at all similar to the postclassical Christian debate? Did Islam impose any limits on a good ruler?
3. What would a Muslim think of the Christian debate about papal versus imperial power?
4. In the final analysis, are there major differences between Christian and Muslim definitions of a good ruler? Do the religions differ in their beliefs about what to do if a ruler is bad?

For Further Discussion

1. Why did both Christian and Muslim leaders urge obedience to the state in almost all circumstances?
2. Which approach, the Christian or the Muslim, would produce more responsible government?
3. Are differences between Christian and Muslim political traditions—complex as both traditions were—still visible in the world today? Do you agree that Christian ideas help explain a limited state concept in the West? What state concept most logically follows from Muslim ideals?

A MUSLIM VIEW: NIZAM AL-MULK

Nizam al-Mulk was a Persian bureaucrat who served sultans for the Seljuk Turks for thirty years during the eleventh century, at a time when the Seljuks controlled much of the Middle East (it was the Seljuks who a bit later opposed the Christians in the Crusades). This treatise in some ways resembles a host of works throughout history that were designed to please kings. King-pleaser treatises flattered rulers by telling them how to get and keep power and generally insisting on their importance to their people. But this was a Muslim statement, and religion is very much present in the kinds of responsibilities and restraints Nizam al-Mulk insists upon in the name of God. The document refers to the title *caliph*, taken by the prophet Muhammad's Arab successors, who claimed wide religious powers and duties. It frequently invokes the holy book the Quran (Koran).

• • •

1. In every age and time God (be He exalted) chooses one member of the human race and, having adorned and endowed him with kingly virtues, entrusts him with the interests of the world and the well-being of His servants; He charges that person to close the doors of corruption, confusion and discord, and He imparts to him such dignity and majesty in the eyes and hearts of men, that under his just rule they may live their lives in constant security and ever wish for his reign to continue.

2. Whenever—Allah be our refuge!—there occurs any disobedience or disregard of divine laws on the part of His servants, or any failure in devotion and attention to the commands of The Truth (be He exalted), and He wishes to chasten them and make them taste the retribution for their deeds—may God not deal us such a fate, and keep us far from such a calamity!—verily the wrath of The Truth overtakes those people and He forsakes them for the vileness of their disobedience; anarchy rears its head in their midst, opposing swords are drawn, [and] blood is shed. . . .

3. Then by divine decree one human being acquires some prosperity and power, and according to his deserts The Truth bestows good fortune upon him and gives him wit and wisdom, wherewith he may employ his subordinates every one according to his merits and confer upon each a dignity and a station proportionate to his powers. He selects ministers and their functionaries from among the people, and giving a rank and post to each, he relies upon them for the efficient conduct of affairs spiritual and temporal. If his subjects tread the path of obedience and busy themselves with their tasks he will keep them untroubled by hardships, so that they may pass their time at ease in the shadow of his justice. If one of his officers or ministers commits any impropriety or oppression, he will only keep him at his post provided that he responds to correction, advice or punishment,

From Nizam al-Mulk, *The Book of Government on Rules for Kings*, trans. Hubert Darke (London: Routledge and Kegan Paul, 1960), 9–13, 62–65. Reprinted by permission of the publisher.

and wakes up from the sleep of negligence; if he fails to mend his ways, he will retain him no longer, but change him for someone who is deserving; and when his subjects are ungrateful for benefits and do not appreciate security and ease, but ponder treachery in their hearts, shewing unruliness and overstepping their bounds, he will admonish them for their misdeeds, and punish them in proportion to their crimes. Having done that he will cover their sins with the skirt of pardon and oblivion. Further he will bring to pass that which concerns the advance of civilization, such as constructing underground channels, digging main canals, building bridges across great waters, rehabilitating villages and farms, raising fortifications, building new towns, and erecting lofty buildings and magnificent dwellings; he will have inns built on the highways and schools for those who seek knowledge; for which things he will be renowned for ever; he will gather the fruit of his good works in the next world and blessings will be showered upon him. . . .

4. . . . [God] furnished [the King] with powers and merits such as had been lacking in the princes of the world before him, and endowed him with all that is needful for a king—such as a comely appearance, a kindly disposition, integrity, manliness, bravery, horsemanship, knowledge, [skill in] the use of various kinds of arms and accomplishment in several arts, pity and mercy upon the creatures of God, [strictness in] the performance of vows and promises, sound faith and true belief, devotion to the worship of God and the practice of such virtuous deeds as praying in the night, supererogatory fasting, respect for religious authorities, honouring devout and pious men, winning the society of men of learning and wisdom, giving regular alms, doing good to the poor, being kind to subordinates and servants, and relieving the people of oppressors. Following all this God gave him power and dominion as befitted his worthiness and good faith, and made all the world subject to him, causing his dignity and authority to reach all climes; all the dwellers on earth are his tributaries, and as long as they seek his favour they are protected by his sword. . . .

On Recognizing the Extent of God's Grace towards Kings

3. It has come down in a tradition from The Prophet (may Allah bless him and save him) that on the day of the resurrection, when anyone is brought forward who [in his life] wielded power and command over God's creatures, his hands will be bound; if he has been just, his justice will loose his hands and send him to paradise; but if he has been unjust, his injustice will cast him into hell as he is, with his hands bound in chains.

4. There is also a tradition that on resurrection day whoever had any command in this world over God's creatures, even over the inhabitants of his own house or over his own underlings, will be questioned about it; likewise the shepherd who tended his sheep will be required to answer for that too.

5. They say that at the time of his father's leaving this world [caliph] 'Abd Allah ibn 'Umar ibn al Khattab (may Allah be pleased with them both) asked, 'O father, where and when shall I see you again?' 'Umar said, 'In the next world.' 'Abd Allah

said, 'I would it were sooner.' He said, 'You will see me in a dream tonight, tomorrow night, or the next night.' Twelve years passed by without his appearing in a dream. Then one night he saw him in a dream and said, 'O father, did you not say that within three nights I should see you?' He said, 'O son, I was occupied, because in the country around Baghdad a bridge had become dilapidated and officials had not attended to repairing it. One day a sheep's forefoot fell into a hole on that bridge and was broken. Till now I have been answering for that.'

6. Of a certainty The Master of the World (may Allah perpetuate his reign) should know that on that great day he will be asked to answer for all those of God's creatures who are under his command, and if he tries to transfer [his responsibility] to someone else he will not be listened to. Since this is so it behoves the king not to leave this important matter to anyone else, and not to disregard the state of God's creatures. To the best of his ability let him ever acquaint himself, secretly and openly, with their conditions; let him protect them from extortionate hands, and preserve them from cruel tyrants, so that the blessings resulting from those actions may come about in the time of his rule, if Allah wills. . . .

1. It is incumbent upon the king to enquire into religious matters, to be acquainted with the divine precepts and prohibitions and put them into practice, and to obey the commands of God (be He exalted); it is his duty to respect doctors of religion and pay their salaries out of the treasury, and he should honour pious and abstemious men. Furthermore it is fitting that once or twice a week he should invite religious elders to his presence and hear from them the commands of The Truth; he should listen to interpretations of the Quran and traditions of The Prophet (may Allah pray for him and give him peace); and he should hear stories about just kings and tales of the prophets (upon them be peace). During that time he should free his mind from worldly cares and give his ears and attention [wholly] to them. Let him bid them take sides and hold a debate, and let him ask questions about what he does not understand; when he has learnt the answers let him commit them to memory. After this has gone on for some time it will become a habit, and it will not be long before he has learnt and memorized most of the precepts of divine law, the meanings of the Quran and the traditions of The Prophet (upon him be peace). Then the way of prudence and rectitude in both spiritual and temporal affairs will be open to him; no heretic or innovator will be able to turn him from that path. His judgment will be strengthened and he will increase in justice and equity; vanity and heresy will vanish from his kingdom and great works will spring from his hands. The roots of wickedness, corruption and discord will be cut out in the time of his empire. The hand of the righteous shall become strong and the wicked shall be no more. In this world he shall have fame, and in the next world he shall find salvation, high degree and inestimable reward. In his age men will more than ever delight in gaining knowledge. . . .

3. The most important thing which a king needs is sound faith, because kingship and religion are like two brothers; whenever disturbance breaks out in the country

religion suffers too; heretics and evil-doers appear; and whenever religious affairs are in disorder, there is confusion in the country; evil-doers gain power and render the king impotent and despondent; heresy grows rife and rebels make themselves felt. . . .

The Story of 'Umar ibn 'Abd al 'Aziz and the Famine

10. They say that in the days of 'Umar ibn 'Abd al 'Aziz (Allah's mercy be upon him) there was a famine and the people were in distress. A party of Arabs approached him and complained saying, 'O Commander of the Faithful, we have consumed our own flesh and blood in the famine (that is, we have become thin), and our cheeks have turned yellow because we have not enough to eat. We need what is in your treasury; and as for that treasure, it belongs either to you or to God or to the servants of God. If it belongs to God's servants it is ours; if it belongs to God, He has no need of it; if it is yours, then [as the Quran 12. 88 says] "be charitable unto us, for Allah will requite the charitable" . . . ; and if it is ours let us have it that we may escape from these straits, for the skin is withered on our bodies.' 'Umar ibn 'Abd al 'Aziz was moved to sympathy for them, and tears came into his eyes; he said, 'I will do as you have said,' and in the same hour he gave orders for their requests to be attended to and their wants to be supplied. When they were about to get up and go, 'Umar ibn 'Abd al 'Aziz (Allah's mercy be upon him) said, 'O men where are you going? As you presented your case and that of the rest of God's servants to me, so do you present my case to God' (meaning: remember me in your prayers). Then those Arab tribesmen lifted their eyes to heaven and said, 'O Lord, by Thy glory [we pray] that Thou wilt do unto 'Umar ibn 'Abd al 'Aziz as he did unto Thy servants.'

11. When they had done praying, immediately a cloud came up and it began to rain heavily; a hailstone fell upon the bricks of 'Umar's palace; it broke in two and a piece of paper fell from inside it. They looked at it and there was written upon it [in Arabic], 'This is a grace from Allah The Mighty to 'Umar ibn 'Abd al 'Aziz [exempting him] from the fire.'

A CHRISTIAN DEBATE: CANON LAWYERS IN THE TWELFTH CENTURY

The growth of state power, including the claims of the emperor of Germany, raised new church-state issues in Europe by the eleventh and twelfth centuries. A famous controversy in the eleventh century had pitted Pope Gregory VII against

From Brian Tierney, *The Crisis of Church and State, 1050–1300* (Englewood Cliffs, N.J.: Prentice-Hall, 1964), 122–26.

the emperor Henry IV over the issue of whether secular rulers had any right to appoint bishops. Gregory insisted on the supremacy of the church in religious matters and, by absolving Germans of religious obligations to obey their ruler, got the emperor to back down. The following debate, from the end of the twelfth century, is between two eminent jurists. Church (canon) law was becoming more elaborate, and the revival of Roman law provided different arguments about the state. In this debate Huguccio favors the emperor's side. Alanus uses interpretations of the Bible, including the idea that Christ conveyed his authority to Peter, who became the first pope, plus claims about the power Constantine gave the church, to support papal supremacy.

· · ·

HUGUCCIO: *After the coming of the Truth.* Up until the coming of Christ the imperial and pontifical rights were not separated, for the same man was emperor and pontiff. . . . But the offices and rights of the emperor and the pontiff were separated by Christ and some things, namely temporal affairs, were assigned to the emperor, others, namely spiritual affairs, to the pontiff, and this was done for the sake of preserving humility and avoiding pride. If the emperor or the pontiff held all offices he would easily grow proud but now since each needs the other and sees that he is not fully self-sufficient he is made humble. . . . Here it can clearly be gathered that each power, the apostolic and imperial, was instituted by God and that neither is derived from the other and that the emperor does not have the sword from the apostle. . . . All these contrary arguments seem to imply that the emperor receives the power of the sword and the imperial authority from the apostle and that the pope makes him emperor and can depose him. I believe however, that the emperor has the power of the sword and the imperial dignity from election by the princes and people, . . . for there was an emperor before there was a pope, an empire before a papacy. Again the words, "Behold, here are two swords" (Luke 22:38), were spoken to symbolize the fact that the two powers, namely the apostolic and imperial, are distinct and separate. If, therefore, it is anywhere stated or implied that the emperor has the power of the sword from the pope, I understand it as meaning the unction and confirmation which he has from the pope when he swears fidelity to him; for before this, although he is not called emperor, he is an emperor as regards dignity though not as regards unction, and before this he has the power of the sword and exercises it. When it is said that the pope can depose him I believe this to be true, but by the will and consent of the princes if he is convicted before them. Then I take it, in the last resort, if he has been convicted and admonished and will not desist or give satisfaction, he should be excommunicated and all should be removed from [loyalty] to him. . . . If still he is not corrected then finally he is justly smitten with a sentence and rightly expelled by armed force, and another legitimately elected. But by whom is the sentence pronounced? By the lord pope before whom he was convicted or by his princes if the Roman pontiff has approved this.

ALANUS: This indeed is certain according to everyone, that the pope has jurisdiction over the emperor in spiritual matters so that he can bind and loose him . . . but, according to Huguccio, by no means in temporal matters though the pope can judge him in temporal matters and depose him by the wish of the princes who elect him according to customary law. According to Huguccio the emperor has the sword from God alone and not from the pope except as regards coronation and confirmation, and he has full imperial jurisdiction beforehand although he is not called emperor.

But in truth, and according to the Catholic faith, he is subject to the pope in spiritual matters and also receives his sword from him, for the right of both swords belongs to the pope. This is proved by the fact that the Lord had both swords on earth and used both as is mentioned here, and he established Peter as his vicar on earth and all Peter's successors. Therefore today Innocent has by right the material sword. If you deny this you are saying that Christ established a secular prince as his vicar in this regard. Again Peter said to the Lord, "Behold, here are two swords" (Luke 22:38), so the material sword too was with Peter. Again if the emperor was not subject to the pope in temporalities he could not sin against the church in temporalities. Again the church is one body and so it shall have only one head or it will be a monster.

This opinion is not invalidated by the fact that there were emperors before there were popes, because they were only *de facto* emperors, and none except those who believed in the true God had a right to the sword; nor do infidel rulers have it nowadays. Likewise it is not invalidated by the fact that Constantine conferred temporal jurisdiction on [pope] Sylvester. . . .

From his plenitude of right the pope could take away the City and other possessions even if the emperor was unwilling.

The emperor then has the sword from the pope. The electors indeed confer it on him, not the pope, but every bishop has his bishopric from the pope and yet the pope does not confer it but rather canonical election of the clergy does. The pope therefore is the ordinary judge of the emperor in both temporal and spiritual affairs and can depose him. . . . But can he depose him for any crime? I answer, rather for none, unless he is determined to persist in it, and even then perhaps not for any offence but only for those which harm the people, as for instance the continued discord of heresy. But could the pope keep the material sword for himself if he wished? I answer no, because the Lord divided the swords as is said here, and the church would be gravely disturbed by this. . . .

CHAPTER 9

CONDITIONS OF WOMEN IN ISLAM, BYZANTINE CHRISTIANITY, AND WESTERN CHRISTIANITY

The major world religions were at pains to deal with conditions for women, through their treatments of family law and in more general discussions of women's role in human society. Both Christianity and Islam faced a major tension in principle: they granted women souls and the chance of salvation, but they regarded women as inferior, more prone to evil. Neither religion undermined patriarchy. But both religions granted women opportunities for religious expression: they could go on pilgrimages, for example. Both Muhammad and some early Christian leaders believed they were giving women important new opportunities through family law and religious prescriptions.

Attention to women's conditions is an important aspect of world history in the postclassical period. It involves two kinds of calculations: the first is the comparison of similarities and differences among major societies, such as the two Christian religions and Islam; the second is assessment of change over time, when patterns are compared to those of the classical period.

The following selections come from laws and commentary in the Byzantine Empire, the center of Orthodox Christianity; from Catholic Western Europe; and from Islam. There are many similarities in the complex statements of patriarchy in all three religions, and these should be the first points to identify. Are there also differences?

The Byzantine Empire obviously shared Christianity with Western Europe, though its Orthodox institutions were separate. Orthodox Christianity continued to allow priests to marry, which may have signaled less fear about sexuality and contamination through contact with women than arose in the West. Because the Byzantine Empire preserved Roman laws and political institutions, it might also have offered some extra protections for women—Rome had been rather careful to combine patriarchy with legal conditions.

Islam poses some obvious problems for interpretation, both in the postclassical period and today. Arab peoples before Islam had a strongly patriarchal society in which women's family rights were not well established. Muhammad believed he added important protections for women—allowing them to divorce, for example, which was simply not possible in Christianity. On the other hand,

Islam did not make women equal; they even prayed separately from men. Some Muslims continue the debate today, arguing that feminism is less necessary in Islam than in Christian cultures, because women's rights were more carefully protected in the religion itself. Are there bases for this argument in the materials derived from religious history?

Questions

1. How does the distinctive power of a particular woman, such as Anna Comnena, the mother of a Byzantine emperor, affect interpretations of women's conditions more generally? Does it suggest that the patriarchal system had been modified?
2. Why did canon law punish men for adultery more than women (at least in principle)? How does this relate to patriarchal views about women?
3. How did the Quran and Christian church (canon) law reflect beliefs in the spiritual equality of both genders?
4. What were the crucial tensions in Islam concerning women's spiritual status, rights, and treatment?
5. In what ways is it clear that Byzantium, Western Europe, and the Islamic Middle East were all patriarchal societies, with women held to be distinctly inferior?
6. Did specific religions (along with other factors) change women's lives?
7. Why were Byzantium and Islam both at pains to distinguish between women's private roles and rights and their public roles? Did religion have anything to do with this distinction?
8. In which society were women's property rights better protected, Islam or Western Christianity? Can you think of factors besides religion that might contribute to the difference? Was the Muslim provision of divorce, compared to Christian family law, a distinct advantage for women (even though their divorce rights were inferior to those of men)?

For Further Discussion

1. Compared to the patriarchal systems of classical civilizations (see chapter 5), were women's conditions improved by the impact of world religions such as Islam and Christianity? In which cultural system, Confucianism or Islam, would a woman be most protected? Which system would be most hostile to female infanticide, and why? How and why did the cultures differ about divorce?
2. Assuming you were an upper-class woman, in which of the three societies would you prefer to have lived during the postclassical period, and why—or do you regard them all as equally confining?

3. **Why do some women in the contemporary Middle East argue that Western-style feminism is not necessary because women's rights can be maintained through Islam?**

WOMEN IN ISLAM

The prophet Muhammad devoted considerable attention to women in the Quran, the holy book of Islam held to be inspired by Allah. The strong Islamic tendency to offer rules for various human affairs is demonstrated in detailed family laws, which in turn reveal both key principles applied to women and practical features of women's lives in Islamic societies. The second selection is from the Hadith, which consists of collections of traditions attributed to Muhammad and other early leaders from the seventh century onward; the Hadith set forth further rules and guidelines for Muslims. A short third selection, from Islamic law in the eleventh century, deals with public issues.

• • •

THE QURAN

O people, observe your Lord; the One who created you from one being and created from it its mate, then spread from the two many men and women. . . .

You shall not covet the qualities bestowed on each other by God; the men enjoy certain qualities, and women enjoy certain qualities. . . .

The men are made responsible for the women, since God endowed them with certain qualities, and made them the bread earners. The righteous women will cheerfully accept this arrangement, and observe God's commandments, even when alone in their privacy. If you experience opposition from the women, you shall first talk to them, then [you may use such negative incentives as] deserting them in bed, then you may beat them. If they obey you, you are not permitted to transgress against them. . . .

The Muslim men, the Muslim women, the believing men, the believing women, the obedient men, the obedient women, the truthful men, the truthful women, the steadfast men, the steadfast women, the reverent men, the reverent women, the charitable men, the charitable women, the fasting men, the fasting women, the chaste men, the chaste women, and the men who commemorate God frequently, and the commemorating women; God has prepared for them forgiveness and a great recompense. . . .

From *The Koran*, trans. George Sale (New York: R.L. Burt, 1902). Selections are from the following suras and verses: 2:221–23, 226–31, 233–37, 240–41, 282; 4:16, 19–25, 32, 34–35; 24:32–33, 60; 33:35–59. Reprinted by permission of the publisher.

Inheritance

Men ought to have a part of what their parents and kindred leave behind them when they die: and women also ought to have a part of what their parents and kindred leave, whether it be little, or whether it be much; a definite part is due to them.

GOD hath thus commanded you concerning your children. A male shall have as much as the share of two females; but if they be females only, and above two in number, they shall have two third parts of what the deceased shall leave; and if there be but one, she shall have the half.

O true believers, it is not lawful for you to be heirs of women against their will, nor to hinder them from marrying others, that ye may take away part of what ye have given them in dowry; unless they have been guilty of a manifest crime: but converse kindly with them. And if ye hate him, it may happen that ye may hate a thing wherein GOD hath placed much good.

Divorce

Those who intend to estrange their wives shall wait four months [for cooling off]; if they reconcile, then God is Forgiver, Most Merciful. If they go through with the divorce, then God is Hearer, Knower. The divorced women shall wait three menstruations [before marrying another man]. It is not lawful for them to conceal what God has created in their wombs, if they believe in God and the Last Day. [In case of pregnancy,] the husband's wishes shall supersede the wife's wishes if he wants to remarry her. The women have rights, as well as obligations, equitably. Thus, the men's wishes prevail [in case of pregnancy]. God is Almighty, Most Wise. . . .

The divorcees also shall be provided for, equitably. This is a duty upon the righteous. . . .

If you wish to marry another wife, in place of your present wife, and you had given the latter a great deal, you shall not take back anything you had given her. Would you take it fraudulently, maliciously, and sinfully? How could you take it back, after you have been intimate with each other, and after they have taken from you a solemn pledge? . . .

If a couple fears separation, you shall appoint an arbitrator from his family and an arbitrator from her family; if they decide to reconcile, God will help them get together. . . .

They consult you; say, "GOD decrees for you the inheritance statutes concerning the loner. If one dies and leaves no children, and he had a sister, she gets half the inheritance. If there were two sisters, they get two-thirds of the inheritance. If the siblings are men and women, the male gets a share equal to that of two females." God thus clarifies for you, lest you go astray. God is fully aware of all things. . . .

The thief, male or female, you shall mark their hands as a punishment for their crime, and to serve as a deterrent from GOD. GOD is Almighty, Most Wise. . . .

Anyone who works righteousness, male or female, while believing, we will surely grant them a happy life in this world, and we will surely pay them their full recompense (*on the Day of Judgment*) for their righteous works.

THE HADITH

He who shows concern for the widows and the unfortunate [ranks as high] as one who goes on Jihād in the way of Allah, or one who fasts by day and who rises at night [for prayer].

To look at a woman is forbidden, even if it is a look without desire, so how much the more is touching her.

Said he—upon whom be Allah's blessing and peace—: "Avoid seven pernicious things." [His Companions] said: "And what are they, O Apostle of Allah?" He answered: "Associating anything with Allah, sorcery, depriving anyone of life where Allah has forbidden that save for just cause, taking usury, devouring the property of orphans, turning the back on the day of battle, and slandering chaste believing women even though they may be acting carelessly."

Said the Prophet—upon whom be Allah's blessing and peace—: "I had a look into Paradise and I saw that the poor made up most of its inhabitants, and I had a look into Hell and saw that most of its inhabitants were women."

Treat women-folk kindly for woman was created of a rib. The crookedest part of a rib is its upper part. If you go to straighten it out you will break it, and if you leave it alone it will continue crooked. So treat women in kindly fashion.

Rules For Muslim Government, Eleventh Century

Exclusion of Women

Nobody may be appointed to the office of qadi [judge] who does not comply fully with the conditions required to make his appointment valid and his decisions effective. . . . The first condition is that he must be a man. This condition consists of two qualities, puberty and masculinity. As for the child below puberty, he cannot be held accountable, nor can his utterances have effect against himself; how much less so against others. As for women, they are unsuited to positions of authority, although judicial verdicts may be based on what they say. Abu Hanifa said that a woman can act as qadi in matters on which it would be lawful for her to testify, but she may not act as qadi in matters on

From Arthur Jeffery, ed., *A Reader on Islam* (New York: Books for Libraries. Division of Arno Press, 1980). Reprinted by permission of Ayer Company Publishers, Inc., North Stratford, NH 03590.

which it would not be lawful for her to testify. Ibn Jarir al-Tabari, giving a divergent view, allows a woman to act as qadi in all cases, but no account should be taken of an opinion which is refuted by both the consensus of the community and the word of God. "Men have authority over women because of what God has conferred on the one in preference to the other" [Koran 4:38], meaning by this, intelligence and discernment. He does not, therefore, permit women to hold authority over men.

The Byzantine Empire

Byzantine family law, not surprisingly, reflected Roman principles, particularly early in the empire. The most important early Byzantine emperor, Justinian (483–565), had codified Roman law. A marriage contract of the eighth century reflects careful concern for legal equity. The Byzantine Empire also produced some extraordinary individual women. Justinian's wife, the empress Theodora, probably made key policy decisions. During the eleventh and twelfth centuries the Comnenus family dominated the imperial line, producing a period of stable, enlightened rule. The princess Anna was a noteworthy historian, and in the second selection below she describes the role of her grandmother, an empress, in affairs of state. Finally, another law code, from about 900 in the reign of Leo VI, suggests another facet of gender relations in the empire. Does it represent a change from the principles expressed in the earlier marriage contract?

• • •

A MARRIAGE CONTRACT

The marriage of Christians, man and woman, who have reached years of discretion, that is for a man at fifteen and for a woman at thirteen years of age, both being desirous and having obtained the consent of their parents, shall be contracted either by deed or by parol.

A written marriage contract shall be based upon a written agreement providing the wife's marriage portion; and it shall be made before three credible witnesses according to the new decrees auspiciously prescribed by us. The man on his part agreeing by it continually to protect and preserve undiminished the wife's marriage portion, and also such additions as he may naturally make thereto in augmentation thereof; and it shall be recorded in the agreement made on that behalf by him, that in case there are no children, one-fourth part thereof shall be secured in settlement.

From Bernard Lewis, ed. and trans. *Islam: From the Prophet Muhammed to the Capture of Constantinople*, vol. 2, *Religion and Society* (New York: Oxford University Press, 1974), 40. Reprinted by permission of Oxford University Press.

Woman d/b -will decides
men d/b woman gets all

If the wife happens to predecease the husband and there are no children of the marriage, the husband shall receive only one-fourth part of the wife's portion for himself, and the remainder thereof shall be given to the beneficiaries named in the wife's will or, if she be intestate, to the next of kin. If the husband predeceases the wife, and there are no children of the marriage, then all the wife's portion shall revert to her, and so much of all her husband's estate as shall be equal to a fourth part of his portion shall also inure to her as her own, and the remainder of his estate shall revert either to his beneficiaries or, if he be intestate, to his next of kin.

If the husband predecease the wife and there are children of the marriage, the wife being their mother, she shall control her marriage portion and all her husband's property as becomes the head of the family and household.

A HISTORY OF ANNA COMNENA (TWELFTH CENTURY, GRANDDAUGHTER OF EMPEROR ALEXIUS I)

One might be amazed that my father accorded his mother such high honor in these matters and that he deferred to her in all respects, as if he were turning over the reins of the empire to her and running alongside her while she drove the imperial chariot, contenting himself simply with the title of emperor. Indeed, he had already passed beyond the period of boyhood, an age especially when lust for power grows in men of such nature [as Alexius]. He took upon himself the wars against the barbarians and whatever battles and combats pertained to them, while he entrusted to his mother the complete management of [civil] affairs: the selection of civil magistrates, the collection of incoming revenues and the expenses of the government. A person who has reached this point in my text may blame my father for entrusting management of the empire to the *gynaiconites* [women's section of the palace]. But if he had known this woman's spirit, how great she was in virtue and intellect and how extremely vigorous, he would cease his reproach and his criticism would be changed into admiration. For my grandmother was so dextrous in handling affairs of state and so highly skilled in controlling and running the government, that she was not only able to manage the Roman empire but could have handled every empire under the sun. She had a vast amount of experience and understood the internal workings of many things: she knew how each affair began and to what result it might lead, which actions were destructive and which rather were beneficial. She was exceedingly acute in discerning whatever course of action was necessary and in carrying it out safely. She was not only acute in her thought, but was no less proficient in her manner of speech. Indeed, she was a persuasive orator, neither verbose nor stretching her phrases out at great length;

From *A Manual of Roman Law*, trans. E. Freslfield (Cambridge: Bowes and Bowes, 1926), 72–74. Reprinted with the permission of Cambridge University Press.
From Anna Comnena, *Alexiade*, vol. 1 (London, 1928), 123–25.

nor did she quickly lose the sense of her argument. What she began felicitously she would finish even more so. . . .

But, as I was saying, my father, after he had assumed power, managed by himself the strains and labors of war, while making his mother a spectator to these actions, but in other affairs he set her up as ruler, and as if he were her servant he used to say and do whatever she ordered. The emperor loved her deeply and was dependent upon her advice (so much affection had he for his mother), and he made his right hand the executor of her orders, his ears paid heed to her words, and everything which she accepted or rejected the emperor likewise accepted or rejected. . . . Everything which she decided or ordered he found satisfactory. Not only was he very obedient to her as is fitting for a son to his mother, but even more he submitted his spirit to her as to a master in the science [*episteme*] of ruling. For he felt that she had attained perfection in everything and far surpassed all men of that time in prudence and in comprehension of affairs.

LEGAL STATUS

I do not know why the ancient authorities, without having thoroughly considered the subject, conferred upon women the right of acting as witnesses. It was, indeed, well known, and they themselves could not fail to be aware that it was dishonorable for them to appear frequently before the eyes of men, and that those who were modest and virtuous should avoid doing so. For this reason, as I have previously stated, I do not understand why they permitted them to be called as witnesses, a privilege which resulted in their frequently being associated with great crowds of men, and holding conversation with them of a character very unbecoming to the sex. . . .

And, indeed, the power to act as witnesses in the numerous assemblies of men with which they mingle, as well as taking part in public affairs, gives them the habit of speaking more freely than they ought, and, depriving them of the morality and reserve of their sex, encourages them in the exercise of boldness and wickedness which, to some extent, is even insulting to men. For is it not an insult, and a very serious one, for women to be authorized to do something which is especially within the province of the male sex?

Wherefore, with a view to reforming not only the errors of custom, but also of law, We hereby deprive them of the power of acting as witnesses, and by this constitution forbid them to be called to witness contracts under any circumstances. But, so far as matters in which they are exclusively interested are concerned, and when men cannot act as witnesses, as, for instance, in confinements, and other things where only women are allowed to be present, they can give testimony as to what is exclusively their own, and which should be concealed from the eyes of men.

From S. P. Scott, ed., *The Civil Law,* vol. 17, *The Novels of Emperor Leo VI* (Cincinnati: Central Trust Co., 1932), 249.

WESTERN EUROPE: CITY AND CANON LAW

The following two documents outline both secular and religious laws concerning women and their rights in marriage. The city of Magdeburg, in northern Germany, was a prosperous center by the thirteenth century, and many merchant families would have had considerable disposable wealth. The codification of canon law on marriage was part of the general systematization of church law— and the rise of lawyers—as European society became more elaborate with economic advance, the growth of cities, and cultural change. An obvious question: were the provisions of the two types of law, city and church, essentially compatible, even as they focused on different sets of details?

• • •

A GERMAN CITY'S LAWS, 1261

14. If a man dies leaving a wife, she shall have no share in his property except what he has given her in court, or has appointed for her dower. She must have six witnesses, male or female, to prove her dower. If the man made no provision for her, her children must support her as long as she does not remarry. If her husband had sheep, the widow shall take them. . . .

18. No one, whether man or woman, shall, on his sick-bed, give away more than three shillings' worth of his property without the consent of his heirs, and the woman must have the consent of her husband. . . .

55. When a man dies his wife shall give [to his heirs] his sword, his horse and saddle, and his best coat of mail. She shall also give a bed, a pillow, a sheet, a tablecloth, two dishes and a towel. Some say that she should give other things also, but that is not necessary. If she does not have these things, she shall not give them, but she shall give proof for each article that she does not have it. . . .

57. If the children are minors, the oldest male relative on the father's side, if he is of the same rank by birth, shall receive all these things and preserve them for the children. . . . He shall also be the guardian of the widow until she remarries, if he is of the same rank as she is.

58. After giving the above articles the widow shall take her dower and all that belongs to her; that is, all the sheep, geese, chests, yarn, beds, pillows, . . . etc., and there are many other trinkets which belong to her. . . . But uncut cloth, and unworked gold and silver do not belong to her.

From Oliver J. Thatcher and Edgar H. McNeal, eds., *A Source Book for Mediæval History* (New York: Charles Scribner's, 1907), 592, 594–95, 600–601.

CHURCH (CANON) LAW ON MARRIAGE, TWELFTH CENTURY

1. [According to John Chrysostom, a leading early theologian:] "Coitus does not make a marriage; consent does; and therefore the separation of the body does not dissolve it, but the separation of the will. Therefore he who forsakes his wife, and does not take another, is still a married man. For even if he is now separated in his body, yet he is still joined in his will. When therefore he takes another woman, then he forsakes fully. Therefore he who forsakes is not the adulterer, but he who takes another woman."

2. . . . . When therefore there is consent, which alone makes a marriage, between those persons, it is clear that they have been married. . . .

22. A man may not make a monastic vow without his wife's consent. . . .

If any married man wishes to join a monastery, he is not to be accepted, unless he has first been released by his wife, and she makes a vow of chastity. For if she, through incontinence, marries another man while he is still living, without a doubt she will be an adulteress. . . .

24. A husband is not permitted to be celibate without his wife's consent. . . .

26. A wife is not permitted to take a vow of celibacy, unless her husband chooses the same way of life. . . .

Betrothals may not be contracted before the age of seven. For only the consent is contracted, which cannot happen unless it is understood by each party what is being done between them. Therefore it is shown that betrothals cannot be contracted between children, whose weakness of age does not admit consent. . . . Therefore those who give girls to boys while they are still in the cradle, and vice versa, achieve nothing, even if the father and mother are willing and do this, unless both of the children consent after they have reached the age of understanding. . . .

14. Childbirth is the sole purpose of marriage for women. . . .

23. Adultery in either sex is punished in the same way. . . .

1. A fornicator cannot forsake his wife for fornication. . . .

4. Men are to be punished more severely for adultery than women.

From Emilie Amt, ed., *Women's Lives in Medieval Europe: A Sourcebook* (New York: Routledge, 1993), 79. Reproduced by permission of Routledge / Taylor & Francis Group, LLC.

CHAPTER 10

FEUDALISM IN WESTERN EUROPE AND JAPAN

Along with the impact of the world religions on the state, a key development in the postclassical period was the formation of governments in new areas. This chapter focuses on distinctive features of that process in Western Europe and Japan, providing another opportunity to deal with key political developments in the postclassical period.

The general issue was this: societies that arose on the fringes of the classical world—including Russia and parts of sub-Saharan Africa, as well as Japan and northwestern Europe—often were forming governments with no particular historical precedent. At most, very loose, essentially tribal kingships had emerged before (save in parts of Africa, where more elaborate states preceded this period). In the absence of highly developed economies, well-established political legitimacy, or even many trained officials, it was difficult to form elaborate states. Western Europe tried briefly to revive the Roman Empire (under the emperor Charlemagne, around 800 C.E.) but did not succeed. Japan made an attempt to imitate the Chinese Empire in the seventh century but could not.

In Japan and Western Europe, the political relationships known as feudalism provided a less demanding political system. Feudalism linked local and regional military leaders—the lords—with some other military personnel. This was a system for elites: it did not directly involve the masses of ordinary people. A lord formed ties with other people who had the equipment (horses, some armor, and weaponry) necessary to fight. He offered them protection and often his support or some land, or both, in return for their loyalty and their service in war. This was the essence of the feudal system. It could provide some orderliness in individual regions, as opposed to endemic local fighting; when it was extended to larger units, through feudal ties among great lords themselves, it could even support a monarchy.

Both Japan and Western Europe established this system in the postclassical period, out of similar needs. They were not in contact with each other, so it is not surprising that the two feudalisms, though remarkably similar, had some differences—differences that would affect the two areas long after feudalism itself had perished. In both cases, however, central rulers (like later English Kings or shoguns from the Minamoto family) could use feudalism to organize larger networks of royalty. Here, then, is another comparison of societies without contact, developing separately but resembling each other to an intriguing degree.

Feudalism in these two societies, at opposite ends of Eurasia, though remarkably similar in origins and structure, had somewhat different consequences in the long run. European feudalism developed into efforts to institutionalize contractual relationships between rulers and vassals; it led in turn to early versions of parliaments set up to try to make sure that rulers would stay within agreed-upon bounds. Japanese feudalism's greater stress on loyalty led not to parliaments—which would arrive only through much later imitation of the West—but to a sense of group cohesiveness that still describes aspects of Japanese management style and political life.

Questions

1. What basic characteristics of feudalism emerge from the European and Japanese materials? What did lords and vassals gain from a feudal tie? What were their respective obligations?
2. How was the Magna Carta a feudal document? How had the king violated feudalism, and what remedies were proposed?
3. In what ways is it clear that vassals, though required to be loyal to their lords, were basically in the same social class and not to be treated as social inferiors?
4. How much difference was there between the loyalty emphases in Japanese feudalism and those in the European version? Would European vassals have agreed with the extent of devotion displayed in the Japanese *Tale of the Heike*? Would Japanese vassals have agreed with the approach taken in the Magna Carta?

For Further Discussion

1. What conditions account for the emergence of such similar political systems in Western Europe and Japan?
2. What would a Confucian bureaucrat think of feudalism? On what grounds would he criticize it? Would he prefer the Western or the Japanese version?
3. Are there any remnants of feudal ideas and institutions in the Western world today? Why do some observers argue that the special qualities of Japanese feudalism, removed from specific feudal institutions, are still useful in Japan today?
4. How could western feudal elites move to the idea of parliaments, composed of these and other elites who advised the king as feudal lord? Why would this particular evolution of feudalism be more difficult in Japan?
5. What are the differences between feudal and modern ideas of limited government?

European Feudalism

Feudal documents were legal records for the most part, and often short. What follows are various documents dating from the seventh to the twelfth centuries that treat different aspects of French and English feudalism.

In the first document, a pagan, that is non-Christian, Viking duke whose people had conquered Normandy is induced to enter a feudal relationship with the king of France, along with marriage to one of the king's daughters. What would each party get out of this relationship? Two documents then describe common feudal property grants and a standard oath of loyalty in what was a very ritual relationship. Next, a well-known French bishop offers a more general description—obviously somewhat idealized—of what feudalism involved. Then a document describes conditions of separation, while another document highlights standard vassal obligations.

The final document offers excerpts from the English Magna Carta, or great charter, which the feudal barons imposed by force of arms on King John in 1215 in defense of feudal rights. John had been trying to extend government powers, and the passages suggest how new parliamentary-style institutions might emerge from feudalism.

• • •

EUROPEAN FEUDAL DOCUMENTS

1. Granting Normandy (Tenth Century)

Immediately Charles [French king], having consulted with them, sent Franco, Archbishop of Rouen, to Rollo, Duke of the [Viking] Pagans. Coming to him he began to speak with mild words. "Most exalted and distinguished of dukes, will you quarrel with the Franks as long as you live? Will you always wage war on them? What will become of you when you are seized by death? Whose creature are you? Do you think you are God? Are you not a man formed from filth? Are you not dust and ashes and food for worms? Remember what you are and will be and by whose judgment you will be condemned. You will experience Hell I think, and no longer injure anyone by your wars. If you are willing to become a Christian you will be able to enjoy peace in the present and the future and to dwell in this world with great riches. Charles, a long-suffering king, persuaded by the counsel of his men, is willing to give you this coastal province that you and Halstigno have grievously ravaged. He will also give you his daughter, Gisela, for a wife in order that peace and concord and a firm, stable and continuous friendship may endure for all time between you and him. . . ."

From Brian Tierney, *Sources of Medieval History*, vol. 1 (New York: Alfred A. Knopf, 1978), 126–29, 131, 133-35.

At the agreed time Charles and Rollo came together at the place that had been decided on. . . . Looking on Rollo, the invader of France, the Franks said to one another, "This duke who has fought such battles against the warriors of this realm is a man of great power and great courage and prowess and good counsel and of great energy too." Then, persuaded by the words of the Franks, Rollo put his hands between the hands of the king, a thing which his father and grandfather and great-grandfather had never done; and so the king gave his daughter Gisela in marriage to the duke and conferred on him the agreed lands from the River Epte to the sea as his property in hereditary right, together with all Brittany from which he could live. . . .

2. Granting Fiefs (Landed Estates) (Seventh Century)

Those who from their early youth have served us or our parents faithfully are justly rewarded by the gifts of our munificence. Know therefore that we have granted to that illustrious man (name), with greatest good will, the villa called (name), situated in the county of (name), with all its possessions and extent, in full as it was formerly held by him or by our treasury. Therefore by the present charter which we command to be observed forever, we decree that the said (name) shall possess the villa of (name), as has been said, in its entirety, with lands, houses, buildings, inhabitants, slaves, woods, pastures, meadows, streams, mills, and all its appurtenances and belongings, and with all the subjects of the royal treasury who dwell on the lands, and he shall hold it forever with full immunity from the entrance of any public official for the purpose of exacting the royal portion of the fines from cases arising there: to the extent finally that he shall have, hold, and possess it in full ownership, no one having the right to expect its transfer, and with the right of leaving it to his successors or to anyone whom he desires, and to do with it whatever else he wishes.

3. Oaths of Loyalty

Thus shall one take the oath of fidelity:

By the Lord before whom this sanctuary is holy, I will to N. be true and faithful, and love all which he loves and shun all which he shuns, according to the laws of God and the order of the world. Nor will I ever with will or action, through word or deed, do anything which is unpleasing to him, on condition that he will hold to me as I shall deserve it, and that he will perform everything as it was in our agreement when I submitted myself to him and chose his will.

It is right that those who offer to us unbroken fidelity should be protected by our aid. And since *such and such* a faithful one of ours, by the favor of God, coming here in our palace with his arms, has seen fit to swear trust and fidelity to us in our hand, therefore we decree and command by the present precept that for the future *such and such* above mentioned be counted with the number of [followers]. And if anyone perchance should presume to kill him, let him know that he will be judged guilty of his [value] of 600 shillings.

4. Fulbert, Bishop of Chartres, on Feudal Obligations (1020)

To William most glorious duke of the Aquitanians, bishop Fulbert the favor of his prayers.

Asked to write something concerning the form of fealty, I have noted briefly for you on the authority of the books the things which follow. He who swears fealty to his lord ought always to have these six things in memory; what is harmless, safe, honorable, useful, easy, practicable. Harmless, that is to say that he should not be injurious to his lord in his body: safe, that he should not be injurious to him in his secrets or in the defenses through which he is able to be secure; honorable, that he should not be injurious to him in his justice or in other matters that pertain to his honor; useful, that he should not be injurious to him in his possessions; easy or practicable, that that good which his lord is able to do easily, he make not difficult, nor that which is practicable he make impossible to him.

However, that the faithful vassal should avoid these injuries is proper, but not for this does he deserve his holding: for it is not sufficient to abstain from evil, unless what is good is done also. It remains, therefore, that in the same six things mentioned above he should faithfully counsel and aid his lord, if he wishes to be looked upon as worthy of his benefice and to be safe concerning the fealty which he has sworn.

The lord also ought to act toward his faithful vassal reciprocally in all these things. And if he does not do this he will be justly considered guilty of bad faith, just as the former, if he should be detected in the avoidance of or the doing of or the consenting to them, would be perfidious and perjured. . . .

5. Lords and Vassals (816)

If anyone shall wish to leave his lord (*seniorem*), and is able to prove against him one of these crimes, that is, in the first place, if the lord has wished to reduce him unjustly into servitude; in the second place, if he has taken counsel against his life; in the third place, if the lord has committed adultery with the wife of his vassal; in the fourth place, if he has wilfully attacked him with a drawn sword; in the fifth place, if the lord has been able to bring defence to his vassal after he has commended his hands to him, and has not done so; it is allowed to the vassal to leave him. If the lord has perpetrated anything against the vassal in these five points it is allowed the vassal to leave him.

6. Military Service (1072)

William, king of the English, to Aethelwig, abbot of Evesham, greeting. I command you to summon all those who are under your charge and administration that they shall have ready before me at Clarendon on the octave of Pentecost all the knights that they owe me. Come to me likewise yourself on that day, and bring ready with you those five knights that you owe me from your abbey.

THE MAGNA CARTA

John, by the grace of God, king of England, lord of Ireland, duke of Normandy and Aquitaine, and count of Anjou, to the archbishops, bishops, abbots, earls, barons, justiciars, foresters, sheriffs, stewards, servants, and to all his bailiffs and loyal persons, greeting. Know that, having regard to God and for the salvation of our souls, and those of all our predecessors and heirs, and unto the honour of God and the advancement of Holy Church, and for the reform of our realm, by the counsel of our venerable fathers . . . we have granted:

XII. No scutage [tax] or aid shall be imposed on our kingdom, unless by common counsel of our kingdom, except for ransoming our person, for making our eldest son a knight, and for marrying our eldest daughter once; and for them there shall not be levied more than a reasonable aid. In like manner it shall be done concerning aids from the city of London.

XXIX. No constable shall compel any knight to give money in stead of castle guard, when he is willing to perform it in his own person, or (if he himself cannot do it from any reasonable cause) then by another reliable man; and if we have led him or sent him upon military service, he shall be quit of guard, in proportion to the time during which he has been on service because of us.

XXXIX. No freeman shall be taken or imprisoned . . . or exiled or in anyway destroyed, nor will we go upon him nor send upon him, except by the lawful judgement of his peers or by the law of the land.

LV. All fines made by us unjustly and against the law of the land, shall be entirely remitted, or else it shall be done concerning them according to the decision of the five-and-twenty barons of whom mention is made below in (the clause for) securing the peace, or according to the judgement of the majority of the same. . . .

LXI. Since, moreover, for God and the amendment of our kingdom and for the better allaying of our quarrel that has arisen between us and our barons, we have granted all these concessions, desirous that they should enjoy them in complete and firm stability for ever, we give and grant to them the underwritten security, namely, that the barons choose five-and-twenty barons of the kingdom, whomsoever they will,

From *Statutes of the Realm*, vol. 1 (London, 1810), 1 5ff.

[handwritten margin notes: "King & Nobles not above the law", "Keeps his word", "Supreme Court"]

who shall be obliged, to observe and hold, and cause to be observed, with all their might, the peace and liberties which we have granted and confirmed to them by this our present Charter, so that if we, or our justiciar, or our bailiffs or any one of our officers, shall in anything be at fault towards anyone, or shall have broken any one of the articles of the peace or of this security, and the offence be notified to four barons of the aforesaid five-and-twenty, the said four barons shall come to us (or to our justiciar, if we are out of the realm) and, laying the transgression before us, petition to have that transgression redressed without delay. And if we shall not have corrected the transgression . . . within forty days, . . . the four barons aforesaid shall refer the matter to the rest of the five-and-twenty barons, and those five-and-twenty barons shall, together with the community of the whole land, distrain and distress us in all possible ways, namely, by seizing our castles, lands, possessions, and in any other way they can, until redress has been obtained as they deem fit. . . .

JAPANESE FEUDALISM

Japanese feudalism and its origins can be tracked in part through government decrees. Japan had an emperor from the sixth century onward. But decrees between the ninth and the twelfth centuries make it clear that the government encountered increasing difficulties in maintaining order or even disciplining its own officials. In the late twelfth and thirteenth centuries, a leading family, the Kamakura (Minamoto), gained central authority (separate from the emperor, now a largely religious figurehead). The government, called a shogunate, established feudal ties with other lords, treating them as vassals with mutual obligations. Documents 3 and 4 suggest some of the characteristics, advantages, and limitations of this feudal monarchy system. The final two documents describe Japanese feudal ideals. The *Tale of the Heike* was a well-known story of the wars that led up to the Kamakura shogunate, written shortly thereafter; it is followed by a letter from a samurai—the characteristic vassal-warrior—to his son.

• • •

JAPANESE FEUDAL DOCUMENTS

1. On Matters Relating to the Business of a Province (1114)

1. Preventing riotous behavior.

When a newly appointed governor travels to the province to which he is assigned, some of his *rōtō* [entourage] and other followers either rob things from other persons or engage in quarrels among themselves. It is therefore ordered that a newly appointed governor must select from among his *rōtō*, pure and strong persons who can engage in the task of stopping this kind of behavior.

2. Do not permit members of your household (*ienoko*) to speak ill of others, and prevent unruly actions of your high ranking *rōtō*.

If on reflection one does not stop those conditions which lead to the use of foul language, and permit one's *rōtō* to engage freely in slandering or heaping abuse on others . . . as these things continue to multiply, people will start ridiculing you. When you take the responsibility of serving the public, you are really performing something good for yourself too. But if you do not put a stop to the abuse that some of your followers—whether they be your own most beloved children or *rōtō*—heap on others, and let this continue [those who are the object of abuse will not serve you]. In this way, you may not be able to collect taxes and send them to the central government. You will then gain the reputation of being an ineffectual governor. If your children and *rōtō* cannot uphold one another and also help you, your term of office will be one of emptiness. If all your followers will pursue their own follies, you will be left with no followers day and night. Then what benefit is there [of becoming a governor]?

2. Establishment of Relationship between Lord and Vassals (1184)

Following the destruction of the Ichinotani fortification in Settsu Province in the Second Month, members of the Heike have been plundering the various provinces in the west, and Genji troops have been sent into the region to check the Heike. One of the means employed has been the sending of Tachibana Kiminari and his men as an advance column into Sanuki Province to secure the support of the local lords. They have since submitted to the Minamoto, and a roster containing their names has been transmitted to Kamakura [central government]. Today, His Lordship has sent instructions to the local lords of Sanuki to take their orders from Kiminari.

[Yoritomo's monogram]

"Ordered to: Immediate vassals of Sanuki Province

"To submit forthwith to the command of Tachibana Kiminari and to join in the Kyushu campaign.

"At this time when the Heike are plundering your lands, you have indicated your submission to me. A roster of your names has been submitted to me. It is indeed a most loyal act on your part. Submit forthwith to the command of Kiminari and conduct yourselves in a loyal and meritorious manner. Thus ordered."

3. The Kamakura Shogunate (1232)

Of the duties devolving on Protectors (*shugō*) in the provinces. In the time of the august Right General [Yoritomo's] House, it was settled that those duties should be the calling out and despatching of the Grand Guard for service at the capital, the suppression of conspiracies and rebellion and the punishment of murder and violence (which included night attacks on houses, gang robbery and piracy). . . .

Be it noted that no person, even if his family were for generations vassals (*gokenin*) of the august House of Minamoto is competent to impress [people] for military service unless he has an investiture [to the land] of the present date.

4. Tale of the Heike

Recognizing each other, master and retainer spurred their horses to join each other. Seizing Kanehira's hands, Yoshinaka said: "I would have fought to the death on the banks of the Kamo at Rokujō. Simply because of you, however, I have galloped here through the enemy swarms."

"It was very kind of you, my lord," replied Kanehira. "I too would have fought to the death at Seta. But in fear of your uncertain fate, I have come this way."

"We are still tied by karma," said Yoshinaka. "There must be more of my men around here, for I have seen them scattered among the hills. Unroll the banner and raise it high!" . . .

At this challenge, [the enemy commander] Tadayori shouted to his men: "Now, hear this! He is the commander of our enemy. Let him not escape! All men—to the attack!" . . . When Yoshinaka found himself alone with Kanehira, he sighed: "My armor has never weighed upon me before, but today it is heavy."

"You do not look tired at all, my lord," replied Kanehira, "and your horse is still fresh. What makes it feel so heavy? If it is because you are discouraged at having none of your retainers but me, please remember that I, Kanehira, am a match for a thousand. Since I still have seven or eight arrows left in my quiver, let me hold back the foe while you withdraw to the Awazu pine wood. Now I pray you to put a peaceful end to yourself."

No sooner had he spoken to his master than another band of soldiers confronted them. "Please go to the pine wood, my lord," said Kanehira again. "Let me fight here to keep them away from you."

"I would have died in the capital!" replied Yoshinaka. "I have come this far with no other hope but to share your fate. How can I die apart from you? Let us fight until we die together!"

With these words, Yoshinaka tried to ride neck and neck with Kanehira. Now Kanehira alighted from his horse, seized the bridle of his master's mount, and pleaded in tears: "Whatever fame a warrior may win, a worthless death is a lasting shame for

From Hiroshi Kitagawa and Bruce T. Tsuchida, trans., *The Tale of the Heike* (Tokyo: University of Tokyo Press, 1975), 520–23. Reprinted by permission of the publisher.

him. You are worn out, my lord. Your horse is also exhausted. If you are surrounded by the enemy and slain at the hand of a low, worthless retainer of some unknown warrior, it will be a great shame for you and me in the days to come. How disgraceful it would be if such a nameless fellow could declare, 'I cut off the head of Yoshinaka, renowned throughout the land of Japan!'"

Yoshinaka finally gave in to Kanehira's entreaty and rode off toward the pine wood of Awazu. Kanehira, riding alone, charged into the band of some fifty horsemen. Rising high in his stirrups, he cried out in a thunderous voice: "You have often heard of me. Now take a good look. I am Imai no Shirō Kanehira, aged thirty-three, a foster brother of Lord Yoshinaka. As I am a valiant warrior among the men of Lord Yoshinaka, your master, Yoritomo, at Kamakura must know my name well. Take my head and show it to him!"

Kanehira had hardly uttered these words when he let fly his remaining eight arrows one after another without pause. Eight men were shot from their horses, either dead or wounded. He then drew his sword and brandished it as he galloped to and fro. None of his opponents could challenge him face to face, though they cried out: "Shoot him down! Shoot him down!"

Sanehira's soldiers let fly a shower of arrows at Kanehira, but his armor was so strong that none of them pierced it. Unless they aimed at the joints of his armor, he could never be wounded.

Yoshinaka was now all alone in the pine wood of Awazu. It was the twenty-first day of the first month. Dusk had begun to fall. Thin ice covered the rice fields and the marsh, so that it was hard to distinguish one from the other. Thus it was that Yoshinaka had not gone far before his horse plunged deep into the muddy slime. Whipping and spurring no longer did any good. The horse could not stir. Despite his predicament, he still thought of Kanehira. As Yoshinaka was turning around to see how he fared, Tamehisa, catching up with him, shot an arrow under his helmet. It was a mortal wound. Yoshinaka pitched forward onto the neck of his horse. Then two of Tamehisa's retainers fell upon Yoshinaka and struck off his head. Raising it high on the point of his sword, Tamehisa shouted: "Kiso no Yoshinaka, renowned throughout the land of Japan as a valiant warrior, has been killed by Miura no Ishida Jirō Tamehisa!"

Kanehira was fighting desperately as these words rang in his ears. At that moment he ceased fighting and cried out: "For whom do I have to fight now? You, warriors of the east, see how the mightiest warrior in Japan puts an end to himself!" Thrusting the point of his sword into his mouth, he flung himself headlong from his horse so that the sword pierced his head.

Yoshinaka and Kanehira died valiant deaths at Awazu. Could there have been a more heroic battle?

5. A Samurai Instructs His Son

. . . In dealing with subordinates do not make an obvious distinction between good and not-good. Use the same kind of language, give the same kind of treatment to all, and thus you will get the best out of the worst. But you yourself must not lose sight of the distinction between good character and bad character, between capable and incapable. You must be fair, but in practice you must not forget the difference between men who are useful and men who are not. Remember that the key to discipline is fair treatment in rewards and in punishments. But make allowance for minor misdeeds in young soldiers and others, if their conduct is usually good.

Do not be careless or negligent in the presence of subordinates, especially of older men. Thus do not spit or snuffle or lounge about on a chest with your legs dangling. This only gives men the impression that you do not care for their good opinion. Preserve your dignity. If you behave rudely, they will tell their families and gossip will spread. You must treat all servants with proper consideration and generosity. . . .

Remember, however, that there are times when a commander must exercise his power of deciding questions of life or death. In those circumstances since human life is at stake you must give most careful thought to your action. Never kill or wound a man in anger, however great the provocation. Better get somebody else to administer the proper punishment. Decisions made in haste before your feelings are calm can only lead to remorse. Close your eyes and reflect carefully when you have a difficult decision to make.

When accusations are brought to you, always remember that there must be another side to the question. Do not merely indulge in anger. To give fair decisions is the most important thing not only in commanding soldiers but also in governing a country.

Excerpted from George Sanson, *A History of Japan to 1334* (Stanford, Calif.: Stanford University Press, 1958), 336. © 1961 by the Board of Trustees of the Leland Stanford Junior University. Reprinted by permission of the publisher.

CHAPTER 11

THE CRUSADES

Muslim and European Reactions

Increasing interactions among civilizations can work in many different ways. They can promote mutual influence and imitation. But contact can also heighten mutual hostilities or establish new enmities. This chapter deals with the clash between Christians and Muslims during the Crusades. Enduring tension between Christian and Muslim was not the only product of this episode, for the sources suggest other consequences as well.

During the postclassical period, both religions spread widely. Islam was clearly more successful, however, partly because it took root in a dynamic, politically and commercially successful region. Often genuinely tolerant of Christians, whom Muhammad had regarded as partially enlightened, Muslims nevertheless looked down on Western Europe in this period as a backward, boorish place. Muslim wealth, cities, science, and learning easily surpassed European levels, and Muslim leaders were well aware of this fact.

For their part, Christians viewed Islam as an infidel, false religion, all the more galling given Muslim success. There was far less tolerance in principle, and tension was exacerbated by European awareness that Muslims surpassed them, during this period, in economic and political achievements.

Christian crusades against Muslim control of the Holy Land (Jerusalem and its environs) were first called for at the end of the eleventh century, at a point when the Arab Caliphate was beginning to decline and Turks controlled considerable territory. Feudal warriors from Western Europe volunteered to fight in the Middle East, for a time carving out a Christian kingdom of Jerusalem. The Third Crusade, 1188–1192, involving kings of England, France, and the Holy Roman Empire, responded to successful Muslim attacks on Jerusalem, under the leadership of the great Turkish warrior Saladin. This crusade led to negotiations that established temporary Christian access to, though not control of, Jerusalem.

The Crusades provided unusual contacts between people, mainly warriors, of two different cultures. Europeans learned much about the economically more advanced Middle East, despite their deep hatred of Islam as a false religion and their frequent attempt to portray Muslims as idol worshipers. Muslims formed or confirmed a variety of opinions about Europeans. How much lasting impact did impressions of this sort have?

Treatments of the same event—such as the Crusades—by people from opposite sides have some fairly standard features. The other side commits atrocities, which contrast with the purity and high aims of our side. Individual participants may develop a grudging respect for the heroism or the simple humanity of opponents, a respect that sometimes contradicts expressions of hatred.

But the accounts offer more than the "you're another" type of mutual hostility. The economic gap between the two sides is evident in comments about Muslim luxury and European awe. To the extent that the Crusades confirmed not only some dislike of European Christians but also a sense of their backwardness, they contributed to a Muslim reluctance to pay attention to changes in Europe in succeeding centuries that might have warranted greater openness.

The Crusades were an interesting episode in the postclassical period, not an earthshaking event. They stemmed from significant cultural and other tensions, and they unintentionally provided materials by which two important civilizations can be compared. They also had some lasting, if largely unexpected, side effects in world history later on, including increasing European interest in trade with Asia. Intriguingly, contemporary Islamic extremists have revived the idea that the West is engaged in a "crusade" against their religion, a sign that a historic conflict can resurface in memory.

Questions

1. In what ways were Christian and Muslim accounts of the Crusades similar? In what terms might each side praise the other?

2. How did the Christian account try to arouse sentiment against Muslim treatment of the Christian religion? How did Muslim accounts try to arouse sentiment against Christian mistreatment of or scorn for Islam?

3. What elements of Islam prompt Ibn-Mundiqh, in the final passage, to simultaneously praise Christ and express shock at the idea of showing God as a child? What clearly inaccurate reference to Islam is included in the Christian account—and why would it have been included?

4. What references in the Muslim accounts particularly suggest a disdain for European backwardness? What is the jealousy passage all about: given Muslim (and Christian) views about men's rights concerning women, why was this probably a backhanded insult, designed to stimulate further disdain against Christians?

5. As expressed in these accounts, were the reasons for Christian and Muslim dislike of each other similar?

For Further Discussion

1. Which of the three accounts—all clearly partisan—strikes you as most accurate, and why? (Or do they all seem equally biased?) Which reference, in any of the accounts, seems most clearly distorted? What criteria help sort out accuracy when the historical sources are clearly tainted?
2. How do the Crusades and Muslim and Christian accounts of them demonstrate how these two religions resembled each other more than either one resembled Buddhism, during the postclassical period?
3. What were the most important results of the Crusades?

A Christian Account

This account was written by Richard of the Holy Trinity, probably Richard de Templo, who was later selected as Prior of the Holy Trinity but who served King Richard as knight or chaplain during the Crusade. His account suggests not only Christian views of Muslims but also key feudal military values (see chapter 9). The subject of his biography, King Richard, known as the Lion-Hearted, won a huge reputation in England as a noble warrior, even though (or because) he spent little time at home (but he did spend considerable English revenues). King Richard fought against his brothers and father and then in 1190 departed for the Third Crusade. His attack on the city of Acre, in alliance with the King of France, failed, but he was able to negotiate access to the holy places in Jerusalem with the Muslim leader Saladin. He was captured and held for ransom on the way home and was later killed in a war with France. Richard's reputation as a brave and good king, enhanced by accounts such as this, entered into other English legends such as that of Robin Hood, and it contrasted with the image of his brother, later King John.

• • •

THE CRUSADE OF RICHARD I

King Richard was not yet quite recovered from his illness; yet, anxious to be doing something, he turned his thoughts to the capture of the city, and had it attacked by his men in the hopes of gaining some success with God's assistance. Accordingly he had a kind of hurdle-shed (commonly called a *circleia*) made and brought up to the ditch outside the city wall. Under its shelter were placed his most skilful crossbowmen;

From T. A. Archer, ed., *The Crusade of Richard I* (New York: G. P. Putnam's, 1885), 92–95, 97–98, 99, 101–2, 103, 126–27.

whilst, to hearten his own men for the combat and to dispirit the Saracens [Muslims] by his presence, he had himself carried there on silken cushions. From this position he worked a crossbow, in the management of which he was very skilful, and slew many of the foes by the bolts and quarrels he discharged. His miners also, approaching the tower against which his stone-casters were being levelled, by an underground passage dug down towards the foundations, filling the gaps they made with logs of wood, to which they would set fire, thus causing the walls, which had already been shaken by the stone-casters, to fall down with sudden crash.

Thereupon the king, seeing how difficult the work was and how valiant were the enemies, knowing also how needful it was to kindle men's valour at critical moments, thought it more fitting to encourage the young [warriors] on by promises of reward than to urge them on by harsh words. For who is there whom the prospect of gain will not entice? Accordingly he proclaimed that he would give two gold pieces to any one who would detach a stone from the wall near the before-mentioned tower. Later he promised three and even four gold-pieces for each stone. Then might you see the young men with their followers leap forth and rush against the wall and set themselves zealously to lugging out the stones—and this as much for the sake of praise as of pay. . . . The height of the wall was very great and it was of no slight thickness; yet, dispelling danger, by courage, they extracted many a stone. The Turks rushing against [the assailants] in bands strove to cast them down from the walls; and, while thus engaged in driving back their enemies, unwarily exposed themselves to darts; for in their haste they rashly neglected to put on their armour. One of the Turks who to his cost was glorying in the arms of Alberic Clements, with which he had girded himself, did king Richard wound to death, piercing him through the breast, with a dart from his crossbow. Grieving over the death of this warrior the Turks recklessly rushed forward for vengeance, and, just as though energetic action were a cure for pain, showed themselves so bold that it seemed as if they feared neither darts nor any other missile. Never were our men engaged by warriors—of any creed whatever—more valorous or apter at defence. Memory staggers at the recollection of their deeds. In the press of this conflict neither armour of strongest proof nor two-fold coat of mail nor quilted work was strong enough to resist the missiles hurled from the stone-casters. Yet, for all this, the Turks kept countermining from within till they compelled our men to retreat; and then they began to raise a furious cry as though their object had been attained. . . . At last the Pisans [Italians], eager for fame and vengeance, scrambled up the tower itself with a mighty effort; but, bravely as they comported themselves, they too had to retreat before the onset of the Turks, who rushed on as if mad. Never has there been such a people as these Turks for prowess in war. And yet, for all the enemies' valour, the city would on that day have been taken and the whole siege finished if the entire army had displayed an equal valour. For, you must know, by far the larger part of the army was at that hour breakfasting; and, as the attack was made at an unsuitable time, it did not succeed.

Though its walls were partly fallen and partly shaken, though a great part of the inhabitants were slain or weakened by wounds, there still remained in the city 6,000 Turks. . . .

[Then leaders] imagined the Christian army had been very keenly touched at the death of Alberic Clements and at the loss of sons and kinsmen who had fallen in the war; and had determined to die or master the Turks—holding that no other course was consistent with honour. So, by common consent and counsel, the besieged begged a truce while they sent notice of their plight to Saladin, hoping that, in accordance with their Pagan ways, he would ensure their safety—as he ought to do—by sending them speedy aid or procuring leave for them to quit the city without disgrace. To obtain this favour, these two noble Saracens, the most renowned [warriors] in all Paganism, Mestoc and Caracois, came to our kings, promising to surrender the city, if Saladin did not send them speedy aid. They stipulated, however, that all the besieged Turks should have free leave to go wherever they wished with their arms and all their goods. The king of France and almost all the French agreed to this; but king Richard utterly refused to hear of entering an empty city after so long and toilsome a siege. . . .

Meanwhile, the Christians' stone-casters never ceased battering the walls night and day. Seeing this a panic seized the inhabitants and some, in utter despair, giving way to fear, threw themselves headlong from the walls by night. Many of them humbly begged to be baptized and made Christians. There is considerable doubt as to the real merits of these [converts], and not without due reason, since it is to be presumed that it was terror rather than divine grace that caused them to make this request. But the ways of salvation are many. . . .

Thus, on the Friday after the translation of the Blessed Benedict [*i.e.* July 12], the wealthier and nobler emirs were proffered and accepted as hostages, one month being allowed for the restoration of the Holy Cross and the collection of the captive Christians. When the news of this surrender became known, the unthinking crowd was moved with wrath; but the wiser folk were much rejoiced at getting so quickly and without danger what previously they had not been able to obtain in so long a time. Then the heralds made proclamation forbidding any one to insult the Turks by word or deed. No missiles were to be hurled against the walls or against the Turks if they chanced to appear on the battlements. On that day, when these famous Turks, of such wonderful valour and warlike excellence, began strolling about on the city walls in all their splendid apparel, previous to their departure [our men] gazed on them with the utmost curiosity. They were wonder-struck at the cheerful features of men who were leaving their city almost penniless and whom only the very sternest necessity had driven to beg for mercy: men whom loss did not deject, and whose visage betrayed no timidity, but even wore the look of victory. It was only their superstitious rites and their pitiful idolatry that had robbed such warriors of their strength. . . .

On the day of its surrender the city had been in the hands of the Saracens four years. It was surrendered, as has been already said, on the morrow of the translation of St. Benedict. But not without horror could the conquerors see the condition of the churches within the city; nor can they even now remember the shameful sights they witnessed there unmoved. What faithful Christian could, with tearless eyes, see the holy features of the crucified Son of God, or even of the saints, dishonoured and defiled? Who would not shudder when he actually saw the insulting way in which the accursed Turks had overthrown the altars, torn down and battered the holy crosses? Ay, and they had even set up their own images of Mahomet in the holy places, introducing foul Mahommedan superstitions, after casting out all the symbols of human redemption and the Christian religion.

Muslim Accounts

The first selection below was written by Bohadin or Beha-ed-Din, born at Mosul in 1145, a Muslim official of Jerusalem and later of Aleppo. He writes of the same Crusade as did Richard of the Holy Trinity, referring to the kings of England and France. The second account, dealing with a period earlier in the twelfth century, comes from the memoirs of Usamah ibn-Munqidh as an Arab-Syrian warrior. He writes of a time when the Christian crusaders controlled the city of Jerusalem; European reactions to Muslim ways (and ibn-Munqidh's reactions to the Europeans) obviously varied from case to case, as often happens when war and occupation combine with a certain familiarity.

• • •

BEH-ED-DIN

The same day Hossâm ad-Din Ibn Barîc . . . brought news that the king of France had set out for Tyre, and that they had come to talk over the matter of the prisoners and to see the true cross of the Crucifixion if it were still in the Musulman [Muslim] camp, or to ascertain if it really had been sent to Bagdad. It was shewn to them, and on beholding it they shewed the profoundest reverence, throwing themselves on the ground till they were covered with dust, and humbling themselves in token of devotion. These envoys told us that the French princes had accepted the

From T. A. Archer, ed., *The Crusade of Richard I* (New York: G. P. Putnams, 1885), 127–31.

Sultan's proposition, viz., to deliver all that was specified in the treaty by three installments at intervals of a month. The Sultan then sent an envoy to Tyre with rich presents, quantities of perfumes, and fine raiment—all of which were for the king of the French.

. . . Ibn Barîc and his comrades returned to the king of England while the Sultan went off with his bodyguard and his closest friends to the hill that abuts on Shefa'Amr. . . . Envoys did not cease to pass from one side to the other in the hope of laying the foundation of a firm peace. These negotiations continued till our men had procured the money and the tale of the prisoners that they were to deliver to the French at the end of the first period in accordance with the treaty. The first instalment was to consist of the Holy Cross, 100,000 dinars and 1,600 prisoners. Trustworthy men sent by the Franks [French, or Europeans] to conduct the examination found it all complete saving only the prisoners who had been demanded by name, all of whom had not yet been gathered together. And thus the negotiations continued to drag on till the end of the first term. . . .

This proposition the Sultan rejected, knowing full well that if he were to deliver the money, the cross, and the prisoners, while our men were still kept captive by the Franks, he would have no security against treachery on the part of the enemy, and this would be a great disaster to Islam.

Then the king of England, seeing all the delays interposed by the Sultan to the execution of the treaty, acted perfidiously as regards his Musulman prisoners. On their yielding the town he had engaged to grant them life, adding that if the Sultan carried out the bargain he would give them freedom and suffer them to carry off their children and wives; if the Sultan did not fulfil his engagements they were to be made slaves. Now the king broke his promises to them and made open display of what he had till now kept hidden in his heart, by carrying out what he had intended to do after he had received the money and the Frank prisoners. It is thus that people of his nation ultimately admitted.

In the afternoon of Tuesday . . . about four o'clock, he came out on horseback with all the Frankish army. . . . The Franks, on reaching the middle of the plain that stretches between this hill and that of Keisân, close to which place the sultan's advanced guard had drawn back, ordered all the Musulman prisoners, whose martyrdom God had decreed for this day, to be brought before him. They numbered more than three thousand and were all bound with ropes. The Franks then flung themselves upon them all at once and massacred them with sword and lance in cold blood. Our advanced guard had already told the Sultan of the enemy's movements and he sent it some reinforcements, but only after the massacre. The Musulmans, seeing what was being done to the prisoners, rushed against the Franks and in the combat, which lasted till nightfall, several were slain and wounded on either side. On the morrow morning our people gathered at the spot and found the Musulmans stretched out upon the ground as martyrs for the faith. They even recognised some of the dead, and the sight was a great affliction to them. The enemy had only spared the prisoners of note and such as were strong enough to work.

The motives of this massacre are differently told; according to some, the captives were slain by way of reprisal for the death of those Christians whom the Musulmans had slain. Others again say that the king of England, on deciding to attempt the conquest of Ascalon, thought it unwise to leave so many prisoners in the town after his departure. God alone knows what the real reason was.

USAMAH IBN-MUNQIDH

. . . A case illustrating their [the Europeans'] curious medicine is the following:

The lord of al-Munaytirah wrote to my uncle asking him to dispatch a physician to treat certain sick persons among his people. My uncle sent him a Christian physician named Thābit. Thābit was absent but ten days when he returned. So we said to him, "How quickly hast thou healed thy patients!" He said:

> They brought before me a knight in whose leg an abscess had grown; and a woman afflicted with imbecility. To the knight I applied a small poultice until the abscess opened and became well; and the woman I put on diet and made her humor wet. Then a Frankish physician came to them and said, "This man knows nothing about treating them." He then said to the knight, "Which wouldst thou prefer, living with one leg or dying with two?" The latter replied, "Living with one leg." The physician said, "Bring me a strong knight and a sharp ax." A knight came with the ax. And I was standing by. Then the physician laid the leg of the patient on a block of wood and bade the knight strike his leg with the ax and chop it off at one blow. Accordingly he struck it—while I was looking on—one blow, but the leg was not severed. He dealt another blow, upon which the marrow of the leg flowed out and the patient died on the spot. He then examined the woman and said, "This is a woman in whose head there is a devil which has possessed her. Shave off her hair." Accordingly they shaved it off and the woman began once more to eat their ordinary diet—garlic and mustard. Her imbecility took a turn for the worse. The physician then said, "The devil has penetrated through her head." He therefore took a razor, made a deep cruciform incision on it, peeled off the skin at the middle of the incision until the bone of the skull was exposed and rubbed it with salt. The woman also expired instantly. Thereupon I asked them whether my services were needed any longer, and when they replied in the negative I returned home, having learned of their medicine what I knew not before.

From Usamah ibn-Munqidh, *Memoirs: An Arab-Syrian Gentleman and Warrior in the Period of the Crusades*, ed. Philip Hitti, (Princeton, N. J.: Princeton University Press, 1987), 67–68, 70, 162–65. Copyright © Viola Winder.

I have, however, witnessed a case of their medicine which was quite different from that.

The king of the Franks had for treasurer a knight named Bernard [*barnād*], who (may Allah's curse be upon him!) was one of the most accursed and wicked among the Franks. A horse kicked him in the leg, which was subsequently infected and which opened in fourteen different places. Every time one of these cuts would close in one place, another would open in another place. All this happened while I was praying for his perdition. Then came to him a Frankish physician and removed from the leg all the ointments which were on it and began to wash it with very strong vinegar. By this treatment all the cuts were healed and the man became well again. He was up again like a devil. . . .

Newly arrived Franks are especially rough: One insists that Usāmah should pray eastward.—Everyone who is a fresh emigrant from the Frankish lands is ruder in character than those who have become acclimatized and have held long association with the Moslems. Here is an illustration of their rude character.

Whenever I visited Jerusalem I always entered the Aqṣa Mosque, beside which stood a small mosque which the Franks had converted into a church. When I used to enter the Aqṣa Mosque, which was occupied by the Templars [*al-dāwiyyah*], who were my friends, the Templars would evacuate the little adjoining mosque so that I might pray in it. One day I entered this mosque, repeated the first formula, "Allah is great," and stood up in the act of praying, upon which one of the Franks rushed on me, got hold of me and turned my face eastward saying, "This is the way thou shouldst pray!" A group of Templars hastened to him, seized him and repelled him from me. I resumed my prayer. The same man, while the others were otherwise busy, rushed once more on me and turned my face eastward, saying, "This is the way thou shouldst pray!" The Templars again came in to him and expelled him. They apologized to me, saying, "This is a stranger who has only recently arrived from the land of the Franks and he has never before seen anyone praying except eastward." Thereupon I said to myself, "I have had enough prayer." So I went out and have ever been surprised at the conduct of this devil of a man, at the change in the color of his face, his trembling and his sentiment at the sight of one praying towards the *qiblah* [direction of Mecca].

Another wants to show to a Moslem God as a child.—I saw one of the Franks come to al-Amīr Mu'īn-al-Dī (may Allah's mercy rest upon his soul!) when he was in the Dome of the Rock and say to him, "Dost thou want to see God as a child?" Mu'-n-al-Dīn said, "Yes." The Frank walked ahead of us until he showed us the picture of Mary with Christ (may peace be upon him!) as an infant in her lap. He then said, "This is God as a child." But Allah is exalted far above what the infidels say about him!

The Franks are void of all zeal and jealousy. One of them may be walking along with his wife. He meets another man who takes the wife by the hand and steps aside to converse with her while the husband is standing on one side waiting for his wife to conclude the conversation. If she lingers too long for him, he leaves her alone with the conversant and goes away.

Here is an illustration which I myself witnessed:

When I used to visit Nāblus, I always took lodging with a man named Muʿizz, whose home was a lodging house for the Moslems. The house had windows which opened to the road, and there stood opposite to it on the other side of the road a house belonging to a Frank who sold wine for the merchants. He would take some wine in a bottle and go around announcing it by shouting, "So and so, the merchant, has just opened a cask full of this wine. He who wants to buy some of it will find it in such and such a place." The Frank's pay for the announcement made would be the wine in that bottle. One day this Frank went home and found a man with his wife in the same bed. He asked him, "What could have made thee enter into my wife's room?" The man replied, "I was tired, so I went in to rest." "But how," asked he, "didst thou get into my bed?" The other replied, "I found a bed that was spread, so I slept in it." "But," said he, "my wife was sleeping together with thee!" The other replied, "Well, the bed is hers. How could I therefore have prevented her from using her own bed?" "By the truth of my religion," said the husband, "if thou shouldst do it again, thou and I would have a quarrel." Such was for the Frank the entire expression of his disapproval and the limit of his jealousy.

CHAPTER 12

MERCHANTS AND TRADE

The postclassical period witnessed an important expansion of trade, within many civilizations and across their fluid boundaries. Merchants gained a growing role in West Africa, throughout the Islamic world, in Europe (both east and west), and in East Asia. Many traded locally, though international merchants made the biggest impression. Chinese commercial centers grew rapidly, supporting a more urban environment. At the same time, many societies had reservations about merchants. Aristocrats worried about their social claims, rulers might envy their wealth, priests and philosophers questioned their motives. The clash of cultures, between religion and materialism, was particularly intense because of the complex new forces at work in these centuries. A genuine ambivalence about merchants was common throughout the postclassical world—and it could affect merchants themselves, as well as how they were treated.

This chapter deals with trade and its cultural impacts. It provides another set of comparisons among three trading societies and also a chance to deal with change during the period itself.

The description of the twelfth-century British merchant Godric was written by a biographer attracted to his saintly life (most merchants did not, it should be emphasized, become saints). It suggests both actual activities and cultural values. The Muslim description of merchants' vices and merits comes from the great historian and philosopher Ibn Khaldun, a North African who wrote in the fourteenth century. The Chinese essay on merchants was written by Chang Han, early in the sixteenth century (right after the postclassical period and more than a half-century after the Ming dynasty had ended its most vigorous international trade). Chang Han was a Ming official whose family had made a fortune in the textile industry, which helps explain the combination of Confucian and reformist remarks.

Questions

1. What kinds of uneasiness did Muslim observers have about trade? In what way did they support trade?
2. How did Chinese concerns about merchant motives differ from those of Christianity?

3. How did Islam offer a distinctive combination of trade and cultural goals—this one more favorable to trade without slighting religion? In what ways did Islam and Christianity, such similar religions in many respects, differ over the validity of trade; would a Godric story have been probable in Islam?

4. What exceptions or ambiguities do the sources suggest, even as they emphasize high ideals? What kinds of activities in Europe clearly represented crasser motives than those of a holy merchant like Godric? Why, in fact, did Godric not enter a holy calling initially—what kinds of motives drew him to trade?

5. How could merchant activity increase within China—as it did in the postclassical period, as cities and business houses prospered—within an official Confucian framework? How did the Confucian bureaucracy collaborate?

6. Do the sources suggest that Europe was becoming wealthier than China by the late postclassical period?

For Further Discussion

1. In light of the postclassical sources and comparisons, how would you rate the argument that no matter what their professed values, most people and societies are motivated by a desire for profit and will expand commercially whenever they can? Is a desire for economic gain an inherent part of human nature?

2. Which came first in world history: concern about trade or economic limitations? Did Christianity cause Western Europe's initial commercial lag in the postclassical period, or did economic decline encourage Christian concerns? How did Confucianism affect actual Chinese economic patterns in the postclassical period and beyond?

3. How do postclassical discussions of trade and merchants compare with the discussions probable in the modern world?

A MUSLIM VIEW: IBN KHALDUN

Ibn Khaldun was one of the greatest historians and geographers of all time. Born in Tunis, North Africa, he lived from 1332 to 1406. He served as an official in Tunis, Morocco, and Spain and traveled widely, finally settling, as a scholar, in Egypt. His great work was the *Kitab al-Ibar* (universal history), which included comments on the active trade that he saw around him, at the time when Muslim commercial success was still near its height.

• • •

CHARACTERISTICS OF TRADERS

Commerce, as we have said before, is the increasing of capital by buying goods and attempting to sell them at a price higher than their cost. This is done either by waiting for a rise in the market price; or by transporting the goods to another place where they are more keenly demanded and therefore fetch a higher price; or, lastly, by selling them on a long-term credit basis. Commerci
al profit is small, relatively to the capital invested, but if the capital is large, even a low rate of profit will produce a large total gain.

In order to achieve this increase in capital, it is necessary to have enough initial capital to pay in cash the sellers from whom one buys goods; it is also necessary to sell for cash, as honesty is not widespread among people. This dishonesty leads on the one hand to fraud and the adulteration of goods, and on the other to delays in payment which diminish profits because capital remains idle during the interval. It also induces buyers to repudiate their debts, a practice which is very injurious to the merchant's capital unless he can produce documentary evidence or the testimony of eyewitness. Nor are magistrates of much help in such cases, because they necessarily judge on evident proofs.

As a result of all this, the trader can only secure his meagre profits by dint of much effort and toil, or indeed he may well lose not only profits but capital as well. Hence, if he is known to be bold in entering law suits, careful in keeping accounts, stubborn in defending his point of view, firm in his attitude towards magistrates, he stands a good chance of getting his due. Should he not have these qualities, his only chance is to secure the support of a highly placed protector who will awe his debtors into paying him and the magistrates into meting justice out to him. Thus he gets justice spontaneously in the first case, and by compulsion in the second. Should a person, however, be lacking in boldness and the spirit of enterprise and at the same time have no protector to back him up, he had better avoid trade altogether, as he risks losing his capital and becoming the prey of other merchants. The fact of the matter is that most people, especially the mob and the trading classes, covet the goods of others; and but for the restraint imposed by the magistrates all goods would have been taken away from their owners. . . .

The manners of tradesmen are inferior to those of rulers, and far removed from manliness and uprightness. We have already stated that traders must buy and sell and seek profits. This necessitates flattery, and evasiveness, litigation and disputation, all of which are characteristic of this profession. And these qualities lead to a decrease and weakening in virtue and manliness. For acts inevitably affect the soul; thus good acts produce good and virtuous effects in the soul while evil or mean acts produce the opposite. Hence the effects of evil acts will strike root and strengthen themselves, if they should come early in life and repeat themselves; while if they come later they will efface the virtues by imprinting their evil effects on the soul; as is the case with all habits resulting from actions.

These effects will differ according to the conditions of the traders. For those of them who are of mean condition and in direct contact with the cheating and extortion of sellers will be more affected by these evils and further removed from manliness. . . . The other kind of traders are those who are protected by prestige and do not have to undertake directly such operations. Such persons are very rare indeed and consist of those who have acquired wealth suddenly, by inheritance or by other, unusual means. This wealth enables them to get in touch with the rulers and thus to gain prestige and protection so that they are released from practising these things [viz. buying and selling] themselves; instead, they entrust such business to their agents. Moreover the rulers, who are not indifferent to the wealth and liberality of such traders, protect them in their right and thus free them from certain unpleasant actions and their resulting evil effects. Hence they will be more manly and honourable than the other kind of trader; yet certain effects will still make themselves felt behind the veil, inasmuch as they still have to supervise their agents and employees in their doings—but this only takes place to a limited extent and its effects are hardly visible. . . .

. . . Consider, as an example, the lands of the East, such as Egypt, Syria, Persia, India, or China; or the lands lying North of the Mediterranean. Because social life is flourishing there, notice how wealth has increased, the state has grown stronger, towns have multiplied, trade has prospected prospered, conditions have improved. . . .

As for Trade, although it be a natural means of livelihood, yet most of the methods it employs are tricks aimed at making a profit by securing the difference between the buying and selling prices, and by appropriating the surplus. This is why [religious] Law allows the use of such methods, which, although they come under the heading of gambling, yet do not constitute the taking without return of other people's goods. . . .

Should their standard of living, however, rise, so that they begin to enjoy more than the bare necessities, the effect will be to breed in them a desire for repose and tranquillity. They will therefore co-operate to secure superfluities; their food and clothing will increase in quantity and refinement; they will enlarge their houses and plan their towns for defence. A further improvement in their conditions will lead to habits of luxury, resulting in extreme refinement in cooking and the preparation of food; in choosing rich clothing of the finest silk; in raising lofty mansions and castles and furnishing them luxuriously, and so on. At this stage the crafts develop and reach their height. Lofty castles and mansions are built and decorated sumptuously, water is drawn to them and a great diversity takes place in the way of dress, furniture, vessels, and household equipment.

Such are the townsmen, who earn their living in industry or trade. Their gains are greater than those working in agriculture or animal husbandry and their standard of living higher, being in line with their wealth. We have shown, then, that both the nomadic and the urban stages are natural and necessary.

A Christian View: Reginald of Durham on Saint Godric

This excerpt from a biography of Godric, an English merchant who later became a saint, both describes actual merchant activities in Europe and provides an example of an established literary-religious form of writing in Christian Europe in which the main point was to stress the saint's virtues and use biography as an inspiration to others. There may be some distortion of reality here; certainly, some aspects of the merchant condition have to be discovered by reading between the lines.

• • •

This holy man's father was named Ailward, and his mother Edwenna; both of slender rank and wealth, but abundant in righteousness and virtue. . . . When the boy had passed his childish years quietly at home; then, as he began to grow to manhood, he began to follow more prudent ways of life, and to learn carefully and persistently the teachings of worldly forethought. Wherefore he chose not to follow the life of a husbandman, but rather to study, learn and exercise the rudiment of more subtle conceptions. For this reason, aspiring to the merchant's trade, he began to follow the chapman's [peddler's] way of life, first learning how to gain in small bargains and things of insignificant price; and thence, while yet a youth, his mind advanced little by little to buy and sell and gain from things of greater expense. For, in his beginnings, he was wont to wander with small wares around the villages and farmsteads of his own neighborhood; but, in process of time, he gradually associated himself by compact with city merchants. Hence, within a brief space of time, the youth who had trudged for many weary hours from village to village, from farm to farm, did so profit by his increase of age and wisdom as to travel with associates of his own age through towns and boroughs fortresses and cities, to fairs and to all the various booths of the market-place. . . . He went along the high-way, neither puffed up by the good testimony of his conscience nor downcast in the nobler part of his soul by the reproach of poverty. . . .

From Reginald of Durham, "Life of St. Godric," in G. G. Coulton, ed., *Social Life in Britain from the Conquest to the Reformation* (Cambridge: Cambridge University Press, 1918), 415–20. Reprinted with the permission of Cambridge University Press.

Yet in all things he walked with simplicity; and, in so far as he yet knew how, it was ever his pleasure to follow in the footsteps of the truth. For, having learned the Lord's Prayer and the Creed from his very cradle, he oftentimes turned them over in his mind, even as he went alone on his longer journeys; and, in so far as the truth was revealed to his mind, he clung thereunto most devoutly in all his thoughts concerning God. At first, he lived as a [salesman] for four years in Lincolnshire, going on foot and carrying the smallest wares; then he travelled abroad, first to St Andrews in Scotland and then for the first time to Rome. On his return, having formed a familiar friendship with certain other young men who were eager for merchandise, he began to launch upon bolder courses, and to coast frequently by sea to the foreign lands that lay around him. Thus, sailing often to and fro between Scotland and Britain, he traded in many divers wares and, amid these occupations, learned much worldly wisdom. . . . He fell into many perils of the sea, yet by God's mercy he was never wrecked; for He who had upheld St Peter as he walked upon the waves, by that same strong right arm kept this His chosen vessel from all misfortune amid these perils. Thus, having learned by frequent experience his wretchedness amid such dangers, he began to worship certain of the Saints with more ardent zeal, venerating and calling upon their shrines, and giving himself up by wholehearted service to those holy names. In such invocations his prayers were oftentimes answered by prompt consolation; some of which prayers he learned from his fellows with whom he shared these frequent perils; others he collected from faithful hearsay; others again from the custom of the place, for he saw and visited such holy places with frequent assiduity. Thus aspiring ever higher and higher, and yearning upward with his whole heart, at length his great labours and cares bore much fruit of worldly gain. For he laboured not only as a merchant but also as a shipman . . . to Denmark and Flanders and Scotland; in all which lands he found certain rare, and therefore more precious, wares, which he carried to other parts wherein he knew them to be least familiar, and coveted by the inhabitants beyond the price of gold itself; wherefore he exchanged these wares for others coveted by men of other lands. . . . Hence he made great profit in all his bargains, and gathered much wealth in the sweat of his brow; for he sold dear in one place the wares which he had bought elsewhere at a small price.

Then he purchased the half of a merchant-ship with certain of his partners in the trade; and again by his prudence he bought the fourth part of another ship. At length, by his skill in navigation, wherein he excelled all his fellows, he earned promotion to the post of steersman. . . .

[On his travels] he oftentimes touched at the island of Lindisfarne, wherein St Cuthbert had been bishop, and at the isle of Farne, where that Saint had lived as an anchoret, and where St Godric (as he himself would tell afterwards) would meditate on the Saint's life with abundant tears. Thence he began to yearn for solitude, and to hold his merchandise in less esteem than heretofore. . . .

And now he had lived sixteen years as a merchant, and began to think of spending on charity, to God's honour and service, the goods which he had so laboriously acquired. He therefore took the cross as a pilgrim to Jerusalem, and, having visited the Holy Sepulchre, came back to England by way of St James [of Compostella]. Not long afterwards he became steward to a certain rich man of his own country, with the care of his whole house and household. But certain of the younger household were men of iniquity, who stole their neighbours' cattle and thus held luxurious feasts, whereat Godric, in his ignorance, was sometimes present. Afterwards, discovering the truth, he rebuked and admonished them to cease; but they made no account of his warnings; wherefore he concealed not their iniquity, but disclosed it to the lord of the household, who, however, slighted his advice. Wherefore he begged to be dismissed and went on a pilgrimage, first to St Gilles and thence to Rome the abode of the Apostles, that thus he might knowingly pay the penalty for those misdeeds wherein he had ignorantly partaken. I have often seen him, even in his old age, weeping for this unknowing transgression. . . .

On his return from Rome, he abode awhile in his father's house; until, inflamed again with holy zeal, he purposed to revisit the abode of the Apostles and made his desire known unto his parents. Not only did they approve his purpose, but his mother besought his leave to bear him company on this pilgrimage; which he gladly granted, and willingly paid her every filial service that was her due. They came therefore to London; and they had scarcely departed from thence when his mother took off her shoes, going thus barefooted to Rome and back to London. Godric, humbly serving his parent, was wont to bear her on his shoulders. . . .

Godric, when he had restored his mother safe to his father's arms, abode but a brief while at home; for he was now already firmly purposed to give himself entirely to God's service. Wherefore, that he might follow Christ the more freely, he sold all his possessions and distributed them among the poor. Then, telling his parents of this purpose and receiving their blessing, he went forth to no certain abode, but whithersoever the Lord should deign to lead him; for above all things he coveted the life of a hermit.

A Chinese View: Chang Han

This passage was written early in the sixteenth century, right after the postclassical period and more than a half-century after the Ming dynasty had stopped its international trade expeditions. Of the three authors in this chapter, Chang Han came the closest to having merchant experience of his own. He came from a family that had made a fortune in the textile industry, but he himself was sent to

Confucian schools and became an official in the Ming dynasty. His background helps explain the combination of Confucian and reformist remarks.

• • •

ESSAY ON MERCHANTS

Money and profit are of great importance to men. They seek profit, then suffer by it, yet they cannot forget it. They exhaust their bodies and spirits, run day and night, yet they still regard what they have gained as insufficient. . . .

Those who become merchants eat fine food and wear elegant clothes. They ride on beautifully caparisoned, double-harnessed horses—dust flying as they race through the streets and the horses' precious sweat falling like rain. Opportunistic persons attracted by their wealth offer to serve them. Pretty girls in beautiful long-sleeved dresses and delicate slippers play string and wind instruments for them and compete to please them.

Merchants boast that their wisdom and ability are such as to give them a free hand in affairs. They believe that they know all the possible transformations in the universe and therefore can calculate all the changes in the human world, and that the rise and fall of prices are under their command. They are confident that they will not make one mistake in a hundred in their calculations. These merchants do not know how insignificant their wisdom and ability really are. As the *Chuang Tzu* says: "Great understanding is broad and unhurried; little understanding is cramped and busy."

Because I have traveled to many places during my career as an official, I am familiar with commercial activities and business conditions in various places. The capital is located in an area with mountains at its back and a great plain stretching in front. The region is rich in millet, grain, donkeys, horses, fruit, and vegetables, and has become a center where goods from distant places are brought. Those who engage in commerce, including the foot peddler, the cart peddler, and the shopkeeper, display not only clothing and fresh foods from the fields but also numerous luxury items such as priceless jade from K'un-lun, pearls from the island of Hai-nan, gold from Yunnan, and coral from Vietnam. These precious items, coming from the mountains or the sea, are not found in central China. But people in remote areas and in other countries, unafraid of the dangers and difficulties of travel, transport these items step by step to the capital, making it the most prosperous place in the empire. . . .

Profits from selling tea and the officials' income from the tea tax are usually ten to twenty percent of the original investment. By contrast, merchants' profits from selling salt and the officials' income from the salt tax can reach seventy to eighty percent of the original invested capital. In either case, the more the invested capital, the greater the profit; the less the invested capital, the less the profit. The profits from selling tea and salt enrich the nation as well as the merchants. Skillful merchants can make great profits for themselves while the inept ones suffer losses. This is the present state of the tea and salt business.

In our Chekiang province it appears that most of the rich gain their wealth from engaging in salt trade. But the Chia family in Wu-ling became rich from selling tea and have sustained their prosperity for generations. The "Book of Chou" [one of the oldest classics] says: "If farmers do not work, there will be an insufficiency of food; if craftsmen do not work, there will be an insufficiency of tools; if merchants do not work, circulation of the three necessities will be cut off, which will cause food and materials to be insufficient."

Foreigners [in the Northwest] are recalcitrant and their greed knows no bounds. At the present time our nation spends over one million cash yearly from our treasury on these foreigners, still we cannot rid ourselves of their demands. What is more, the greedy heart is unpredictable. If one day they break the treaties and invade our frontiers, who will be able to defend us against them? I do not think our present trade with them will ensure us a century of peace.

As to the foreigners in the Southeast, their goods are useful to us just as ours are to them. To use what one has to exchange for what one does not have is what trade is all about. Moreover, these foreigners trade with China under the name of tributary contributions. That means China's authority is established and the foreigners are submissive. Even if the gifts we grant them are great and the tribute they send us is small, our expense is still less than one ten-thousandth of the benefit we gain from trading with them. Moreover, the Southeast sea foreigners are more concerned with trading with China than with gaining gifts from China. Even if they send a large tribute offering only to receive small gifts in return, they will still be content. In addition, trading with them can enrich our people. So why do we refrain from the trade?

Some people may say that the Southeast sea foreigners have invaded us several times so they are not the kind of people with whom we should trade. But they should realize that the Southeast sea foreigners need Chinese goods and the Chinese need their goods. If we prohibit the natural flow of this merchandise, how can we prevent them from invading us? I believe that if the sea trade were opened, the trouble with foreign pirates would cease. These Southeast sea foreigners are simple people, not to be compared to the unpredictable Northeast sea foreigners. Moreover, China's exports in the Northwest trade come from the national treasury. Whereas the Northwest foreign trade ensures only harm, the sea trade provides us with only gain. How could those in charge of the government fail to realize this?

Turning to the taxes levied on Chinese merchants, though these taxes are needed to fill the national treasury, excessive exploitation should be prohibited. Merchants from all areas are ordered to stop their carts and boats and have their bags and cases examined whenever they pass through a road or river checkpoint. Often the cargoes are overestimated and thus a falsely high duty is demanded. Usually merchants are taxed when they enter the checkpoint and are taxed again at the marketplace. When a piece of goods is taxed once, the merchant can still make some profit while complying with the state's regulations. But today's merchants often are stopped on the road for additional payments and also suffer extortions from the clerks. Such exploitation is hard and bitter enough but, in addition, the merchants are taxed twice. How can they avoid becoming more and more impoverished?

When I was Vice-President of the Board of Public Works in Nanking, I was also in charge of the customs duties on the upper and lower streams of the Black Dragon River. At that time I was working with Imperial Censor Fang K'o-yung. I told him: "In antiquity, taxes on merchants were in the form of voluntary contributions based on official hints, not through levies. Levying taxes on merchants is a bad policy. We should tax people according to their degree of wealth or poverty. Who says we cannot have good government!" Fang agreed with me, so we lowered the taxes on the merchants some twenty percent. After the taxes were lowered, merchants became willing to stop at the checkpoints. All boats stopped when they should and the total tax income received from merchants increased fifty percent. From this example one can see that the people can be moved by benevolent policies.

CHAPTER 13

THE MONGOL ERA

Conquests and Connections

This chapter compares the experiences of China, Russia, and Western Europe during the period of the Mongol conquests in the thirteenth and fourteenth centuries. The development of interlocking Mongol empires, called khanates, produced significant but diverse consequences in world history. Coming on the heels of the decline of Arab world power, the Mongol episode facilitated vital exchanges among previously separate civilizations while producing new tensions in large parts of Asia and Eastern Europe.

The Mongols, a herding people from Central Asia, gained important leadership structure and cultural values from interacting with more formal civilizations such as China. Contacts along China's northern border increased for several centuries. New leadership, and possibly some population pressure, inspired a wave of military ventures in the thirteenth century under the aegis of Chinggis Khan. The Mongols swept through the empire of China from 1206 onward and controlled the society for over a century. They pushed into the Middle East, toppling the Arab caliphate and challenging Turkish forces, and into Southeast Asia. They also conquered Russia (1236), which they loosely controlled for almost two centuries. Mongol victories in Poland and Hungary did not lead to durable conquests in the rest of Europe. Two efforts to conquer Japan also failed, leading to a growing sense of confidence and isolation there. Even the consequences of failure, however, reveal the awesome sweep of Mongol power.

Overall, the Mongol era in world history had two results: it caused disruption and resentment, and it provided unusual, stimulating international contacts.

Mongol overlords were resented in most of their holdings, despite efforts by individual rulers, such as the famous Kublai Khan in China, to adapt to established political and cultural traditions. Although some Chinese officials assisted the Mongols in return for specific gains, such as the preservation of Chinese unity, there were many points of discord. Confucianists believed that the Mongols scorned their commitment to bureaucracy and hierarchy. Kublai Khan praised Confucianism on occasion, but he utilized non-Confucian officials and, along with other leaders, increasingly inclined to the Buddhist religion, which Chinese officialdom had previously rejected.

The Russian situation was somewhat different. The resentment was strong here, too, in part because Mongol leaders concentrated on military coercion and demands for taxes and tribute, rather than the more systematic government developed in China. The cultural clash was different but severe, for Russia was committed to Orthodox Christianity, and its religious leaders condemned the Mongols as pagans, possibly a punitive visitation from God.

If the Mongol period meant resentment and disruption in key civilizations, it meant new opportunity for other peoples. Many Muslims appreciated trade opportunities with Mongol China and reported their awe at the wealth of the leading cities. Western Europeans responded even more eagerly, despite criticism of the Mongol commitment to "pagan" religions. Since Europe was spared any direct Mongol invasions, European religious and commercial leaders took advantage of Mongol tolerance of foreign travelers and trading activities. Direct European contacts with China were established for the first time in world history, and as a result the Europeans gained access to China's superior technology. European appetite for trade with Asia, already encouraged by the Crusades (see chapter 9), increased as well.

The Mongol era, decisive in Eurasian history toward the end of the postclassical millennium, was also brief. China regained independence, with its new Ming dynasty, in 1328. Russia won increasing autonomy by the late fourteenth century, an effort spearheaded by the dukes of the Moscow region, and then attained full autonomy around 1450, pushing the Mongol overlords farther and farther back into central Asia. With these changes, the period of easy Western contact with East Asia ended as well. But after the Mongol period, the Eurasian civilizations did not return to the previous status quo. The diverse results of the Mongol experience continued to affect policies of expansion and isolation, and the heady period of technological exchange continued to be exploited.

Questions

1. What characteristics did even sympathetic Chinese observers assign to the Mongols? Why was it easy to look down on Mongol habits despite the Mongols' success in conquest?
2. What does the Mongol description of the conquest of China suggest about probable Chinese reactions?
3. What does the *Novgorod Chronicle* suggest about Russia's cultural levels and social unity as it encountered Mongol pressures?

4. What was Novgorod's reaction to the Tartars (Mongols)? How did Russian religious authorities describe Tartar characteristics? How did their reactions compare with those of the Chinese?

5. How did Novgorod actually deal with the Tartars? Judging by this city's experience, what were the major impacts of the Mongol invasion on postclassical Russia? Did the Mongols cause or rather reflect the Russian disarray?

6. How did the Mongol approach to Russia differ from Kublai Khan's efforts in China? What did the Mongols want in each case? What might explain the differences in goals?

7. How did the Russian experience with the Mongols compare with that of China? Which society was more disrupted, and why?

8. How did Marco Polo try to appeal both to critical and to envious impressions of Mongol rulers? Why would both reactions seem appropriate to a Western European audience?

9. How did Marco Polo's reactions explain why Western Europe was ready to gain from the new contacts with East Asia? Why did Russia not develop a similar set of contacts?

For Further Discussion

1. How did the Mongol experience affect later Russian policies: what might be predicted about later interests in expansion and about later attitudes toward Asia?

2. What were the long-term consequences of the Mongol experience in China? How and why did Russia's and China's "post-Mongol" policies diverge?

3. Why was the Mongol era important for Western Europe? How did Marco Polo's account compare with earlier European reactions to cultural contact, as suggested by previous travelers and by the tales of the Crusades? What kinds of misperceptions still accompanied Western beliefs about societies such as China, and why?

MONGOLS IN CHINA: LI CHIH-CH'ANG AND
THE SECRET HISTORY OF THE MONGOLS

The first of the following selections is a Taoist emissary's impressions of the Mongols under Chinggis Khan, as the Mongol invasion of China began. Li

From Li Chih-Ch'ang, *The Travels of an Alchemist*, trans. Arthur Weley (Westport, Conn.: Greenwood Press, 1976), 67–68, 106–7. Reprinted by permission of Routledge UK.

Chih-Ch'ang, accompanying a Taoist master summoned by the khan into central Asia, had favorable discussions with the khan, who professed interest in the religion. Li's view, correspondingly, was less jaded than that of Confucian officials later on. But even these Chinese certainly saw the Mongols as very different: how did their reactions predict wider Chinese distaste for Mongol rule? The second selection is by an unknown author, perhaps someone in Chinggis's household writing about his conquests shortly after his death. The account was called *The Secret History of the Mongols.*

· · ·

LI CHIH-CH'ANG

The people live in black waggons and white tents; they are all herdsmen and hunters. Their clothes are made of hides and fur; they live on meat and curdled milk. The men wear their hair in two plaits that hang behind the ears. The married women wear a head-dress of birch-bark, some two feet high. This they generally cover with a black woollen stuff; but some of the richer women use red silk. The end (of this head-dress) is like a duck; they call it *ku-ku.* They are in constant fear of people knocking against it, and are obliged to go backwards and crouching through the doorways of their tents.

They have no writing. Contracts are either verbal or recorded by tokens carved out of wood. Whatever food they get is shared among them, and if any one is in trouble the others hasten to his assistance. They are obedient to orders and unfailing in their performance of a promise. They have indeed preserved the simplicity of primeval times. . . .

Both men and women plait their hair. The men's hats are often like *yüan-shan-mao* [theatrical caps], trimmed with all kinds of coloured stuffs, which are embroidered with cloud-patterns, and from the hats hang tasseled pendants. They are worn by all holders of official rank, from the notables downwards. The common people merely wear round their heads a piece of white muslin about six feet long. The wives of rich or important people wind round their heads a piece of black or purple gauze some six or seven feet long. This sometimes has flowers embroidered on it or woven patterns. The hair is always worn hanging down. Some cover it in a bag of floss-silk which may be either plain or coloured; others wear a bag of cloth or plain silk. Those who cover their heads with cotton or silk look just like Buddhist nuns. It is the women of the common people who do so. Their clothes are generally made of cotton, sewn like a straining-bag, narrow at the top and wide at the bottom, with sleeves sewn on. This is called the under robe and is worn by men and women alike. Their carriages, boats and agricultural implements are made very differently from ours. Their vessels are usually of brass or copper; sometimes of porcelain. They have a kind of porcelain that is very like our Ting [delicate] ware. For holding wire they use only glass. Their weapons are made of steel. In their markets they use gold coins without a hole in the middle. There are native written characters on both sides. The people are often very tall and strong; so much so that they can carry the heaviest load without a carrying-beam. If a woman marries and the husband becomes poor, she may go to another husband. If he goes on a journey and does not come back for three months, his wife is allowed to marry again. Oddly enough some of the women have beards and moustaches. There are certain persons called *dashman* who understand the writing of the country and are in charge of records and documents.

THE SECRET HISTORY OF THE MONGOLS

Conquering Northern China, 1211–1215

After this in the Year of the Sheep
Chingis Khan set out to fight the people of Cathy [Northern
    China].
First he took the city of Fuzhou
then marching through the Wild Fox Pass
he took Xuandefu.
From here he sent out an army under Jebe's command
to take the fortress at the Zhuyongguan.
When Jebe arrived he saw the Zhuyongguan was well defended,
so he said:
"I'll trick them and make them come out in the open.
I'll pretend to retreat
and when they come out I'll attack them."
So Jebe retreated and the Cathayan army cried:
"Let's go after them!"
They poured out of their fortifications
until the valleys and mountainsides were full of their soldiers.
Jebe retreated to Sondi-i-wu Ridge
and there he turned his army around to attack
as the enemy rushed towards him in waves.
The Cathayan army was beaten
and close behind Jebe's forces
Chingis Khan commanding the great Middle Army attacked as
    well,
forcing the Cathayan army to retreat,

killing the finest and most courageous soldiers of Cathay,
the Jurchin and Kara Khitan fighters,
slaughtered them along the sides of Zhuyongguan
so that their bodies lay piled up like rotting trees. . . .

Recruiting Administrators, 1220s

Once he had conquered the Moslem people
Chigis Khan appointed agents to govern in each of their cities.
From the city of Gurganj came two Khawarezm [present-day
    Uzbekistan]
Moslems,
a father and son named Yalavech and Masgud,
who explained to Chingis Khan the customs and laws of these cities
and the customs by which they were governed.
Chingis Khan appointed the Khwarezm Masgud head of the agents
who governed the cities of the Turkestan:
Bukhara, Samarkand, Guranj, Khotan, Kashgar, Yarkand, and
    Kusen Tarim.
And his father Yalavech he made governor of the city of Zhongdu
    in Cathay.
Since among all the Moslems Yalavech and Masgud
were the most skilled at the customs and laws for governing cities,
he appointed them the governors of Cathay,
along with our own agents. . . .

RUSSIAN REACTIONS: THE *NOVGOROD CHRONICLE*

The *Novgorod Chronicle* is one of the most vital documents from postclassical Russia—or what is more properly called Kievan Russia, the first development of a Russian civilization centered in what is now western Russia, Ukraine, and Belarus. Maintained by Orthodox monks and reflecting their fervent religion, the *Chronicle* detailed major events, without much interpretation save that inspired by religious and local loyalties. Novgorod was a trading city of 250,000 people on the route between Scandinavia and Byzantium. As Kievan Rus fell apart in the twelfth century, Novgorod developed an increasingly independent regional government and army. During the mid–thirteenth century (from 1240 to 1263)

From Robert Mitchell and Nevill Forbes, eds., *The Chronicle of Novgorod (1076–1471)* (London: Royal Historical Society, 1914), 186–88. Reprinted by permission of the publisher.

the city was ruled by Prince Alexander Nevsky, who won important victories over Germans and Swedes but submitted to Mongol—called Tartar in the *Chronicle*— tax gatherers in order to buy his city's independence. Alexander also visited Mongol leaders to negotiate for his city. Mongol incursions occurred, but Novgorod remained the only Russian state to escape full Mongol (Tartar) control. Only in the late fourteenth century did the city begin to lose more of its independence, to the expanding Russian government now based in Moscow.

• • •

A.D. 1224. The same year for our sins, unknown tribes came, whom no one exactly knows, who they are, nor whence they came out, nor what their language is, nor of what race they are, nor what their faith is; but they call them Tartars. . . . God alone knows who they are and whence they came out. Very wise men know them exactly, who understand books; but we do not know who they are, but have written of them here for the sake of the memory of the Russian Princes and of the misfortune which came to them from them. For we have heard that they have captured many countries. . . .

A.D. 1238. And the accursed ones having come thence took Moscow, Pereyaslavl, Yurev, Dmitrov, *Volok,* and Tver; there also they killed the son of [King] Yaroslav. And thence the lawless ones came and invested [the city of] Torzhok on the festival of the first Sunday in Lent. They fenced it all round with a fence as they had taken other towns, and here the accursed ones fought with battering rams for two weeks. And the people in the town were exhausted and from Novgorod there was no help for them; but already every man began to be in perplexity and terror. And so the pagans took the town, and slew all from the male sex even to the female, all the priests and the monks, and all stripped and reviled gave up their souls to the Lord in a bitter and a wretched death, on March 5, the day of the commemoration of the holy Martyr Nikon, on Wednesday in Easter week. And there, too, were killed Ivanko the Posadnik of Novi-torg, Yakin Vlunkovich, Gleb Borisovich and Mikhailo Moiseivich. And the accursed godless ones then pushed on from Torzhok by the road of Seregeri right up to Ignati's cross, cutting down everybody like grass, to within [50 miles] of Novgorod. God, however, and the great and sacred apostolic cathedral Church of St. Sophia, and St. Kyuril, and the prayers of the holy and orthodox archbishop, of the faithful Princess, and of the very reverend monks finally ended the attack. . . .

The same winter the accursed raw-eating Tartars, Berkai and Kasachik, came with their wives, and many others, and there was a great tumult in Novgorod, and they did much evil in the provinces, taking contribution for the accursed Tartars. And the accursed ones began to fear death; they said to [Prince] Alexander: "Give us guards, lest they kill us." And the Prince ordered . . . all the sons of the *Boyars* [nobles] to protect them by night. The Tartars said: "Give us your numbers for tribute or we will run away." And the common people would not give their numbers for tribute but said: "Let us die honourably for St. Sophia and for the angelic houses." Then the people were divided: who was good stood by St. Sophia and by the True Faith; and they made opposition; the greater men bade the lesser be counted for tribute. And the accursed ones wanted to escape, driven by the Holy Spirit, and they devised an evil counsel how to strike at the town at the other side, and the others at this side by the lake; and Christ's power evidently forbade them, and they durst not. And becoming frightened they began to crowd to one point to St. Sophia, saying: "Let us lay our heads by St. Sophia." And it was on the morrow, the Prince rode down . . . and the accursed Tartars with him, and by the counsel of the evil they numbered themselves for tribute; for the *Boyars* thought it would be easy for themselves, but fall hard on the lesser men. And the accursed ones began to ride through the streets, writing down the Christian houses; because for our sins God has brought wild beasts out of the desert to eat the flesh of the strong, and to drink the blood of the *Boyars*. And having numbered them for tribute and taken it, the accursed ones went away, and Alexander followed them, having set his son Dmitri on the throne.

THE WEST AND THE MONGOLS: MARCO POLO

Marco Polo was one of the last, and certainly the most famous, Western travelers to Mongol China. It is important to remember that a substantial series of travelers visited in the thirteenth and fourteenth centuries, and many of them wrote accounts. Early emissaries, sent by the Pope, usually saw China and the Mongols in disapproving religious terms, their censure heightened by fear of military prowess. Later travelers, including Marco Polo, took a somewhat more accepting view, though hints of the earlier approach remained. Increasingly, their reports contained wondrous elements mixed with a fairly realistic, if awed, appraisal of China. Marco Polo repeated a number of legends about fabulous wealth and mythical kings, along with some solid data that increased European knowledge of Asia and of the benefits of contact. Marco Polo (1254–1324) came from a Venetian merchant family; his uncle and his father had gone to China in 1266. The family included Marco on a later visit, and he apparently became a favorite of Kublai Khan, who made use of him on business matters and in administering a city. Marco Polo returned to Italy and was later imprisoned during a war with Genoa; it was here that he wrote his account, which long served as the principal source of European information on China. Recent historical scholarship has cast some doubt on his trip; he may not have actually gone to China, but rather repeated his father's and uncle's account, as well as available Persian guide books, while glorifying himself in the best Italian Renaissance fashion. Nevertheless,

From *The Travels of Marco Polo the Venetian*, ed. and trans. William Marsden (New York: Doubleday, 1948), 134–35, 152–53, 178, 211, 216, 218, 221–22, 243–45.

his account reflected and promoted European ideas about the Mongols and about China.

• • •

In the middle of the hall, where the grand khan sits at table, there is a magnificent piece of furniture, made in the form of a square coffer, each side of which is three paces in length, exquisitely carved in figures of animals, and gilt. It is hollow within, for the purpose of receiving a capacious vase, shaped like a jar, and of precious materials, calculated to hold about a tun, and filled with wine. On each of its four sides stands a smaller vessel, containing about a hogshead, one of which is filled with mare's milk, another with that of the camel, and so of the others, according to the kinds of beverage in use. Within this buffet are also the cups or flagons belonging to his majesty, for serving the liquors. Some of them are of beautiful gilt plate. Their size is such that, when filled with wine or other liquor, the quantity would be sufficient for eight or ten men. Before every two persons who have seats at the tables, one of these flagons is placed, together with a kind of ladle, in the form of a cup with a handle, also of plate; to be used not only for taking the wine out of the flagon, but for lifting it to the head. This is observed as well with respect to the women as the men. The quantity and richness of the plate belonging to his majesty [are] quite incredible. Officers of rank are likewise appointed, whose duty it is to see that all strangers who happen to arrive at the time of the festival, and are unacquainted with the etiquette of the court, are suitably accommodated with places; and these stewards are continually visiting every part of the hall, inquiring of the guests if there is anything with which they are unprovided, or whether any of them wish for wine, milk, meat, or other articles, in which case it is immediately brought to them by the attendants. . . .

. . . From the city of Kanbalu there are many roads leading to the different provinces, and upon each of these, that is to say, upon every great high road, at the distance of twenty-five or thirty miles, accordingly as the towns happen to be situated, there are stations, with houses of accommodation for travellers, called *yamb* or post-houses. These are large and handsome buildings, having several well-furnished apartments, hung with silk, and provided with everything suitable to persons of rank. Even kings may be lodged at these stations in a becoming manner, as every article required may be obtained from the towns and strong places in the vicinity; and for some of them the court makes regular provision. At each station four hundred good horses are kept in constant readiness, in order that all messengers going and coming upon the business of the grand khan, and all ambassadors, may have relays, and, leaving their jaded horses, be supplied with fresh ones. Even in mountainous districts, remote from the great roads, where there are no villages, and the towns are far distant from each other, his majesty has equally caused buildings of the same kind to be erected, furnished with everything necessary, and provided with the usual establishment of horses. He sends people to dwell upon the spot, in order to cultivate the land, and attend to the service of the post; by which means large villages are formed. In consequence of these regulations, ambassadors to the court, and the royal messengers, go and return through every province and kingdom of the empire with the greatest convenience and facility; in all of which the grand khan exhibits a superiority over every other emperor, king, or human being. In his dominions no fewer than two hundred thousand horses are thus employed in the department of the post, and ten thousand buildings, with suitable furniture, are kept up. It is indeed so wonderful a system, and so effective in its operation, as it is scarcely possible to describe. If it be questioned how the population of the country can supply sufficient numbers of these duties, and by what means they can be victualled, we may answer, that all the idolaters [Chinese], and like-wise the Saracens [Turks], keep six, eight, or ten women, according to their circumstances, by whom they have a prodigious number of children; some of them as many as thirty sons capable of following their fathers in arms; whereas with us a man has only one wife, and even although she should prove barren, he is obliged to pass his life with her, and is by that means deprived of the chance of raising a family. Hence it is that our population is so much inferior to theirs. . . .

. . . [In Western China] these idolatrous people are treacherous and cruel, and holding it no crime or turpitude to rob, are the greatest thieves in the world. They subsist by the chase and by fowling, as well as upon the fruits of the earth.

Here are found the animals that produce the musk, and such is the quantity, that the scent of it is diffused over the whole country. . . . In the rivers gold-dust is found in very large quantities. . . .

Very different were [the habits] of Kublai-khan, emperor of the Tartars, whose whole delight consisted in thoughts of a warlike nature, of the conquest of countries, and of extending his renown. . . .

Of the province of Nan-ghin. Nan-ghin is the name of a large and distinguished province of Manji, situated towards the west. The people are idolaters, use paper money in currency, are subjects of the grand khan, and are largely engaged in commerce. They have raw silk, and weave tissues of silver and gold in great quantities, and of various patterns. The country produces abundance of corn [grain], and is stored as well with domestic cattle as with beasts and birds that are the objects of the chase, and plenty of tigers. It supplies the sovereign with an ample revenue, and chiefly from the imposts levied upon the rich articles in which the merchants trade. . . .

Sin-gui is a large and magnificent city, the circumference of which is twenty miles. The inhabitants are idolaters, subjects of the grand khan, and use his paper money. They have vast quantities of raw silk, and manufacture it, not only for their own consumption, all of them being clothed in dresses of silk, but also for other markets. There are amongst them some very rich merchants, and the number of inhabitants is so great as to be a subject of astonishment. . . . They have amongst them many physicians of eminent skill, who can ascertain the nature of the disorder, and know how to apply the proper remedies. There are also persons distinguished as professors of learning, or, as we should term them, philosophers, and others who may be called magicians or enchanters. On the mountains near the city, rhubarb grows in the highest perfection, and is from thence distributed throughout the province. Ginger is likewise produced in large quantities, and is sold at so cheap a rate, that forty pounds weight of the fresh root may be had for the value, in their money, of a Venetian silver groat. . . .

Upon leaving the city of Kue-lin-fu, and travelling three days, during which you are continually passing towns and castles, of which the inhabitants are idolaters, have silk in abundance, and export it in considerable quantities, you reach the city of Unguen. This place is remarkable for a great manufacture of sugar, which is sent from thence to the city of Kanbalu for the supply of the court. Previously to its being brought under the dominion of the grand khan, the natives were unacquainted with the art of manufacturing sugar of a fine quality, and boiled it in such an imperfect manner, that when left to cool it remained in the state of a dark-brown paste. But at the time this city became subject to his majesty's government, there happened to be at the court some persons from Babylon who were skilled in the process, and who, being sent thither, instructed the inhabitants in the mode of refining the sugar by means of the ashes of certain woods. . . .

Travelling fifteen miles further in the same direction, you come to the city of Kan-giu. . . . In this place is stationed a large army for the protection of the country, and to be always in readiness to act, in the event of any city manifesting a disposition to rebel. Through the midst of it passes a river, a mile in breadth, upon the banks of which, on either side, are extensive and handsome buildings. In front of these, great numbers of ships are seen lying, having merchandise on board, and especially sugar, of which large quantities are manufactured here also. Many vessels arrive at this port from India, freighted by merchants who bring with them rich assortments of jewels and pearls, upon the sale of which they obtain a considerable profit. . . . The ships coming from India ascend the river as high up as the city, which abounds with every sort of provision, and has delightful gardens, producing exquisite fruits. . . .

. . . At the end of five days' journey, you arrive at the noble and handsome city of Zai-tun, which has a port on the sea-coast celebrated for the resort of shipping, loaded with merchandise, that is afterwards distributed through every part of the province of Manji. The quantity of pepper imported there is so considerable, that what is carried to Alexandria, to supply the demand of the western parts of the world, is trifling in comparison, perhaps not more than the hundredth part.

CHAPTER 14

AFRICA IN THE POSTCLASSICAL WORLD

Major developments took shape in sub-Saharan Africa during the postclassical period. Large kingdoms formed in West Africa, including Ghana and then Mali, in the region the Arabs called the Sudan. Trading cities developed along the east African coast. Islam spread widely and had great influence, though the majority of sub-Saharan Africans remained polytheists. In turn, Africa played a significant role in the world trade of the period, and also developed centers of Islamic learning.

Sources for sub-Saharan Africa in the postclassical period are, however, somewhat limited. The most important written documents come from travelers, mainly North African Arabs but also, by the end of the period, a few Europeans. These accounts have the advantage of an outsider perspective, but they also reflect the biases and the pockets of ignorance foreign visitors often display. They reveal much about the observers themselves, and their cultures of origin—and in the process they help establish the context in which African trade and cultural connections developed.

The three documents in this chapter all deal with the southern Sahara and the Sudanic region, though they focus on different specific places. Two emanate from Islamic travelers, including the most tireless tourist of the postclassical era, Ibn Battuta. One comes from a European merchant. All suggest significant characteristics of this wide zone of Africa.

Questions

1. What common African features do the three documents describe, concerning political, cultural, and economic activity?
2. What are the most important weaknesses of the traveler accounts, in terms of distorting biases or apparent ignorance?
3. Which of the three accounts seems most reliable, and why?
4. Do the accounts suggest significant differences in the evaluation of Africa between Muslim travelers on the one hand and the European Christian on the other? What might explain major differences?
5. What kinds of interregional contacts did the Sudanic kingdoms maintain in the postclassical period?

For Further Discussion

1. **Do the accounts suggest potential differences between the African-Arab relations and the African-European relations that would develop in the next world history period?**
2. **How did the political institutions of sub-Saharan Africa compare with those of the Middle East and Western Europe during the postclassical period?**

ABD AL-AZIZ AL-BAKRI

Abd al-Aziz al-Bakri was a Muslim scholar in Spain in the eleventh century (he died in 1084). He never traveled to Africa directly, but accumulated many other accounts (most of which have since been lost) and also met many travelers and merchants coming from the Sudan. He provides one of the most important sources available on Africa in the period.

• • •

This is the independent kingdom of the Farwiyyun. Among the strange things found there is a pool where water collects and in it a plant grows of which the roots are the surest means of strengthening and aiding sexual powers. The king reserves this for himself and does not allow anyone else to partake of it. He owns an enormous number of women, and when he wants to make the round of them he warns them one day before, takes the medicine, and then takes them all in turn and scarcely flags. One of the neighboring Muslim kings gave him precious gifts, requesting some of this plant in exchange. In return he gave presents of equal value and wrote a letter saying: "Muslims may lawfully wed only a few women, and I fear that if I sent you this medicine you would not be able to restrain yourself and you would commit excesses which your religion makes unlawful. I am however, sending you an herb which will enable an impotent man, if he eats it, to beget children." In the country of the Farwiyyun salt is exchanged for gold.

GHANA AND THE CUSTOMS OF ITS INHABITANTS

Ghana is a title given to their kings; the name of the region is Akwar, and their king today, namely in the year 460/1067–8 is Tunka Manin. He ascended the throne in 455/1063. The name if his predecessor was Basi and he became their ruler at the age of 85. He led a praiseworthy life on account of his love of justice and friendship for the

From N. Levtzion and J. F. P. Hopkins, eds., *Corpus of Early Arabic Sources for West African History*, trans. J. R. Hopkins (Cambridge: Cambridge University Press, 1981), 78–83, 85–87.

Muslims. At the end of his life he became blind, but he concealed this from his subjects and pretended that he could see. When something was put before him he said: "This is good" or "This is bad." His ministers deceived the people by indicating to the king in cryptic words what he should say, so that the commoners could not understand. Basi was a maternal uncle of Tunka Manin. This is their custom and their habit, that the kingship is inherited only by the son of the king's sister. He has no doubt that his successor is a son of his sister, while he is not certain that his son is in fact his own, and he is not convinced of the genuineness of his relationship to him. This Tunka Manin is powerful, rules an enormous kingdom, and possesses great authority.

The city of Ghana consists of two towns situated on a plain. One of these towns, which is inhabited by Muslims, is large and possesses twelve mosques, in one of which they assemble for the Friday prayer. There are salaried imams and muezzins, as well as jurists and scholars. In the environs are wells with sweet water, from which they drink and with which they grow vegetables. The king's town is six miles distant from this one and bears the name of Al-Ghaba. Between these two towns there are continuous habitations. The houses of the inhabitants are of stone and acacia (sunt) wood. The king has a palace and a number of domed dwellings all surrounded with an enclosure like a city wall (sur). In the king's town, and not far from his court of justice, is a mosque where the Muslims who arrive at his court (yafid 'alayh) pray. Around the king's town are domed buildings and groves and thickets where the sorcerers of these people, men in charge of the religious cult, live. In them too are their idols and the tombs of their kings. These woods are guarded and none may enter them and know what is there. In them also are the king's prisons. If somebody is imprisoned there no news of him is ever heard. The king's interpreters, the official in charge of his treasury and the majority of his ministers are Muslims. Among the people who follow the king's religion only he and his heir apparent (who is the son of his sister) may wear sewn clothes. All other people wear robes of cotton, silk, or brocade, according to their means. All of them shave their beards, and women shave their heads. The king adorns himself like a woman [wearing necklaces] round his neck and [bracelets] on his forearms, and he puts on a high cap (tartur) decorated with gold and wrapped in a turban of fine cotton. He sits in audience or to hear grievances against officials (mazalim) in a domed pavilion around which stand ten horses covered with gold-embroidered materials. Behind the king stand ten pages holding shields and swords decorated with gold, and on his right are the sons of the [vassal] kings of his country wearing splendid garments and their hair plaited with gold. The governor of the city sits on the ground before the king and around him are ministers seated likewise. At the door of the pavilion are dogs of excellent pedigree who hardly ever leave the place where the king is, guarding him. Round their necks they wear collars of gold and silver studded with a number of balls of the same metals. The audience is announced by the beating of a drum which they call duba, made from a long hollow log. When the people who profess the same religion as the king approach him they fall on their knees and sprinkle dust on their heads, for this is their way of greeting him. As for the Muslims, they greet him only by clapping their hands.

Their religion is paganism and the worship of idols (dakakir). When their king dies they construct over the place where his tomb will be an enormous dome of saj wood. Then they bring him on a bed covered with a few carpets and cushions and place him beside the dome. At this side they place his ornaments, his weapons, and the vessels from which he used to eat and drink, filled with various kinds of food and beverages. They place there too the men who used to serve his meals. They close the door of the dome and cover it with mats and furnishings. Then the people assemble, who heap earth upon it until it becomes like a big hillock and dig a ditch around it until the mound can be reached at only one place.

They make sacrifices to their dead and make offerings of intoxicating drinks. On every donkey-load of salt when it is brought into the country their king levies one gold dinar, and two dinars when it is sent out. From a load of copper the king's due is five mithquals, and from a load of other goods ten mithqals. The best gold found in his land comes from the town over a country inhabited by tribes of the Sudan whose dwellings are continuous.

The nuggets (nadra) found in all the mines of his country are reserved for the king, only this gold dust (al-tibr al-daqiq) being left for the people. But for this the people would accumulate gold until it lost its value. The nuggets may weigh from an ounce (uqiyya) to a pound (ratl). It is related that the king owns a nugget as large as a big stone. . . .

The king of Ghana, when he calls up his army, can put 200,000 men into the field, more than 40,000 of them archers. The horses in Ghana are very small. . . . the inhabitants sow their crops twice yearly, the first time in the moist earth (thara) during the season of the Nil flood, and later in the earth [that has preserved its humidity].

West of Ghiyaru, on the Nil, is the town of Yarisna, inhabited by Muslims surrounded by polytheists. In Yarisna is a species of small goat. When a goat gives birth to a male it is slaughtered, only females being allowed to live. In this country is a certain tree against which the goats rub themselves and become fecundated by the wood without the medium of the male. This fact is well known to them; none of them deny it and it has been related by many trustworthy Muslims. From Yarisna the Sudan who speak an unintelligible language (a'jam pl. 'ujm) called the Banu Naghmarata, who are merchants, export gold to other countries. . . .

Beyond this country lies another called Malal, the king of which is known as al-musulmani. He is thus called because his country became afflicted with drought one year following another; the inhabitants prayed for rain, sacrificing cattle till they had exterminated almost all of them, but the drought and the misery only increased. The king had as his guest a Muslim who used to read the Koran and was acquainted with the Sunna. To this man the king complained of the calamities that assailed him and his people. The man said; "O King, if you believed in God (who is exalted) and testified that He is One, and testified as to the prophetic mission of Muhammad (God bless him and give him peace) and if you accepted all the religious laws of Islam, I would pray for your deliverance from your plight and that God's mercy would envelop all the people of your country and that your enemies and adversaries might envy you on that account." Thus he continued to press the king until the latter accepted Islam and became a sincere Muslim. The man made him recite from the Koran some easy passages and taught him religious obligations and practices which no one may be excused from knowing. Then the Muslim made him wait till the eve of the following Friday, when he ordered him to purify himself by a complete ablution, and clothed him in a cotton garment which he had. The two of them came out towards a mound of earth, and there the Muslim stood praying while the king, standing at his right side, imitated him. Thus they prayed for part of the night, the Muslim reciting invocations and the king saying "Amen." The dawn had just started to break when God caused abundant rain to descend upon them. So the king ordered the idols to be broken and expelled the sorcerers from his country. He and his descendants after him as well as his nobles were sincerely attached to Islam, while the common people of the kingdom remained polytheists. Since then their rulers have been given the title of almusulmani.

Among the provinces (a'mal) of Ghana is a region called Sama, the inhabitants of which are known as al-Bukm. From that region to Ghana is four days' traveling. The people there go naked; only the women cover their sexual parts with strips of leather which they plait. They leave the hair on the pubis and only shave their heads. Abu 'Abd Allah al-Makki related that he saw one of these women stop in front of an Arab, who had a long beard, and say something that he could not understand. He asked the interpreter about the meaning of her words. He replied that she wished that she had hair like that of his beard on her pubis. The Arab, filled with anger, called down curses upon her. . . .

From Bughrat you go to Tiraqqa and from there across the desert plain to Tadmakka, which of all the towns of the world is the one that resembles Mecca the most. Its name means "the Mecca-like." It is a large town amidst mountains and ravines and is better built than Ghana or Kawkaw. The inhabitants of Tadmakka are Muslim Berbers who veil themselves as the Berbers of the desert do. They live on meat and milk as well as on grain which the earth produces without being tilled. Sorghum and other grains are imported for them from the land of the Sudan. They wear clothes of cotton, nuli, and other robes dyed red. Their kings wears a red turban, yellow shirt, and blue trousers. Their dinars are called "bald" because they are of pure gold without any stamp. Their women are of perfect beauty, unequalled among people of any other country, but adultery is allowed among them. They fall upon any merchant [disputing as to] which of them shall take him to her house. . . .

When a traveler goes from the country of Kawkaw along the bank of the river in a westerly direction he reached the kingdom called Damdam, the people of which eat anyone who falls into their hands. They have a great king to whom minor rulers are subject. In their country there is a huge fortress surmounted by an idol (sanam) in the form of a woman which they worship as their God and to which they go on pilgrimage.

Between Tadamakka and the town of Kawkaw is a distance of nine stages. The Arabs call the inhabitants of the latter the BZRKANYYN. This town consists of two towns, one being the residence of the king and the other inhabited by the Muslims. The king is called Qanda. The clothes of the people there are like those of the other Sudan, consisting of a robe (milhafa) and a garment of skins or some other material, according to each man's individual means. They worship idols (dakakir) as do the other Sudan. When their king sits down [to partake of a meal] a drum is beaten, the Sudanese women dance with their thick hair flowing, and nobody in the town goes about his business until he has finished his repast, the remnants of which are thrown into the Nile. At this [the couriers] shout out boisterously so that the people know that the king has finished his meal. When the king ascends the throne he is handed a signet ring, a sword, and a copy of the Koran which, as they assert, were sent to them by the Commander of the Faithful. Their king is a Muslim, for they entrust the kingship only to Muslims. . . .

IBN BATTUTA

Ibn Battuta (1304–1369) was a North African Arab who visited many African kingdoms during the fourteenth century. An indefatigable traveler, over a thirty-year span he also visited many parts of Asia and islands in the Indian Ocean and proudly wrote about his observations. His account obviously warrants comparison with that of al-Bakri, being a traveler's vs. a scholar's account but also a fourteenth- vs. an eleventh-century account.

• • •

ANECDOTE CONCERNING THE MASSUFA WHO INHABIT IWALATAN

The conditions of these people is strange and their manners outlandish. As for their men, there is no sexual jealous in them. And none of them derives his genealogy from his father but, on the contrary, from his maternal uncle. A man does not pass on inheritance except to the sons of his sister to the exclusion of his own sons. Now that is a thing I never saw in any part of the world except in the country of the unbelievers of the land of Mulaibar [Malabar] among the Indians. As to the former [the Massufa], they are Muslims keeping to the prayers, studying *fiqh* [Islamic jurisprudence],

From Said Hamdum and Noel King, eds., *Ibn Battuta in Black Africa* (London: Rex Collings, 1975), 27–29, 36–39, 47–48. Reprinted by permission of Markus Wiener Publishers, Inc.

and learning the Koran by heart. With regard to their women, they are not modest in the presence of men, they do not veil themselves in spite of their perseverance in the prayers. He who wishes to marry among them can marry, but the women do not travel with the husband, and if one of them wanted to do that, she would be prevented by her family. The women there have friends and companions amongst men outside the prohibited degrees of marriage [other than brothers, fathers, etc.]. Likewise for the men, there are companions from amongst women outside the prohibited degrees. One of them would enter his house to find his wife with her companion and would not disapprove of that conduct. . . .

The sultan [emperor of Mali] has a raised cupola which is entered from inside his house. He sits in it a great part of the time. It has on the audience side a chamber with three wooden arches, the woodwork is covered with sheets of beaten silver and beneath these, three more covered with beaten gold, or, rather, it is silver covered with gilt. The windows have woolen curtains which are raised on a day when the sultan will be in session in his cupola: thus it is known that he is holding a session. When he sits, a silken cord is put out from the grill of one of the arches with a scarf of Egyptian embroidery tied to it. When the people see the scarf, drums are beaten and bugles sounded. Then from the door of the palace come out about three hundred slaves. Some have bows in their hands and some small spears and shields. Some of the spearmen stand on the right and some on the left, the two bowmen sit likewise. Then they bring two mares saddled and bridled, and with the two rams. They say that these are effective against the evil eye. When the sultan has sat down three of his slaves go out quickly to call his deputy, Qanja Musa. The *farariyya* [commanders] arrive, and they are the amirs [officers], and among them are the preacher and the men of *fiqh*, who sit in front of the armed men on the right and left of the place of audience. The interpreter Dugha stands at the door of the audience chamber wearing splendid robes of *zardkhuana* [official] and others. On his head is a turban which has fringes, they have a superb way of tying a turban. He is girt with a sword whose sheath is of gold, on his feet are light boots and spurs. And nobody wears boots that day except he. In his hands there are two small spears, one of gold and one of silver with points of iron. The soldiers, the district governors, the pages and the Massufa and others are seated outside the place of audience in a broad street which has trees in it. Each *farari* [commander] has his followers before him with their spears, bows, drums and bugles made of elephant tusks. Their instruments of music are made of reeds and calabashes, and they beat them with sticks and produce a wonderful sound. Each *farari* has a quiver which is placed between his shoulders. He holds his bow in his hand and is mounted on a mare. Some of his men are on foot and some on mounts.

Inside the audience chamber under the arches a man is standing; he who wants to spead to the sultan speaks to Dugha, Dugha speaks to the man who is standing, and he speaks to the sultan.

An Account of the Session in the Place of Audience

The sultan sits on certain days in the palace yard to give audience. There is a platform under a tree steps which they call banbi. It is covered with silk and has pillows placed on it. The shatr [umbrella] is raised, this is a shelter made of silk with a golden bird like a sparrowhawk above it. The sultan comes out from a gate in the corner of the palace, bow in hand, his quiver between his shoulders, and on his head a cap of gold tied with a golden band which has fringes like thin-bladed knives more than a span long. He often wears a robe which is soft and red, made from Roman cloth . . . *mutanfas*. The singers go out before him carrying gold and silver *qanabir* [guitars] and behind him come three hundred armed armed slaves. The sultan walks slowly and pauses often and sometimes he stops completely. When he comes to the *banbi* he stops and looks at the people. Then he mounts the steps with dignity in the manner of a preacher getting into the pulpit. When he sits down they beat the drums, blow the bugles and the horns, and three of the slaves go out in haste and call the deputy and the *farariyya* [commanders]. They enter and sit down. The two mares are brought in with the two rams. Damugha stands at the door while the rest of the people are in the street under the tree. The blacks are the most humble of men before their king and the most extreme in their self-abasement before him. They swear by his name, saying 'Mansa Sulaimanki' [the law of Mansa Sulaimanki]. When he calls one of them while he is in session in his cupola which we described above, the man invited takes off his clothes and wears patched clothes, takes off his turban, puts on a dirty cap, and goes in raising his clothes and trousers up his legs half-way to his knees. He advances with humility looking like a beggar. He hits the ground with his elbows, he hits it hard. He stands bowed, like one in the *ruku* position in prayer, listening to what the king says. When one of them speaks to the sultan and gives him an answer, he removed his clothes from his back and throw dust on his head and back, as a person does when bathing with water. I used to wonder how they do not blind their eyes. When the sultan speaks in his council, at his word those present take their turbans off their heads and listen to the speech. . . .

Amongst their good qualities is the small amount of injustice amongst them, for of all people they are the furthest from it. Their sultan does not forgive anyone in any matter to do with justice. Among these qualities there is also the prevalence of peace in their country, the traveler is not afraid in it nor is he who lives there in fear of the thief or of the robber by violence. They do not interfere with the property of the white man who dies in their country even though it may consist of great wealth, but rather they entrust it to the hand of someone dependable among the white men until it is taken by the rightful claimant.

Another of the good habits amongst them is the way they meticulously observe the times of the prayers and attendance at them, so also it is with regard to their congregational services and their beating of their children to instill these things in them.

When it is Friday, if a man does not come early to the mosque he will not find a place to pray because of the numbers of the crowd. It is their custom for every man to send his boy with his prayer mat. He spreads it for him in a place commensurate with his position and keeps the place until he comes to the mosque. Their prayer mats are made of the leaves of a tree like a date palm but it bears no fruit.

Among their good qualities is their putting on of good white clothes on Friday. If a man among them has nothing except a tattered shirt, he washes and cleans it and attends the Friday prayer in it. Another of their good qualities is their concern for learning the sublime Koran by heart. They make fetters for their children when they appear on their part to be falling short in their learning of it by heart, and they are not taken off from them until they do learn by heart. I went in to visit the *qadi* on an 'Id day and his children were tied up. I said to him 'Why do you not release them?' He said, 'I shall not do so until they learn the Koran by heart.' One day I passed by a handsome youth from them dressed in fine clothes and on his feet was a heavy chain. I said to the man who was with me, 'What has this youth done—has he killed someone?' The youth heard my remark and laughed. It was told me, 'He has been chained so that he will learn the Koran by heart.'

Among the bad things which they do—their serving women, slave women and little daughters appear before people naked, exposing their private parts. I used to see many of them in this state in Ramadan, for it was the custom of the *farariyya* [commanders] to break the fast in the sultan's house. Everyone of them has his food carried into him by twenty or more of his slave girls and they are naked, every one. Also among their bad customs is the way women will go into the presence of the sultan naked, with out any covering; and the nakedness of the sultan's daughters—on the night of the twenty-seventh of Ramadan, I saw about a hundred slave girls coming out of his palace with food, with them were two of his daughters, they had full breasts and no clothes on. Another of their bad customs is their putting of dust and ashes on their heads as a sign of respect. And another is the laughing matter I mentioned of their poetic recitals. And another is that many of them eat animals not ritually slaughtered, and dogs and donkeys.

AFRICA THROUGH THE EYES OF A EUROPEAN MERCHANT

ANTONIUS MALFANTE

Antonius Malfante wrote from Tuat (Tawat) in the central Sahara in 1447, to a colleague in Genoa. His travels suggest growing European outreach, for contact

From *The Voyages of Cadamosto and Other Documents on Western Africa in the Second Half of the fifteenth Century*, trans. and edited by G. R. Crone, Hakluyt Society Works Ser II: Vol 80, 1937, 85–90. The Hakluyt Society was established in 1846 for the purpose of printing rare or unpublished Voyages and Travels. For further information please see their website at: www.hakluyt.com. Reprinted by permission of the publisher.

with Africa below the Sahara had been limited since the fall of the Roman Empire. Genoa was increasingly active in Mediterranean trade, and presumably Malfante's venture was part of this activity, as his account itself implies. He seems to have traveled fairly widely in the region and was also eager to report what he thought he learned about places he did not visit directly.

• • •

After we had come from the sea, we journeyed on horseback, always southwards, for about twelve days. For seven days we encountered no dwelling—nothing but sandy plains; we proceeded as though at sea, guided by the sun during the day, at night by the stars. At the end of the seventh day, we arrived at an oasis, where dwelt very poor people who supported themselves on water and a little sandy ground. They sow little, living upon the numerous date palms. At this [oasis] we had come into Tueto [Tawat, a group of oases]. In this place there are eighteen quarters, enclosed within one wall, and ruled by an oligarchy. Each ruler of a quarter protects his followers, whether they be in the right or no. The quarters closely adjoin each other and are jealous of their privileges. Everyone arriving here places himself under the protection of one of these rulers, who will protect him to the death: thus merchants enjoy very great security, much greater, in my opinion, than in other North African kingdoms such as Tunis.

Though I am a Christian, no one ever addressed an insulting word to me. They said they had never seen a Christian before. It is true that on my first arrival they were scornful of me, because they all wished to see me, saying with wonder "This Christian has a countenance like ours"—for they believed that Christians had disguised faces. Their curiosity was soon satisfied, and now I can go alone anywhere, with no one to say an evil word to me.

There are many Jews, who lead a good life here, for they are under the protection of the several rulers, each of whom defends his own clients. Thus they enjoy very secure social standing. Trade is in their hands, and many of them are to be trusted with the greatest confidence.

This locality is a mart of the country of the African Muslims, to which merchants come to sell their goods: gold is carried hither, and bought by those who come up from the coast. There are many rich men here. The generality, however, are very poor, for they do not sow, nor do they harvest anything, save the dates upon which they subsist. They eat no meat but that of castrated camels, which are scarce and very dear.

It is true that the Arabs with whom I came from the coast brought with them corn and barley which they sell throughout the year.

It never rains here: if it did, the houses, being built of salt in the place of reeds, would be destroyed. It is scarcely ever cold here: in summer the heat is extreme, wherefore they are almost all blacks. The children of both sexes go naked up to the age of fifteen. These people observe the religion and law of Muhammad. In the vicinity there are 150 to 200 oases.

In the lands of the Blacks, as well as here, dwell the Tuareg, who live, like the Arabs, in tents. They are without number, and hold sway over the land from the borders of Egypt to the shores of the Ocean [present-day Liberia], and over all the neighboring towns of the blacks. They are fair, strong in body and very handsome in appearance. They ride without stirrups, with simple spurs. They are governed by kings, whose heirs are the sons of their sisters—for such is their law. They keep their mouths and noses covered. I have seen many of them here, and have asked them through an interpreter why they cover their mouths and noses thus. They replied: "We have inherited this custom from our ancestors." Their faith is that of the Blacks. Their sustenance is milk and flesh, no corn or barley, but much rice. Their sheep, cattle, and camels are without number. One breed of camel, white as snow, can cover in one day a distance which would take a horseman four days to travel. Great warriors, these people are continually at war amongst themselves.

The states which are under their rule border upon the land of the Blacks. I shall speak of those known to men here, and which have inhabitants of the faith of Muhammad. In all, the great majority are Blacks, but there are a small number of white [i.e. tawny Moors]. . . .

These adhere to the law of Muhammad.

To the south of these are innumerable great cities and territories, the inhabitants of which are all blacks and idolaters, continually at war with each other in defense of their law and faith of their idols. Some worship the sun, others the moon, the seven planets, fire, or water; others a mirror which reflects their faces, which they take to be the images of gods; others groves of trees, the seats of a spirit to whom they make sacrifice; others again, statues of wood and stone, with which, they say, they commune by incantations. They relate here extraordinary things of this people.

The lord in whose protection I am, here, who is the greatest in this land, having a fortune of more than 100,000 *doubles* [a coin], a man worthy of credence, relates that he lived for thirty years in that town, and, as he says, for fourteen years in the land of the Blacks. Every day he tells me wonderful things of these peoples. He says that these lands and peoples extend endlessly to the south: they all go naked, save for a small loincloth to cover their privates. They have an abundance of flesh, milk, and rice, but no corn or barley.

The slaves which the blacks take in their internecine wars are sold at a very low price. These peoples, who cover the land in multitudes, are in carnal acts like the beasts. They breed greatly, for a woman bears up to five at a birth. Nor can it be doubted that they are eaters of human flesh, for many people have gone hence into their country. Neither are there ever epidemics.

When the blacks catch sight of a white man from a distance, they take to flight as though from a monster, believing him to be a phantom. They are unlettered, and without books. They are great magicians, evoking by incense diabolical spirits, with whom, they say, they perform marvels.

The wares for which there is demand here are many: but the principal articles are copper, and salt in slabs, bars and cakes. The copper of Romania [the Byzantine Empire], which is obtained through Alexandria, is always in great demand throughout the land of the Blacks. I frequently enquired what they did with it, but no one could give me a definite answer. I believe it is that there are so many peoples that there is almost nothing but is of use to them.

The Egyptian merchants come to trade in the land of the Black with half a million head of cattle and camels—a figure which is not fantastic in this region.

The place where I am is good for trade, as the Egyptians and other merchants come hither form the land of the Blacks bringing gold, which they exchange for copper and other goods. Thus everything sells well; until there is nothing left for sale. The people here will neither sell nor buy unless at a profit of one hundred per cent. For this reason, I have lost on the goods I brought here, two thousand *doubles*.

From what I can understand, these people neighbor on India. Indian merchants come hither, and converse through interpreters. These Indians are Christians, adorers of the cross. It is said that in the land of the Blacks there are forty dialects, so that they are unable to understand each other.

I often enquired where the gold was found and collected; my patron always replied "I was fourteen years in the land of the Blacks, and I have never heard nor seen anyone who could reply from definite knowledge. That is my experience, as to how it is found and collected. What appears plain is that it comes from a distant land, and, as I believe, from a definite zone." He also said that he had been in places where silver was as valuable as gold.

CHAPTER 15

CHINESE AND PORTUGUESE VOYAGES
IN THE FIFTEENTH CENTURY

One of the last great sets of events of the postclassical period involved the several Chinese voyages through the Indian ocean between 1405 and 1433, under the new Ming dynasty. One of the first great events of the next, early modern period was the voyage of the Portuguese Vasco da Gama around Africa to India. Documents in this chapter compare two Chinese trips, the last one launched in 1430, and da Gama's historic venture.

These were very different expeditions, from very different countries. Accounts of the two voyages clearly allow comparisons of the scopes and some of the motivations involved. Historians continue to debate exactly what the Chinese expeditions were all about—like the Portuguese, they were directly authorized by the ruler—but the sources suggest several of the factors involved. At the same time it is valid to look for similarities as well: after all, these were major expeditions, and it is important to ask why they occurred so close together in time, reaching some of the same places (notably East Africa, the port of Hormuz in the Middle East, and the southwest Indian port of Calicut).

The sources merit assessment as well in terms of possible bias. There is little documentation about the Chinese trips, which were ended in 1433 amid court disfavor, but the artisan who wrote the documents included here surely wanted some credit, if not for himself at least for the expedition as a whole. Vasco da Gama's account was intended for his royal sponsors and other possible supporters back home.

The two series had very different outcomes. China's venture was exceptionally ambitious and in many ways successful, but the fact that it was not continued, as China found other ways to profit from interregional trade, limits its ongoing significance in world history. Historians often, in fact, spend more time discussing why the trips stopped than they do discussing the voyages themselves. Da Gama's venture, later repeated with more firepower, launched a major Portuguese commitment to oceanic trade and colonization in the Indian Ocean and elsewhere, which in turn was part of Western Europe's commercial surge in the early modern centuries.

Questions

1. What were the main motives of the two expeditions? How do they compare?

2. What do the accounts suggest about the nature of the expeditions—their scope and power? What kinds of receptions did the expeditions receive (at least, according to the authors) and how do these compare?

3. What kinds of attitudes toward foreigners did the Chinese and the Portuguese display?

4. Why was there such great interest in the Indian Ocean?

5. What were the motives of people who wrote expedition accounts at this point in history? What kinds of distortions might result?

6. What do the documents suggest about the significance of the two expeditions?

For Further Discussion

1. Why was there new interest in ocean-based commerce in the fifteenth century? What kinds of technologies were involved?

2. Why did China judge that it was sensible to stop its expeditions, whereas Portugal pressed ahead as long as possible?

3. Why were foreign expeditions often well received?

4. How do these expeditions compare with earlier patterns of interregional trade in Africa-Asia-Europe?

MA HUAN

Ma Huan was a woodcutter who probably went on several trips with the great admiral Cheng Ho. The first selection is a poem that he may have written. It appeared in a novel by Lo Mou-teng, written in 1597, which was a very fanciful account; but some historians believe it was actually written in 1416, about an expedition that took place 1413–1415. The second selection refers to the 1430 trip, in an account called *The Overall Survey of the Ocean's Shores*, which Ma Huan wrote in 1433.

Admiral Chengho [handwritten marginal note]

• • •

The Poem

The Emporer's glorious envoy [Cheng Ho] received the divine
    commands,

Silk mention [handwritten marginal note]

'proclaim abroad the silken sounds, and go to the barbarous lands.'
His giant ship on the roaring waves of the boundless ocean rode;

afar, o'er the rolling billows vast and limitless, it strode.

The vast sea's rolling billows in lovely breakers sweep; . . . Java
[Indonesia] he quickly makes.

From the Central Glorious Country Java is distant far,

a noisome steam is heaven's breath, and strange the people are.

With unkempt heads and naked feet, a barbarous tongue they speak;

dresses and hats they use not, nor manners nor virtue seek.

Here when the heavenly writing [the emperor's commands] came, a
happy clamour meeting,

Chieftains and heads of the barbarous tribes all vied to give it
greeting.

Tribute of southern gold, rare gems, from distant parts appear;

The shipmen lifted up their heads; the west with the east they
mixed;

only pointing to the [Polaris] star whereby north and south were fixed.

Mountains high and mighty waves I ere then saw but few;

Unwonted gems and jewels rare I now began to view.

Above to heaven and down to earth I looked—no boundary ran;

To heaven's ends and earth's extremes each one is the sovereign's man.

Union under imperial Ming our grand and great land shares;

from time forgotten until now no [other land] compares.

The Emperor's envoy, dutiful, fears to tarry and delay;

just then he meets the south wind, which points to his homeward way.

O'er waves like swimming dragons huge [the envoy's] vessel rides;

he turns his head back, mist and fog the distant desert hides.

To capital returned, the Palace levee he attended;

in Dragon Court his tribute, every precious thing extended.

One glance of the all-wise eyes [the court advisors], and joy filled
Heaven's face [the emperor],

all dignities, gifts, were bestowed, new pledges of Heaven's grace.

Ma Huan, the mountain-woodcutter of Kuei chi.

• • •

The Overall Survey of the Ocean's Shores

This country of Mecca setting sail from the country of Calicut, you proceed towards
the south-west—the point *shen* on the compass; the ship travels for three moons, and

From Ma Huan, *Ying-yai Sheng-lan* (*The Overall Survey of the Ocena's Shores*), trans. J. V. G. Mills (Cambridge: Cambridge University Press, 1970), 73–75. Reprinted with the permission of Cambridge University Press.

— Five Pillers

then reaches the jetty of this country. They profess the Muslim religion. A holy man first expounded and spread this forth. . . .

Inside the wall [of the mosque], at the four corners, are built four towers; at every service of worship they ascend these towers, call to the company, and chant the ceremonial. On both sides, left and right, are the halls where all the patriarchs have preached the doctrine; these, too, are built with layers of stone, and are decorated most beautifully. . . .

[1430] An order was respectfully received from our imperial court that the principle envoy the grand eunuch Chen Ho and others should go to all the foreign countries to read out the imperial commands and to bestow rewards.

When a division of the fleet reached the country of Calicut, [the chief officer] selected an interpreter and others, seven men in all, and sent them with a load of musk, *trade* porcelain articles, and other such things; [and] they joined a ship of this country [Calicut] and went there. It took them one year to return to China.

They bought all kinds of unusual commodities, and rare valuables, lions, 'camelfowls,' and other such things; in addition they painted an accurate representation of the 'Heavenly Hall,' [and] they returned to the Chinese capital.

The king of the country of Mecca also sent envoys who brought some local articles, accompanied the seven men—the interpreter [and others]—who had originally gone there, and presented the articles to the court.

VASCO DA GAMA

Vasco da Gama was the first European to round Africa and reach India, after many earlier fifteenth-century trips had crawled ever further down the west African coast. He reached present-day South Africa in 1497, India a year later. He was able to profit sufficiently from this first trip to interest Portugal in further efforts; a later, second trip involved more abundant military preparation and use of cannon to intimidate Indian rulers and merchants.

• • •

VASCO DA GAMA: ROUND AFRICA TO INDIA, 1497–1498 C.E.

The inhabitants of this country are tawny-colored. Their food is confined to the flesh of seals, whales and gazelles, and the roots of herbs. They are dressed in skins, and wear sheaths over their virile members. They are armed with poles of olive wood to which a horn, browned in the fire, is attached. Their numerous dogs resemble those of Portugal,

From Oliver Thatcher, ed., *The Library of Original Sources*, vol. 1 (Milwaukee, Wis.: University Research Extension Co.l, 1907), 26–40, scanned by J. S. Arkenberg of California State University Fullerton, who modernized the text.

and bark like them. The birds of the country likewise, are the same as in Portugal, and include cormorants, gulls, turtle doves, crested larks, and many others. The climate is healthy and temperate, and produces good herbage. On the day after we had cast anchor, that is to say on Thursday (November 9) we landed with the captain-major [da Gama referred to himself in the third person], and made captive one of the natives, who was small of stature. This man had been gathering honey in the sandy waste, for in this country the bees deposit their honey at the foot of the mounds around the bushes. He was taken on board the captain-major's ship, and being placed at table he ate of all we ate. On the following day the captain-major had him well dressed and sent ashore.

On the following day (November 10) fourteen or fifteen natives came to where our ship lay. The captain-major landed and showed them a variety of merchandise, with the view of finding out whether such things were to be found in their country. This merchandise included cinnamon, cloves, seed-pearls, gold, and many other things, but it was evident that they had no knowledge whatsoever of such articles, and they were consequently given round bells and tin rings.

On that day Fernaro Velloso, who was with the captain-major, expressed a great desire to be permitted to accompany the natives to their houses, so that he might find out how they lived and what they ate. After a meal they expressed a desire that he should not accompany them any further, but return to the vessels. When Fernao Velloso came abreast of the vessels he began to shout, the negroes keeping in the bush.

We were still at supper; but when his shouts were heard the captain-major rose at once, and so did we others, and we entered a sailing boat. The negroes then began running along the beach, and they came as quickly up with Fernao Velloso as we did, and when we endeavored to get him into the boat they threw their assegais, and wounded the captain-major and three or four others. All this happened because we looked upon these people as men of little spirit, quite incapable of violence, and had therefore landed without first arming ourselves. We then returned to the ships.

1498. Calicut [Arrival.] That night (May 20) we anchored two leagues from the city of Calicut, and we did so because our pilot mistook Capna, a town at that place, for Calicut. Still further there is another town called Pandarani. We anchored about a league and a half from the shore. After we were at anchor, four boats (almadias) approached us from the land, who asked of what nation we were. We told them, and they then pointed out Calicut to us.

The city of Calicut is inhabited by Christians. [The first voyagers to Indian mistook the Hindus for Christians.] They are of tawny complexion. Some of them have big beards and long hair, whilst others clip their hair short or shave the head, merely allowing a tuft to remain on the crown as a sign that they are Christians. They also wear moustaches. They pierce the ears and wear much gold in them. They go naked down to the waist, covering their lower extremities with very fine cotton stuffs. But it is only the most respectable who do this, for the others manage as best they are able. The women of this country, as a rule, are ugly and of small stature. They wear many jewels of gold round the neck, numerous bracelets on their arms, and rings set with precious stones on their toes. All these people are well-disposed and apparently of mild temper. At first sight they seem covetous and ignorant.

When we arrived at Calicut the king was fifteen leagues away. The captain-major sent two men to him with a message, informing him that an ambassador had arrived from the King of Portugal with letters, and that if he desired it he would take them to where the king then was. The king presented the bearers of this message with much fine cloth. He sent word to the captain-major bidding him welcome, saying that he was about to proceed to Calicut. As a matter of fact, he started at once with a large retinue. At this time we were actually in front of the city of Calicut. We were told that the anchorage at the place to which we were to go was good, whilst at the place we were then it was bad, with a stony bottom, which was quite true; and, moreover, that it was customary for the ships which came to this country to anchor there for the sake of safety. We ourselves did not feel comfortable, and the captain-major had no sooner received this royal message than he ordered the sails to be set, and we departed. We did not, however, anchor as near the shore as the king's pilot desired.

PART III

The Early Modern Period, 1450–1750

BEGINNING IN THE MID–FIFTEENTH CENTURY, several new themes began to shape the larger patterns of world history, compelling all major civilizations to come to terms with some unexpected forces. The world did not become more homogeneous as a result, because different regions reacted quite differently to the common themes. But every society was altered in the process. New technologies, particularly guns and improved navigational devices, changed world politics and trade. Western Europe expanded its commercial role and created new empires. The Europeans eagerly sought new prospects, and internal rivalries pushed individual states to seek colonies.

The rise of Western power soon brought Europe into contact with the Americas. Exploitation of American resources and the establishment of colonies propelled the Americas into international contacts for the first time since the arrival of people from Asia many millennia before. European control and also European diseases and animals now came to the Americas; and American crops such as corn and potatoes were taken to many other parts of the world, encouraging rapid population growth from China to Europe itself. American trade stimulated world commerce. Europe, particularly, began to increase its manufacturing sector, while relying on fairly traditional technologies and home-and shop-based production. It traded these finished goods for raw materials, precious metals, and spices from other parts of the world. Europe also managed to dominate most ocean-going trade, setting up huge commercial companies that provided another source of profits. Asian producers also benefited; China gained much of the American silver, which the Europeans used to pay for silks and porcelain.

The intensifying commercial contacts around the world created a new set of international inequalities. Some areas, such as Latin America, produced cheap materials for export, depending on forced labor and lacking a large merchant class. They became heavily dependent on European trade initiatives. Africa, though not colonized like Latin America, was brought into this system through the slave trade; millions of Africans were conscripted by African merchants and government agents and sold to Europeans for transport to the Americas. Indonesia was drawn in, through trade for spices and then because of Dutch-run colonies and estate agriculture. India became open to growing European penetration by the eighteenth century.

European gains, the inclusion of the Americas, and the formation of a more intensive international economy were not the only themes of the period. A new set of land-based empires formed, aided by the use of gunpowder and cannons. In the most dramatic change, the Turkish-led Ottoman Empire covered a large part of the Middle East, Egypt, and southeastern Europe; it replaced the loosening Arab political control and pushed back Christianity in the northern part of the region. The fall of Constantinople in 1453 essentially completed the conquest of the Christian Byzantine Empire. India experienced a new, Muslim-led Mughal Empire that dominated the Hindu majority during the sixteenth and seventeenth centuries. The Russian Empire began its expansion into central and eastern Asia and further into Eastern Europe. Some of these empires, along with the more traditional Chinese Empire, began to weaken somewhat toward the end of the early modern period, but their power, political hold, and internal cultural impact shaped the regions involved for several centuries. This was also a period of dramatic innovation in Japan, under the Tokugawa shogunate, a kind of feudal monarchy.

The early modern period saw no sweeping cultural changes of international scope. Islamic gains continued in parts of Asia. Christianity advanced particularly in the Americas, on the heels of European conquest. Confucianism gained ground in Japan, along with an extensive educational system. In Western Europe, a more scientific outlook accompanied massive discoveries in physics and biology; only in the eighteenth century, however, was this new intellectual framework exported, haltingly, to places like Russia and the British colonies of North America.

Comparative analysis unquestionably helps focus key issues in understanding world history in the early modern period. Comparisons in this chapter focus on four basic developments in the early modern period; first, contacts among peoples that had known each other little if at all previously, as global relationships were shaken up particularly by the new European sea power; second, the installation of new or vastly intensified labor systems to deal with problems of controlling workers and producing goods often central to the growing world trade; third, the expansion of land empires (which involved much continuity in China but important new developments in the Ottoman Empire and Russia); and finally, outright interaction with Western Europe, both by peoples now part of European colonies and by societies independent but exposed to new or potential influences.

EUROPEANS AND AMERICAN INDIANS

Explorers, Conquerors, and Aztec Reactions

The encounter between European explorers and settlers and Native Americans was one of the most fascinating and, from the Indian standpoint, tragic, in world history. Europeans came with technologies, animals, diseases, and religious views for which the Indians had no prior preparation. Some Indians proved quite adaptable to the context that European arrival established, gaining skill with horses, learning new political forms, and so on. Overall, however, Europeans brought greater force, devastating diseases, and an attitude of superiority that would combine to severely restrict Indian life.

Comparisons in this chapter involve an unusual, highly significant case of encounter, but also the interactions that developed key features of the Columbian exchange. Early European arrivals, such as Columbus himself, often focused on the naïveté and timidity of the Indians they encountered, wondering at their nakedness and lack of metals and weapons but confident that they could proceed in friendship. Columbus's report on the 1492 voyage to the Caribbean islands shows this early openness, but also the menace that underlay it: "I have also established the greatest friendship with the king of that country, so much so that he took pride in calling me his brother, and treating me as such. Even should these people change their intentions towards us and become hostile, they do not know what arms are, but, as I have said, go naked, and are the most timid people in the world; so that the men I have left could, alone, destroy the whole country."

Later accounts changed, and terms like *deceitful* and *lazy,* as well as *pagan,* began to be applied to Indians. The following European accounts come from Diego Alvarez Chanca, a surgeon on Columbus's 1493 return to the Caribbean, who later published a somewhat "ethnographic," if hostile, account in his hometown of Seville, Spain; from Hernando Cortés, in letters to the Spanish government as he began the conquest of Mexico in 1519; and from the French explorer Champlain, in a diary kept as he traveled the coasts of Maine and Cape Code in the early seventeenth century.

The nature of the sources varies. Champlain and Chanca wrote accounts for general interest; Cortés was reporting to the Spanish royalty. Which kind of account is more accurate, less likely to exaggerate?

What of the Indian views implied in the European accounts? Why does their outlook toward different Europeans vary—or does it? Why did Europeans pick up different signals about Indian reactions to the first presentations of Christianity? There are few direct accounts of initial Indian responses, so it is important to speculate on the basis of European descriptions of varying behaviors. Also, is there any sign of a distinction, in dealing with Europeans, between the Indians of New England or the Caribbean islands, who combined agriculture and hunting, and the Indians in that part of Mexico long embraced in the elaborate civilizations of the Aztecs and Mayans, whom Cortés first encountered?

Finally, there is the reaction from the Indians themselves. The Aztec Empire, founded in the fourteenth century and building on earlier civilizations in the region, was the key political power in Mexico and much of Central America. A set of Aztec accounts provides an unusual insight into initial contacts from the Indian side—interestingly, the comments refer to the same first encounters that the Cortés account deals with. The ruler of the vast Aztec empire, Montezuma (Motecuhzoma in the Aztec account), sent a mission to contact Cortés, and the results are documented in this passage, along with later observations about some of the biological impact of the Spanish arrival. Aztec response reflected among other things an old belief in a beneficent civilizer-god, Quetzalcoatl, who would return from the east in a particular type of year in the Aztec calendar, which 1519 happened to be. With this document, one set of Indian perceptions of Europeans can be directly compared with European reactions to the Indians; the same document suggests the complex mix of factors that explain why the Indian response combined resistance with various kinds of accommodation.

Questions

1. What were the dominant attitudes of the Europeans? Why did they feel justified in killing Indians? Were there also "good" Indians, and how were they defined?

2. Why do the accounts of Cortés and Chanca differ? Who were their audiences, and how might this factor have affected their emphases?

3. Which of the three European accounts was most optimistic about possibilities of dealing with the Indians, and why?

4. What did the Europeans believe Indian reactions to their arrival were?

5. Which looms larger in the European accounts: religious motivations or greed? Do the European accounts suggest an early form of racism?

6. How did Cortés treat Indians in Mexico? What were his basic assumptions?

7. Why did some Indians fight and others not? Why did the Aztecs not simply resist European intrusion in every possible way?

8. What suggestions does the Aztec account offer as to why Spanish conquest succeeded?

9. How do the Aztec account and the comments of Cortés compare? How do the two groups evaluate the religious factor? Which side was more aggressive? Which side had more deeply rooted assumptions of superiority, and why?

For Further Discussion

1. Why were small numbers of Europeans able to conquer the numerous, often well-organized American peoples?

2. Were European incursions into the Americas one of the great tragedies of world history?

3. Why might hunting-and-gathering Indians be harder for Europeans to deal with than those in the civilizations of the Aztecs and the Incas?

SPANISH REACTIONS: CHANCA AND CORTÉS

Dr. Chanca's comments on Indians came from his experience with the second Columbus expedition of 1493, which visited various Caribbean islands. Dr. Chanca was interested in titillating his Spanish readership. Hernando Cortés (1485–1547) reported to the Spanish royal government from 1519 onward. He had been assigned an official expedition to Mexico and was able to converse with Indian representatives through his two interpreters, one a Spaniard previously abandoned in the Yucatan, one an Indian woman. Cortés used a combination of alliances with dissident Indian groups and outright fighting to defeat the Aztecs by 1521.

• • •

DR. DIEGO ALVAREZ CHANCA ON THE CARIBE INDIANS

The way of life of these *caribe* people is bestial. There are three islands, this one is called *Turuqueira*, the other, which we saw first, is called *Ceyre*, and the third is called *Ayai*. They are all agreed, as if they were of one lineage, doing no harm to each other. All together they make war on all the other neighbouring islands, going 150 leagues by sea to make raids in the many canoes which they have, which are small 'fustas' made

From Peter Hulme and Noel Whitehead, eds., *Wild Majesty: Encounters with Caribes from Columbia to the Present Day* (Oxford: Clarendon Press, 1992), 13–14.

of a single piece of wood. Their arms are arrows rather than iron weapons, because they do not possess any iron: they fix on points made of tortoise-shell, others from another island fix on fish bones which are jagged, being like that naturally, like very strong saws, a thing which, for an unarmed people, as they all are, can kill and do great injury, but for people of our nation are not arms greatly to be feared.

These people raid the other islands and carry off the women whom they can take, especially the young and beautiful ones, whom they keep to serve them and have them as concubines, and they carry off so many that in fifty houses nobody was found, and of the captives more than twenty were young girls. These women also say that they are treated with a cruelty which seems incredible, for sons whom they have from them are eaten and they only rear those whom they have from their native women. The men whom they are able to take, those who are alive they bring to their houses to butcher for meat, and those who are dead are eaten there and then. They say that men's flesh is so good that there is nothing like it in the world, and it certainly seems so for the bones which we found in these houses had been gnawed of everything they could gnaw, so that nothing was left on them except what was much too tough to be eaten. In one house there a man's neck was found cooking in a pot. They cut off the male member of the boys they take prisoner and make use of them until they are men, and then when they want to make a feast, they kill and eat them, for they say that the flesh of boys and of women is not good to eat. Of these boys, three came fleeing to us, and all three had had their members cut off.

CORTÉS IN MEXICO

H. Cortés accordingly left Cuba and began his voyage with ten ships and four hundred fighting men, among whom were many knights and gentlemen, seventeen being mounted. The first land they touched was the Island of Cozumel, now called Santa Cruz, as we mentioned, and on landing at the part of San Juan de Portalatina the town was found entirely deserted, as if it had never been inhabited. Cortés wishing to know the cause of such a flight ordered the men to disembark and took up his abode in the town. It was not long before he learnt from three Indians captured in a canoe as they were making for the mainland of Yucatán that the chiefs of the Island at the sight of the Spanish ships approaching had left the town and retired with all the Indians to the woods and hills, being very afraid of the Spaniards as not knowing what their intentions might be. Cortés, replying by means of the native interpreter whom he had with him, informed them he was going to do them no harm but admonish them and bring them to the knowledge of our Holy Catholic Faith, that they might become vassals of

From Hernando Cortés, *Five Letters of Cortes to the Emperor*, trans. J. Bayard Morris (New York: Norton, 1991), 50–52, 92–94. Translation copyright © 1969 by J. Bayard Morris. Reprinted by permission of W. W. Norton & Company, Inc.

your Majesty and serve and obey him, as had all the Indians and peoples of those parts which are already peopled with Spanish subjects of your Majesties. On the Captain reassuring them in this manner they lost much of their former fear, and replied that they would willingly inform their chieftains who had taken refuge in the hills. The Captain thereupon gave them a letter by which the chiefs might approach in safety and they departed with it promising to return within the space of five days. After waiting for the reply some three or four days longer than the allotted time and seeing that they had not reappeared Cortés decided to search out the coast on either side of him, in order that the Island should not remain entirely deserted, and accordingly sent out two captains each with a hundred men, ordering them to proceed to either extremity of the Island and to hold conversations with any Indians they might meet, telling them that he was awaiting them in the port of San Juan de Portalatina in order to speak with them on behalf of your Majesty; such Indians they were to beg and urge as best they could to come to the said port but were to be careful not to do any harm to them, in their persons, their houses or their goods, lest the natives should be rendered more timid and deceitful than they were already. The two captains departed as they were commanded and returning within four days reported that all the towns which they had come across were desolate. They brought with them, however, ten or a dozen people whom they had managed to persuade, among whom was an Indian chieftain to whom Cortés spoke by means of his interpreter bidding him go and inform the chiefs that he would in no wise depart from the Island without seeing and speaking to them. The chieftain agreeing left with the second letter for the chiefs and two days later returned with the head chief to inform Cortés that he was the ruler of the Island and was come to see what he wanted. The Captain informed him that he wished them no harm, but that they should come to the knowledge of the true faith, and should know that we acknowledged as lords the greatest princes of the earth and that these in their turn obeyed a greater prince than he, wherefore what he desired of them was not otherwise than that the chiefs and Indians of that Island should likewise obey your Majesties, and that doing so they would be favoured, no-one being able to do them harm. The chief replied that he was content so to do and sent for all the other chieftains of the Island, who coming rejoiced greatly at all that the Captain Hernando Cortés had spoken to their chief, and were reassured in such manner that within a very few days the towns were as full of people as before, and the Indians went about among us with as little fear as if they had already had dealings with us for many years. . . .

Accordingly, as the Captain Hernando Cortés saw that stores were already beginning to run short and that the men would suffer much from hunger should he delay there any longer, and the true object of his voyage rest unattained, he decided, his men agreeing, to depart; and so hoisting sail they left that Island of Cozumel, now Santa Cruz, very peaceably inclined, so much so that if it were proposed to found a colony there the natives would be ready without coercion to serve their Spanish masters. The chiefs in particular were left very contented and at ease with what the Captain had told them on behalf of your Majesties and with the numerous articles of finery which he had given them for their own persons. I think there can be no doubt that all Spaniards who may happen to come to this Island in the future will be as well received as if they were arriving in a land which had been a long time colonized. The Island of Cozumel is small, without so much as a single river or stream; all the water that the Indians drink is from wells. The soil is composed solely of rocks and stones, a certain portion of it being woody. The Indians' only produce is that obtained from bee-keeping, and our procurators are sending to your Majesties samples both of the land and of the honey for your Majesties' inspection.

Your Majesties must know that when the Captain told the chiefs in his first interview with them that they must live no longer in the pagan faith which they held they begged him to acquaint them with the law under which they were henceforth to live. The Captain accordingly informed them to the best of his ability in the Catholic Faith, leaving them a cross of wood which was fixed on a high building and an image of Our Lady the Virgin Mary, and gave them to understand very fully what they must do to be good Christians, all of which they manifestly received with very good will, and so we left them very happy and contented. . . .

On arriving at the first town we found the Indians in boats drawn up on the shore near the water. . . . Early next morning a few Indians approached us in a canoe bringing several chickens and enough maize to make a meal for a few men and bidding us accept these and depart from their land. The Captain however spoke to them through the interpreters giving them to understand that in no wise would he depart from that land before he had found out the secret of it in order to be able to send your Majesties a true account, and again begged them not to be offended at his project nor to deny him entrance for they also were subjects of your Majesties. However they still forbade us to make a landing and urged us to depart. On their return to the town the Captain decided to move, and ordered one of his captains to go with two hundred men by a path which had been discovered during the preceding night to lead to the village. He himself embarked with some eighty men on the brigs and boats and took up his position in front of the town ready to land if they would permit him to do so: even as he approached he found the Indians in war paint and armed with bows and arrows, lances and small round shields, yelling that if we would not leave their land and wanted war it should begin at once, for they were men to defend their own homes. Cortés attempted to speak with them four times (your Majesties' notary who accompanied him witnessed to the same to the effect that he did not desire war) but seeing that it was the determined will of the Indians to resist his landing and that they were beginning to shoot their arrows against us, ordered the guns which we carried to be fired and an attack to be made. Immediately after the discharge of our guns and in the landing which followed a few of our men were wounded, but finally the fury of our onslaught and the sudden attack of our comrades who had come up in the rear of the enemy forced them to fly and abandon the village, which we accordingly took and settled ourselves in what appeared to be the strongest part of it. In the evening of the following day two Indians arrived from their chiefs bringing a few very inferior gold ornaments of small value and told the Captain that they offered him these in order that in exchange he might leave the land as it was before and do them no hurt. Cortés replied saying that as to doing them no hurt it pleased him well, but as to leaving the land they should know that from henceforward they must acknowledge as lords the greatest princes of the earth and must be their subjects and serve them; by doing which they would obtain many favours from your Majesties who would help them and defend them from their enemies. On this they replied that they were content to do this, but nevertheless still begged him to leave their land, and so we arrived at friendly terms.

Having patched up this friendship the Captain pointed out that the Spanish troops who were with him in the village had nothing to eat and had brought nothing from their ships. He therefore asked them to bring us sufficient food so long as we remained on land, which they promised to do on the following day, and so departed. But the next day and another passed without any food arriving so that we were faced with extreme shortness of provisions, and on the third day a few Spanish soldiers asked leave of the Captain to visit some of the near-lying farms and see if they could obtain some food. . . . Proceeding in this order the vanguard came upon a large body of Indians who were advancing to attack our camp, so that had we not gone out to meet them that day it is very possible we should have been hard put to it. And again the captain of artillery made certain representations (as your notary can bear witness) to the Indians whom he met in full war paint, crying to them by means of the native heralds and interpreters that we wanted not war but peace with them: their only answer was given not in words but in arrows which began to fall very thickly. The leading party was thus already engaged with the Indians when the two officers in command of the rearguard came up, and it was not until two hours later that Cortés arrived in a part of the wood where the Indians were beginning to encircle the Spaniards in the rear, and there he continued fighting against the Indians for about an hour; moreover such was their number that neither those among the Spaniards who were fighting on foot perceived those on horseback nor knew in what part of the field they were, nor could those on horseback so much as perceive one another as they surged hither and thither among the Indians. However, as soon as the Spaniards perceived the horsemen they attacked still more briskly and almost immediately the Indians were put to flight, the pursuit lasting half a league. . . . And so having attended to the wounded and laid them upon stretchers, we regained our camp taking with us two Indians who were captured there. These Cortés ordered to be loosed, and sent them with letters to the chieftains telling them that if they were willing to come to where he was he would pardon them the evil they had done and would be their friend. Accordingly the very same evening two Indians who purported to be chieftains arrived, declaring that they were very grieved at what had occurred and that the chieftains as a body begged him to pardon them and not punish them further for what was passed nor kill any more of their people, for over two hundred and twenty Indians had fallen; the past was past and henceforward they were willing to be subjects of that prince of whom he had spoken, and such they already held themselves to be, and bound themselves to do him service whenever anything in your Majesties' name should be desired of them.

In this wise they sat down and peace was made. The Captain then enquired of them by the interpreter what people it was who had fought in that battle, and they replied that tribes from eight provinces had joined together in that place and that according to the reckoning and lists which they possessed they would be about forty thousand men, for they could well reckon up to such a number. Thus your Majesties may truly believe that this battle was won rather by the will of God than by our own strength, for of what avail are four hundred (and we were no more) against forty thousand warriors?

FRENCH REACTIONS: CHAMPLAIN

Samuel de Champlain (1567–1635), was the chief French explorer in North America and a key founder of New France, in Canada. He made his first fur-trading expedition to the region in 1603 and subsequently participated in a number of other expeditions, sometimes joining in attacks on the Iroquois Indians by the Huron tribe. He wrote accounts of his travels in several editions, with a definitive edition completed in exile (during a period when the English had conquered New France) in 1632. In his later years, both before and after the English disruption, he served as virtual governor of New France, and he was buried in Quebec.

• • •

FRENCH ENCOUNTERS IN NORTH AMERICA

Now I will drop this discussion to return to the savages who had conducted me to the falls of the river Norumbegue, who went to notify Bessabez, their chief, and other savages, who in turn proceeded to another little river to inform their own, named Cabahis, and give him notice of our arrival.

From *Voyages of Samuel de Champlain*, 1604–1618, ed. W. L. Grant (New York: Charles Scribner's, 1907), 49–50, 71–74, 97–100.

The 16th of the month there came to us some thirty savages on assurances given them by those who had served us as guides. There came also to us the same day the above-named Bessabez with six canoes. As soon as the savages who were on land saw him coming, they all began to sing, dance, and jump, until he had landed. Afterwards, they all seated themselves in a circle on the ground, as is their custom, when they wish to celebrate a festivity, or an harangue is to be made. Cabahis, the other chief, arrived also a little later with twenty or thirty of his companions, who withdrew to one side and greatly enjoyed seeing us, as it was the first time they had seen Christians. A little while after, I went on shore with two of my companions and two of our savages who served as interpreters. I directed the men in our barque to approach near the savages, and hold their arms in readiness to do their duty in case they noticed any movement of these people against us. Bessabez, seeing us on land, bade us sit down, and began to smoke with his companions, as they usually do before an address. They presented us with venison and game.

I directed our interpreter to say to our savages that they should cause Bessabez, Cabahis, and their companions to understand that Sieur de Monts had sent me to them to see them, and also their country, and that he desired to preserve friendship with them and to reconcile them with their enemies, the Souriquois and Canadians, and moreover that he desired to inhabit their country and show them how to cultivate it, in order that they might not continue to lead so miserable a life as they were doing, and some other words on the same subject. This our savages interpreted to them, at which they signified their great satisfaction, saying that no greater good could come to them than to have our friendship, and that they desired to live in peace with their enemies, and that we should dwell in their land, in order that they might in future more than ever before engage in hunting beavers, and give us a part of them in return for our providing them with things which they wanted. After he had finished his discourse, I presented them with hatchets, paternosters, caps, knives, and other little knickknacks, when we separated from each other. All the rest of this day and the following night, until break of day, they did nothing but dance, sing, and make merry, after which we traded for a certain number of beavers. Then each party returned, Bessabez with his companions on the one side, and we on the other, highly pleased at having made the acquaintance of this people. . . .

On the 23d of July, four or five seamen having gone on shore with some kettles to get fresh water, which was to be found in one of the sand-banks a short distance from our barque, some of the savages, coveting them, watched the time when our men went to the spring, and then seized one out of the hands of a sailor, who was the first to dip, and who had no weapons. One of his companions, starting to run after him, soon returned, as he could not catch him, since he ran much faster than himself. The other savages, of whom there were a large number, seeing our sailors running to our barque, and at the same time shouting to us to fire at them, took to flight. At the time there were some of them in our barque, who threw themselves into the sea, only one of whom we were able to seize. Those on the land who had taken to flight, seeing them swimming, returned straight to the sailor from whom they had taken away the kettle, hurled several arrows at him from behind, and brought him down. Seeing this, they ran at once to him, and despatched him with their knives. Meanwhile, haste was made to go on shore, and muskets were fired from our barque: mine, bursting in my hands, came near killing me. The savages, hearing this discharge of fire-arms, took to flight, and with redoubled speed when they saw that we had landed, for they were afraid when they saw us running after them. There was no likelihood of our catching them, for they are as swift as horses. We brought in the murdered man, and he was buried some hours later. Meanwhile, we kept the prisoner bound by the feet and hands on board of our barque, fearing that he might escape. But Sieur de Monts resolved to let him go, being persuaded that he was not to blame, and that he had no previous knowledge of what had transpired, as also those who, at the time, were in and about our barque. Some hours later there came some savages to us, to excuse themselves, indicating by signs and demonstrations that it was not they who had committed this malicious act, but others farther off in the interior. We did not wish to harm them, although it was in our power to avenge ourselves.

All these savages from the Island Cape wear neither robes nor furs, except very rarely: moreover, their robes are made of grasses and hemp, scarcely covering the body, and coming down only to their thighs. They have only the sexual parts concealed with a small piece of leather; so likewise the women, with whom it comes down a little lower behind than with the men, all the rest of the body being naked. Whenever the women came to see us, they wore robes which were open in front. The men cut off the hair on the top of the head like those at the river Choüacoet. I saw, among other things, a girl with her hair very neatly dressed, with a skin colored red, and bordered on the upper part with little shellbeads. A part of her hair hung down behind, the rest being braided in various ways. These people paint the face red, black, and yellow. They have scarcely any beard, and tear it out as fast as it grows. Their bodies are well-proportioned. I cannot tell what government they have, but I think that in this respect they resemble their neighbors, who have none at all. They know not how to worship or pray; yet, like the other savages, they have some superstitions, which I shall describe in their place. As for weapons, they have only pikes, clubs, bows and arrows. It would seem from their appearance that they have a good disposition, better than those of the north, but they are all in fact of no great worth. Even a slight intercourse with them gives you at once a knowledge of them. They are great thieves and, if they cannot lay hold of any thing with their hands, they try to do so with their feet, as we have oftentimes learned by experience. I am of opinion that, if they had any thing to exchange with us, they would not give themselves to thieving. They bartered away to us their bows, arrows, and quivers, for pins and buttons; and if they had had any thing else better they would have done the same with it. It is necessary to be on one's guard against this people, and live in a state of distrust of them, yet without letting them perceive it. They gave us a large quantity of tobacco, which they dry and then reduce to powder. When they eat Indian corn, they boil it in earthen pots, which they make in a way different from ours. They bray it also in wooden mortars and reduce it to flour, of which they then make cakes, like the Indians of Peru. . . .

Now, in view of what Sieur de Poutrincourt had seen, and the order which it had been told him they observed when they wished to play some bad trick, when we passed by some cabins, where there was a large number of women, we gave them some bracelets and rings to keep them quiet and free from fear, and to most of the old and distinguished men hatchets, knives, and other things which they desired. This pleased them greatly, and they repaid it all in dances, gambols, and harangues, which we did not understand at all. We went wherever we chose without their having the assurance to say anything to us. It pleased us greatly to see them show themselves so simple in appearance. . . .

The next day, in the morning, the 15th of October, the savages did not fail to come and see in what condition our men were, whom they found asleep, except one, who was near the fire. When they saw them in this condition, they came, to the number of four hundred, softly over a little hill, and sent them such a volley of arrows that to rise up was death. Fleeing the best they could towards our barque, shouting, "Help! they are killing us!" a part fell dead in the water; the others were all pierced with arrows, and one died in consequence a short time after. The savages made a desperate noise with roarings, which it was terrible to hear.

Upon the occurrence of this noise and that of our men, the sentinel, on our vessel, exclaimed, "To arms! They are killing our men!" Consequently, each one immediately seized his arms; and we embarked in the shallop, some fifteen or sixteen of us, in order to go ashore. But, being unable to get there on account of a sandbank between us and the land, we threw ourselves into the water, and waded from this bank to the shore, the distance of a musket-shot. As soon as we were there, the savages, seeing us within arrow range, fled into the interior. To pursue them was fruitless, for they are marvellously swift. All that we could do was to carry away the dead bodies and bury them near a cross, which had been set up the day before, and then to go here and there to see if we could get sight of any of them. But it was time wasted, therefore we came back. Three hours afterwards, they returned to us on the sea-shore. We discharged at them several shots from our little brass cannon; and, when they heard the noise, they crouched down on the ground to avoid the fire. In mockery of us, they beat down the cross and disinterred the dead, which displeased us greatly, and caused us to go for them a second time; but they fled, as they had done before. We set up again the cross, and reinterred the dead, whom they had thrown here and there amid the heath, where they kindled a fire to burn them. We returned without any result, as we had done before, well aware that there was scarcely hope of avenging ourselves this time, and that we should have to renew the undertaking when it should please God.

AZTEC REACTIONS: *THE BROKEN SPEARS*

The Broken Spears is a compilation of a number of Aztec and other Indian records from the sixteenth century, assembled in the 1960s by a Spanish scholar. The materials include codices originally written in the Nahuat language (one of the Aztec-stem languages) that escaped the general Spanish destruction of native-language documents, plus later recollections written by Indians in Spanish. The reassembly of the materials in rough chronological order, by the book's editor, permits unique insight into one whole side of this fateful encounter.

• • •

Then Motecuhzoma gave the messengers his final orders. He said to them: "Go now, without delay. Do reverence to our lord the god. Say to him: 'Your deputy, Motecuhzoma, has sent us to you. Here are the presents with which he welcomes you home to Mexico.'" . . .

One by one they did reverence to Cortes by touching the ground before him with their lips. They said to him: "If the god will deign to hear us, your deputy Motecuhzoma has sent us to render you homage. He has the City of Mexico in his care. He says: 'The god is weary.'"

Then they arrayed the Captain in the finery they had brought him as presents. With great care they fastened the turquoise mask in place, the mask of the god with its crossband of quetzal feathers. A golden earring hung down on either side of this mask. They dressed him in the decorated vest and the collar woven in the petatillo style—-the collar of *chalchihuites,* with a disk of gold in the center.

Next they fastened the mirror to his hips, dressed him in the cloak known as "the ringing bell" and adorned his feet. . . . In his hand they placed the shield with its fringe and pendant of quetzal feathers, its ornaments of gold and mother-of-pearl. Finally they set before him the pair of black sandals. As for the other objects of divine finery, they only laid them out for him to see.

The Captain asked them: "And is this all? Is this your gift of welcome? Is this how you greet people?"

They replied: "This is all, our lord. This is what we have brought you."

Then the Captain gave orders, and the messengers were chained by the feet and by the neck. When this had been done, the great cannon was fired off. The messengers lost their senses and fainted away. They fell down side by side and lay where they had fallen. But the Spaniards quickly revived them: they lifted them up, gave them wine to drink and then offered them food.

From Miguel Leon-Portilla, *The Broken Spears* (expanded and updated edition, Boston: Beacon, 1992). © by Miguel Leon-Portilla. Reprinted by permission of Beacon Press, Boston.

The Captain said to them: "I have heard that the Mexicans are very great warriors, very brave and terrible. If a Mexican is fighting alone, he knows how to retreat, turn back, rush forward and conquer, even if his opponents are ten or even twenty. But my heart is not convinced. I want to see it for myself. I want to find out if you are truly that strong and brave."

Then he gave them swords, spears and leather shields. He said: "It will take place very early, at daybreak. We are going to fight each other in pairs, and in this way we will learn the truth. We will see who falls to the ground!"

They said to the Captain: "Our lord, we were not sent here for this by your deputy Motecuhzoma! We have come on an exclusive mission, to offer you rest and repose and to bring you presents. What the lord desires is not within our warrant. If we were to do this, it might anger Motecuhzoma, and he would surely put us to death." . . .

Then they left in great haste and continued to the City of Mexico. They entered the city at night, in the middle of the night.

The messengers went to the House of the Serpent, and Motecuhzoma arrived. The two captives were then sacrificed before his eyes: their breasts were torn open, and the messengers were sprinkled with their blood. This was done because the messengers had completed a difficult mission: they had seen the gods, their eyes had looked on their faces. They had even conversed with the gods!

When the sacrifice was finished, the messengers reported to the king. They told him how they had made the journey, and what they had seen, and what food the strangers ate. Motecuhzoma was astonished and terrified by their report, and the description of the strangers' food astonished him above all else.

He was also terrified to learn how the cannon roared, how its noise resounded, how it caused one to faint and grow deaf. The messengers told him: "A thing like a ball of stone comes out of its entrails: it comes out shooting sparks and raining fire. The smoke that comes out with it has a pestilent odor, like that of rotten mud. This odor penetrates even to the brain and causes the greatest discomfort. If the cannon is aimed against a mountain, the mountain splits and cracks open. If it is aimed against a tree, it shatters the tree into splinters. This is a most unnatural sight, as if the tree had exploded from within."

The messengers also said: "Their trappings and arms are all made of iron. They dress in iron and wear iron casques on their heads. Their swords are iron; their bows are iron; their shields are iron; their spears are iron. Their deer carry them on their backs wherever they wish to go. These deer, our lord, are as tall as the roof of a house.

"The strangers' bodies are completely covered, so that only their faces can be seen. Their skin is white, as if it were made of lime. They have yellow hair, though some of them have black. Their beards are long and yellow, and their moustaches are also yellow. Their hair is curly, with very fine strands.

"As for their food, it is like human food. It is large and white, and not heavy. It is something like straw, but with the taste of a cornstalk, of the pith of a cornstalk. It is a little sweet, as if it were flavored with honey; it tastes of honey, it is sweet-tasting food. . . .

When Motecuhzoma heard this report, he was filled with terror. It was as if his heart had fainted, as if it had shriveled. It was as if he were conquered by despair.

While the Spaniards were in Tlaxcala, a great plague broke out here in Tenochtitlan [the Aztec capital, now Mexico City]. It began to spread during the thirteenth month and lasted for seventy days, striking everywhere in the city and killing a vast number of our people. Sores erupted on our faces, our breasts, our bellies; we were covered with agonizing sores from head to foot.

The illness was so dreadful that no one could walk or move. The sick were so utterly helpless that they could only lie on their beds like corpses, unable to move their limbs or even their heads. They could not lie face down or roll from one side to the other. If they did move their bodies, they screamed with pain.

A great many died from this plague, and many others died of hunger. They could not get up to search for food, and everyone else was too sick to care for them, so they starved to death in their beds.

Some people came down with a milder form of the disease; they suffered less than the others and made a good recovery. But they could not escape entirely. Their looks were ravaged, for wherever a sore broke out, it gouged an ugly pockmark in the skin. And a few of the survivors were left completely blind.

CHAPTER 17

THE SPREAD OF SLAVERY AND THE ATLANTIC
SLAVE TRADE

Atlantic history, as a category, is gaining increasing attention. The ocean became a world trade artery for the first time in the fifteenth century. More important were the human connections formed, as peoples from both sides of the Atlantic, and from north and south, interacted in various ways. New creativity and new suffering both resulted.

This chapter deals with the unprecedented transatlantic trade in African slaves, which began in the sixteenth century and continued for three hundred years. This trade had a host of impacts in world history and in the development of all the regions involved.

The capture and purchase of millions of Africans, who were sent as slaves to South and North America and the Caribbean by European slave traders from the sixteenth century until the early nineteenth, mainly for plantation work, constitute one of the key episodes of early modern world history. The result weakened internal trade balance and population size in West Africa, though individual merchants and rulers benefited. The profits helped fuel Europe's commercial economy. The spread of slavery and the impact of diverse African cultures left durable marks on the Americas.

Slavery was an old institution. Most river valley civilizations had held slaves, often captives in war. Greek and Roman societies had depended heavily on slaves, who provided domestic service but also did vital, brutal work in mines and on agricultural estates. Roman use of slaves for agricultural labor indeed provided the clearest prior precedent for the new slavery of the early modern period. Slavery also existed within Africa, again involving captures in war and the ensuing hereditary status of their descendants. Though the numbers of slaves were relatively small, Africa obviously contained a preestablished group of slave merchants.

Nevertheless, the volume, speed, and displacement of the new transatlantic slave trade had no precedent. Europeans in the Americas hoped to find gold and other easy wealth. In fact, they discovered the profitability of some mining and also export agricultural production. Yet local labor was scarce, in large part because the majority of the American Indian population died off in contact with

European diseases. Africa, newly explored by European voyagers, seemed to provide the answer, in a context where Europeans now ruled the seas.

Here, clearly, was a radically new international contact, which affected Europe, Africa, and the Americas. The impact on Africa has been much debated. Population loss and diversion of trade away from the Muslim world, as transatlantic commerce replaced trans-Saharan, definitely made a difference. On the other hand, strong governments persisted in Africa, as did older cultural forms. Europe was most obviously affected by the money its merchants made, which increased wealth and capital—helping to fuel further economic change, including ultimately the industrial revolution. More subtly, European views of Africans, though not yet as thoroughly racist as they would become in the nineteenth century, became hardened in ways that still affect world history. The massive new labor force in the Americas enhanced the ability to generate exports such as sugar for the world economy. Africans also brought their cultures and their experience of the slave voyage and of slavery itself, which would contribute vital ingredients to the history of the Americas from this time onward.

Finally, of course, there was the impact on the slaves themselves, for whom this was an unquestionably dreadful experience. Deaths and mistreatment on the slave ships were compounded by harsh treatment in the Americas—though there were different levels of awfulness. The fear and indignity of the experience affected surviving slaves more perhaps than the physical torment. Here, too, were important ingredients of early modern world history that would have ongoing impacts on the large African American minorities in the Caribbean and on both American continents.

In the following selections, a European slave trader presents his observations, indirectly highlighting some of the attitudes that would allow him to accept his active commercial role. Then, from a hundred years later, in the eighteenth century, an African former slave presents his view of the same process. We are able to juxtapose two different vantage points, that of the actors and that of the acted upon, to determine how they evaluated the same basic historical process and what larger consequences their perspectives suggest.

The slave trade constitutes one of those common events with at least two radically different sides, the winners and the losers. Comparison can help sort out what really happened, while sharpening the analysis of the experience of both parties.

Questions

1. **What did Europeans offer Africans in the slave trade? How were slaves obtained from the African interior? Do Barbot and Equiano agree on the methods used?**

2. Why were European traders so nonchalant about their own involvement, and so willing to be involved?

3. What impact did Europeans think they were having on Africa itself, including African states and rulers?

4. How did Christianity interact with the slave trade? Does Barbot reflect Christian criteria in his slave trader account?

5. Were the European traders aware of slaves as humans? Could they distinguish good from bad treatment? How did they understand and deal with the reactions of slaves themselves to the experience of capture and trade?

6. Are there any similarities between European and African descriptions of the trade? How did Africans react to European technology and material culture? What was the role of beliefs in magic? Did Africans have the fears of Europeans that the slave traders claimed? What motives did they ascribe to Europeans?

7. Slave traders and slaves both were potentially partisan. Does either of the following accounts seem exaggerated? Does Barbot show any signs of distorting his descriptions to make himself look good, or does he not believe he has to bother? Does Equiano exaggerate problems or ignore benefits?

For Further Discussion

1. Which account most helps you to understand the slave trade and the experiences involved? Which is more informative? Which provides the better basis for assessing the effects of the slave trade?

2. Judging by Barbot's discussion, were slave traders racist? Scholars debate whether Western racism helped cause the European treatment of slaves or was a result of it. What does Barbot's account suggest? Is this a useful question for the early modern period?

3. What impact would the trade and the passage across the Atlantic have in the later lives of the slaves and their descendants? Does either of the accounts in this chapter suggest probable impacts?

4. What was different about slavery and the slave trade in the Americas from more traditional forms of slavery? What accounts for the differences?

THE SLAVE TRADER'S VIEW: JOHN BARBOT

John Barbot was an employee of a French slave trading company. He made several trips to West Africa in the 1670s and 1680s. His account is unusually detailed,

From Elysbeth Doman, ed., *Documents Illustrative of the History of the Slave Trade to America* (Washington, D.C.: Carnegie Institute, 1930), 282–85, 286–90, 293, 294–95.

suggesting an active intellect, whatever his other attributes were. And he clearly harbored some internal ambivalence about the treatment he saw and participated in—though it's possible to argue that he did almost nothing about his qualms.

•   •   •

Goods for Trade

. . . the French import common red, blue, and scarlet cloth, silver and brass rings, or bracelets, chains, little bells, false crystal, ordinary and coarse hats; Dutch pointed knives, pewter dishes, silk sashes, with false gold and silver fringes; blue serges, French paper, steels to strike fire . . . brass kettles, yellow amber, maccatons, that is, beads of two sorts, pieces of eight of the old stamp, some silver pieces of 28 sols value, either plain or gilt, Dutch cutlaces, strait and bow'd, clouts, galet, martosdes, two other sorts of beads, of which the Blacks make necklaces for women, white sugar, musket balls, iron nails, shot, white and red frize, looking-glasses in gilt and plain frames, cloves, cinnamon, scissors, needles, coarse thread of sundry colours, but chiefly red, yellow, and white. . . . Particularly at Goeree, the company imports ten thousand or more every year, of those which are made in the province of Brittany, all short and thin, which is called in London narrow flat iron, or half flat iron of Sweden; but each bar shortened, or cut off at one end to about 16 or 18 inches, so that about eighty of these bars weigh a ton, or twenty hundred weight English. It is to be observ'd, that such voyage-iron, as called in London, is the only sort and size used throughout all Nigritia, Guinea, and West-Ethiopia, in the way of trade. Lastly, a good quantity of Coignac brandy, both in hogsheads and rundlets, single and double, the double being eight, the single four gallons.

The principal goods the French have in return for these commodities from the Moors and Blacks, are slaves, gold-dust, elephants teeth, bees-wax, dry and green hides, gum-arabick, ostrich feathers, and several other odd things. . . .

The French have built a small fort, mounted with eight guns. . . . There they buy slaves in considerable numbers . . . which they convey down to their factory every year. . . .

The country of little Brak affords them slaves. . . .

At the villages of Bozaert, or Bozar, and Caye, near the factory they have slaves. . . .

Slaves

Those sold by the Blacks are for the most part prisoners of war, taken either in fight, or pursuit, or in the incursions they make into their enemies' territories; others stolen away by their own countrymen; and some there are, who will sell their own children, kindred, or neighbours. This has been often seen, and to compass it, they desire the

person they intend to sell, to help them in carrying something to the factory by way of trade, and when there, the person so deluded, not understanding the language, is sold and deliver'd up as a slave, notwithstanding all his resistance, and exclaiming against the treachery. I was told of one, who design'd to sell his own son, after that manner; but he understanding French, dissembled for a while, and then contriv'd it so cunningly as to persuade the French, that the old man was his slave, and not his father, by which means he deliver'd him up into captivity; and thus made good the Italian Proverb, *A furbo furbo e mezzo;* amounting to as much as, Set a thief to catch a thief, or Diamond cuts Diamond. However, it happened soon after, that the fellow was met by some of the principal Blacks of the country, as he was returning home from the factory, with the goods he had receiv'd for the sale of his father, all which they took away, and order'd him to be sold for a slave.

The kings are so absolute, that upon any slight pretence of offences committed by their subjects, they order them to be sold for slaves, without regard to rank, or possession. Thus a Marabout, or Priest, as I believe, was sold to me at Goeree, by the Alcaide of Rio Fresco, by special order of king Damel, for some misdemeanors. I took notice, that this Priest was above two months aboard the ship, before he would speak one word. . . .

Abundance of little Blacks of both sexes are also stolen away by their neighbours, when found abroad on the roads, or in the woods; or else in the Cougans, or cornfields, at the time of the year, when their parents keep them there all day, to scare away the devouring small birds, that come to feed on the millet, in swarms, as has been said above.

In times of dearth and famine, abundance of those people will sell themselves, for a maintenance, and to prevent starving. When I first arriv'd at Goeree, in December, 1681, I could have bought a great number, at very easy rates, if I could have found provisions to subsist them; so great was the dearth then, in that part of Nigritia.

To conclude, some slaves are also brought to these Blacks, from very remote inland countries, by way of trade, and sold for things of very inconsiderable value; but these slaves are generally poor and weak, by reason of the barbarous usage they have had in traveling so far, being continually beaten, and almost famish'd; so inhuman are the Blacks to one another. . . .

The great wealth of the Fantineans [Fantyn, a West African country] makes them so proud and haughty, that an European trading there must stand bare to them. . . . A good slave sells there, as at all other trading places on the Gold-Coast westward, at the rate of one Benda of gold, which is two ounces. . . .

In time of war, it [Accra] furnishes so great a number of slaves, that it amounts to, at least, as many as are sold all along the rest of the coast. This country is continually in war with some of the neighbouring nations, which are very populous, and from whom they take very many prisoners, most of whom, they sell to the Europeans. The slaves are commonly purchased for coesvelt linen, slyziger, lywat, sheets, sayes, perpetuanas, firelocks, powder, brandy, bugles, knives, top-sails, nicannees, and other goods, according to the times. The natives carry those commodities to Abonee market, which is four leagues beyond Great Acra northward, for the Accanez people, who resort thither three times a week; as do other Blacks from the country of Abonee, Aquamboe, and Aquimera, who all buy those goods of the Acra men, at such rates as they think fit to put upon them, the king refusing to permit those strangers to go down themselves to the European warehouses on the coast; for which reason, those Blacks pay often double the value for what they buy. The king has there an overseer, who has the power to set the price on all goods, between buyer and seller. This general overseer is assisted by several officers to act for him, where he cannot be present himself. Those employments are much sought after there, as being both honourable and advantageous; because, both the king's and their perquisites are very considerable. . . .

The king and chief Blacks of Acra were, in my time, very rich in slaves and gold, through the vast trade the natives drove with the Europeans on the coast, and the neighbouring nations up the country. . . .

The trade of slaves is in a more peculiar manner the business of kings, rich men, and prime merchants, exclusive of the inferior sort of Blacks.

These slaves are severely and barbarously treated by their masters, who subsist them poorly, and beat them inhumanly, as may be seen by the scabs and wounds on the bodies of many of them when sold to us. They scarce allow them the least rag to cover their nakedness, which they also take off from them when sold to Europeans; and they always go bare-headed. The wives and children of slaves, are also slaves to the master under whom they are married; and when dead, they never bury them, but cast out the bodies into some by place, to be devoured by birds, or beasts of prey.

This barbarous usage of those unfortunate wretches, makes it appear, that the fate of such as are bought, and transported from the coast to America, or other parts of the world, by Europeans, is less deplorable, than that of those who end their days in their native country; for aboard ships all possible care is taken to preserve and subsist them for the interest of the owners, and when sold in America, the same motive ought to prevail with their masters to use them well, that they may live the longer, and do them more service. Not to mention the inestimable advantage they may reap, of becoming christians, and saving their souls, if they make a true use of their condition. . . .

I also remember, that I once, among my several runs along that coast, happened to have aboard a whole family, man, wife, three young boys, and a girl, bought one after another, at several places; and cannot but observe here, what mighty satisfaction those poor creatures expressed to be so come together again, tho' in bondage. For several days successively they could not forbear shedding tears of joy, and continually embracing and caressing one another; which moving me to compassion, I ordered they should be better treated aboard than commonly we can afford to do it, where there are four or five hundred in a ship; and at Martinico, I sold them all together to a considerable planter, at a cheaper rate than I might have expected, had they been disposed of severally; being informed of that gentleman's good-nature, and having taken his word, that he would use that family as well as their circumstances would permit, and settle them in some part by themselves.

I have elsewhere spoke of the manner of valuing and rating the slaves among the Blacks, and shall conclude this chapter, which proves to be one of the longest, with an odd remark; which is, That many of those slaves we transport from Guinea to America are prepossessed with the opinion, that they are carried like sheep to the slaughter, and that the Europeans are fond of their flesh; which notion so far prevails with some, as to make them fall into a deep melancholy and despair, and to refuse all sustenance, tho' never so much compelled and even beaten to oblige them to take some nourishment: notwithstanding all which, they will starve to death; whereof I have had several instances in my own slaves both aboard and at Guadalupe. And tho' I must say I am naturally compassionate, yet have I been necessitated sometimes to cause the teeth of those wretches to be broken, because they would not open their mouths, or be prevailed upon by any intreaties to feed themselves; and thus have forced some sustenance into their throats. . . .

As the slaves come down to Fida from the inland country, they are put into a booth, or prison, built for that purpose, near the beach, all of them together; and when the Europeans are to receive them, they are brought out into a large plain, where the surgeons examine every part of every one of them, to the smallest member, men and women being all stark naked. Such as are allowed good and sound, are set on one side, and the others by themselves; which slaves so rejected are there called Mackrons, being above thirty five years of age, or defective in their limbs, eyes or teeth; or grown grey, or that have the venereal disease, or any other imperfection. These being so set aside, each of the others, which have passed as good, is marked on the breast, with a red-hot iron, imprinting the mark of the French, English, or Dutch companies, that so each nation may distinguish their own, and to prevent their being chang'd by the natives for worse, as they are apt enough to do. In this particular, care is taken that the women, as tenderest, be not burnt too hard. . . .

If there happens to be no stock of slaves at Fida, the factor must trust the Blacks with his goods, to the value of a hundred and fifty, or two hundred slaves; which goods they carry up into the inland, to buy slaves, at all the markets, for above two hundred leagues up the country, where they are kept like cattle in Europe; the slaves sold there being generally prisoners of war, taken from their enemies, like other booty, and perhaps some few sold by their own countrymen, in extreme want, or upon a famine; as also some as a punishment of heinous crimes: tho' many Europeans believe that parents sell their own children, men their wives and relations, which, if it ever happens, is so seldom, that it cannot justly be charged upon a whole nation, as a custom and common practice. . . .

As to the slaves, and the trade of them, whereof I have before spoke at large, it will be proper to observe here, that commonly the slaves we purchase at Fida and

Ardra, are brought down to the coast from several countries, two and three hundred leagues up the inland; where the inhabitants are lusty, strong, and very laborious people: thence it is, that tho' they are not so black and fine to look at as the North-Guinea and Gold-Coast Blacks, yet are they fitter for the American plantations, than any others; especially in the sugar islands, where they require more labour and strength than in the other colonies of Europeans, at which the Fida and Ardra slaves are found, by constant experience, to hold out much longer, and with less detriment to themselves, than the other slaves transported thither from the other abovementioned parts of Guinea. One thing is to be taken notice of by sea-faring men, that these Fida and Ardra slaves are of all the others, the most apt to revolt aboard ships, by a conspiracy carried on amongst themselves; especially such as are brought down to Fida, from very remote inland countries, who easily draw others into their plot: for being used to see men's flesh eaten in their own country, and publick markets held for that purpose, they are very full of the notion, that we buy and transport them to the same purpose; and will therefore watch all opportunities to deliver themselves, by assaulting a ship's crew, and murdering them all, if possible: whereof, we have almost every year some instances, in one European ship or other, that is filled with slaves.

The African Slave Experience: Olaudah Equiano

Most slaves, needless to say, had no opportunity to write about their experience. Olaudah Equiano's account is unusual because of its existence, but the experience reported is not necessarily unusual. Equiano was born in a Nigerian village, Isseke, in 1745. He was kidnapped and in 1756 taken to Barbados and then to Virginia. Finally able to buy his freedom from his Quaker master, he went to England in 1767. He became active in the antislavery movement, publishing his memoirs in 1788 as a protest against the whole institution of slavery. His writings were among the first antislavery books by an ex-slave.

• • •

My father, besides many slaves, had a numerous family, of which seven lived to grow up, including myself and sister, who was the only daughter. As I was the youngest of the sons, I became, of course, the greatest favorite with my mother, and was always with her; and she used to take particular pains to form my mind. I was trained up from my earliest years in the art of war: my daily exercise was shooting and throwing javelins, and my mother adorned me with emblems, after the manner of our greatest

From *The Interesting Narrative of the Life of Olaudah Equiano*, ed. Robert J. Allison (Boston: Bedford Books, 1995), 46–58. (Follows the first American printing [New York, 1791]). Includes modernized spelling.

warriors. In this way I grew up till I had turned the age of eleven, when an end was put to my happiness in the following manner. . . .

One day, when all our people were gone out to their works as usual, and only I and my dear sister were left to mind the house, two men and a woman got over our walls, and in a moment seized us both, and, without giving us time to cry out, or make resistance, they stopped our mouths, and ran off with us into the nearest wood. Here they tied our hands, and continued to carry us as far as they could, till night came on, when we reached a small house, where the robbers halted for refreshment, and spent the night. We were then unbound, but were unable to take any food; and, being quite overpowered by fatigue and grief, our only relief was some sleep, which allayed our misfortune for a short time. The next morning we left the house, and continued travelling all the day. For a long time we had kept the woods, but at last we came into a road which I believed I knew. I had now some hopes of being delivered; for we had advanced but a little way before I discovered some people at a distance, on which I began to cry out for their assistance; but my cries had no other effect than to make them tie me faster and stop my mouth, and then they put me into a large sack. They also stopped my sister's mouth, and tied her hands; and in this manner we proceeded till we were out of sight of these people. When we went to rest the following night, they offered us some victuals, but we refused it; and the only comfort we had was in being in one another's arms all that night, and bathing each other with our tears. But alas! we were soon deprived of even the small comfort of weeping together.

The next day proved a day of greater sorrow than I had yet experienced; for my sister and I were then separated, while we lay clasped in each other's arms. It was in vain that we besought them not to part us; she was torn from me, and immediately carried away, while I was left in a state of distraction not to be described.

From the time I left my own nation, I always found somebody that understood me till I came to the sea coast. The languages of different nations did not totally differ, nor were they so copious as those of the Europeans, particularly the English. They were therefore easily learned; and, while I was journeying thus through Africa, I acquired two or three different tongues. . . .

The first object which saluted my eyes when I arrived on the coast, was the sea, and a slave ship, which was then riding at anchor, and waiting for its cargo. These filled me with astonishment, which was soon converted into terror, when I was carried on board. I was immediately handled, and tossed up to see if I were sound, by some of the crew; and I was now persuaded that I had gotten into a world of bad spirits, and that they were going to kill me. Their complexions, too, differing so much from ours, their long hair, and the language they spoke (which was very different from any I had ever heard), united to confirm me in this belief. Indeed, such were the horrors of my views and fears at the moment, that, if ten thousand worlds had been my own, I would have freely parted with them all to have exchanged my condition with that of the meanest slave in my own country. When I looked round the ship too, and saw a large furnace of copper boiling, and a multitude of black people of every description chained together, every one of their countenances expressing dejection and sorrow, I no longer doubted of my fate; and, quite overpowered with horror and anguish, I fell motionless on the deck and fainted. When I recovered a little, I found some black people about me, who I believed were some of those who had brought me on board, and had been receiving their pay; they talked to me in order to cheer me, but all in vain. I asked them if we were not to be eaten by those white men with horrible looks, red faces, and long hair. They told me I was not. . . .

I now saw myself deprived of all chance of returning to my native country, or even the least glimpse of hope of gaining the shore, which I now considered as friendly; and I even wished for my former slavery in preference to my present situation, which was filled with horrors of every kind, still heightened by my ignorance of what I was to undergo. I was not long suffered to indulge my grief; I was soon put down under the decks, and there I received such a salutation in my nostrils as I had never experienced in my life: so that, with the loathsomeness of the stench, and crying together, I became so sick and low that I was not able to eat, nor had I the least desire to taste anything. I now wished for the last friend, death, to relieve me; but soon, to my grief, two of the white men offered me eatables; and, on my refusing to eat, one of them held me fast by the hands, and laid me across, I think, the windlass, and tied my feet, while the other flogged me severely. I had never experienced anything of this kind before, and, although not being used to the water, I naturally feared that element the first time I saw it, yet, nevertheless, could I have got over the nettings, I would have jumped over the side, but I could not; and besides, the crew used to watch us very closely who were not chained down to the decks, lest we should leap into the water; and I have seen some of these poor African prisoners most severely cut, for attempting to do so, and hourly whipped for not eating. This indeed was often the case with myself.

In a little time after, amongst the poor chained men, I found some of my own nation, which in a small degree gave ease to my mind. I inquired of these what was to be done with us? They gave me to understand, we were to be carried to these white people's country to work for them. I then was a little revived, and thought, if it were no worse than working, my situation was not so desperate; but still I feared I should be put to death, the white people looked and acted, as I thought, in so savage a manner; for I had never seen among any people such instances of brutal cruelty; and this not only shown towards us blacks, but also to some of the whites themselves. One white man in particular I saw, when we were permitted to be on deck, flogged so unmercifully with a large rope near the foremast, that he died in consequence of it; and they tossed him over the side as they would have done a brute. This made me fear these people the more; and I expected nothing less than to be treated in the same manner. I could not help expressing my fears and apprehensions to some of my countrymen; I asked them if these people had no country, but lived in this hollow place (the ship)?

They told me they did not, but came from a distant one. "Then," said I, "how comes it in all our country we never heard of them?" They told me because they lived so very far off. . . . I therefore wished much to be [away] from . . . them, for I expected they would sacrifice me; but my wishes were vain—for we were so quartered that it was impossible for any of us to make our escape. . . .

At last, when the ship we were in, had got in all her cargo, they made ready with many fearful noises, and we were all put under deck, so that we could not see how they managed the vessel. But this disappointment was the least of my sorrow. The stench of the hold while we were on the coast was so intolerably loathsome, that it was dangerous to remain there for any time, and some of us had been permitted to stay on the deck for the fresh air; but now that the whole ship's cargo were confined together, it became absolutely pestilential. The closeness of the place, and the heat of the climate, added to the number in the ship, which was so crowded that each had scarcely room to turn himself, almost suffocated us. This produced copious perspirations, so that the air soon became unfit for respiration, from a variety of loathsome smells, and brought on a sickness among the slaves, of which many died—thus falling victims to the improvident avarice, as I may call it, of their purchasers. This wretched situation was again aggravated by the galling of the chains, now became insupportable, and the filth of the necessary tubs, into which the children often fell, and were almost suffocated. The shrieks of the women, and the groans of the dying, rendered the whole a scene of horror almost inconceivable. Happily perhaps, for myself, I was soon reduced so low here that it was thought necessary to keep me almost always on deck; and from my extreme youth I was not put in fetters. In this situation I expected every hour to share the fate of my companions, some of whom were almost daily brought upon deck at the point of death, which I began to hope would soon put an end to my miseries. Often did I think many of the inhabitants of the deep much more happy than myself. I envied them the freedom they enjoyed, and as often wished I could change my condition for theirs. Every circumstance I met with, served only to render my state more painful, and heightened my apprehensions, and my opinion of the cruelty of the whites.

One day they had taken a number of fishes; and when they had killed and satisfied themselves with as many as they thought fit, to our astonishment who were on deck, rather than give any of them to us to eat, as we expected, they tossed the remaining fish into the sea again, although we begged and prayed for some as well as we could, but in vain; and some of my countrymen, being pressed by hunger, took an opportunity, when they thought no one saw them, of trying to get a little privately; but they were discovered, and the attempt procured them some very severe floggings.

One day, when we had a smooth sea and moderate wind, two of my wearied countrymen who were chained together (I was near them at the time), preferring death to such a life of misery, somehow made through the nettings and jumped into the sea; immediately, another quite dejected fellow, who, on account of his illness, was suffered to be out of irons, also followed their example; and I believe many more would very soon have done the same, if they had not been prevented by the ship's crew, who were instantly alarmed. . . .

At last we came in sight of the island of Barbados, at which the whites on board gave a great shout, and made many signs of joy to us. We did not know what to think of this; but as the vessel drew nearer, we plainly saw the harbor, and other ships of different kinds of sizes, and we soon anchored amongst them, off Bridgetown. Many merchants and planters now came on board, though it was in the evening. They put us in separate parcels, and examined us attentively. They also made us jump, and pointed to the land, signifying we were to go there. We thought by this, we should be eaten by these ugly men, as they appeared to us; and, when soon after we were all put down under the deck again, there was much dread and trembling among us, and nothing but bitter cries to be heard all the night from these apprehensions, insomuch, that at last the white people got some old slaves from the land to pacify us. They told us we were not to be eaten, but to work, and were soon to go on land, where we should see many of our country people. This report eased us much. And sure enough, soon after we were landed, there came to us Africans of all languages.

We were conducted immediately to the merchant's yard, where we were all pent up together, like so many sheep in a fold, without regard to sex or age. As every object was new to me, everything I saw filled me with surprise. What struck me first, was, that the houses were built with bricks and stories, and in every other respect different from those I had seen in Africa; but I was still more astonished on seeing people on horseback. I did not know what this could mean; and, indeed, I thought these people were full of nothing but magical arts. While I was in this astonishment, one of my fellow prisoners spoke to a countryman of his, about the horses, who said they were the same kind they had in their country. I understood them, though they were from a distant part of Africa; and I thought it odd I had not seen any horses there; but afterwards, when I came to converse with different Africans, I found they had many horses amongst them, and much larger than those I then saw.

We were not many days in the merchant's custody, before we were sold after their usual manner, which is this: On a signal given (as the beat of a drum), the buyers rush at once into the yard where the slaves are confined, and make choice of that parcel they like best. The noise and clamor with which this is attended, and the eagerness visible in the countenances of the buyers, serve not a little to increase the apprehension of terrified Africans, who may well be supposed to consider them as the ministers of that destruction to which they think themselves devoted. In this manner, without scruple, are relations and friends separated, most of them never to see each other again.

I remember, in the vessel in which I was brought over, in the men's apartment, there were several brothers, who, in the sale, were sold in different lots; and it was very moving on this occasion, to see and hear their cries at parting. O, ye nominal Christians! might not an African ask you—Learned you this from your God, who says unto you, Do unto all men as you would men should do unto you? Is it not enough that we are torn from our country and friends, to toil for your luxury and lust of gain? Must every tender feeling be likewise sacrificed to your avarice? Are the dearest friends and relations, now rendered more dear by their separation from their kindred, still to be parted from each other, and thus prevented from cheering the gloom of slavery, with the small comfort of being together, and mingling their sufferings and sorrows? Why are parents to lose their children, brothers their sisters, or husbands their wives? Surely, this is a new refinement in cruelty, which, while it has no advantage to atone for it, thus aggravates distress, and adds fresh horrors even to the wretchedness of slavery.

CHAPTER 18

THE SCIENTIFIC REVOLUTION AND GLOBAL IMPACT

During the seventeenth century, major scientific discoveries occurred in Western Europe, along with increasingly precise statements of the general scientific method. Western science built on earlier contacts, particularly with Arab science, but now it pressed further. Some discoveries provided Europeans with an understanding scientists in other societies had assumed for some time—for example, that the earth is not the center of the universe. Others provided brand new knowledge. Along with the specific findings came an excitement about science, a belief (among some) that science should serve as the centerpiece for all knowledge—and these features had never before developed in any culture, despite important scientific traditions dating back many centuries.

The scientific revolution, and the disputes it roused, particularly with religious authorities, quickly had major impact within Europe. Religion declined, though it hardly disappeared. Scientific approaches began to be applied to social topics, as well as topics in the physical universe. New relationships between science and technological innovation began to develop. Much of this extension occurred during the eighteenth century, in the Enlightenment.

Ultimately, Western science would spread widely, and indeed many societies would begin to contribute to modern scientific work. During the early modern period, however, reactions were somewhat more mixed and tentative. The Ottoman Empire, for example, with a proud scientific tradition of its own, hesitated to import much Western science. Japan, fairly isolated culturally during the seventeenth century, began to allow translations of Western scientific work after about 1720; the Japanese encountered this work through their trading contacts with the Dutch. China, again with an important scientific tradition of its own, maintained some contact with Western discoveries but would not begin to incorporate them thoroughly until the late nineteenth century. Russia (see chapter 19) by the eighteenth century tried actively to import new kinds of scientific training.

The documents that follow highlight some of the key features of the scientific revolution itself. They also allow consideration of several different reactions, where comparison becomes essential. They help explain why the new science, though Western in origin, would ultimately spur global changes in intellectual life and in education.

Questions

1. How did the new science relate to established religion in Western Europe? How did scientists seek to deal with religious objections?
2. What kind of broader intellectual attitudes did the scientific revolution encourage?
3. What was new about the Enlightenment idea of progress?
4. What advantages did Japanese intellectuals begin to see in Western science? How did this science seem to relate to their own traditions?
5. Why did many Ottoman officials hesitate to embrace Western science?
6. What was the early modern Chinese interaction with Western science? Why did it not immediately lead to broader incorporation of modern science?
7. Why did some societies open up to Western science earlier than others?

For Further Discussion

1. How did Western science affect interregional cultural contacts? How would it affect Western attitudes toward other parts of the world?
2. Why might Russia or Japan take an earlier interest in Western science than China or the Ottoman empire?
3. To what extent has modern science led to religious decline in world history during the past three centuries?

Galileo

Galileo, an Italian scientist of the early seventeenth century, made major discoveries about gravity and about planetary motion. He also suggested some of the intellectual style that could accompany the new science. His clashes with the Church ultimately landed him in prison, though in fairly luxurious conditions. The following letter was written in 1617.

• • •

GALILEO'S LETTER TO THE GRAND DUCHESS OF TUSCANY

To the Most Serene Grand Duchess Mother:

Some years ago, as Your Serene Highness well knows, I discovered in the heavens many things that had not been seen before our own age. The novelty of these things, as well as some consequences which followed from them in

From Modern History Sourcebook, http://www.fordham.edu/halsall/mod/galileo-tuscany.html.

contradiction to the physical notions commonly held among academic philosophers, stirred up against me no small number of professors—as if I had placed these things in the sky with my own hands in order to upset nature and overturn the sciences. They seemed to forget that the increase of known truths stimulates the investigation, establishment, and growth of the arts; not their diminution or destruction.

Showing a greater fondness for their own opinions than for truth they sought to deny and disprove the new things which, if they had cared to look for themselves, their own senses would have demonstrated to them. To this end they hurled various charges and published numerous writings filled with vain arguments, and they made the grave mistake of sprinkling these with passages taken from places in the Bible which they had failed to understand properly, and which were ill-suited to their purposes.

These men would perhaps not have fallen into such error had they but paid attention to a most useful doctrine of St. Augustine's, relative to our making positive statements about things which are obscure and hard to understand by means of reason alone. Speaking of a certain physical conclusion about the heavenly bodies, he wrote: "Now keeping always our respect for moderation in grave piety, we ought not to believe anything inadvisedly on a dubious point, lest in favor to our error we conceive a prejudice against something that truth hereafter may reveal to be not contrary in any way to the sacred books of either the Old or the New Testament."

Well, the passage of time has revealed to everyone the truths that I previously set forth; and, together with the truth of the facts, there has come to light the great difference in attitude between those who simply and dispassionately refused to admit the discoveries to be true, and those who combined with their incredulity some reckless passion of their own. Men who were well grounded in astronomical and physical science were persuaded as soon as they received my first message. There were others who denied them or remained in doubt only because of their novel and unexpected character, and because they had not yet had the opportunity to see for themselves. These men have by degrees come to be satisfied. But some, besides allegiance to their original error, possess I know not what fanciful interest in remaining hostile not so much toward the things in question as toward their discoverer. No longer being able to deny them, these men now take refuge in obstinate silence, but being more than ever exasperated by that which has pacified and quieted other men, they divert their thoughts to other fancies and seek new ways to damage me.

I should pay no more attention to them than to those who previously contradicted me—at whom I always laugh, being assured of the eventual outcome—were it not that in their new calumnies and persecutions I perceive that they do not stop at proving themselves more learned than I am (a claim which I scarcely contest), but go so far as to cast against me the imputations of crimes which must be, and are, more abhorrent to me than death itself. I cannot remain satisfied merely to know that the injustice of this is recognized by those who are acquainted with these men and with me, as perhaps it is not known to others.

Persisting in their original resolve to destroy me and everything mine by any means they can think of, these men are aware of my views in astronomy and philosophy. They know that as to the arrangement of the parts of the universe, I hold the sun to be situated motionless in the center of the revolution of the celestial orbs while the earth revolves about the sun. They know also that I support this position not only by refuting the arguments of Ptolemy and Aristotle, but by producing many counter-arguments; in particular, some which relate to physical effects whose causes can perhaps be assigned in no other way. In addition there are astronomical arguments derived from many things in my new celestial discoveries that plainly confute the Ptolemaic system [the system that held the earth to be center of the universe] while admirably agreeing with and confirming the contrary hypothesis. Possibly because they are disturbed by the known truth of other propositions of mine which differ from those commonly held, and therefore mistrusting their defense so long as they confine themselves to the field of philosophy, these men have resolved to fabricate a shield for their fallacies out of the mantle of pretended religion and the authority of the Bible. These they apply with little judgment to the refutation of arguments that they do not understand and have not even listened to. . . .

CONDORCET AND THE ENLIGHTENMENT IDEA OF PROGRESS

Condorcet was a French aristocrat and an eager participant in the Enlightenment. His *Sketch for a Historical Picture of the Progress of the Human Mind* (1793) extended the implications of the new science. Ironically, Condorcet was arrested during the radical phase of the French Revolution and committed suicide rather than wait for execution.

• • •

No one has ever believed that the human mind could exhaust all the facts of nature, all the refinements of measuring and analyzing these facts, the interrelationship of objects, and all the possible combinations of ideas. . . .

But because, as the number of facts known increases, man learns to classify them, to reduce them to more general terms; because the instruments and the methods of

observation and exact measurement are at the same time reaching a new precision; . . .
the truths whose discovery has cost the most effort, which at first could be grasped
only by men capable of profound thought, are soon carried further and proved by
methods that are no longer beyond the reach of ordinary intelligence. If the methods
that lead to new combinations are exhausted, if their application to problems not yet
solved requires labors that exceed the time or the capacity of scholars, soon more general methods, simpler means, come to open a new avenue for genius. . . .

•   •   •

Applying these general reflections to the different sciences, we shall give, for each,
examples of their successive improvement that will leave no doubt as to the certainty of the future improvements we can expect. We shall indicate particularly the
most likely and most imminent progress in those sciences that are now commonly
believed to be almost exhausted. We shall point out how more universal education
in each country, by giving more people the elementary knowledge that can inspire
them with a taste for more advanced study and give them the capacity for making
progress in it, can add to such hopes; how [these hopes] increase even more, if a
more general prosperity permits a greater number of individuals to pursue studies,
since at present, in the most enlightened countries, hardly a fiftieth part of those
men to whom nature has given talent receive the education necessary to make use
of their talents; and that, therefore, the number of men destined to push back the
frontiers of the sciences by their discoveries will grow in the same proportion [as
universal education increases].

We shall show how this equality of education, and the equality that will arise between nations, will speed up the advances of those sciences whose progress depends
on observations repeated in greater number over a larger area; all that mineralogy,
botany, zoology, meteorology can be expected to gain thereby; and finally what an
enormous disproportion exists, in these sciences, between the weakness of the means
that nevertheless have led us to so many useful and important truths, and the great
scope of the means men will in the future be able to deploy.

•   •   •

If we now turn to the mechanical arts, we shall see that their progress can have no
other limit than the reach of the scientific theories on which they depend; that the
methods of these arts are capable of the same improvement, the same simplifications
as methods in the sciences. Instruments, machines, looms will increasingly supplement the strength and skill of men; will augment at the same time the perfection and
the precision of manufactures by lessening both the time and the labor needed to produce them. Then the obstacles that still impede this progress will disappear, and along
with them accidents that will become preventable and unhealthy conditions in general, whether owing to work, or habits, or climate.

Then a smaller and smaller area of land will be able to produce commodities of greater use or higher value; wider enjoyment will be obtained with less outlay; the same manufacturing output will call for less expenditure of raw materials or will be more durable. For each kind of soil people will know how to choose, from among crops that satisfy the same kind of need, those crops that are most versatile, those that satisfy [the needs of a greater mass of users, requiring less labor and less real consumption. Thus, without any sacrifice, the methods of conservation and of economy in consumption will follow the progress of the art of producing the various commodities, preparing them and turning them into manufactures.

Thus not only will the same amount of land be able to feed more people; but each of them, with less labor, will be employed more productively and will be able to satisfy his needs better.

• • •

But in this progress of industry and prosperity . . . each generation . . . is destined to fuller enjoyment; and hence, as a consequence of the physical constitution of the human species, to an increase of the population. Will there not come a time when . . . the increase in population surpassing its means of subsistence, the result would necessarily be—if not a continuous decline in wellbeing and number of people, a truly retrograde movement—at least a kind of oscillation between good and bad? Would not such oscillations in societies that have reached this point be an ever-present cause of more or less periodic suffering? Would this not mark the limit beyond which all improvement would become impossible . . . ?

No one will fail to see how far removed from us this time is; but will we reach it one day. It is impossible to speak for or against an event that will occur only at a time when the human species will necessarily have acquired knowledge that we cannot even imagine. And who, in fact, would dare to predict what the art of converting the elements to our use may one day become?

But supposing a limit were reached, nothing terrible would happen, regarding either the happiness or the indefinite perfectibility of mankind. We must also suppose that before that time, the progress of reason will have gone hand in hand with progress in the arts and sciences; that the ridiculous prejudices of superstition will no longer cover morality with an austerity that corrupts and degrades it instead of purifying and elevating it. Men will know then that if they have obligations to beings who do not yet exist, these obligations do not consist in giving life, but in giving happiness. Their object is the general welfare of the human species, of the society in which people live, of the family to which they belong and not the puerile idea of filling the earth with useless and unhappy beings. The possible quantity of the means of subsistence could therefore have a limit, and consequently so could the attainable level of population, without resulting in the destruction . . . of part of the living.

Among the progress of the human mind that is most important for human happiness, we must count the entire destruction of the prejudices that have established inequality between the sexes, fatal even to the sex it favors. One would look in vain for reasons to justify it, by differences in physical constitution, intelligence, moral sensibility. This inequality has no other source but the abuse of power, and men have tried in vain to excuse it by sophisms.

We shall show how much the destruction of customs authorized by this prejudice, of the laws it has dictated, can contribute to the greater happiness of families, and to the spread of the domestic virtues, the first foundation of all other virtues. It will promote the progress of education, because [education] will be extended to both sexes more equally, and because education cannot become general, even among men, without the cooperation of mothers.

• • •

All these causes of the improvement of the human species, all these means that assure it, will by their nature act continuously and acquire a constantly growing momentum. We have explained the proofs of this . . . ; we could therefore already conclude that the perfectibility of man is unlimited, even though, up to now, we have only supposed him endowed with the same natural faculties and organization. What then would be the certainty and extent of our hopes if we could believe that these natural faculties themselves and this organization are also susceptible of improvement? This is the last question remaining for us to examine.

The organic perfectibility or degeneration of races in plants and animals may be regarded as one of the general laws of nature.

This law extends to the human species; and certainly no one will doubt that progress in medical conservation [of life], in the use of healthier food and housing, a way of living that would develop strength through exercise without impairing it by excess, and finally the destruction of the two most active causes of degradation—misery and too great wealth—will prolong the extent of life and assure people more constant health as well as a more robust constitution. We feel that the progress of preventive medicine as a preservative, made more effective by the progress of reason and social order, will eventually banish communicable or contagious illnesses and those diseases in general that originate in climate, food, and the nature of work. It would not be difficult to prove that this hope should extend to almost all other diseases, whose more remote causes will eventually be recognized. Would it be absurd now to suppose that the improvement of the human race should be regarded as capable of unlimited progress? That a time will come when death would result only from extraordinary accidents or the more and more gradual wearing out of vitality, and that, finally, the duration of the average interval between birth and wearing out has itself no specific limit whatsoever? No doubt man will not become immortal, but cannot the span constantly increase between the moment he begins to live and the time when naturally, without illness or accident, he finds life a burden?

FATHER DE HALDE AND SCIENCE IN CHINA

Father de Halde was a Catholic missionary who discussed science at the court of the Qing emperor, in the late seventeenth century. His comments date from around 1680. Catholic missionaries had long sought to interest Chinese officials in science and in specific technologies like Western clocks, as a means of winning opportunities for direct missionary work. Is this account an accurate representation of Chinese reactions?

• • •

This nation, naturally proud, looked upon themselves as the most learned in the world, and they enjoyed this reputation without disturbance because they were acquainted with no other people more knowing than themselves; but they were undeceived by the ingenuity of the missionaries who appeared at court. The proof which they gave of their capacity served greatly to authorize their ministry and to gain esteem for the religion which they preached. The late emperor, Kang xi, whose chief delight was to acquire knowledge, was never weary of seeing or hearing them. On the other hand, the Jesuits, perceiving how necessary the protection of this great prince was to the progress of the Gospel, omitted nothing that might excite his curiosity and satisfy this natural relish for the sciences.

They gave him an insight into optics by making him a present of a semi-cylinder of a light kind of wood. In the middle of its axis was placed a convex glass, which, being turned toward any object, painted the image within the tube to a great nicety. The emperor was greatly pleased with so unusual a sight, and desired to have a machine made in his garden at Peking, wherein, without being seen himself, he might see everything that passed in the streets and neighboring places. They prepared for this purpose an object-glass of much greater diameter, and made in the thickest garden wall a great window in the shape of a pyramid, the basis of which was towards the garden, and the point toward the street. At the point they fixed the glass eye over against the place where there was the greatest concourse of people; at the basis was made a large closet, shut up close to all sides and very dark. It was there the emperor came with his queens to observe the lively images of everything that passed in the street; and this sight pleased him extremely; but it charmed the princesses a great deal more, who could not otherwise behold this spectacle, the custom of China not allowing them to go out of the palace. [Another missionary] gave another wonderful spectacle by his skill in optics in the Jesuits' Garden at Peking, which greatly astonished the grandees of the emperor. They made upon four walls four human figures, every one being of the same length as

From Eva March Tappan, ed., *The World's Story. Vol. 1, China, Japan, and the Islands of the Pacific* (Boston: Houghton Mifflin, 1914), 155–62.

the wall, which was fifty feet. As he had perfectly observed the optic rules, there was nothing seen on the front but mountains, forests, chases, and other things of this nature; but at a certain point they perceived the figure of a man well made and well-proportioned. The emperor honored the Jesuits' house with his presence, and beheld these figures a long time with admiration. The grandees and principal mandarins, who came in crowds, were equally surprised; but that which struck them most was to see the figures so regular and so exact upon irregular walls that in several places had large windows and doors. In catoptrics they presented the emperor with all sorts of telescopes, as well for astronomical observations as for taking great and small distances upon the earth; and likewise glasses for diminishing, magnifying, and multiplying. Among other things, they presented him with a tube made like a prism having eight sides, which being placed parallel with the horizon, presented eight different scenes so lifelike that they might be mistaken for the objects themselves; this being joined to the variety of painting entertained the emperor a long time. They likewise presented another tube wherein was a polygon glass, which by its different facets collected into one image several parts of different objects, insomuch that instead of a landscape, woods, flocks, and a hundred other things represented in a picture, there was seen distinctly a human face or some other figure very exact. There was also another machine which contained a lighted lamp, the light of which came through a tube, at the end whereof was a convex glass, near which several small pieces of glass painted with divers figures were made to slide. These figures were seen upon the opposite wall of a size proportioned to the size of the wall. This spectacle in the nighttime or in a very dark place frightened those who were ignorant of the artifice as much as it pleased those who were acquainted with it. [The missionaries also] offered the emperor a machine the principal parts of which were only four notched wheels and an iron grapple. With the help of this machine, a child raised several thousand weight without difficulty, and stood firm against the efforts of twenty strong men. With respect to hydrostatics, they made for the emperor pumps, canals, siphons, wheels, and several other machines proper to raise water out of the river, called the ten thousand springs, and to carry it into the ground belonging to the emperor's demesnes, as he had desired. [They] also made a present to the emperor of a hydraulic machine of a new type. There appeared in it a clock that went very true, the motions of the heavens, and an accurate alarm. The pneumatic machines also did no less excite the emperor's curiosity. They caused a wagon to be made of light wood about two feet long. In the middle of it they placed a brazen vessel full of live coals, and upon that an aeolipile, the wind of which came through a little pipe upon a sort of wheel made like the sails of a windmill. This little wheel turned another with an axle-tree, and by that means set the wagon in motion for two hours together; but lest room should be wanting to proceed constantly forward, it was contrived to move circularly in the following manner: To the axle-tree of the two hind wheels was fixed a small beam, and at the end of this beam another axle-tree, which went through the center of another wheel somewhat larger than the rest.

They did not fail afterwards to comply with the emperor's taste for great quantities of curious things were sent out of Europe by Christian princes, who had the conversion of this great empire at heart, insomuch that the emperor's cabinet was soon filled with various rarities, especially clocks of the most recently invented and most curious workmanship.

They also presented the emperor with thermometers to show the several degrees of heat and cold, to which was added a very nice hygrometer to discover the several degrees of moisture and dryness. It was a barrel of a large diameter, suspended by a thick string made of catgut of a proper length and parallel to the horizon. The least change in the air contracts or relaxes the string, and causes the barrel to turn sometimes to the right, sometimes to the left, and stretches or loosens to the right or left upon the circumference of the barrel a small string which draws a little pendulum and marks the several degrees of humidity on one, and on the other those of dryness.

All these different inventions of human wit, till then unknown to the Chinese, abated something of their natural pride and taught them not to have too contemptible an opinion of foreigners; nay, it so far altered their way of thinking that they began to look upon Europeans as their masters.

SCIENCE IN THE OTTOMAN EMPIRE: LADY MONTAGUE

Lady Montague was wife of the British ambassador to the Ottoman Empire, who wrote in the early eighteenth century (her husband began his service in 1717). She here describes a system of inoculation against smallpox, which she used on her own children. This system was extended by Edward Jenner in Europe later in the eighteenth century, through use of a serum cultivated in cattle.

• • •

A propos of distempers, I am going to tell you a thing that will make you wish yourself here. The small-pox, so fatal, and so general amongst us, is here entirely harmless, by the invention of engrafting, which is the term they give it. There is a set of old women, who make it their business to perform the operation, every autumn, in the month of September, when the great heat is abated. People send to one another to know if any of their family has a mind to have the small-pox; they make parties for this purpose, and when they are met (commonly fifteen or sixteen together) the old woman comes with a nut-shell full of the matter of the best sort of small-pox, and asks what vein you please to have opened. She immediately rips open that you offer to her, with a large needle (which give you no more pain that a common scratch) and puts into the vein as much matter as can lie upon the head of her needle, and after that, binds up the little wound with a hollow bit of shell, and in this matter opens up four or five veins. The Grecians have commonly the superstition of opening one in the middle of the forehead, one in each arm, and one on the breast, to mark the sign of the cross; but this has a very ill effect, all these wounds leaving little scars, and is not done by those that are not superstitious, who cause to have them in the legs, or that part of the arm that is concealed. The children or young patients play together all the rest of the day, and are in perfect health to the eighth. Then the fever begins to seize them, and they keep their beds two days, very seldom three. They have very rarely above twenty or thirty in their faces, which never mark, and in eight days time they are as well as before their illness. Where they were wounded, there remains running sores during the distemper, which I don't doubt is a great relief to it. Every year, thousands undergo this operation, and the French Ambassador says pleasantly, that they take the smallpox here by way of diversion, as they take the waters in other countries. There is no example of any one that had dies of it, and you may believe I am well satisfied of the safety of this experiment, since I intend to try it on my dear little son. I am patriot enough to take the pains to bring this useful invention into fashion in England, and I should not fail to write to some of our doctors very particularly about it, if I knew any one of them that I thought had virtue enough to destroy such a considerable branch of their revenue, for the good of mankind. But that distemper is too beneficial to them, not to expose to all their resentment, the hardy weight that should undertake to put an end to it. Perhaps if I live to return, I may, however, have courage to war with them. Upon this occasion, admire the heroism in the heart of your friend.

REACTION IN JAPAN: SUGITA GENPAKU

Sugita Genpaku, 1733–1817, was a member of the so-called Dutch school, because of his involvement in translations from Dutch scientific works.

• • •

The corpse of the criminal was that of an old woman of about 50 years, nicknamed Aocha Bab, born in Kyoto. I was an old butcher who made the dissection. We had been promised an *eda* named Toramatsu, known for his skill in dissection, but because he was sick his grandfather came instead. He was ninety years old, but healthy, and he told us he had been doing this since his youth. According to him up until this time people had left it up to him, and he had not shown them where the lungs, kidneys, and other organs were. They would pretend that they had studied the internal structure of the body directly. But the parts naturally weren't labeled, and they had to be satisfied with the way he pointed them out. He knew where everything was, but he

From Marius Jansen, *The Making of Modern Japan* (Cambridge, Mass.: Harvard University Press, 2002), 213.

had not learned their proper names. . . . Some of the things turned out to be arteries, veins, and suprarenal bodies according to our [Dutch] anatomical tables. . . . We found that the structure of the lungs and liver and the position and shape of the stomach were quite different from what we had believed according to old Chinese theory. . . . I suggested that we decipher the *Tafel Anatomica* (the book they were using) without the aid of the interpreters in Nagasaki, and translate it into Japanese. . . . the next day we met and began. . . . Gradually we got so we could decipher ten lines or more a day. After two or three years of hard study everything became clear to us; the joy of it was as the chewing of sweet sugar cane.

CHAPTER 19

THE GUNPOWDER EMPIRES

One of the great developments of the early modern period was the emergence of new land-based empires in various parts of Asia and Eastern Europe. These are sometimes called gunpowder empires because their conquests depended in part on the use of cannon. They arose at the same time that Western Europeans were constructing overseas empires, also using superior force. Interestingly, Western Europeans were often considerably awed by the Asian empires, whose administrative personnel, armies, and cities far surpassed those available in the national monarchies back home.

The documents that follow deal with three new empires—the Ottoman, Mughal, and Russian. They also all involve relationships with the West. Two documents come from Western observers, noting the strengths though also some of the constraints of the great empires. A cluster of documents from Russia (which was not so highly esteemed by Western observers) deal with efforts to use Western contacts to effect internal reforms around 1700. Russia's westernization, though highly selective, was in marked contrast to the lack of interest of many Asian leaders in Western example.

The empires discussed here were dazzling at the time, during most of the early modern period, clearly demonstrating superior military and political capacity. Two of them, however, would ultimately decline: the Mughal began to loosen its grip by the eighteenth century, the Ottoman by the nineteenth. And in both cases increasing European intrusion would result. It is vital to remember the achievements that preceded decline and that could have continuing impact in the regions. The same applies to Russia, which would encounter new challenges as a multinational empire at the end of the twentieth century though it managed to maintain vast holdings.

Questions

1. Why were European observers awed by the Ottoman and Mughal Empires? Were the reasons similar or different in the two cases?
2. Why might European observers exaggerate strengths in the empires?
3. Do the comments suggest why the Mughal Empire declined much sooner than the Ottoman?

4. In what ways was Russia more interested in active contacts with the West than the Ottoman or Mughal Empires? Why was this the case?

5. What did Peter the Great seek to westernize, and what did he leave untouched?

For Further Discussion

1. What were some significant contributions of the Ottoman and Mughal Empires to their regions, the Middle East and India, respectively?

2. Why did the Russian Empire last longer than the other two empires?

3. What were some characteristic weaknesses in the gunpowder empires?

THE OTTOMAN EMPIRE: BUSBECQ

Ogier Chiselin be Busbecq, of Flemish origin (in what is now Belgium), was an ambassador from the Holy Roman Empire to the Ottoman sultan, in Constantinople, from 1555 to 1562. His letters provide important data on the Ottomans. He was, however, eager to see reform in the Holy Roman Empire, and actively shaped his observations of the Ottoman Empire to encourage change back home.

• • •

At Buda I made my first acquaintance with the Janissaries; this is the name by which the Turks call the infantry of the royal guard. The Turkish state has 12,000 of these troops when the corps is at its full strength. They are scattered through every part of the empire, either to garrison the forts against the enemy, or to protect the Christians and Jews from the violence of the mob. There is no district with any considerable amount of population, no borough or city, which has not a detachment of Janissaries to protect the Christians, Jews, and other helpless people from outrage and wrong.

The Turkish monarch going to war takes with him over 400 camels and nearly as many baggage mules, of which a great part are loaded with rice and other kinds of grain. These mules and camels also serve to carry tents and armour, and likewise tools and munitions for the campaign. . . . The invading army carefully abstains from encroaching on its [supplies] at the outset; as they are well aware that when the season for campaigning draws to a close, they will have to retreat over districts wasted by the enemy, or scraped bare by countless hordes of men and droves of hungry animals, as if they had been devastated by locusts; accordingly they reserve their stores as much as possible for this emergency.

From C. T. Forster and F. H. Daniel, eds., *The Life and Letters of Ogier Chiselin de Busbecq*, vol. 1 (London: Kegan Paul, 1881) 86–88, 219–22.

From this you will see that it is the patience, self-denial and thrift of the Turkish soldier that enable him to face the most trying circumstances and come safely out of the dangers that surround him. What a contrast to our men! Christian soldiers on a campaign refuse to put up with their ordinary food, and call for thrushes, beccaficos [a small bird esteemed a dainty, as it feeds on figs and grapes], and suchlike dainty dishes! . . . It makes me shudder to think of what the result of a struggle between such different systems must be; one of us must prevail and the other be destroyed, at any rate we cannot both exist in safety. On their side is the vast wealth of their empire, unimpaired resources, experience and practice in arms, a veteran solidery, and uninterrupted series of victories, readiness to endure hardships, union, order, discipline, thrift and watchfulness. On ours are found an empty exchequer, luxurious habits, exhausted resources, broken spirits, a raw and insubordinate soldiery, and greedy quarrels; there is no regard for discipline, license runs riot, the men indulge in drunkenness and debauchery, and worst of all, the enemy are accustomed to victory, we to defeat. Can we doubt what the result must be? The only obstacle is Persia, whose position on his rear forces the invader to take precautions. The fear of Persia gives us a respite, but it is only for a time.

No distinction is attached to birth among the Turks; the deference to be paid to a man is measured by the position he holds in the public service. There is no fighting for precedence; a man's place is marked out by the duties he discharges. In making his appointments the Sultan pays no regard to any pretensions on the score of wealth or rank, nor does he take into consideration recommendations or popularity, he considers each case on its own merits, and examines carefully into the character, ability, and disposition of the man whose promotion is in question. It is by merit that men rise in the service, a system which ensures that posts should only be assigned to the competent. Each man in Turkey carries in his own hand his ancestry and his position in life, which he may make or mar as he will. Those who receive the highest offices from the Sultan are for the most part the sons of shepherds or herdsmen, and so far from being ashamed of their parentage, they actually glory in it, and consider it a matter of boasting that they owe nothing to the accident of birth; for they do not believe that high qualities are either natural or hereditary, nor do they think that they can be handed down from father to son, but that they are partly the gift of God, and partly the result of good training, great industry, and unwearied zeal; arguing that high qualities do not descend from a father to his son or heir, any more than a talent for music, mathematics, or the like; and that the mind does not derive its origin from the father, so that the son should necessarily be like the father in character, or emanates from heaven, and thence infused into the human body. Among the Turks, therefore, honours, high posts, and judgeships are the rewards of great ability and good service. If a man be dishonest, or lazy, or careless, he remains at the bottom of the ladder, an object of contempt; for such qualities there are no honours in Turkey.

This is the reason that they are successful in their undertakings, that they lord it over others, and are daily extending the bounds of their empire. These are not our ideas, with us there is no opening left for merit; birth is the standard for everything; the prestige of birth is the sole key to advancement in the public service.

THE MUGHAL EMPIRE: MONSERATE AND BERNIER

Antonio Monserate was a Jesuit who visited the great Emperor Akbar's court from 1580 to 1583, at the benefit of the Mughal power. The following are excerpts from his Commentary. François Bernier, a Frenchman, was the personal physician of the Mughal emperor Aurangzeb for twelve years. He wrote the first European work dealing with racial classifications of humans, and in 1684 he published his *Travels to the Mughal Empire* to detail his experiences in India.

• • •

MONSERATE

This Prince is of a stature and type of countenance well fitted to his royal dignity, so that one could easily recognize even at first glace that he is the king. . . . His forehead is broad and open, his eyes so bright and flashing that they seem like a sea shimmering in the sunlight. . . . He creates an opportunity almost every day for any of the common people or of the nobles to see him and converse with him. It is remarkable how great an effect this courtesy and affability has in attaching to him the minds of his subjects . . . he has an acute insight, and shows much wise foresight both in avoiding dangers and in seizing favorable opportunities for carrying out his designs. . . . Unlike the palaces built by other Indian kings, his are lofty [and] their total circuit is so large that it easily embraces four great royal dwellings. . . . Not a little is added to the beauty of the palaces by charming pigeon cotes. . . . The pigeons are cared for by eunuch and servant maids. Their evolutions are controlled at will, when they are flying, by means of certain signals, just as those of a well trained soldiery. . . . It will seem little short of miraculous when I affirm that when sent out they dance, turn somersaults all together in the air, flying orderly rhythm, and return to their starting point, all at the sound of a whistle. [Akbar's] empire is wonderfully rich and fertile both for cultivation and pasture, and has a great trade both in exports and imports. . . . Indian towns appear very pleasant from afar; they are adorned with many towers and high buildings in a very beautiful manner. But when one enters them, one finds that the narrowness, aimless crookedness and ill planning of the streets deprive these cities of all beauty. . . . The common people live in lowly huts and tiny cottages, and hence if a traveler has seen one of these cities, he has seen them all.

EUROPEAN AWE AT OTHER EMPIRES

BERNIER

The Moguls have left and communicated their name to the strangers that now govern Indostan, the country of the Indians; though those that are employed in public charges and offices, and even those that are listed in the militia, be not all of the race of the Moguls, but strangers and nations gathered out of all countries, most of them Persians, some Arabians, and some Turks. For, to be esteemed a mogul it is enough to be a stranger, white of face, and a Muslim; in distinction as well to the Indians, who are brown and pagans, as to the Christians of Europe, who are called Franguis [i.e., "Ferengis" or "Franks"]. . . .

My lord, you may have seen before this, by the maps of Asia, how great every way is the extent of the empire of the Great Mogul, which is commonly called India or Indostan. I have not measured it mathematically; but to speak of it accordingly to the ordinary journeys of the country, after the rate of three whole months' march, traversing from the frontiers of the kingdom of Golconda as far as beyond Kazni near Kandahar, which is the first town of Persia, I cannot but persuade myself otherwise but that it is at least five times as far as from Paris to Lyons—that is about five hundred common leagues. . . .

In this same extent of country there are sundry nations which the Mogul is not full master of, most of them still retaining their particular sovereigns and lord that neither obey him nor pay him tribute but from constraint; many that do little, some that do nothing at all, and some also that receive tribute from him. . . .

. . . Of the like sort are more than an hundred rajahs, or considerable heathen sovereigns, dispersed through the whole empire, some near to, others remote from, Agra and Delhi; amongst whom there are about fifteen or sixteen that are very rich and puissant [several of them princes]; are so great and powerful that if they three alone should combine they would hold him [i.e. the Great Moghul] back; each of them being able in a very short time to raise and bring into the field twenty-five thousand horse, better troops than the Mogul's. These cavaliers are called rajipous, or children of the rajahs. These are men who, as I have said elsewhere, carry swords from father to son, and to whom the rajahs allot land on condition that they be always ready to appear on horseback when the rajah commands. They can endure much hardship, and they want nothing but good order and discipline to make them good soldiers. . . .

The Mogul is obliged to keep these rajas in his service for sundry reasons: the first, because the militia of the rajahs is a very good (as we said above) and because there are rajash (as was intimated also) any one of whom can bring into the field

From James Harvey Robinson, ed., *Readings in European History*, vol. 2 (Boston: Ginn, 1906), 336–38.

above twenty-five thousand men; the second, the better to bridle the other rajahs and to reduce them to reason, when they cantonize, or when they refuse to pay tribute, or when, out of fear or other cause, they will not leave their country to serve in the army when the Mogul requires it; the third, the better to nourish jealousies and keenness among them, by favoring and caressing one more than the other, which is done to that degree that they proceed to fight with one another very frequently.

THE RUSSIAN EMPIRE: PETER THE GREAT (1682–1725)

The first of the following decrees from the czar involved the creation of a Governing Senate (council), which reflected some of the changes he sought in administration and state functions. A second decree, from 1714, established so-called compulsory education for the nobles (though this was not actually fully enforceable); a related "instruction" urged selective study abroad. A 1721 decree (number 4) was designed to encourage manufacturing, but through a very distinctive means. Finally, a 1724 decree set up an academy modeled on Western associations—such as the Royal Society in England, which had been established in the seventeenth century—to encourage discussion of science. Which reforms probably had the greatest impact? Which would be most likely to encounter resistance? What groups and activities were left untouched?

• • •

The *ukaz* [decree] should be made known. We have decreed that during our absence administration of the country is to be [in the hands of] the Governing Senate [Peter then names its new members]. . . .

Each *gubernia* [region] is to send two officials to advise the Senate on judicial and legislative matters. . . .

In our absence the Senate is charged by this *ukaz* with the following:

1. To establish a just court, to deprive unjust judges of their offices and of all their property, and to administer the same treatment to all slanderers.
2. To supervise governmental expenditures throughout the country and cancel unnecessary and, above all, useless things.
3. To collect as much money as possible because money is the artery of war.
4. To recruit young noblemen for officer training, especially those who try to evade it; also to select about 1,000 educated boyars for the same purpose.
5. To reform letters of exchange and keep these in one place.
6. To take inventory of goods leased to offices or *gubernias*.
7. To farm out the salt trade in an effort to receive some profit [for the state].
8. To organize a good company and assign to it the China trade.

9. To increase trade with Persia and by all possible means to attract in great numbers Armenians [to that trade]. To organize inspectors and inform them of their responsibilities.

2. Education Decree

Send to every *gubernia* [region] some persons from mathematical schools to teach the children of the nobility—except those of freeholders and government clerks—mathematics and geometry; as a penalty [for evasion] establish a rule that no one will be allowed to marry unless he learns these [subjects]. Inform all prelates to issue no marriage certificates to those who are ordered to go to schools. . . .

The Great Sovereign has decreed: in all *gubernias* children between the ages of ten and fifteen of the nobility, of government clerks, and of lesser officials, except those of freeholders, must be taught mathematics and some geometry. Toward that end, students should be sent from mathematical schools [as teachers], several into each *gubernia*, to prelates and to renowned monasteries to establish schools. During their instruction these teachers should be given food and financial remuneration of three *altyns* and two *dengas* per day from *gubernia* revenues set aside for that purpose by personal orders of His Imperial Majesty. No fees should be collected from students. When they have mastered the material, they should then be given certificates written in their own handwriting. When the students are released they ought to pay one ruble each for their training. Without these certificates they should not be allowed to marry nor receive marriage certificates.

3. Navigation Study Abroad

1. Learn [how to draw] plans and charts and how to use the compass and other naval indicators.
2. [Learn] how to navigate a vessel in battle as well as in a simple maneuver, and learn how to use all appropriate tools and instruments; namely sails, ropes, and oars, and the like matters, on row boats and other vessels.
3. Discover as much as possible how to put ships to sea during a naval battle. Those who cannot succeed in this effort must diligently ascertain what action should taken by the vessels that do and those that do not put to sea during such a situation [naval battle]. Obtain from [foreign] naval officers written statements, bearing their signatures and seals, of how adequately you [Russian students] are prepared for [naval] duties.
4. If, upon his return, anyone wishes to receive [from the Tsar] greater favors for himself, he should learn, in addition to the above enumerated instructions, how to construct those vessels aboard which he would like to demonstrate his skills.
5. Upon his return to Moscow, every [foreign-trained Russian] should bring with him at his own expense, for which he will later be reimbursed, at least two experienced masters of naval science. They [the returnees] will be assigned soldiers, one soldier

per returnee, to teach them [what they have learned abroad]. And if they do not wish to accept soldiers they may teach their acquaintances or their own people. The treasure will pay for transportation and maintenance of soldiers. And if anyone other than soldiers learns [the art of navigation] the treasurer will pay 100 rubles for the maintenance of every such individual. . . .

4. Right of Factories to Buy Villages

Previous decrees have denied merchants the right to obtain villages. This prohibition was instituted because those people, outside their business, did not have any establishments that could be of any use to the state. Nowadays, thanks to Our decrees, as every one can see, many merchants have companies and many have succeeded in establishing new enterprises for the benefit of the state; namely: silver, copper, iron, coal and the like, as well as silk, linen, and woolen industries, many of which have begun operations. As a result, by this Our *ukaz* aimed at the increase of factories, We permit the nobility as well as merchants to freely purchase villages for these factories, with the sanction of the Mining and Manufacturing College, under one condition: that these villages be always integral parts of these factories. Consequently, neither the nobility nor merchants may sell or mortgage these villages without the factories because of pressing needs, it must be done with the permission of the Mining and Manufacturing College. And whoever violates this procedure will have his possessions confiscated.

And should someone try to establish a small factory for the sake of appearance in order to purchase a village, such an entrepreneur should not be allowed to purchase anything. The Mining and Manufacturing College should adhere to this rule very strictly. Should such a thing happen, those responsible for it should be deprived of all their movable and immovable property.

5. Founding the Academy

His Imperial Majesty decreed the establishment of an academy, wherein languages as well as other science and important arts could be taught, and where books could be translated. On January 22, [1724], during his stay in the Winter Palace, His Majesty approved the project for the Academy, and with his own hand signed a decree that stipulates that the Academy's budget of 24,912 rubles annually should come from revenues from custom dues and export-import license fees collected in the following cities: Narva, Dorpat, Pernov and Arensburg. . . .

Usually two kinds of institutions are used in organizing arts and sciences. One is known as a university; the other as an Academy or society of arts and sciences.

1. A University is an association of learned individuals who teach the young people the development of such distinguished science as theology and jurisprudence (the

legal skill), and medicine and philosophy. An Academy, on the other hand, is an association of learned and skilled people who not only know their subjects to the same degree [as their counterparts in the University] but who, in addition, improve and develop them through research and inventions. They have no obligation to teach others.

2. While the Academy consists of the same scientific disciplines and has the same members as the University, these two institutions, in other states, have no connection between themselves in training many other well-qualified people who could organize different societies. This is done to prevent interference into the activity of the Academy, whose sole task is to improve arts and science through theoretical research that would benefit professors as well as students of universities. Freed from the pressure of research, universities can concentrate on educating the young people.

3. Now that an institution aimed at the cultivation of arts and sciences is to be chartered in Russia, there is no need to follow the practice that is accepted in other states. It is essential to take into account the existing circumstances of this state [Russia], consider [the quality of Russian] teachers and students, and organize such an institution that would not only immediately increase the glory of this [Russian] state through the development of sciences, but would also, through teaching and dissemination [of knowledge], benefit the people [of Russia] in the future.

4. These two aims will not be realized if the Academy of Sciences alone is chartered, because while the Academy may try to promote and disseminate arts and sciences, these will not spread among the people. The establishment of a university will do even less, simply because there are no elementary schools, gymnasia or seminaries [in Russia], where young people could learn the fundamentals before studying more advanced subjects [at the University] to make themselves useful. It is therefore inconceivable that under these circumstances a university would be of some value [to Russia].

5. Consequently what is needed most [in Russia] is the establishment of an institution that would consist of the most learned people, who, in turn, would be willing: (a) to promote and perfect the sciences while at the same time, wherever possible, be willing (b) to give public instruction to young people (if they feel the latter are qualified) and (c) instruct some people individually so that they in turn could train young people [of Russia] in the fundamental principles of all sciences.

CHAPTER 20

COFFEE IN EARLY MODERN WORLD HISTORY

One of the key features of the early modern period involved the circulation of new goods among different regions, and the related development of new consumer tastes. Tobacco, cotton, and silver, and their literally global exchange, began to play serious roles in shaping world history—through consumption, production, and trade, and the regional relationships involved.

Coffee was a major player as well. Native to northeastern Africa, it spread initially through the Middle East during the sixteenth century. Europeans encountered it there, and coffee enjoyed growing popularity from the seventeenth century onward. In both regions, and later more widely still, coffee affected not only personal consumption but also, potentially, health and sleep and, above all, new patterns of sociability and exchange of news and views.

Coffee was also controversial—like many novel products, but with some particularly interesting disputes and debates. The following documents, from the Middle East and Europe, suggest key issues in coffee's progress. They must be compared, so that we can get at the nature of clashing viewpoints. They must be subtly analyzed, so that we can look between the lines of the critiques to assess coffee's impact. And of course they invite consideration of the relationship between Middle Eastern and European patterns.

Questions

1. What were some of the main objections to coffee?
2. Why did coffee gain steadily in popularity?
3. Were there significant differences between coffee's early history in the Middle East and that in Western Europe? What might account for major differences and similarities?
4. What were some of the political and social implications of coffee? Were there also gender implications?
5. What types of people opposed coffee, and why? What types of people favored it?

For Further Discussion

1. **Is a humble product like coffee a significant subject for world history?**
2. **To what extent did attacks on coffee fail, and why?**
3. **Did the spread of coffee relate to other significant developments in early modern Middle Eastern or European history?**
4. **Does the history of coffee suggest analogies to reactions to other kinds of new products, either in the past or today?**

A Middle Eastern Account

This selection comes from an Arab manuscript written in the seventeenth or early eighteenth century.

Schehabeddin Ben, an Arabian author of the ninth century of the Gegira, or fifteenth of the Christians, attributes to Gemaleddin, Mufti of Aden [the Arabian Gulf], who was nearly his contemporary, the first introduction into that country, of drinking Coffee. He tells us, that Gemaleddin, having occasion to travel into Persia, during his abode there, saw some of his countrymen drinking Coffee, which at that time he did not much attend to; but, on his return to Aden, finding himself indisposed, and remembering that he had seen his countrymen drinking Coffee in Persia, in hopes of reviving some benefit from it, he determined to try it on himself; and, after making the experiment, not only recovered his health, but perceived other useful qualities in that liquor; such as relieving the headache, enlivening the spirits, and, without prejudice to the constitution, preventing drowsiness. This last quality he resolved to turn to the advantage of his profession: he took it himself, and recommended it to the Dervishes, or religious Muslims, to enable them to pass the night in prayer, and other exercises of their religions, with greater zeal and attention. Soon men of letters, and persons belonging to the law, adopted the use of it. These were followed by the tradesmen, and artisans that were under a necessity of working in the night, and such as were obliged to travel later after sunset. At length the custom become general in Aden; and it was not only drunk in the night by those who were desirous of being kept awake, but in the day for the sake of its other agreeable qualities.

Coffee, being thus received at Aden, where it has continued in use ever since without interruption, passed by degrees to many neighboring towns; and not long after reached Mecca, where it was introduced, as at Aden, by the Dervishes, and for the same purposes of religion. The inhabitants of Mecca, were at last so fond of this liquor,

From John Ellis, *A Historical Account of Coffee with an Engraving, and Botanical Description of the Tree* (London: Edward and Charles Dilly, 1774).

that, without regarding the intention of the religious, and other studious persons, they at length drank it publicly in coffeehouses, where they assembled in crowds to pass the time agreeably, making that the pretense: here they played at chess, and such other kind of games, and that even for money. In these houses they amused themselves likewise with singing, dancing, and music, contrary to the manners of the rigid Muslims, which afterwards was the occasion of some disturbances.

From hence the custom extended itself to many other towns of Arabia, and particularly to Medina, and then to Grand Cairo in Egypt.

But at length the rigid Muslims began to disapprove the use of Coffee, as occasioning frequent disorders, and too nearly resembling wine in its effects; the drinking of which is contrary to the tenets of their religion. Government was therefore obliged to interfere, and at times refrain from the use of it. However, it had become so universally liked, that it was found afterwards necessary to take off all restraint for the future.

[By 1554 coffee reached Constantinople, and two Syrian merchants] sold Coffee publicly, in rooms fitted up in an elegant manner; which were presently frequented by men of learning, and particularly poets and other persons, who came to amuse themselves with a game of chess, or draughts; or to make acquaintance, and pass their time agreeably at small expense.

These houses and assemblies insensibly became so much in vogue, that they were frequented by people of all professions, and even by the officers of the ferablio, the pachas, and persons of the first rank about the court. However, when they seemed to be the most firmly established, the Imans, or officers of the Mosques, complained loudly of their being deserted, while the Coffeehouses were full of company. . . .

The chief of the Law . . . pronounced that the drinking of Coffee was contrary to the law of Mohammed. Immediately all the Coffeehouses were shut, and the officers of the police were commanded to prevent any one from drinking coffee. However, the habit was become so strong, and the use of it so generally agreeable, that the people continued, notwithstanding all prohibitions, to drink it in their own houses. The officers of the police, seeing they could not suppress the use of it, allowed . . . the drinking of it, provided it was not done openly; so that it was drunk in particular places, with the doors shut, or in the back room of some of the shopkeepers' houses.

ENGLISH ACCOUNTS

The first selection is from *The Nature of the drink Kauhi, or Coffe, and the Berry of which it is made, Described by an Arabian Phisitian* (Oxford: Henry Hall, 1659). The second selection is from *A Character of Coffee and Coffee-Houses* (London, 1661).

• • •

Coffee is by experience
Found to conduce to the drying of
Rheumes, and flegmatick coughes and
Distillations, and the opening of obstructions,
And the provocation of urin
When it is dried and thoroughly boyled,
It allayes the ebullition of the blood,
is good against the small poxe and measles,
and bloudy pimples; yet causeth
vertiginous headheach, and maketh lean
much, occasioneth waking, and the Emrods,
and asswageth lust, and sometimes
breeds melancholy. He that would drink
it for livelinesse sake, and to discusse
slothfulnesse, and the other properties that
we have mentioned, let him use much
sweet meates with it, and oyle of pistaccioes,
and butter. Some drink it with
milk, but it is an error, and such as may
bring in danger of the leprosy.

• • •

Six or seven years ago was [coffee] first brought into England,
When the Palats of the English were as Fanatical, as
Their
Brains. Like Apes, the English imitate all other people
In their ridiculous Fashions. As Slaves they submit to
The
Customes even of Turky and India. . . .
With the Barbarous Indian he smoaks Tobacco.
With the Turk he drinks Coffee. . . .
Even the Deserts of Arabia are ransackt for a Berry,
Which made into a drink, is as thick as puddle-water,
And ugly in colour and taste, . . .
'Tis extolled for drying up the Crudities of the
Stomack, and for expelling Fumes out of the Head.
Excellent Berry! Which can cleanse the English-man's
Stomak of Flegm, and expel Giddinesse out of his Head.
Yet it is certain, that for the small space of an hour or
Thereabouts it hath expelled out of his Head and
Stomack these infirmities. But Physicians say that

Coffee causeth the Migraine and other Giddinesses in the
Head. Of these dayly experiment may be made: For
If you set Short-hand-writers to take down the
Discourse of the Company, who prattle over Coffee, it
Will be evident on reading the Notes, that the talk is
Extravagant and exactly like that of the Academians of
Bedlam, and such, as any others, would be ashamed of
But themselves.
The other sex hath just cause to curse the day, in
Which it was brought into England; Had Women any sense of sprit
They would remonstrate to his Majestie, that Men in
Former times were more able, than now, . . .
Men drink so [much]
They are grown as impotent as Age, as dry and as
Unfruitful, as the Deserts of Africk. . . .
In this Age Men tattle more than Women,
And particularly at the Coffee-house, when the number hath
Been but six, five of them have talked at one time. The
Company here have out-talk'd an equal number of
Gossipping Women, and made a greater noise than a Bake-house.
The Relater hereof hath heard
A young gentleman affirm, that he used to go to the Coffee-house
Purposely to vent his strange and wild Conceits, . . .
[An] opinion, how foolish or fond soever,
Here received entertainment. . . .

Two Descriptions of English Coffee Houses

The first description is from 1673, the second from 1675.

• • •

THE CHARACTER OF A COFFEE-HOUSE, 1673 A.D.

A coffee-house is a lay conventicler, good-fellowship turned puritan, ill-husbandry in masquerade, whither people come, after toping all day, to purchase, at the expense of their last penny, the repute of sober companions: A Rota [i.e. club room], that, like Noah's ark, receives animals of every sort, from the precise diminutive band, to the

From Charles W. Colby, ed., *Selections from the Sources of English History, B.C. 55–A.D. 1832* (London: Longmans, Green, 1920), 208–12. Text modernized by Jerome S. Arkenberg.

hectoring cravat and cuffs in folio; a nursery for training up the smaller fry of virtuosi in confident tattling, or a cabal of knitting [i.e. carping] critics that have only learned to spit and mew; a mint of intelligence, that, to make each man his pennyworth, draws out into petty parcels, what the merchant receives in bullion: he, that comes often, saves twopence a week in Gazettes, and has his news and his coffee for the same charge, as at a threepenny ordinary they give in broth to your chop of mutton; it is an exchange, where haberdashers of political small-wares meet, and mutually abuse each other, and the public, with bottomless stories, and heedless notions; the rendezvous of idle pamphlets, and persons more idly employed to read them; a high court of justice, where every little fellow in a camlet cloak takes upon him to transpose affairs both in church and state, to show reasons against acts of parliament, and condemn the decrees of general councils.

COFFEE-HOUSES VINDICATED, 1675 A.D.

Though the happy Arabia, nature's spicery, prodigally furnishes the voluptuous world with all kinds of aromatics, and divers other rarities; yet I scare know whether mankind be not still as much obliged to it for the excellent fruit of the humble coffee-shrub, as for any other of its more specious productions: for, since there is nothing we here enjoy, next to life, valuable beyond health, certainly those things that contribute to preserve us in good plight and *eucrasy* (such a due mixture of qualities as constitutes health), and fortify our weak bodies against the continual assaults and batteries of disease, deserve our regards much more than those which only gratify a liquorish palate, or otherwise prove subservient to our delights. As for this salutiferous berry, of so general a use through all the regions of the east, it is sufficiently known, when prepared, to be moderately hot, and of a very drying attenuating and cleansing quality; whence reason infers, that its decoction must contain many good physical properties, and cannot but be an incomparable remedy to dissolve crudities, comfort the brain, and dry up ill humors in the stomach. In brief, to prevent or redress, in those that frequently drink it, all cold drowsy rheumatic distempers whatsoever, that proceed from excess of moisture, which are so numerous, that but to name them would tire the tongue of a mountebank.

Lastly, for diversion. Now, whither shall a person, wearied with hard study, or the laborious turmoils of a tedious day, repair to refresh himself? Or where can young gentlemen, or shop-keepers, more innocently and advantageously spend an hour or two in the evening, than at a coffee-house? Where they shall be sure to meet company, and, by the custom of the house, not such as at other places, stingy and reserved to themselves, but free and communicative; where every man may modestly begin his story, and propose to, or answer another, as he thinks fit.

In brief, it is undeniable, that, as you have here the most civil, so it is, generally, the most intelligent society; the frequenting whose converse, and observing their discourses and deportment, cannot but civilize our manners, enlarge our understanding, refine our language, teach us a generous confidence and handsome mode of address, and brush off the *pudor rubrusticus* (as, I remember, Tully somewhere calls it), that clownish kind of modesty frequently incident to the best natures, which render them sheepish and ridiculous in company.

PART IV

The Long Nineteenth Century

BEGINNING ABOUT 1750, changes in Europe's economy and politics began to create the conditions for another reshaping of the framework of world
history. Some elements of this reshaping—the rise of industry and new kinds of
powered equipment, for example, or new ideals of democracy—still persist
today. But the changes initially generated a surge of European power in the
world that has not endured in full force. In this sense a world history period that
begins with European revolutions in the eighteenth century and ends in 1914, on
the eve of Europe's relative decline in world affairs, constitutes an obviously coherent unit. Many historians call this period the long nineteenth century. With
the long nineteenth century, in other words, the world's industrial era began,
and it is still unfolding. At the same time, a shorter but significant period of European dominance prevailed during the period as well, based on temporary monopoly of industrial power.

During the late eighteenth century the industrial revolution developed in
Britain. It featured the rise of factory industry and the use of the new powered machinery, with the invention of a usable steam engine being the central
technological innovation. Industrialization fairly quickly spread to other parts
of Western Europe and to the United States. It allowed a massive increase in the
production of goods, including new kinds of weaponry, plus more rapid systems
of transportation and communication. During the same period, a series of Western revolutions and wars of independence were also launched, stretching from
the United States to Western Europe and back to Latin America.

These changes helped set in motion a massive increase in the power of the
West in the world at large. Technology and military power were crucial. Western
armies could now defeat much larger landed forces; the naval advantage was enhanced as well. Western victories or successful intimidations in Ottoman territory
(1798), in China (1839–42), in Japan (1853), and in Russia (1854–55) demonstrated the new international balance of power. Massive imperialist conquests in
Africa, Southeast Asia, and the Pacific brought direct European control to new
areas. Even Latin America, though now technically independent, found itself
more fully dominated by Western commercial interests than ever before.

Massive changes in the West itself, accompanying the rise of an industrial society and the gradual emergence of political democracy, were matched, in world history, by the need to react both to Western power and to Western values. These reactions varied, which means that comparative issues in world history remain complicated. Japan quickly saw the need to reform (though not to become Western), while China lagged. India's changes, as a colony, obviously differed from those of the Ottoman Empire, which remained technically independent though increasingly beleaguered. Africa, seized late in the imperialist surge and then exploited vigorously, displayed distinctive patterns of its own. Important new areas of the world, including the United States, Canada, Australia, and New Zealand, formed societies in many ways Western in orientation but tempered by frontier conditions and an unusual mixture of races. Attention to careful comparisons is vital in order to get reactions to early industrialization and to Western imperialism amid very diverse settings.

This section deals with several key issues of world history in the long nineteenth century in a number of comparative groupings. The new political ideas and revolutions that rocked the Atlantic regions from the late eighteenth century to 1848 launched the period. Comparing revolutionary ideas and some unexpected consequences, including the powerful modern force of nationalism, involves Europe and the Americas alike.

Growing European power and decidedly undemocratic attitudes toward other peoples spawned the new wave of imperialism. Europeans' forced entry into China, from 1839 onward, represented the imperialist thrust while marking a tremendous—and very difficult—transition in Chinese history. The Chinese were forcefully opened to the world and at a great disadvantage. There is a clear opportunity here to compare European imperialist ideas with the reactions of a proud but weakened civilization.

New political ideas accompanied by complex economic changes produced important shifts in the conditions of women, leading to new ideas and new complaints. Changes in the West, accompanying imperialism, also caused shifts in colonial areas such as India, although westernization was incomplete where women were concerned.

The end of widespread slavery (save in a few important pockets) and harsh serfdom was one of the great events of nineteenth-century world history, extending from emancipations accompanying the revolutionary era up to the final decades of the century. Emancipations occurred in response to some of the same economic and cultural forces the world over, but the precise forms and consequences varied. Many dissatisfactions remained, as labor was incompletely freed despite great legal change and as existing upper classes and dominant races worked to retain key advantages. Again, comparison helps pinpoint the crucial issues.

While industrialization was largely a Western achievement during the long nineteenth century, by the 1890s, both Japan and Russia had managed to launch significant factory industry, imitating Western patterns in part but supplying special ingredients from their own cultural and institutional frameworks. Differences between Japanese and Western economic styles, still operative today, can be traced to the long nineteenth century, even though Japan openly copied the West in many respects. Russia and Japan also generated notable resistance to Western values, using nationalism to defend certain traditions and "inventing" others that would help preserve distinctive identities amid change. Here was an important reminder that, even in a century of triumphant Western power, the world remained diverse and many societies sought the means to limit Western influence.

CHAPTER 21

THE AGE OF ATLANTIC REVOLUTIONS

This chapter and the next (on nationalism) are closely linked. Both involve major political changes that took shape first in Europe and the Americas in the later eighteenth century but exerted global impact over ensuing decades. This chapter focuses on the revolutionary principles themselves (and objections to them). The subsequent section on nationalism allows comparison of the relationship between the core revolutionary values and the political force that emerged alongside them.

The American Revolution, bursting forth in 1776, and the French Revolution of 1789 both enunciated universal principles of human rights. They deserve careful comparison: similarities are obvious, but are there any suggestive differences? Two other documents add to the comparative mix: a critique of the French Revolution, which needs to be compared to what the revolutionaries thought they were establishing ; and another French revolutionary document that suggests the social force of this revolution, beyond political change.

In the wake of these revolutions, a major revolt broke out in Haiti, which ultimately overthrew French control and abolished slavery. How do the principles of this revolution, and objections to it, compare with the other Atlantic cases?

Questions

1. What were the shared principles of the Atlantic revolutions? What explains their similarities? What were the underlying definitions of human nature and the characteristics of a good government?
2. What differences existed in the statements of rights and liberties?
3. How does the Haitian Revolution reflect the revolutionary process more generally? What were some of its distinctive features?
4. How did the social aspects of the French and Haitian Revolutions relate to the political goals? Were they entirely consistent, or could they raise some complications with statements of rights and liberties?
5. What kinds of objections were raised to the revolutionary principles? Did the critics reject the revolutionary principles themselves or merely the disruption and violence of the revolutionary process? How did Burke begin to define a new kind of conservatism?

For Further Discussion

1. Some historians have argued that the American Revolution is best interpreted as an independence war, not a real revolution at all, if the French revolution is used as the standard. What was "unrevolutionary" about the American revolution?
2. Why did the revolutionary principles, which spread so quickly in Europe and the Americas, not spread more widely, to other parts of the globe, during the same period?

THE AMERICAN REVOLUTION

This document emanated from the First Continental Congress (October 1774). The Revolutionary War had not broken out, and there was still some effort to reach accommodation with England. But the principles that would lead to revolt and to the construction of the later United States Constitution were clearly enunciated.

• • •

DECLARATION AND RESOLVES OF THE FIRST CONTINENTAL CONGRESS (OCTOBER 1774)

Whereas, since the close of the last war, the British parliament, claiming a power of right to bind the people of America by statute in all cases whatsoever, hath, in some acts expressly imposed taxes on them, and in others, under various pretenses, but in fact for the purpose of raising a revenue, hath imposed rates and duties payable in these colonies, established a board of commissioners with unconstitutional powers, and extended the jurisdiction of courts of Admiralty not only for collecting the said duties, but for the trial of causes merely arising within the body of a county.

And whereas, in consequence of other statutes, judges who before held only estates at will in their offices, have been made dependent on the Crown alone for their salaries, and standing armies kept in times of peace. And it has lately been resolved in Parliament, that by force of a statute made in the thirty-fifth year of the reign of king Henry the Eighth, colonists may be transported in England, and tried there upon accusations for treasons and misprisons, or concealments of treasons committed in the colonies; and by a late statute, such trials have been directed in cases therein mentioned.

And whereas, in the last session of Parliament, three statutes were made; one entitled "An act to discontinue, in such manner and for such time as are therein mentioned, the landing and discharging, lading, or shipping of goods, wares and merchandise, at the town, and within the harbor of Boston in the province of Massachusetts-bay, in North America"; another, entitled "An act for the better regulating the government of the province of the Massachusetts-bay in New England"; and another, entitled "An act for

223

the impartial administration of justice, in the cases of persons questioned for any act done by them in the execution of the law, or for the suppression of riots and tumults, in the province of the Massachusetts-bay, in New England." And another statute was then made, "for making more effectual provision for the government of the province of Quebec, etc. All which statues are impolitic, unjust, and cruel, as well as unconstitutional, and most dangerous and destructive of American rights.

And whereas, Assemblies have been frequently dissolved, contrary to the rights of the people, when they attempted to deliberate on grievances; and their dutiful, humble, loyal, and reasonable petitions to the crown for redress, have been repeatedly treated with contempt, by His Majesty's ministers of state:

The good people of the several Colonies of New Hampshire, Massachusetts bay, Rhode Island and Providence plantations, Connecticut, New York, New Jersey, Pennsylvania, Newcastle Kent and Sussex on Delaware, Maryland, Virginia, North Carolina, and South Carolina, justly alarmed at these arbitrary proceedings of parliament and administration, have severally elected, constituted, and appointed deputies to meet, and set in general Congress, in the city of Philadelphia, in order to obtain such establishment, as that their religion, laws, and liberties, may not be subverted:

Whereupon the deputies so appointed being now assembled, in a full and free representation of these Colonies, taking into their most serious consideration the best means of attaining the ends aforesaid, do in the first place, as Englishmen their ancestors in like cases have usually done, for asserting and vindicating their rights and liberties, declare,

That the inhabitants of the English Colonies in North America, by the immutable laws of nature, the principles of the English constitution, and the several charters or compacts, have the following rights:

1. That they are entitled to life, liberty, and property, and they never ceded to any sovereign power whatever, a right to dispose of either without their consent.
2. That our ancestors, who first settled these colonies, were at the time of their emigration from the mother country, entitled to all the rights, liberties, and immunities of free and natural born subjects within the realm of England.
3. That by such emigration they by no means forfeited, surrendered, or lost any of those rights, but that they were, and their descendants now are entitled to the exercise and enjoyment of all such of them, as their local and other circumstances enable them to exercise and enjoy.
4. That the foundation of English liberty, and of all free government, is a right in the people to participate in their legislative council: and as the English colonists are not represented, and from their local and other circumstances, cannot properly be represented in the British parliament, they are entitled to a free and exclusive power of legislation in their several provincial legislatures, where their right of representation can alone be preserved, in all cases of taxation and internal polity, subject only to the negative of their sovereign, in such manner as has been heretofore used and

accustomed. But, from the necessity of the case, and a regard to the mutal interest of both countries, we cheerfully consent to the operation of such acts of the British parliament, as are bona fide restrained to the regulation of our external commerce, for the purpose of securing the commercial advantages of the whole empire to the mother country, and the commercial benefits of its respective members excluding every idea of taxation, internal or external, for raising a revenue on the subjects in America without their consent.

5. That the respective colonies are entitled to the common law of England, and more especially to the great and inestimable privilege of being tried by their peers of the vincinage, according to the course of that law. . . .

6. That they have a right peaceably to assemble, consider of their grievances, and petition the King; and that all prosecutions, prohibitory proclamations, and commitments for the same, are illegal.

7. That the keeping a Standing army in these colonies, in times of peace, without the consent of the legislature of that colony in which such army is kept, is against law.

8. It is indispensably necessary to good government, and rendered essential by the English constitution, that the constituent branches of the legislature be independent of each other; that, therefore, the exercise of legislative power in several colonies, by a council appointed during pleasure, by the crown, is unconstitutional, dangerous, and destructive to the freedom of American legislation.

All and each of which the aforesaid deputies, in behalf of themselves, and their constituents, do claim, demand, and insist on, as their indubitable rights and liberties; which cannot be legally taken from them, altered or abridged by any power whatever, without their own consent, by their representatives in their several provincial legislatures.

The French Revolution

The Declaration of the Rights of Man was one of the early proclamations of the new National Assembly, the body that succeeded the traditional Third Estate. It was called on August 26, 1789.

• • •

DECLARATION OF THE RIGHTS OF MAN

The representatives of the French people, organized as a National Assembly, believing that the ignorance, neglect, or contempt of the rights of man are the sole cause of public calamities and of the corruption of governments, have determined to set forth in a

From Cybercasting Services Division of the National Public Telecommuting Network. http://www.yale.edu/lawweb/avalon/rightsof.htm.

solemn declaration the natural, unalienable, and sacred rights of man, in order that this declaration, being constantly before all the members of the Social body, shall remind them continually of their rights and duties; in order that the acts of the legislative power, as well as those of the executive power, may be compared at any moment with the objects and purposes of all political institutions and may thus be more respected, and, lastly, in order that the grievances of the citizens, based hereafter upon simple and incontestable principles, shall tend to the maintenance of the constitution and redound to the happiness of all. Therefore the National Assembly recognizes and proclaims, in the presence and under the auspices of the Supreme Being, the following rights of man and of the citizen: Articles:

1. Men are born and remain free and equal in rights. Social distinctions may be founded only upon the general good.
2. The aim of all political associations is the preservation of the natural and imperceptible rights of man. These rights are liberty, property, security, and resistance to oppression.
3. The principle of all sovereignty resides essentially in the nation. No body nor individual may exercise any authority which does not proceed directly from the nation.
4. Liberty consists in the freedom to do everything which injures no one else; hence the exercise of the natural rights of each man has no limits except those which assure to the other members of the society the enjoyment of the same rights. These limits can only be determined by law.
5. Law can only prohibit such actions as are hurtful to society. Nothing may be prevented which is not forbidden by law, and no one may be forced to do anything not provided for by law.
6. Law is the expression of the general will. Every citizen has a right to participate personally, or through his representative, in its foundation. It must be the same for all, whether it protects or punishes. All citizens, being equal in the eyes of the law, are equally eligible to all dignities and to all public positions and occupations, according to their abilities, and without distinction except that of their virtues and talents.
7. No person shall be accused, arrested, or imprisoned except in the cases and according to the forms prescribed by law. Any one soliciting, transmitting, executing, or causing to be executed, any arbitrary order, shall be punished. But any citizen summoned or arrested in virtue of the law shall submit without delay, as resistance constitutes an offense.
8. The law shall provide for such punishments only as are strictly and obviously necessary, and no one shall suffer punishment except it be legally inflicted in virtue of a law passed and promulgated before the commission of the offense.
9. As all persons are held innocent until they shall have been declared guilty, if arrest shall be deemed indispensable, all harshness not essential to the securing of the prisoner's person shall be severely repressed by law.

10. No one shall be disquieted on account of his opinions, including his religious views, provided their manifestation does not disturb the public order established by law.

11. The free communication of ideas and opinions is one of the most precious of the rights of man. Every citizen may, accordingly, speak, write, and print with freedom, but shall be responsible for such abuses of this freedom as shall be defined by law.

12. The security of the rights of man and of the citizen requires public military forces. These forces are, therefore, established for the good of all and not for the personal advantage of those to whom they shall be entrusted.

13. A common contribution is essential for the maintenance of the public forces and for the cost of administration. This should be equitably distributed among all the citizens in proportion to their means.

14. All the citizens have a right to decide, either personally or by their representatives, as to the necessity of the public contribution; to grant this freely; to know to what uses it is put; and to fix the proportion, the mode of assessment and of collection and the duration of the taxes.

15. Society has the right to require of every public agent an account of his administration.

16. A society in which the observance of the law is not assured, nor the separation of powers defined, has no constitution at all.

17. Since property is an inviolable and sacred right, no one shall be deprived thereof except where public necessity, legally determined, shall clearly demand it, and then only on condition that the owner shall have been previously and equitably indemnified.

DECREE ABOLISHING FEUDALISM

This decree, adopted officially on August 11, 1789, followed from reports of widespread peasant attacks on landed estates and manorial records. The goal was to pacify the peasantry, but the results involved sweeping social change.

• • •

The Decree Abolishing the Feudal System, August 11, 1789

Article I. The National Assembly hereby completely abolishes the feudal system. It decrees that, among the existing rights and dues, [including] feudal [dues], all those originating in or representing real or personal serfdom shall be abolished without indemnification. All other dues are declared redeemable, the terms and mode of redemption to be fixed by the National Assembly. Those of the said dues which are

From J. H. Robinson ed., *Readings in European History*, vol. 2 (Boston: Ginn, 1906), 404–9.

not extinguished by this decree shall continue to be collected until indemnification shall take place.

III. The exclusive right to hunt and to maintain unenclosed warrens is likewise abolished, and every landowner shall have the right to kill, or to have destroyed on his own land, all kinds of game, observing, however, such police regulations as may be established with a view to the safety of the public. . . .

IV. All perpetual ground rents, payable either in money or in kind, of whatever nature they may be, whatever their origin and to whomsoever they may be due, . . . shall be redeemable at a rate fixed by the Assembly. No due shall in the future be created which is not redeemable.

VI. The sale of judicial and municipal offices shall be abolished forthwith. Justice shall be dispensed gratis. Nevertheless the magistrates at present holding such offices shall continue to exercise their functions and to receive their emoluments until the Assembly shall have made provision for indemnifying them. . . .

IX. Pecuniary privileges, personal or real, in the payment of taxes are abolished forever. Taxes shall be collected from all the citizens, and from all property, in the same manner and in the same form. Plans shall be considered by which the taxes shall be paid proportionally by all, even for the last six months of the current years. . . .

XI. All citizens, without distinction of birth, are eligible to any office or dignity, whether ecclesiastical, civil, or military; and no profession shall imply any derogation.

EDMUND BURKE

Edmund Burke became a pioneering spokesman for antirevolutionary conservatism, as he increasingly attacked the French Revolution from his position in the British House of Commons. His *Reflections on the Revolution in France* was published in 1790.

• • •

Abstractly speaking, government, as well as liberty, is good; yet could I, in common sense, ten years ago, have congratulated France on her enjoyment of a government (for she then had a government) without enquiry what the nature of that government was, or how it was administered? Can I now congratulate the same nation upon its freedom?

From Edmund Burke, *Select Works of Edmund Burke*, vol. 2 (London: Payne, 1876), 93–94.

Is it because liberty in the abstract may be classed amongst the blessings of mankind, that I am seriously to felicitate a madman, who has escaped from the protecting restraint and wholesome darkness of his cell, on his restoration to the enjoyment of light and liberty? Am I to congratulate a highwayman and murderer, who has broke prison, upon the recovery of his natural rights?

When I see the spirit of liberty in action, I see a strong principle at work; and this, for a while, is all I can possibly know of it. The wild gas, the fixed air, is plainly broke loose: but we ought to suspend our judgment until the first effervescence is a little subsided, til the liquor is cleared, and until we see something deeper than the agitation of a troubled and frothy surface. I must be tolerably sure, before I venture publicly to congratulate men upon a blessing, that they have really received one. Flattery corrupts both the receiver and the giver; and adulation is not of more service to the people than to kings. I should therefore suspend my congratulations on the new liberty of France, until I was informed how it had been combined with government; with public force; with the discipline and obedience of armies; with the collection of an effective and well-distributed revenue; with morality and religion; with the solidity of property; with peace and order; with civil and social manners. All these (in their way) are good things too; and without them, liberty is not a benefit whilst it lasts, and is not likely to continue long. The effect of liberty to individuals is, that they may do what they please: we ought to see what it will please them to do, before we risk congratulations, which may be soon turned into complaints. Prudence would dictate this in the case of separate insulated private men; but liberty, when men act in bodies, is power. Considerate people, before they declare themselves, will observe the use which is made of power; and particularly of so trying a thing as new power in new persons, of whose principles, tempers, and dispositions, they have little or no experience. . . .

The Haitian Revolution

The following proclamation, issued by several Haitian leaders, including Jean-Jacques Dessalines, was issued in 1803. It refers among other things to the possibility of interference by France; Napoleon bitterly opposed the revolution, which led to Haitian independence from France, though he was unable to act effectively.

• • •

Preliminary Declaration

Art. 1. The people inhabiting the island formerly called St. Domingo, hereby agree to form themselves into a free state sovereign and independent of any other power in the universe, under the name of empire of Hayti.

2. Slavery is forever abolished.

From Marcus Rainsford, *An Historical Account of the Black Empire of Hayti* (London, 1805), 439–41.

3. The Citizens of Hayti are brothers at home; equality in the eyes of the law is incontestably acknowledged, and there cannot exist any titles, advantages, or privileges, other than those necessarily resulting from the consideration and reward of services rendered to liberty and independence.

4. The law is the same to all, whether it punishes, or whether it protects.

5. The law has no retroactive effect.

6. Property is sacred, its violation shall be severely prosecuted. [But later: all property which formerly belonged to white Frenchemen, is incontestably and of right confiscated to the use of the state.]

9. No person is worthy of being a Haitian who is not a good father, a good son, a good husband, and especially a good soldier.

12. No white man of whatever nation he may be, shall put his foot on this territory with the title of master or proprietor, neither shall he in future acquire any property therein.

13. The preceding article cannot in the smallest degree affect white women who have been naturalized Haytians by Government, nor does it extend to children already born, or that may be born of the said women.

14. All [designation] of colour among the children of one and the same [national] family, of whom the chief magistrate is the father, being necessarily to cease, the Haytians shall hence forward be known only by the generic appellation of Blacks.

Of Worship

50. The law admits of no predominant religion.

51. The freedom of worship is tolerated.

52. The state does not provide for the maintenance of any religious institution, nor or any minister.

FROM A FRENCH NEWSPAPER

This article appeared in the *Courier francais* on August 23, 1796, as the Haitian revolution began. It was based on a letter sent by a French plantation owner.

• • •

Since my first letter, which accompanies this, there has occurred, and there is still occurring, what follows:

At Port-au-Prince, and in the environs, the Negroes are in a state of insurrection; they have burnt many habitations, which had remained untouched til this day. The Negroes will not work.

From *Pennsylvania Gazette*, Sept. 28, 1796.

On this side of Grand Rivière, there is a great rising; the Brigand Negroes have killed a Negro chief named Gagnet, who commanded for the [French] Republic, his family, and the état-major. Fifteen thousand men taken from the principal posts are to go against the revolters; they doubt much the success of these new Republicans. I deplore the unhappy fate of the inhabitants of St. Domingo. It is impossible for them to come with security to their habitations. The Negroes who have returned to their habitations will not absolutely attend to speak to their masters; they are willing enough to be Republicans, but point de travail [no work]; they think it is contrary to Republican rights; by this title they are to be supplied with all that is necessary.

The mask is thrown off—the Negroes say, haughtily, that St. Domingo belongs to them; on this condition they will work, otherwise not.

CHAPTER 22

NATIONALISM

Nationalism is one of the great forces of modern history, so much so that it is sometimes hard to step back and realize what a new kind of loyalty it is. Despite some hints of nationalist-type beliefs earlier, most people in 1750 identified themselves in terms of locality and, often, religion, not nation. From 1750 onward, however, first in Europe and then more globally, intellectual advocacy of nationalism, growing social changes—such as urbanization—that weakened traditional ties, and increasing interregional contacts all promoted nationalism.

Nationalism sprang in part from the revolutionary era of the late eighteenth century. The idea of citizen links with government helped nationalism in France, for example, where the world's first national anthem originated. Later, however, nationalism could be used as a conservative force, defending against social protests and often using adventures abroad to distract from tensions back home.

Rising nationalism played a role in many revolutions, from the American and French Revolutions onward. It supported major changes like the Latin American wars of independence and the Italian and the German unifications. It provided one of the major bases for opposition to European imperialism. It contributed to numerous wars.

Nationalism embodied a number of analytical tensions, beyond the liberal-conservative divide. How would nationalists react to nations other than their own? How would a nationalist balance national goals with other goals such as liberal institutions or economic advance—in other words, where would nationalism fit in a priority list? How would a nationalist balance appeals to national traditions, real or imagined, with a desire to promote more modern development?

The documents that follow offer insights into several aspects of nationalism, including its somewhat elusive basic definition. A proclamation by the French Revolution's National Convention helps explain how the revolution could promote nationalism in adjacent conquered territories (like western Germany or Spain) both intentionally and unintentionally. A treatise by the German philosopher Fichte was one of the first deliberate statements of nationalism and shows its intellectual bases; two quick followups in later German history (one from the French revolutionary period, one from the national unifications period of the 1860s) show how nationalism could later be used. Finally, Simon Bolivar suggests the nature of Latin American nationalism, as it was defined as part of the wars of independence.

Questions

1. How did the French Revolution stimulate nationalism both at home and in Europe more generally? Did the revolutionaries see themselves as nationalists or universalists?
2. How did the nationalism that emerged around the French Revolution relate to the more explicit purposes of revolution discussed in the previous chapter?
3. What was Fichte's philosophical basis for nationalism? What ideas was he arguing against in promoting nationalism?
4. How did Frederick William reflect the impact of revolutionary ideas in urging opposition to Napoleonic France? How and why did he suggest German nationalism?
5. How did Bismarck define and use nationalism?
6. Did German nationalism remain consistent from Fichte through Frederick William to Bismarck, or were there significant changes?
7. Looking at the French and the German documents, discuss how nationalism could be both a liberal and a conservative force. Was German nationalism consistently conservative?
8. How does Bolivar's nationalism compare to the European versions? What special Latin American issues does he reflect? Where does his nationalism fit on a liberal-conservative spectrum?

For Further Discussion

1. What factors explain the rise of nationalism in Europe and theAmericas?
2. How and why could nationalism turn against liberal ideals?
3. Did leaders like Bolivar assume that Latin America was part of Western civilization, or did they assume that it was very different? What civilizational framework works best for understanding Latin American history in the nineteenth century?
4. Are the forces that sustained nationalism declining in the twenty-first century?

THE FRENCH REVOLUTION AND NATIONALISM:
A 1792 DECREE

The following decree came from the National Convention in France, elected in 1792. France had begun to fight off foreign attack and had annexed Belgium in the process; Belgian resistance stimulated the decree.

• • •

The National Convention, having heard the report of its combined Committees of Finance, War, and Diplomacy; faithful to the principles of the sovereignty of the people, which do not permit it to recognize any institutions detrimental thereto, and wishing to establish the rules to be followed by the generals of the armies of the Republic in territories where they bear arms, decrees:

1. In territories which are or may be occupied by the armies of the Republic, the generals shall proclaim immediately, in the name of the French nation, the sovereignty of the people, the suppression of all established authorities and of existing imposts or taxes, the [manorial] abolition of the tithe, of feudalism, of seigniorial rights, . . . of nobility, and generally of all privileges.

2. They shall announce to the people that they bring it peace, aid, fraternity, liberty, and equality, and they shall convoke it thereafter in primary or communal assemblies, in order to create and organize a provisional administration and justice; they shall supervise the security of persons and property; they shall have the present decree and the proclamation annexed thereto printed in the language or idiom of the territory and posted and executed without delay in every commune.

3. All agents and civil or military officials of the former government, as well as individuals heretofore considered noble, or members of any corporation heretofore privileged, shall be, for this time only, inadmissible to vote in the primary or communal assemblies, and they may not be elected to positions in the provisional administration or judiciary.

4. The generals shall place, consecutively, under the safeguard and protection of the French Republic all real and personal property belonging to the public treasury, to the prince, his abettors, adherents, and voluntary satellites, to public establishments, and to lay and ecclesiastical bodies and communities; they shall have a detailed statement thereof drafted promptly and dispatched to the Executive council, and they shall take all measure within their power in order that such properties be respected.

5. The provisional administration, elected by the people, shall be responsible for the surveillance and administration of matters placed under the safeguard and protection of

From John Hall Stewart, ed., *A Documentary Survey of the French Revolution* (New York: Macmillan, 1951), 381–84. Reprinted by permission of Pearson Education, Inc. Upper Saddle River, NJ.

the French Republic; it shall supervise the security of persons and property; it shall have the laws now in force relative to the trial of civil and criminal suites, to the police, and to public security put into effect; it shall be in charge of regulating and paying local expenses and those necessary for the common defense; it may institute taxes, provided, however, that they are not borne by the indigent and hard-working portion of the population.

6. As soon as the provisional administration has been organized, the National Convention shall appoint commissioners from within its own body to go to fraternize with it.

7. The Executive Council also shall appoint national commissioners who shall go, consecutively, to the places, to consult the generals and the provisional administration elected by the people concerning measures to be taken for the common defence and concerning the means to be employed to procure the clothing and provisions necessary for the armies, and to pay ther [i.e., the armies'] expenses during their sojourn on its territory.

Henceforth the French nation proclaims the sovereignty of the people, the suppression of all civil and military authorities which have governed you up to the present, and of all taxes which you sustain, in whatever form they exist; the abolition of the tithe, of feudalism, of seigniorial rights, . . . fixed or contingent, of *banalités* of real and personal servitude, of hunting and fishing privileges, [labor service and all manorial taxes], and generally of every species of contributions with which you have been burdened by your usurpers; it proclaims also the abolition among you of every corporation, noble, sacerdotal, and others, of all prerogative and privileges that are contrary to equality. You are henceforth, brothers and friends, all citizens, all equal in rights, and all equally summoned to govern, to serve, and to defend your *Patrie* [fatherland].

FICHTE

Johann Gottlieb Fichte (1762–1814) was a German philosopher who supported the French Revolution and its ideals but then rethought his position as the French extended controls over Germany. This address occurred in 1806, in French-occupied Berlin.

• • •

The first, original, and truly natural boundaries of states are beyond doubt their internal boundaries. Those who speak the same language are joined to each other by a multitude of invisible bonds by nature herself, long before any human art begins;

From Johann Gottlieb Fichte, *Addresses to the German Nation,* ed. George A. Kelly (New York: Harper Torchbooks, 1968), 19,091, 19,394, 19,798, in public domain.

they understand each other and have the power of continuing to make themselves understood more and more clearly; they belong together and are by nature one and an inseparable whole. Such a whole, if it wishes to absorb and mingle with itself any other people of different descent and language, cannot do so without itself becoming confused, in the beginning at any rate, and violently disturbing the even progress of its culture. From this internal boundary, which is drawn by the spiritual nature of man himself, the marking of the external boundary by dwelling place results as a consequence; and in the natural view of things it is not because men dwell between certain mountains and rivers that they are a people, but, on the contrary, men dwell together—and, if their luck has so arranged it, are protected by rivers and mountain—because they were a people already by a law of nature which is much higher.

Thus was the German nation place—sufficiently united within itself by a common language and a common way of thinking, and sharply enough severed from the other peoples—in the middle of Europe, as a wall to divide races not akin. . . .

That things should remain thus did not suit the selfishness of foreign countries, whose calculations did not look more than one moment ahead. They found German bravery useful in waging their wars and German hands useful to snatch the booty from their rivals. A means had to be found to attain this end, and foreign cunning won an easy victory over German ingenuousness and lack of suspicion. It was foreign countries which first made use of the division of mind produced by religious disputes in Germany—Germany, which presented on a small scale the features of Christian Europe as a whole—foreign countries, I say, made use of these disputes to break up the close inner unity of Germany into separate and disconnected parts. . . .

Now at last, let us be bold enough to look at the deceptive vision of a universal monarchy, which people are beginning to hold up for public veration in place of that equilibrium which for some time has been growing more and more preposterous, and let us perceive how hateful and contrary to reason that vision is. . . . Only when each people, left to itself, develops and forms itself in accordance with its own peculiar quality, and only when in every people each individual develops himself in accordance with that common quality, as well as in accordance with his own peculiar quality—then, and then only, does the manifestation of divinity appear in its true mirror as it ought to be. . . . Only in the invisible qualities of nations, which are hidden from their own eyes—qualities as the means whereby these nations remain in touch with the source of original life—only therein is to be found the guarantee of their presence and future worth, virtue, and merit.

A PROCLAMATION BY THE PRUSSIAN KING, 1813

Frederick William was king of Prussia. He issued this proclamation as he prepared to join the war against Napoleon. The Prussian monarchy had a long history of careful military activity and promotion of its dynasty. The proclamation reflects

the monarch's interest but in new ways that showed the influence of revolutionary ideals, including nationalism.

• • •

THE KING OF PRUSSIA ROUSES HIS PEOPLE AGAINST NAPOLEON

There is no need of explaining to my loyal subjects, or to any German, the reasons for the war which is about to begin. They lie plainly before the eyes of awakened Europe. We succumbed to the superior force of France. The peace which followed deprived me of my people and, far from bringing us blessings, it inflicted upon us deeper wounds than the war itself, sucking out the very marrow of the country. Our principal fortresses remained in the hand of the enemy, and agriculture, as well as the highly developed industries of our towns, was crippled. The freedom of trade was hampered and thereby the sources of commerce and prosperity cut off. The country was left a prey to the ravages of destitution.

I hoped, by the punctilious fulfillment of the engagements I had entered into, to lighten the burdens of my people, and even to convince the French emporer that it would be to his own advantage to leave Prussia her independence. But the purest and best of intentions on my part were of no avail against insolence and faithlessness, and it became only too plain that the emperor's treaties would gradually ruin us even more surely than his wars. The moment is come when we can no longer harbor the slightest illusion as to our situation.

Brandenburgers, Prussians, Silesians, Pomeranians, Lithuanians! You know what you have borne for the past seven years; you know the sad fate that awaits you if we do not bring this war to a honorable end. Think of the times gone by,—of the Great Elector, the great Frederick! Remember the blessings for which your forefathers fought under their leadership and which they paid for with their blood,—freedom of conscience, national honor, independence, commerce, industry, learning. Look at the great example of our powerful allies, the Russians; look at the Spaniards, the Portuguese. For such objects as these even weaker peoples have gone forth against the mightier enemies and returned in triumph. Witness the heroic Swiss and the people of the Netherlands.

Great sacrifices will be demanded from every class of the people, for our undertaking is a great one, and the number and resources of our enemies far from insignificant. But would you not rather make these sacrifices for the fatherland and for your own rightful king than for a foreign ruler, who, as he has shown by many examples, will use you and your sons and your uttermost farthing for ends which are nothing to you?

Faith in God, perseverance, and the powerful aid of our allies will bring us victory as the reward of our honest efforts. Whatever sacrifices may be required of us as

From James Harvey Robinson, ed., *Readings in European History*, vol. 2 (New York: Ginn, 1928), 522–23.

individuals, they will be outweighed by the sacred rights for which we make them, and for which we must fight to a victorious end unless we are willing to cease to be Prussians or Germans. This is the final, the decisive struggle; upon it depends on our independence, our prosperity, our existence. There are no other alternatives but an honorable peace or a heroic end. You would willingly face even the latter for honor's sake, for without honor no Prussian or German could live.

However, we may confidently await the outcome. God and our own firm purpose will bring victory to our cause and with it an assured and glorious peace and the return of happier times.

Frederick William.
Breslau, March 17, 1813.

BISMARCK

Otto von Bismarck was the chief architect of German unification (1866–1871) from a welter of individual kingdoms, the largest of which was Prussia. Bismarck used nationalism, and German unification both built on and encouraged national loyalties; but his own motiviations had more to do with enhancing Prussian power. This brief comment suggests the complexities of his approach.

• • •

In order that German patriotism should be active and effective, it needs as a rule to hang on the peg of dependence upon a dynasty; independent of dynasty it rarely comes to the rising point, though in theory it daily does so, in parliament, in the press, in public meeting; in practice the German needs either attachment to a dynasty or the goad of anger, hurrying him into action; the latter phenomenon, however, by its own nature is not permanent. It is as a Prussian, a Hanoverian, a Wurtemberger, a Bavarian or Hessian, rather than a German, that he is disposed to give unequivocal proof of a patriotism; and in the lower orders and the parliamentary groups it will be long before it is otherwise. We cannot say that the Hanoverian, Hessian, and other dynasties were at any special pains to win the affections of their subjects; but nevertheless the German patriotism of their subjects is essentially conditioned by their attachment to the dynasty after which they call themselves. . . . The German's love of Fatherland has need of a prince on whom it can concentrate its attachment. Suppose that all the German dynasties were suddenly deposed; there would then be no likelihood that the German national sentiment would suffice to hold all Germans together from the point of view of international law amid the friction of European politics, even in the form

From Otto von Bismarck, *Memoirs* (in Bismarck, *The Man and the Statesman*, New York; Harper and Brothers, 1899).

of federated Hanse towns and imperial village communes. The Germans would fall a prey to more closely welded nations if they once lost the tie which resides in the princes' sense of community of rank. History shows for Germany the Prussian stock is that of which the individual character is most strongly stamped.

POLITICAL IDEALS AND NATIONALISM IN LATIN AMERICA: SIMÓN BOLÍVAR

Simon Bolivar (1783–1830) was one of the principle leaders in Latin America's successful struggle for independence early in the nineteenth century. A Creole— that is, American born but of European stock, Bolivar was keenly aware of the political ideas of the European Enlightenment and the French and American Revolutions. He led the battles against the Spaniards in Venezuela, Columbia, and the northern Andes region, hoping to form one great state. He was selected as the initial leader but was unable to maintain the political structure or the unity he had intended, as the region soon split into separate, smaller countries. The following selections come from a proclamation calling Venezuelans to arms in the fight against Spanish occupation, which occurred in 1813, and an address to the legislature in Venezuela soon after independence, in 1819.

•   •   •

THE 1813 PROCLAMATION

Venezuelans: An army of your brothers, sent by the Sovereign Congress of New Granada [present-day Columbia] has come to liberate you. Having expelled the oppressors from the provinces of Mérida and Trujillo, it is now among you.

We are sent to destroy the Spaniards, to protect the Americans, and to reestablish the republican governments that once formed the Confederation of Venezuela. The states defended by our arms are again governed by their former constitutions and tribunals, in full enjoyment of their liberty and independence, for our mission is designed only to break the chains of servitude which still shackle some of our towns, and not to impose laws or exercise acts of dominion to which the rules of war might entitle us.

Moved by your misfortunes, we have been unable to observe with indifference the afflictions you were forced to experience by the barbarous Spaniards, who have ravished you, plundered you, and brought you death and destruction. They have violated the sacred rights of nations. They have broken the most solemn agreements and treaties. In fact, they have committed every manner of crime, reducing the Republic

From Vicente Lecuna, ed., *Selected Writings of Bolivar* (New York: Colonial Press, 1951), 31–32.

of Venezuela to the most frightful desolation. Justice therefore demands vengeance, and necessity compels us to exact it. Let the monsters who infest Columbian soil, who have drenched it in blood, be cast out forever; may their punishment be equal to the enormity of their perfidy, so that we may eradicate the stain of our ignominy and demonstrate to the nations of the world that the sons of America cannot be offended with impunity.

Despite our just resentment toward the iniquitous Spaniards, our magnanimous heart still commands us to open to them for the last time a path to reconciliation and friendship; they are invited to live peacefully among us, if they will abjure their crimes, honestly change their ways, and cooperate with us in destroying the intruding Spanish government and in the reestablishment of the Republic of Venezuela.

Any Spaniard who does not, by every active and effective means, work against tyranny in behalf of this just cause, will be considered an enemy and punished; as a traitor to the nation, he will inevitably be shot by a firing squad. On the other hand, a general and absolute amnesty is granted to those who come over to our army with or without their arms, as well as those who render aid to the good citizens who are endeavoring to throw off the yoke of tyranny. Army officers and civil magistrates who proclaim the government of Venezuela and join with us shall retain their positions; in a word, those Spaniards who render outstanding service to the State shall be regarded and treated as Americans.

And you Americans who, by error or treachery, have been lured from the paths of justice, are informed that your brothers, deeply regretting the error of your ways, have pardoned you as we are profoundly convinced that you cannot be truly to blame, for only the blindness and ignorance in which you have been kept up to now by those responsible for your crimes could have induced you to commit them. . . . You are hereby assured, with absolute impunity, of your honor, lives, and property. The single title, "Americans," shall be your safeguard and guarantee. Our arms have come to protect you, and they shall never be raised against a single one of you, your brothers.

THE 1819 PROCLAMATION

We are not Europeans; we are not Indians; we are but a mixed species of aborigines and Spaniards. Americans by birth and Europeans by law, we find ourselves engaged in a dual conflict: we are disputing with the natives for titles of ownership, and at the same time we are struggling to maintain ourselves in the country that gave us birth against the opposition of the invaders. Thus our position is most extraordinary and complicated. But there is more. As our role has always been strictly passive and political existence nil, we find that our quest for liberty is now even more difficult of

From: Simón Bolívar, *An Address of Bolivar at the Congress of Angostura*, February 15, 1819. (Reprint ed., Washington, D.C.: Press of B.S. Adams, 1919), passim.

accomplishment; for we, having been placed in a state lower than slavery, had been robbed not only of our freedom but also of the right to exercise an active domestic tyranny. . . . We have been ruled more by deceit than by force, and we have been degraded more by vice than by superstition. Slavery is the daughter of darkness: an ignorant people is a blind instrument of its own destruction. Ambition and intrigue abuse the credulity and experience of men lacking all political, economic, and civic knowledge; they adopt pure illusion as reality; they take license for liberty, treachery for patriotism, and vengeance for justice. If a people perverted by their training, succeed in achieving their liberty, they will soon lose it, for it would be of no avail to endeavor to explain to them that happiness consists in the practice of virtue; that the rule of law is more powerful than the rule of tyrants, because as the laws are more inflexible, everyone should submit to their beneficent austerity; that proper morals, and not force, are the bases of law; and that to practice justice is to practice liberty.

Although those people [North Americans], so lacking in many respects, are unique in the history of mankind, it is a marvel, I repeat, that so weak and complicated a government as the federal system has managed to govern them in the difficult and trying circumstances of their past. But, regardless of the effectiveness of this form of government with respect to North America, I must say that it has never for a moment entered my mind to compare the position and character of two states as dissimilar as the English-American and the Spanish-American. Would it not be most difficult to apply to Spain the English system of political, civil, and religious liberty: Hence, it would be even more difficult to adapt to Venezuela the laws of North America.

CHAPTER 23

THE OPIUM WAR

Chinese and English Views

One of the key events in nineteenth-century history was the West's forcing open of China. Like the Crusades many centuries before (see chapter 10), when Europe attacked Islam, the confrontation of the West and China allows a comparison of two societies' reactions to a single event. Unlike the Crusades, however, this event involved a decisive Western victory and a lasting impact on China because that society was on the losing end. The whole episode was a crucial stage in expanding Western imperialism. Comparison facilitates understanding imperialism from two sides rather than accepting a winner's narrative alone, while also suggesting some reasons for later Chinese policies devoted to eliminating outside control.

Since the rise of the West in the world trade in the fifteenth century, China had adopted a cautious policy, trading actively but with careful supervision of contacts. The nation had no need for Western goods, and it distrusted these aggressive barbarians. British requests for access to Chinese markets were rudely declined as late as 1796: China could stand alone.

Two developments altered this situation by the 1830s. In the first place, China's government was weakening, its hold over its bureaucracy and its tax revenues both slipping. The desire to maintain a traditional policy of isolation and rebuff remained, but the ability to implement it had declined.

More important was the greater strength of Britain and the West, thanks to early industrialization. The West had more wealth, which created a greater appetite for Chinese luxury goods such as silk and porcelain. It engaged in more production, which aroused some interest in gaining access to Chinese markets. It had better technology and better and more abundant armaments, which meant it could now give the Chinese a run for their money if it came to battle.

It was still true that the West had little to offer China economically, for the great empire had its own preindustrial manufacturing and elaborate internal trade. That is why the final ingredient to this unhappy puzzle involved pressure to sell opium. All these elements drew together in the first (of two) opium wars in the late 1830s. With a small military force, the British compelled the Chinese to back down; China began to be open to foreign trade, though a second war was needed to confirm these results. The Opium War, in turn, was not only pivotal in Chinese history, ushering in many decades of disarray and Western intervention. It also signaled the beginning of the massive nineteenth-century explosion of European imperialism virtually worldwide.

Between 1839 and 1842, British forces, supplemented by other Western troops, successfully battled Chinese coastal contingents over the right to import opium and more generally to trade freely in China. The war demonstrated that the West could easily capture coastal cities. Chinese opposition to Western demands was based on its long-standing suspicion of foreigners ("barbarians") and foreign trade, plus a keen awareness of the effects of opium, which had not been widely used before the late eighteenth century. The imperial government attempted to assert its normal strong control over internal affairs. Britain was battling for access to lucrative Chinese products and markets, the old commercial goal that Western military superiority could not attain. Opium, produced in British holdings in India, was a desirable means of earning Chinese currency to exchange for eagerly sought silks and craft goods—for the Chinese were not wildly enthusiastic about what the West itself had for sale. The war began a process of growing Western interference and internal confusion as China was reluctantly dragged into new international involvements.

Views of the war varied. The first selections reflect the official policy, backed by centuries of imperial confidence and responsibility. But reports from officials on the spot show the nation's weakness in fact, which made the emperor's goals unrealizable. An English participant, J. Elliot Bingham, gives an English explanation, offering a much different view of the opium issue, the quality of Chinese society, and the benefits of Western power. It is a classic imperialist statement. How does it compare to the views about non-Westerners prevalent in the slave trade and the conquest of the Americas (chapters 16 and 17)? Finally, a reforming official, Wei Yuan, offers a plan in 1842 for reviving China and defeating the West. His views long remained unheeded.

Questions

1. What was official Chinese policy? How did it reflect traditional Confucian ideas about the role and legitimacy of government? How did the emperor evaluate the Europeans (called barbarians by the Chinese)?
2. What kind of concessions did the imperial commissioner urge in 1842? What were his motives?
3. How did a British official justify the use of force and the sale of opium to the Chinese? How did his view of the Chinese compare with the Chinese view of the Europeans?
4. On what bases did the British now find the Chinese inferior? What, according to Bingham, might ultimately bring the Chinese up to civilized levels? What

evidence does Bingham offer about why the British were now able to defeat the Chinese?

5. Is Bingham a characteristic European imperialist, in his motives and his arguments? Using his statements, how would you define the imperialist approach?

6. What were the key ingredients of Wei Yuan's Defense Plan? What elements of traditional Chinese policy does he propose to change? Would his reforms have gone far enough to make China capable of resisting further European intervention? How would Bingham react to Wei Yuan's plan?

For Further Discussion

1. What impact did the Opium War have on long-term Chinese attitudes toward the West? Would China (and the eventual Chinese-Western relations) have been better served if the West had simply taken the nation over as a colony, as was done with India, rather than exploiting it economically without taking full responsibility?

2. Was Wei Yuan proposing a "modernization" of China? Why did China not at least quickly move to accept this kind of strategy? Why was China slow to reform, at a time when the West and other neighboring societies were clearly changing so rapidly?

3. Did many Westerners really believe their own rationales for imperialism, or was this simply a naked power grab?

4. How would a British history and a Chinese history, using these documents around 1900, when imperialist assumptions still reigned in Europe, differ in their accounts of the Opium War?

CHINA: OFFICIAL STATEMENTS

The following two documents, both issued in 1842 after the war had begun, come respectively from the emperor himself, outlining an official policy of resistance, and from a regional commissioner reporting on the actual course of the fighting.

• • •

IMPERIAL EDICT TO THE GRAND SECRETARIAT, JUNE 5, 1842

On account of the widespread evil of opium in depraving the lives of our people, I issued edicts in a preceding year commanding the various provinces strictly to prohibit the drug. The warning was repeated many times thereafter. And since Canton is the

From P. C. Kuo, *A Critical Study of the First Anglo-Chinese War* (Shanghai: Commercial Press, 1935), 289–92, 293, 296, 298. Reproduced by permission of the Commercial Press (Hong Kong) Limited.

port where the outer barbarians come to trade, Lin Tsê-hsü was specially delegated to go there to examine the affairs. The barbarian merchants of all nations obeyed the restrictions imposed by the Commissioner. The English barbarian rebel Elliot alone started disturbances on the pretext that our government had destroyed their opium. . . .

Yet the rebellious barbarians were cunning and fickle. Their demands knew no bounds. They evidently knew that Yishan was bent upon peaceful diplomacy and that he was not backed by force. Hence they dared to start hostilities by suddenly attacking the forts at Taikok and Shakok, killing our officials and disturbing the inhabitants. It is thus apparent that the rebellious barbarians began hostilities on account of smuggling opium. Then, they pretended to request favors, while in the meantime they enfolded their dark schemes. Such sheer insincerity and ingratitude should arouse the wrath of both the gods and men. When I called forth our punitive expedition, it was prompted by this consideration.

Later, when Yishan and his colleagues arrived at Canton, the rebellious barbarians had invaded the inner river and were besieging the provincial city itself. The provincial authorities thereupon agreed that the rebels sought only material profit and wished the restoration of trade. They prayed that the [merchant] debts be paid back to them. As I always treated things with true generosity, I thought that this negligible sum hardly deserved much consideration and that it was certainly not worth while to find an enemy in these rotten people, if by the grant the barbarians would abstain from creating further troubles. Thus again, I made an unusual concession out of a love for the lives of our people.

But, contrary to my expectations, the barbarians cherished mischievous ideas, offending heaven and ignoring reason itself. For no sooner had they composed the quarrels at Canton than fresh troubles arose in Fukien and Chekiang. They invaded Tinghai for the second time and took other cities in succession. It led to the suicide of our Governor and the martyrdom of our generals. The guilt of their depredation upon the lives of our people was beyond the power of redemption.

Therefore, we dispatched Yikin and others to extirpate them with our troops. During the past few months, the enemy withdrew from Ningpo, but captured Chapu in its stead. Thus these rebels first begged our favors while in Canton and fled. Then, in Chekiang, they filled their stores by robbery or depredation. Judged by their rapacious conduct, their guilt has really amounted to the full measure. While it will certainly receive the punishment from the heaven, yet there is no reason why the people should suffer this wise.

When I deliberate upon this situation, I feel tormented by it. So long as the evil were not eradicated, there is no salvation for the sufferings of the people. I censure myself for the inadequacy of my virtue, and can scarcely rest in peace. The generals, secretaries, governors, and all other officials should understand my mind and strive to relieve the sufferings of the people. They should not procrastinate, lest they should spoil the situation at present. Nor should they hope to evade their duties, lest they should perpetuate ill repute in the future.

As to the officers and soldiers in the army, there is a current belief among them that the sturdy ships and fierce cannons of the barbarians are irresistible. Hence, they gave up fighting the moment they saw the enemies on the battlefields. But they should know that the cause of the invasion of the enemies was our concession at the beginning. Should every one go forth bravely and with the coöperation of the village braves, it must be obvious that not only there is great difference between us the hosts and them the strangers, but also there is no comparison between the numerical strength of the two parties. Fighting with the advantage of knowing our own geography, there is no difficulty for us to achieve success. Thus it is apparent that the violence of the rebellious barbarians is all attributable to the inefficiency of our own troops. . . .

I am the ruler of all the people. If I should be content with peace for the time being, and not seek for the great and the far, and let the evil of the opium go its way without any prohibition, that would mean that I am betraying my ancestors who intrusted to me the care of the empire, and that I am unable to afford due protection to the lives of my subjects. Thinking about these points, how can I rest without strictly prohibiting it, how dare I not strictly prohibit it?

Although the barbarians are becoming daily more violent and rapacious, you commanders and governors, occupying important posts of the government, should arouse your conscience and enforce the laws of prohibition with vigor. Those who exert their energy will certainly receive rewards. Those who procrastinate will likewise receive penalties. When things are conducted this wise, I see no reason what attack launched by us cannot achieve success, nor what defense made by us is not impregnable. . . .

In a word, the prohibition of opium has its object in the saving of the lives of the people, while the defense against the invaders has its object in the protection of the same. I am obsessed by these tasks all the time. You ministers of the state must alike give united support to the cause, encouraging the troops to fight with persistence. Certainly it will result in the extermination of the rebels, and the eradication of violence along the coast. By that time, all of us can share with the people a universal peace.

REPORTS BY KIYING, IMPERIAL COMMISSIONER, 1842

As I examined into the said principles, I found that they truly indicate, as your Majesty had said, their [Western] insistence upon material profit. I believed that it was a good occasion for us to get them under our control. . . .

. . . Should we still persist in resistance and should the city fall to the barbarians, the loss of our own lives is an insignificant matter. But we fear that once this city, the metropolis of three provinces, should be upset, not only would the route of Chinkiang be cut off, but the barbarians could easily sail direct to the capitals of Anhwei, Kiangsi, and Hupeh. Moreover, according to a report of the magistrate of Yangchow, Pang I-chu, the barbarians had declared that if they fight and lose, they will employ native traitors to instigate troubles from within. Should this be true, the disaster would be still more inconceivable.

We believe that, although the demands of the barbarians are indeed rapacious, yet they are little more than a desire for ports and for the privilege of trade. There are no dark schemes in them. Compared with war which will inevitably entail great disasters, we would rather see assent be given to their demands, and thus save the whole country south of the Yangtze. . . .

In settling the barbarian affairs this time, we are governed at every hand by the inevitable and we concede that the policy is the least commendable. What we have been doing is to choose between danger and safety, not between right and wrong. For instance, the barbarians asked for as many as 21,000,000 dollars, and five ports. Although we are ignorant, yet we realize that the public revenues of our government are limited, that the coastal frontiers are important, and that we should not give concessions easily. But the spirit of the invaders is running high. They occupy our important cities. The illness on the limbs is becoming one in the heart of a person. Should we fail to take advantage of the present occasion, and to ease the situation by soothing the barbarians, they will run over our country like beasts, doing anything they like.

Moreover, during the past two years, we assembled the troops of several provinces. No matter whether it was for extirpation or for defense, it was of no avail. At present, the additional warships of the barbarians have almost doubled the number they used to have before. If it should happen that Nanking falls, they can easily ascend the river. The waters are deep and the banks extended; while the spots of defense are scattered, the man power available at each point must necessarily be feeble. It would be hard to erect forts at one stroke. Judged by these circumstances, the possibilities of victory or defeat must be manifest. Should their force cut off our communication between the south and the north, it is still more difficult to foretell the disasters.

The ships of the barbarians are sturdy and their cannons fierce. Previously this was only hearsay. But now we have been on their ships and personally have seen their cannons. After this experience, we are the more convinced that we cannot control them by force. It is because of the inevitable that we asked, in our previous memorial, to grant large sums of money in order to save the country.

Britain: A View from a Participant

J. Elliot Bingham was a navy officer and the son of a clergyman (the latter fact is particularly interesting in view of some of his moralizing statements and moral blind spots). Bingham wrote his account right after the war, seeking to glorify the British cause to an adoring public back home—though popular enthusiasm for imperialism was not yet at the pitch it would attain a few decades later.

• • •

Now it might be supposed from the foregoing extracts, that the Chinese have been very ill-used, and that the opium trade has been forced on them; but such was not at all the case. I must beg my readers to divest themselves of such an idea; for be it remembered, while the Chinese statesmen pencil their highly moral edicts and memorials with one hand against the admission of this poisonous drug, with the other they receive bribes and fees, levied for the secret admission of this baneful enchantment. Nay, they themselves, in secret, revel in all the luxury of the opium pipe; a luxury which, when once indulged in, it is almost impossible to shake off. . . .

To *suppress* this traffic is utterly impossible, until the whole character of the Chinese nation becomes altered. Opium they will have; and experience has proved that all the obstacles and difficulties thrown in the way of its introduction have only tended to increase it, and extend its use. It would be just as easy to put down beer and gin drinking in England. I much question whether there are not as many English gin sufferers as there are Chinese opium sufferers, for the opium is used by them in the least deleterious manner, viz., by smoking.

But, as I have before observed, it is not the question of health or morality with the Chinese. The fact is, our imports have given a great balance in our favour, as is shown in the following table:—

	£.
Our purchases for the year ending June 30, 1838, for teas, silk, and all other articles, amount to	3,147,481
Our sales of opium, metals, and cotton, to	5,637,052
Balance in favour of British	2,489,571

which was generally paid in sycee, the export of which, in 1837–8, amounted to nearly nine millions of dollars.

Thus we see what was the chief and true reason for attempting to stop the trade in opium, and accordingly the edicts previously or subsequently to this year, enlarged more on the abstraction of the sycee than on the morals of the people. . . .

Active hostilities therefore ceased, and the Emperor's assent to the provisions of the treaty having been intimated by an imperial edict on the 29th, vessels were despatched to the different Chinese ports to remove the embargoes on their trade.

During the preliminary arrangements of peace the Chinese authorities visited the Cornwallis, where they were received in great state and shown round the ship. The formidable appointments of *the barbarian sanpan* somewhat astonished the mind of their excellencies, while bumpers of cherry brandy upset the equilibrium of several

From John Elliot Bingham, *Narrative of the Expedition to China from the Commencement of the War to Its Termination in 1842.* . . . (London: Henry Colburn, 1843), 22–23, 34–39, 363–66, 369–72.

jolly members of their suite. The entertainment was duly returned, when shamsoo took the place of cherry brandy. . . .

Conclusion

The dispute with "the celestial empire" having been brought, by the energetic measures of our present Government, to a triumphant conclusion, and that, not so much by the mere destruction of junks and forts as by the consequent pressure on the trade of the country, nothing more remains for me to do, than to offer a few general remarks in concluding this narrative of events.

The military tactics of the Chinese must be regarded as far below mediocrity; and can it be otherwise with a people, among whom the recommendation of a general for employment is not his intimate acquaintance with the arts of war, but rather his acuteness to frame and his effrontery to utter the most unblushing falsehoods, in order to deceive his opponents? No deceit is too gross, no artifice too mean and dirty for a mandarin, whether soldier, magistrate, or statesman, to stoop to. The following Chinese maxim illustrates the justness of this stricture:—"When the territory of our sovereign is in difficulty we ought immediately to deliver it. What would be the use of adhering bigotedly to a little bit of good faith, thereby involving doubts and delays?"

That individuals possessing personal courage are to be found, both among Chinese and Tartars, many a single combat has shown. The latter, indeed, both at Chapoo and Tchang-kiang, when all retreat was cut off, fought with a determination that was not expected. However, upon giving the subject our consideration, we shall find that this originated not so much from the *esprit de corps* of soldiers, as from the desperation of men fighting for their wives and children, whom they fully expected would be treated by their conquerors with the same inhuman barbarity as they would have inflicted upon us, had we lost the day. . . . And most assuredly they would have made us *pay*; for hundreds of English would have been chopped up at Pekin to evince the triumph of the empire over the rebel barbarians.

"The Chinese," says the late Doctor Morrison, who had ample opportunity of forming a correct opinion, "are specious, but insincere, jealous, envious, and distrustful to a high degree; they are generally selfish, coldblooded, and inhuman." Can we, I would add, accord to them a single virtue? We might allow them one, filial affection, if that virtue, great and redeeming as it would otherwise be, did not arise more from the force of education and habit, than from the outpouring of a generous and humane heart.

The losses of the enemy, to say nothing of the wounded (vast numbers of whom probably died), cannot have fallen much short of twenty thousand, exclusive of such as perished by disease. This must of course be regarded as a rough calculation, their habit of carrying off their killed and wounded whenever by any exertion they could do so, rendering it impossible in any one instance to discover the exact number of the slain. Much as we may lament the necessity of inflicting so severe a chastisement on a people whose rulers alone were in fault, these losses are but a mere drop in comparison of the resources of an empire which maintains at least one million of men for military service, whom it draws from one-third of the human race. . . . It may also behoove us to maintain for some time a commanding force in the China seas, not forgetting the perfidious character of a nation who, having despised us before as barbarians, now hate us as their conquerors. It will be long ere their pride will forgive us for the humiliating discipline we have applied to them.

It will be our wisdom, however, to maintain the vantage ground which, through the blessing of the Almighty upon our arms, we have acquired, as well as to embrace every opportunity of making them understand the real character of the great nation they have to deal with; and in order to do this, we must treat them with firmness combined with liberality. Let us hope that the way may thus be opened for enlightening their minds with the truths of that Christianity which is the real basis of Britain's glory.

Much opposed as the government of China has ever been to the Christian religion, I do not despair of the arrival of that day, when under the influence of the spirit of the Most High the disciples of Christ shall abound and be protected even in the cities of "the central flowery land." Why should not Japan too, ere long, under the results of similar operations, be induced to open her ports to the Christian trader, and respect that cross of Christ on which she now tramples? . . .

Wei Yuan's Defense Plan, 1842

Wei Yuan was a government official, trained in Confucianism, writing in the wake of China's defeat in the first Opium War. He proposed to the emperor a number of changes, both in diplomacy and in military policy. His ideas were far too imaginative for a conservative, weak government to accept. Nevertheless, some of his proposals contain some interesting mistakes, particularly in Russian and Indian geography; why was an otherwise alert official in China prone to mistakes of this sort?

• • •

India is on the southwest of the Onion Range, and adjacent to our further Tibet, the Gurkhas, and Burma. From the homeland of the British barbarians, India is several myriad *li*. The British barbarians used warships and occupied the three parts of India, in the east, the south, and center. The Russian troops then, from the space between the Black Sea and the Caspian Sea, attacked and subdued the various nomadic tribes and made connection with the two western and central parts of India. They were only separated by the Himalayas. Each side was guarded by heavy garrisons of troops. From Bengal to Malwa in East India and from Bombay to Madras in South India opium is prevalent. The British barbarians annually collect from opium taxes more than ten million (taels) silver, and the Russians are jealous. When the British barbarians mobilized Indian . . . troops and warships to invade China, they were greatly afraid that Russia might take advantage of their weakness to invade Hindustan. . . . Therefore, the British barbarians' fear of Russia lies not in her national capital but in India. This is one opportunity which might be used. . . .

There is no better method of attacking England by sea than to use France and America. France is very close to the English barbarians, being separated only by an arm of the sea. America and the English barbarians, on the other hand, are separated by a great ocean. Beginning from the period at the end of the Ming and the beginning of this dynasty, France colonized the northeast territory of America. Cities and towns were built, markets and ports were opened. The British barbarians suddenly attacked and seized them. Thereupon the French barbarians and the English barbarians became bitter enemies. . . .

Let us establish a shipyard and an arsenal at two spots, Chuenpi and Taikoktow outside of the Bogue in Kwangtung, and select one or two persons from among the foreign headmen who have come from France and America, respectively, to bring Western craftsmen to Canton to take charge of building ships and making arms. In addition, we should invite Western helmsmen to take charge of teaching the methods of navigating ships and of using cannon, following the precedent of the barbarian officials in the Imperial Board of Astronomy. We should select clever artisans and good soldiers from Fukien and Kwangtung to learn from them, the craftsmen to learn the casting of cannon and building of ships, and the good soldiers to learn their methods of navigating and attack. . . . In Kwangtung there should be ten thousand soldiers; in Fukien, ten thousand; in Chekiang, six thousand; and in Kiangsu, four thousand. In assigning soldiers to the ships we must rely on selection and training. . . . Eight out of ten should be taken from among the fishermen and smugglers along the sea coast. Two out of ten should be taken from the old encampments of the water forces. All the padded rations and extra rations of the water force should be . . . used for the recruiting and maintenance of good soldiers. We must make the water forces of China able to navigate large (lit., "storied") ships overseas, and able to fight against foreign barbarians on the high seas.

CHAPTER 24

THE EMANCIPATIONS AND THEIR CONSEQUENCES

Widespread abolition of slavery and serfdom in the nineteenth century was one of the big developments in world history. Documents in this section encourage discussion of the reasons for this change; the actual nature of the change; and the gaps between reform professions and actual results—all in a comparative context. Latin American countries abolished slavery between 1810 and 1890, and the institution was also attacked in Africa. Serfdom ended in Europe. Forms of work and power that had existed virtually since the origin of civilization were opposed and put down.

Historians continue to debate the origins of the unprecedented movement to abolish the most blatant forms of coercive labor. New democratic and humanitarian ideals played a role. Christian humanitarians began agitating against the Atlantic slave trade in the late eighteenth century. Enlightenment political theorists joined in. Russian reformers picked up these sentiments as well, urging fundamental reform in Russia; American abolitionists stepped up the attack on slavery in the United States by the 1820s (after many northern states had ended the institution in the wake of the American Revolution). But new ideas, sincerely held, were not the only motivation. Some historians also point to the importance of new forms of capitalist labor, which demonstrated that workers could be exploited as "free" wage labor and that slavery might in fact not be efficient enough for the commercial needs of the nineteenth century. Antislavery campaigns might also distract industrial workers from their own plight, by pointing to miseries elsewhere. Rising global population levels provided alternative sources of labor.

Discussions of the complex causes of the emancipation current relate also to the question of results. On paper, emancipation ended legal servitude. But even the humanitarians had not necessarily thought much about the real conditions that would prevail for former serfs and slaves. And powerful interested parties, such as the estate owners, had obvious reasons to try to limit the impact of change. Emancipation, though real, in this sense set up further problems.

Russia, the United States, and Brazil in the nineteenth century invite comparison. All three were huge, expanding countries beginning to have a growing impact in world affairs. All three abolished deeply rooted labor systems between 1800 and 1890, but all three faced important social tensions thereafter.

Two major moves occurred almost simultaneously: Russia's Emancipation of the Serfs in 1861 and Lincoln's Emancipation Proclamation of 1863. Circumstances differed. Lincoln acted during civil war, to rally support for the Union cause. Russia hoped to reduce peasant discontent and also build a more flexible economy and labor force, as it lagged behind industrial Western Europe. Russia was spurred by its embarrassing loss to Britain and France in the Crimean War (1854–55), which seemed to prove that change was essential. But some similar humanitarian ideals were involved in each case, at least on the part of certain reformers, plus a belief that "free" wage labor was economically more productive than its forced equivalent. What are the professed intentions behind the two emancipations, as reflected in the initial documents below? Are they part of a single movement in world history, in two rather different societies? Brazil's movement came later, but with much less debate. It too, however, can be compared with other emancipations in terms of principles, process, and probable results.

Both Russia and the United States experienced continued disruption after these major reforms. Russian serfs immediately complained of mistreatment, and their protest continued for decades. As Southern whites regained political control in the 1870s after the Reconstruction period ended, African Americans in the region experienced a loss of economic opportunities and other rights. Why was reform incomplete in both countries? Brazilian ex-slaves faced economic challenges as well in a society that defined racism differently than the United States did. Today, Afro-Brazilians with darker skin color continue to face discrimination, but there is less sense that having some African ancestry puts everyone in a single racial category.

Questions

1. How do the three emancipations compare? How do their justifications differ? Which pays more attention to the conditions likely to result from emancipation? In what sense can all three reform measures be judged to be rather limited, despite their role in ending long-standing institutions of labor?
2. Why did Russia's peasants begin immediately protesting the conditions of emancipation? What institution did they think could fix the problems? Why did the kinds of problems and expectations expressed in these protests ultimately—a half-century later—help lead to revolution?
3. In what ways did black protest in the American South differ from that of the Russian peasants? What were some similar complaints?
4. What happened to the social structure (class, or race) of the three societies after emancipation? How did postemancipation reactions of the Russian aristocracy and the Southern planter class compare? Was either more violent than the other—and if so, for what reasons?

5. Why were there such gaps between the apparent intent of emancipations and their actual results?

6. To what extent was Brazilian emancipation distinctive? What are the likely causes of distinctiveness?

For Further Discussion

1. What caused the emancipation movements? Were the causes basically the same in Russia, the United States, and Brazil?

2. Which political system was more open to protest, that of Russia or that of the United States? Why did the protests of former serfs in Russia ultimately lead to revolution, whereas protests by former slaves in the United States did not?

3. On balance, did reform fail or succeed in Russia? In the United States? In either case, can you think of ways reform could have been done more successfully, with better long-term results?

4. What results did Brazilian emancipation and the abolitionism that preceded it suggest for freed slaves and the postslavery economy?

THE EMANCIPATION MANIFESTO, 1861

Russia's emancipation of the serfs had been debated off and on for almost a century, as a reform element developed in the Western-oriented aristocracy. The loss of the Crimean War, when the industrially sustained armies of Britain and France beat Russia on its own southern border, accelerated the discussion. A new, reform-minded czar, Alexander II, resolved to act. The measure was the first of many reforms over the next two decades. Nonetheless, the emancipation clearly took into account the vital position of the Russian nobility; it was not intended to be a social revolution.

• • •

By the Grace of God We, Alexander II, Emperor and Autocrat of All Russia, King of Poland, Grand Duke of Finland, etc., make known to all Our faithful subjects:

Called by Divine Providence and by the sacred right of inheritance to the throne of Our Russian ancestors, We vowed in Our heart to respond to the mission which is entrusted to Us and to surround with Our affection and Our Imperial solicitude all Our faithful subjects of every rank and condition, from the soldier who nobly defends the country to the humble artisan who works in industry; from the career official of the state to the plowman who tills the soil.

From Basil Dmytryshyn, *Imperial Russia: A Sourcebook, 1700–1917* (New York: Holt, Rinehart and Winston, 1967), 221–23, 225.

Examining the condition of classes and professions comprising the state, We became convinced that the present state legislation favors the upper and middle classes, defines their obligations, rights, and privileges, but does not equally favor the serfs, so designated because in part from old laws and in part from custom they have been hereditarily subjected to the authority of landowners, who in turn were obligated to provide for their well being. Rights of nobles have been hitherto very broad and legally ill defined, because they stem from tradition, custom, and the good will of the noblemen. In most cases this has led to the establishment of good patriarchal relations based on the sincere, just concern and benevolence on the part of the nobles, and on affectionate submission on the part of the peasants. Because of the decline of the simplicity of morals, because of an increase in the diversity of relations, because of the weakening of the direct paternal attitude of nobles toward the peasants, and because noble rights fell sometimes into the hands of people exclusively concerned with their personal interests, good relations weakened. The way was opened for an arbitrariness burdensome for the peasants and detrimental to their welfare, causing them to be indifferent to the improvement of their own existence. . . .

We thus became convinced that the problem of improving the condition of serfs was a sacred inheritance bequeathed to Us by Our predecessors, a mission which, in the course of events, Divine Providence has called upon Us to fulfill.

We have begun this task by expressing Our confidence toward the Russian nobility, which has proven on so many occasions its devotion to the Throne, and its readiness to make sacrifices for the welfare of the country.

We have left to the nobles themselves, in accordance with their own wishes, the task of preparing proposals for the new organization of peasant life—proposals that would limit their rights over the peasants, and the realization of which would inflict on them [the nobles] some material losses. Our confidence was justified. Through members of the *gubernia* committees, who had the trust of the nobles' associations, the nobility voluntarily renounced its right to own serfs. These committees, after collecting the necessary data, have formulated proposals on a new arrangement for serfs and their relationship with the nobles.

These proposals were diverse, because of the nature of the problem. They have been compared, collated, systematized, rectified and finalized in the main committee instituted for that purpose; and these new arrangements dealing with the peasants and domestics of the nobility have been examined in the Governing Council.

Having invoked Divine assistance, We have resolved to execute this task.

On the basis of the above mentioned new arrangements, the serfs will receive in time the full rights of free rural inhabitants.

The nobles, while retaining their property rights on all the lands belonging to them, grant the peasants perpetual use of their domicile in return for a specified obligation; and, to assure their livelihood as well as to guarantee fulfillment of their obligations toward the government, [the nobles] grant them a portion of arable land fixed by the said arrangements, as well as other property.

While enjoying these land allotments, the peasants are obliged, in return, to fulfill obligations to the noblemen fixed by the same arrangements. In this state, which is temporary, the peasants are temporarily bound.

At the same time, they are granted the right to purchase their domicile, and, with the consent of the nobles, they may acquire in full ownership the arable lands and other properties which are allotted them for permanent use. Following such acquisition of full ownership of land, the peasants will be freed from their obligations to the nobles for the land thus purchased and will become free peasant landowners. . . .

We leave it to the nobles to reach a friendly understanding with the peasants and to reach agreements on the extent of the land allotment and the obligations stemming from it, observing, at the same time, the established rules to guarantee the inviolability of such agreements. . . .

What legally belongs to nobles cannot be taken away from them without adequate compensation, or through their voluntary concession; it would be contrary to all justice to use the land of the nobles without assuming responsibility for it.

And now We confidently expect that the freed serfs, on the eve of a new future which is opening to them, will appreciate and recognize the considerable sacrifices which the nobility has made on their behalf.

The Emancipation Proclamation, 1862

Abraham Lincoln did not come easily to the decision to emancipate the slaves. He was opposed to slavery, but his opinions had wavered over his adult life. He believed in property, and he did not want to antagonize the South more than necessary. But in the second year of the Civil War, with northern abolitionists pressing for action, it became clear that emancipation might improve support for the war and also help raise black resistance in the South, thus weakening the secessionist war effort. Lincoln's proclamation differed from the czar's in many ways, reflecting a very different political and religious system. But it expressed some similar cautions. As in Russia, this reform was followed by others, when the North took over the South during the Reconstruction period. As in Russia also, the reform era ended by the late 1870s or the 1880s.

• • •

Whereas on the 22d day of September, A.D. 1862, a proclamation was issued by the President of the United States, containing, among other things, the following, to wit:

"That on the 1st day of January, A.D. 1863, all persons held as slaves within any State or designated part of a State the people whereof shall then be in rebellion against the

THE LONG NINETEENTH CENTURY

United States shall be then, thenceforward, and forever free; and the executive government of the United States, including the military and naval authority thereof, will recognize and maintain the freedom of such persons and will do no act or acts to repress such persons, or any of them, in any efforts they may make for their actual freedom. . . .

And by virtue of the power and for the purpose aforesaid, I do order and declare that all persons held as slaves within said designated States and parts of States are, and henceforward shall be, free; and that the Executive Government of the United States, including the military and naval authorities thereof, will recognize and maintain the freedom of said persons.

And I hereby enjoin upon the people so declared to be free to abstain from all violence, unless in necessary self-defense; and I recommend to them that, in all cases when allowed, they labor faithfully for reasonable wages.

And I further declare and make known that such persons of suitable condition will be received into the armed service of the United States to garrison forts, positions, stations, and other places, and to man vessels of all sorts in said service.

And upon this act, sincerely believed to be an act of justice, warranted by the Constitution upon military necessity, I invoke the considerate judgment of mankind and the gracious favor of Almighty God.

JOACHIM NABUCO AND BRAZILIAN ABOLITIONISM

Joachim Nabuco was a leader in Brazilian abolitionism after a failed effort in 1871. The following extracts were part of a book he published in 1881 in which he lays out his arguments against slavery and his vision of a postslavery Brazil.

• • •

The need for rapid abolition is recognized by all who are dissatisfied with the concept of Brazil as a new [colonial economy] in America. The necessity of this operation has been demonstrated, just as surgical science can prove the need to amputate a gangrenous arm or leg in order to save a human life.

Unfortunately for slavery, however, as it undermined the entire nation, it weakened itself as well; while corrupting everything else, it was also self-corrupting. As a result, [this] proslavery army is a mixed and undisciplined mob eager to flee the field of combat. The clientele of slavery are ashamed of living upon the scraps they are tossed, of depending upon slavery's indulgence. The people who survive like vagrants on lands not their own, when given the hope of legitimately possessing those lands where they are now suffered to squat as pariahs, will reject their present serflike status.

From Joachim Nabuco, *Abolitionism: The Brazilian Antislavery Struggle*, trans. Robert Conrad (Urbana: University of Illinois Press, 1977), 148, 149, 150–51, 171, 173.

In regard to the several social forces, slavery has made them so weak, timid, and unreliable that they will be the first to welcome any change which brings their own downfall and reconstructs them with new elements. . . .

Public opinion, as it is now developing, possesses strength and has its effects upon the government. It represents the nation before the world, holds within its grasp the leadership of a huge political complex which would be amenable to emancipation if it were not for the coffee districts in the provinces of São Paulo, Minas Gerais, and Rio de Janeiro, a political mass which is each day more and more impelled by the national conscience to abandon the orbit which slavery marked out for it.

However vast the power of slavery, however impressive the credit it can command in the banks, however huge the value of its mortgaged estates, it stands like a dogmatic aberration in the face of established truth. An ounce of science is worth more, in the final analysis, than a ton of faith. Similarly, the smallest particle of high-minded sentiment on behalf of humanity will eventually destroy the largest monopoly erected against humanity's interests. I do not attribute any metaphysical power to principles when there is nobody to impose them, when the human mass to which such principles might be applied is unreceptive to them. Yet, setting private interests aside, I do not elevate too highly the character, tendencies, and aspirations of the Brazilian people when I say that all their sympathies are on the side of freedom and against slavery.

Yet the following truth must also be recognized: the reluctant attitude of the government—the one force capable of destroying slavery—the still inconsequential extent of its response to public opinion, and the slowness of the latter's development do not allow us to hope that the break between the government and slavery will occur soon. If the abolitionist pressure did not exist, the government would delay even more than it does. Consequently, our strength will grow as we are able to arouse such opinion, as we call each class to action based upon its understanding that slavery not only degrades our country but undermines it physically. The instrument of success exists and is known to us; this instrument is power. The way to produce power, which is also known to us, is through public concern. What remains to be done is to endow that public opinion with the needed energy, to draw it out of the lassitude which renders it useless, to prove to it that prolonged inactivity is suicidal.

Compare the Brazil of today and its slavery with the ideal of a motherland which we, the abolitionists, uphold. The latter is a country where all are free, where European immigration, attracted by the openness of our institutions and by the freedom of our system, will endlessly send to the tropics a current of lively, energetic, and healthy Caucasian blood which we can absorb without danger, instead of that Chinese wave with which the large landholders hope to contaminate and corrupt our race even further. What we wish is a country which may work in her own unique way for the good of humanity and the development of South America. . . .

[The] past whose collapse we are now witnessing will give way to an order of things founded upon an entirely different concept of our duties toward life, property, the individual, the family, personal rights, honor, and individual integrity. That past will make way for a society in which there is a new regard for our fellowman, for the individual before the nation, for personal freedom, for civilization, for equal legal protection, for established social achievements, for humanity itself, which inspires us with the will to participate in this immense heritage of our species, which in fact tacitly delivers this heritage over to the protection of each one of us.

The abolitionists include all those who believe in a Brazil without slaves, all those who anticipate the miracles of free labor, all those who suffer *slavery* as a detested vassalage imposed upon the entire nation by some in the interests of some. They include those who now gasp in the foul air which slaves and masters freely breathe—those who do not believe that Brazil with slavery gone, will lie down to die, as did the Roman in the age of the Caesars because he had lost his liberty.

This means that we are seeking our country's highest interests, her civilization, the future rightfully hers, the mission to which her place in America calls her. But, between us and those who are blocking the path, who will win? This, indeed, is the very enigma of Brazil's national destiny. Slavery injected fanaticism into her bloodstream, and she is now doing nothing to grasp control of her fate from those blind and indifferent forces which now silently lead her on.

BRAZILIAN ABOLITION

LAW NO. 3353, ABOLISHING SLAVERY IN BRAZIL,

MAY 13, 1888

The Princess Imperial Regent, in the name of His Majesty the Emperor Dom Pedro II, makes known to all subjects of the Empire that the General Assembly has decreed, and she has sanctioned, the following law:

Art. 1. From the date of this law slavery is declared extinct in Brazil.
Art. 1. All provisions to the contrary are revoked.

She orders, therefore, all the authorities to whom the knowledge and execution of this Law belong to carry it out, and cause it to be fully and exactly executed and observed.

RUSSIAN PEASANTS AFTER EMANCIPATION:
PEASANT PETITIONS

Discontent with the conditions of emancipation surfaced almost immediately in Russia. For a time, petitions rained in. Over a longer period, major peasant protests surged, in which remaining estates might be occupied and records of redemption payments that peasants owed for the land they had received burned.

The petitions require some care in interpretation. They include detail that needs to be sorted out to find the main points. They include some hyperbole, because the peasants hoped to win the czar's attention by elaborate expressions of trust and obedience. What were the main grievances? How did peasants decide they could best define the justice of their case?

• • •

PETITION FROM PEASANTS IN BALASHOV DISTRICT (SARATOV PROVINCE)
TO GRAND DUKE KONSTANTIN NIKOLAEVICH, 25 JANUARY 1862

Your Imperial Excellency! Most gracious sire! Grand Duke Konstantin Nikolaevich!

Most magnanimous prince, given by God for the welfare of people in the Russian Empire! The countless acts of mercy and humanitarianism of Your Imperial Excellency toward the loyal subjects have emboldened us to fall to your feet and plead:

Show your steadfast and just protection of oppressed humanity! Following the example of our fathers, grandfathers and ancestors, we have always and without complaint obeyed the laws of Russian monarchs and the authority of its rulers. . . .

The monarch's mercy—which has no precedent in the chronicles of all peoples in the universe—has now changed the attitude of our squire, who has reduced us 1,500 peasants to a pitiable condition. . . . After being informed of the Imperial manifesto on the emancipation of peasants from serfdom in 1861 (which was explained to us by the constable of township 2 of Balashov District), we received this [news] with jubilation, as a special gift from heaven, and expressed our willingness to obey the squire's will in every respect during the coming two-year [transition] period [and to remain] on the fertile land which we occupy, where we could realise our life. . . . [sic]

But from this moment, our squire ordered that the land be cut off from the entire township. But this is absolutely intolerable for us: it not only denies us profit, but threatens us with a catastrophic future. He began to hold repeated meetings and [tried to] force us to sign that we agreed to accept the above land allotment. But, upon seeing so unexpected a change, and bearing in mind the gracious manifesto, we refused. . . . But when [the nobles] saw that this did not succeed, they had a company of soldiers sent in and said that they had been sent—by the Tsar!—to restore peace between us and the squires. . . . Then [Col.] Globbe came from their midst, threatened us with exile to Siberia, and ordered the soldiers to strip the peasants and to punish seven people by flogging in the most inhuman manner. They still have not regained consciousness.

From Gregory L. Freeze, ed., *From Supplication to Revolution: A Documentary Social History of Imperial Russia* (New York: Oxford University Press, 1988), 171–79. Reprinted by permission of the publisher.

The inhuman acts and intolerable oppression have forced us to fall to the sacred feet of Your Imperial Excellency: 1,500 voices most humbly ask for just, most august defense, which can save weeping families from certain death, and [we ask] that You issue a decree [on our case].

PETITION FROM PEASANTS IN PODOSINOVKA (VORONEZH PROVINCE)
TO ALEXANDER II, MAY 1863

The most merciful manifesto of Your Imperial Majesty from 19 February 1861, with the published rules, put a limit to the enslavement of the people in blessed Russia. But some former serfowners—who desire not to improve the peasants' life, but to oppress and ruin them—apportion land contrary to the laws, choose the best land from all the fields for themselves, and give the poor peasants (who are just emerging from their domination) the worst and least usable lands. . . . Of our fields and resources, [our landlord] chose the best places from amidst our strips and, like a cooking ring in a hearth, carved off 300 dessiatines for herself. Other places—characterized by sand, hills, knolls and ravines (with the sparsest amount of hayland)—were designated as the peasant allotment; altogether, including the household plots, we were given four dessiatines per soul and assessed a quitrent of 12 rubles per soul. But our community refused to accept so ruinous an allotment and requested that we be given an allotment in accordance with the local Statute [of emancipation], without injury, even if the quitrent must be increased. . . . The provincial governor—without making any investigation and without interrogating a single person—ordered that the birch rods be brought and that the punishment commence, which was carried out with cruelty and mercilessness. They punished up to 200 men and women; 80 people were at four levels (with 500, 400, 300 and 200 blows); some received lesser punishment. . . .

Having explained the inhuman acts of our local authorities and our final ruination through the oppressive allotment of unusable land in strips, we dare to implore you, Orthodox emperor and our merciful father, not to reject the petition of a community with 600 souls, including wives and children. . . .

AFRICAN AMERICANS AFTER SLAVERY:
PETITIONS IN THE SOUTH

During the 1870s, former slaves often petitioned the federal government for new opportunities, in a context in which Reconstruction state governments allowed them voice. While most land remained in the hands of former plantation owners, blacks managed to purchase some. They also set up schools and other community institutions. But the end of Reconstruction showed how vulnerable the former slave population was.

JOINT AFFIDAVIT FROM GEORGE UNDERWOOD, BEN HARRIS, AND ISIAH FULLER

Caddo Parish, La., August 3, 1875

We worked, or made a contract to work, and make a crop on shares on Mr. McMoring's place, and worked for one-third (⅓) of the crop, and he (McMoring) was to find us all of our provisions; and in July, 1875, we was working alone in the field, and Mr. McMoring and McBounton came to us and says, "Well, boys, you all got to get away from here; and that they had gone as far as they could go, and you all must live agreeable, or you shall take what follows"; and the two white men went and got sticks and guns, and told us that we must leave the place; and we told them that we would not leave it, because we don't want to give up our crop for nothing; and they told us that we had better leave, or we would not get anything; and we wanted to have justice, but he would not let us have justice; and we told them that we would get judges to judge the crop, to say what it is worth; and the white men told us that no judge should come on his place; and we did not want to leave the place, but they beat Isiah Fuller, and whipped him, and then we got afraid, and we left the place; and we got about thirty acres in cotton, and the best cotton crop in that part of the parish; and we have about twenty-nine acres of corn, and about the best corn in the parish, and it is ripe, and the fodder ready to pull, and our cotton laid by; and runned us off from the place, and told us not to come back any more; and we were due McMoring the sum of one hundred and eighty dollars ($180) and they told us that if they ever heard of it any more that they would fix us; and all the time that we were living and working on the place they would not half feed us; and we had to pay for all, or half of our rashings, or what we had to eat, and that is all that was due them for; and we worked for them as though we were slaves, and then treated like dogs all the time.

MEMORIAL FROM ALABAMA NEGROES

To His Excellency the President of the United States, and the honorable the Congress of the United States:

The colored people of the State of Alabama, who by virtue of the three latest amendments to the Constitution of the United States became emancipated, and also became citizens of the United States, feeling anxiously and solemnly impressed by

From Herbert Aptheker, ed., *A Documentary History of the Negro People in the United States* (New York: Citadel Press, 1951), 586, 600–603.

their past and present condition in the State of Alabama, and by the grave and menacing dangers that now surround and threaten them and their constitutional rights, have as a race and as a people assembled together in convention to consider their situation, and to take solemn counsel together as to what it becomes them to do for their self-preservation.

We, therefore, for your better information upon the subject, do humbly present for your consideration and action the following memorial:

That as a race, and as citizens, we never have enjoyed, except partially, imperfectly, and locally, our political and civil rights in this State. Our right to vote in elections has been, in a large portion of this State, denied, abridged, and rendered difficult and dangerous ever since we became voters. The means used by our political opponents to destroy or impair their right have been various; but have chiefly consisted of violence in the form of secret assassination, lynching, intimidation, malicious and frivolous prosecutions and arrests, and by depriving or threatening to deprive us of employment and the renting of lands, which many of us, in our poverty and distress, were unable to disregard. These acts of lawlessness have been repeated and continued since our first vote in 1868, and their effect has been such that from ten to fifteen thousand of the votes of our race have in each election been either repressed or been given under compulsion to our political opponents. . . .

Nor have we fared better in our civil rights of life, liberty, and property which have come for adjudication before the State courts. It is true that republican judges have generally presided over the superior courts of this State, and have generally shown a disposition to do us justice, but even these have been to some extent, warped by local pressure. But the main reasons for this failure of justice are that the sheriffs, probate judges and clerks of courts have almost universally, throughout the State, in plain violation of State laws, failed or refused to put men of our race on grand and petit juries in most of the counties in Alabama, and it has followed, as a consequence, that the lives, liberties, and property of black men have been decided by grand and petit juries composed exclusively of white men who are their political opponents. In controversies between our race and white men, and in criminal trials where the accused or the injured is a black man, it is almost if not quite impossible for a black man to obtain justice. . . . Our lives, liberties, and properties are made to hang upon the capricious, perilous, and prejudiced judgments of juries composed of a hostile community of ex-slaveholders who disdain to recognize the colored race as their peers in anything, who look upon us as being *by nature an inferior race,* and by right their chattel property. . . .

Pressed around with these wrongs, misfortunes, and dangers, and solemnly impressed with their gravity, no resource or hope suggests itself to us but an earnest, prayerful, and we hope not unavailing, appeal to the President and the Congress of the United States, who still have the power and the agencies that may, in some measure, right our wrongs and diminish our misfortunes.

The question which our case and condition presents to you is simply this: whether our constitutional rights as citizens are to be a reality or a mockery, a protection and a boon or a danger and a curse; whether we are to be freemen in fact or only in name; and whether the late amendments to the Constitution are to be practically enforced or to become a nullity and stand only "as dead letters on the statute-book."

CHAPTER 25

RUSSIAN AND JAPANESE CONSERVATISM

Conservatism is not a standard world history topic. However, conservatism experienced a number of crucial changes in the long nineteenth century, in a number of different societies, while remaining a vigorous force, sometimes a dominant force, in political life. The need to articulate reactions to change and foreign influence, and the increasing ability to use nationalism to help shape conservative response, were widespread developments that warrant explicit comparative treatment. Japanese and Russian conservatisms were important in their own right, but they also raise larger issues.

Conservatism is as old as human politics. Any political situation involves some people a bit more eager for change and others insistent that current arrangements should be preserved. These latter are conservatives. Some political cultures, because of an emphasis on order, are more dominated by conservatism than others—China before the twentieth century is an example frequently cited. But the general phenomenon is a common one in history.

During the nineteenth century so many changes were occurring, because of new political ideas (including ideas spread by the French Revolution), industrialization, and imperialism, that conservatives in many areas were inclined to become more explicit about their viewpoint and even to organize as a political movement. Formal conservatism, as opposed to more informal groupings of like-minded leaders, thus emerged in Europe during the French revolutionary era, around 1800. Further, outside Europe, pressures to import political and social ideas and institutions from the dynamic West prompted conservatives to worry about foreignness as well as about change in general. Many conservatives found themselves defending against Western corruption what they saw as vital elements of their own cultural and political traditions.

Because political changes and Western influence were particularly widespread in Japan from the Meiji era (beginning in 1868) onward and in Russia under Alexander II (1855–81), conservatism in these two countries gained unusual importance and complexity. Conservatives were forced to define what aspects of the contemporary West and what resultant reform proposals were particularly objectionable. But they might also identify certain ingredients that, altered to preserve national essentials, could be accepted as change. In both countries conservatives wielded great influence, shaping much of the reform process in Japan and, in Russia, preventing certain kinds of reforms altogether.

Conservatism in the nineteenth century was rarely simple-minded. Many conservatives recognized the need for some change: they merely insisted that many older values and institutions should be essentially preserved and that change should not be blindly embraced. Many Russian conservatives after 1861, for example, clearly recognized that the emancipation of the serfs had been a desirable reform; they did not argue for a return to serfdom, though they rarely wanted many more concessions to the aggrieved peasantry. Russian conservatives also saw that their country should participate in the kinds of scientific research being spearheaded in Western Europe; there was danger in lagging behind here. Japanese conservatives were even more flexible: they granted that the old system of feudalism and the shogunate should not be restored (though they sometimes sought to maintain some of the older values, including military honor). Conservatives in both countries utilized the new force of nationalism. Interpreting modern conservatism as it began to develop in response to the massive changes of the long nineteenth century thus requires some subtlety: what did conservatives insist on keeping intact, and where were they willing to bend?

Russian conservatives were in the ascendancy after Alexander II was assassinated by terrorists in 1881. Although they did not oppose all change (industrialization continued), they definitely resisted any further alterations to the political and social structure. Their obstinacy helped develop an atmosphere of inflexibility and repression that led to the revolutions of 1905 and 1907. Japanese conservatives gained ground in the 1880s also, with the backing of the emperor, amid a widespread sense that disorder was spreading, for example, in the schools.

Russian conservatism was not uniform, though all its leading spokesmen favored nationalism, czarist autocracy, and the Orthodox church. Some conservative nationalists praised the Russian people in the abstract while defining distinctive views of the state and progress. Leaders such as Nikolai Danilevsky, in the 1860s, bitterly opposed the West, but they could grant the need for some limited change. After the terrorist assassination of czar Alexander II in 1881, however, Russian conservatism became more defensive. Constantine Pobedonostsev became Russia's conservative leader. A lawyer, he gained positions both in the government and in the Orthodox church, spurring reactionary policies between 1881 and 1905. Pobedonostsev was outspoken in his hostility to key Western principles and institutions.

In Japan, Yamagata Arimoto was the most conservative of the leading statesmen of the Meiji era and was closely associated with the army. He, too, objected to many Western values, but he also saw how certain Western practices, such as universal military conscription, though radical in terms of Japanese tradition, could actually benefit a conservative Japanese state. Here, he tried to show how history set a Japanese precedent for a practice that was apparently new.

Comparing these two conservative currents requires the now-familiar balance between noting the important points they have in common—do Russian and Japanese leaders agree about Western political fallacies, for example?—and discerning the ways in which they differ in degree of openness to limited change.

Questions

1. How did Danilevsky define Russian superiority? What, in his view, were Russia's key strengths?
2. What did Danilevsky mean by freedom? What recent reform was he willing to defend? What few aspects of the West did he admire?
3. How do Danilevsky and Pobedonostsev compare as Russian nationalists and conservatives? Did they agree on the qualities of a strong state? How do their emphases differ?
4. Which version of Russian conservatism do Yamagata Arimoto's views most resemble: Danilevsky's or Pobedonostsev's?
5. Why and how did Russian conservatism change between the 1860s (Danilevsky, and the 1880s (Pobedonostsev)?
6. What aspects of Western politics did Yamagata Arimoto, Danilevsky, and Pobedonostsev all criticize? Did they agree in their reactions to the West?
7. How did Yamagata Arimoto and Pobedonostsev view voting and political parties and the remedies for divisiveness?
8. How did Yamagata Arimoto's Confucianism compare with Pobedonostsev's conservative ideals? Would Russian conservatives' advice to soldiers be different from Yamagata Arimoto's? What are the implications of these differences? By Russian conservative standards, is it accurate to call Yamagata Arimoto a conservative at all?
9. What kinds of differences in national setting did the two conservative movements suggest? In which country did conservatives have an easier time defending the status quo in the 1880s and 1890s?

For Further Discussion

1. What is conservative nationalism? How does it differ from liberal or radical nationalism?
2. Why did both Japanese and Russian conservatives emphasize the importance of an emperor and a strong state?

3. What aspects of the West were most likely to be criticized by foreign observers in the late nineteenth century? Are the same aspects still likely to be criticized today, or has the list changed?
4. Can Japan's greater success in combining change and stability be traced in the nature of its conservatism? How did Russia's version of conservatism play a role in the conditions that led to major revolution?

DANILEVSKY

The following selection was authored by an ardent Slavic nationalist, Nikolai Danilevsky, in a multiple-edition book called *Russia and Europe,* first issued in 1869. Danilevsky asserts the special virtues of the Slavic peoples as against other Europeans, and the dominance of Russia among the Slavs. Elements of his argument might seem comical: he twists history, he glosses over ongoing problems such as peasant discontent after emancipation, and he ludicrously promises stability in a country almost foredoomed to revolution. But Danilevsky's views about Russian distinctiveness and Western evil were widely shared, even by people opposed to the existing czarist regime. The complexities of his outlook were widely shared also, as he talked about some selective borrowing from the West. Complexities of this sort outlived the czarist regime and flourished after the Communist revolution of 1917.

· · ·

And now let us turn to the Slav world, and chiefly to Russia, its only independent representative, in order to examine the results and the promises of this world, a world still only at the beginning of its cultural-historical life. We must examine it from the viewpoint of the above four foci of reference: religion, culture, politics, and socio-economic structure, in order to elucidate what we rightfully expect as well as hope from the Slav cultural-historical type.

Religion constituted the most essential element of ancient Russian life, and at the present time, the overwhelming spiritual interest of the ordinary Russian is also involved in it; in truth, one cannot but wonder at the ignorance and the impertinence of these people who could insist (to gratify their fantasies) on the religious indifference of the Russian people.

From an objective, factual viewpoint, the Russian and the majority of Slav peoples became, with the Greeks, the chief guardians of the living tradition of religious truth, Orthodoxy, and in this way they continued the high calling, which was the destiny of Israel and Byzantium: to be the chosen people. . . .

From Nikolai Danilevsky, *Russia and Europe,* in *The Mind of Modern Russia,* ed. Hans Kohn (New Brunswick, N.J.: Rutgers University Press, 1955), 200–211.

. . . The religious aspect of the cultural activity belongs to the Slav cultural type and to Russia in particular; it is its inalienable achievement, founded on the psychology of its people and on its guardianship of religious truth. . . .

Whatever the future may bring we are entitled, on the evidence of the past alone, to consider the Slavs among the most gifted families of the human race in political ability. Here we may turn our attention to the special character of this political ability and show how it manifested itself during the growth of the Russian state. The Russians do not send out colonists to create new political societies, as the Greeks did in antiquity or the English in modern times. Russia does not have colonial possessions, like Rome or like England. The Russian state from early Muscovite times on has been Russia herself, gradually, irresistibly spreading on all sides, settling neighboring non-settled territories, and assimilating into herself and into her national boundaries foreign populations. This basic character of Russian expansion was misunderstood because of the distortion of the original Russian point of view through Europeanization, the origin of every evil in Russia. . . .

But the expansion of the state, its attainment of stability, strength, and power, constitutes only one aspect of political activity. It has still another one, consisting of the establishment of equal relationships between the citizens themselves and between them and the state, i.e., in the establishment of civil and political freedom. A people not endowed with this freedom cannot be said to possess a healthy political sense. Is the Russian people capable of freedom?

Naturally our "well-wishers" give a negative answer: some regard slavery as a natural element of the Russians, and others are afraid, or pretend to be afraid, that freedom in Russian hands must lead to all sorts of excesses and abuses. But on the basis of Russian history and with knowledge of the views and traits of the Russian people, one can only form an opinion diametrically opposed to this view—namely, that there hardly ever has existed or exists a people so capable of enduring such a large share of freedom as the Russians and so little inclined to abuse it, due to their ability and habit to obey, their respect and trust in the authorities, their lack of love for power, and their loathing of interference in matters where they do not consider themselves competent. If we look into the causes of all political troubles, we shall find their root not in the striving after freedom, but in the love for power and the vain cravings of human beings to interfere in affairs that are beyond their comprehension. . . .

This nature of the Russian people is the true reason why Russia is the only state which never had (and in all probability never will have) a political revolution, i.e., a revolution having as its aim the limitation of the power of the ruler. . . .

With legality in the succession of the throne secured . . . and finally with the liberation of the peasants, all the reasons which in former times had agitated the people disappeared; and even an ordinary rebellion, going beyond the limits of a regrettable misunderstanding, has become impossible in Russia so long as the moral character of the Russian people does not change. . . .

. . . Thus we may conclude that the Russian people, by their attitude towards the power of the state, by their ability to sacrifice to it their own personal interests, and by their attitude towards the use of political and civil freedom, are gifted with wonderful political sense.

In the socio-economic sphere, Russia is the only large state which has solid ground under its feet, in which there are no landless masses, and in which, consequently, the social edifice does not rest on the misery of the majority of the citizens and on the insecurity of their situation. In Russia only there cannot and does not exist any contradiction between political and economic ideals. . . . The factors that give such superiority to the Russian social structure over the European, and give it an unshakable stability, are the peasant's land and its common ownership. On this health of Russia's socio-economic structure we found our hope for the great socio-economic significance of the Slav cultural-historical type. This type has been able for the first time to create a just and normal system of human activity, which embraces not only human relations in the moral and political sphere, but also man's mastery of nature, which is a means of satisfying human needs and requirements. Thus it establishes not only formal equality in the relations between citizens, but a real and concrete equality.

However, as regards the prominent place of the Slav cultural-historical type in the field of culture proper, one must admit that so far the Russian and other Slav achievements in the sciences and in the arts are insignificant in comparison with the accomplishments of the two great cultural types, the Greek and the European. . . .

Scientific and artistic activity can thrive only under conditions of leisure, of an overflow of forces that remain free from daily toil. Could much leisure be left over among Russians and Slavs? . . . All these considerations fully answer, it seems to me, the question why until now Russia and the other Slav countries could not occupy a respected position in purely cultural activities. . . . But indications of these aptitudes, of these spiritual forces, which are necessary for brilliant achievements in the fields of science and art are now indisputably present among the Slav peoples in spite of all the unfavorable conditions of their life; and, consequently, we are justified in expecting that with a change in these conditions, these peoples will bring forth remarkable creations. . . .

The Slav cultural type has already produced enough examples of artistic and, to a lesser degree, scientific achievements to allow us to conclude that it has attained a significant degree of development in these fields. The relative youth of the race and the concentration of all its forces upon other, more urgent types of activity have not, until now, given the Slavs the opportunity of acquiring cultural significance, in the exact meaning of the phrase. This should not embarrass us; rather, it points to the right path in our development. As long as there is no strong foundation, we cannot and we must not think of the erection of a durable edifice; we can only set up temporary buildings, which cannot be expected to display the talents of the builder in every respect. The political independence of the race is the indispensable foundation of culture, and consequently all the Slav forces must be directed towards this goal. Independence is indispensable . . . [for] without the consciousness of Slav racial unity, as distinct from other races, an independent culture is impossible. . . .

The requisite preliminary achievement of political independence has still another importance in the cultural as well as in all other spheres: the struggle against the Germano-Roman world (without which Slav independence is impossible) will help to eradicate the cancer of imitativeness and the servile attitude towards the West, which through unfavorable conditions has eaten its way into the Slav body and soul.

POBEDONOSTSEV

Constantine Pobedonostsev (1827–1907) was a statesman and jurist, trained in the law. He tutored the future czar Alexander II, then served in the holy synod of the Russian Orthodox Church (1880–1905), where he became the leading spokesman of religious orthodoxy, nationalism, and autocracy. He had great influence over czar Alexander III and encouraged policies of rigorous censorship, persecution of religious minorities, and repression of all political opposition. He also supported an activist foreign policy designed to enhance Russia's national prestige. He wrote widely on Russian law and also authored a number of attacks on Western rationalism and liberalism.

• • •

What is this freedom by which so many minds are agitated, which inspires so many insensate actions, so many wild speeches, which leads the people so often to misfortune? In the democratic sense of the word, freedom is the right of political power, or, to express it otherwise, the right to participate in the government of the State. This universal aspiration for a share in the government has no constant limitations, and seeks no definite issue, but incessantly extends. . . . Forever extending its base, the new Democracy now aspires to universal suffrage—a fatal error, and one of the most remarkable in the history of mankind. By this means, the political power so passionately demanded by Democracy would be shattered into a number of infinitesimal bits, of which each citizen acquires a single one. What will he do with it, then? How will he employ it? In the result it has undoubtedly been shown that in the attainment of this aim Democracy violates its sacred formula of "Freedom indissolubly joined with Equality." It is shown that this apparently equal distribution of "freedom" among all involves the total destruction of equality. Each vote, representing an inconsiderable fragment of power, by itself signifies nothing; an aggregation of votes alone has a

From Konstantin P. Pobyedonostsev, *Reflections of a Russian Statesman,* trans. Robert Crozier Long (London: Grant Richard, 1898), 23–30, 32–46, 52–54, 62–74.

relative value. The result may be likened to the general meetings of shareholders in public companies. By themselves individuals are ineffective, but he who controls a number of these fragmentary forces is master of all power, and directs all decisions and dispositions. We may well ask in what consists the superiority of Democracy. Everywhere the strongest man becomes master of the State; sometimes a fortunate and resolute general, sometimes a monarch or administrator with knowledge, dexterity, a clear plan of action, and a determined will; in a Democracy, the real rulers are the dexterous manipulators of votes, with their place-men, the mechanics who so skillfully operate the hidden springs which move the puppets in the arena of democratic elections. Men of this kind are ever ready with loud speeches lauding equality; in reality, they rule the people as any despot or military dictator might rule it. . . . Experience proves a very different thing. The history of mankind bears witness that the most necessary and fruitful reforms—the most durable measures—emanated from the supreme will of statesmen, or from a minority enlightened by lofty ideas and deep knowledge, and that, on the contrary, the extension of the representative principle is accompanied by an abasement of political ideas and the vulgarization of opinions in the mass of the electors. . . .

. . . Even in the classic countries of Parliamentarism [democracy] it would satisfy not one of [its criteria]. The elections in no way express the will of the electors. The popular representatives are in no way restricted by the opinions of their constituents, but are guided by their own views and considerations, modified by the tactics of their opponents. In reality, ministers are autocratic, and they rule, rather than are ruled by Parliament. They attain power, and lose power, not by virtue of the will of the people, but through immense influence . . . and they fear no censure while they enjoy the support in Parliament of a majority which they maintain by the distribution of bounties from the rich tables which the State has put at their disposal. In reality, the ministers are as irresponsible as the representatives of the people. Mistakes, abuse of power, and arbitrary acts, are of daily occurrence, yet how often do we hear of the grave responsibility of a minister? It may be once in fifty years a minister is tried for his crimes, with a result contemptible when compared with the celebrity gained by the solemn procedure. . . .

. . . It is sad to think that even in Russia there are men who aspire to the establishment of this falsehood among us; that our professors glorify to their young pupils representative government as the ideal of political science; that our newspapers pursue it . . . , under the name of justice and order, without troubling to examine without prejudice the working of the parliamentary machine. Yet even where centuries have sanctified its existence, faith already decays; the Liberal intelligence exalts it, but the people groans under its despotism, and recognizes its falsehood. We may not see, but our children and grandchildren assuredly will see, the overthrow of this idol, which contemporary thought in its vanity continues still to worship. . . .

The prevalent doctrine of the perfection of Democracy and of democratic government stands on the same delusive foundation. This doctrine presupposes the capacity of the people to understand subtleties of political science which have a clear and substantial existence in the minds of its apostles only. Precision of knowledge is attainable only by the few minds which constitute the aristocracy of intellect; the mass, always and everywhere, is *vulgus,* and its conceptions of necessity are vulgar.

Democracy is the most complicated and the most burdensome system of government recorded in the history of humanity. For this reason it has never appeared save as a transitory manifestation, with few exceptions giving place before long to other systems. It is in no way surprising. The duty of the State is to act and to ordain: its dispositions are manifestations of a single will; without this, government is inconceivable. But how can a multitude of men, or a popular assembly act with a single will? . . . Such conditions inevitably lead to anarchy, from which society can be saved alone by dictatorship—that is, by the rehabilitation of autocracy in the government of the world.

YAMAGATA ARIMOTO

Yamagata Arimoto (1838–1922) was born a samurai but backed the Meiji side in the turmoil of 1860s. He studied military science in Europe and in the 1870s led in the restructuring of the Japanese army, copying German organizational models. In the 1880s he concentrated more on domestic affairs, encouraging more Confucian elements in the schools and repressing political opposition. He also supported Japanese imperialism and a strong military influence in the government. Clearly opposed to the more westernizing reformers in Japan, Yamagata Arimoto has been the subject of some debate among historians of Japan, who argue about whether a "conservative" label is really appropriate for this formative and dynamic leader in modern Japanese history.

• • •

On Military Conscription, 1872

In the system in effect in our country in the ancient past everyone was a soldier. In an emergency the emperor became the Marshal, mobilizing the able-bodied youth for military service and thereby suppressing rebellion. When the campaign was over the men returned to their homes and their occupations. . . . When the State suffers disaster, the people cannot escape being affected. Thus, the people can ward off disaster to themselves by striving to ward off disaster to the State. And where there is a state,

From Ryusako Tsunoda, William Theodore de Bary, and Donald Keene, eds., *Sources of Japanese Tradition* (New York: Columbia University Press, 1958), 704–7, 709–10, 712–13. Reprinted by permission of the publisher.

there is military defense; and if there is military defense there must be military service. It follows, therefore, that the law providing for a militia is the law of nature and not an accidental, man-made law. As for the system itself, it should be made after a survey of the past and the present, and adapted to the time and circumstance. The Occidental countries established their military systems after several hundred years of study and experience. Thus, their regulations are exact and detailed. However, the difference in geography rules out their wholesale adoption here. We should now select only what is good in them, use them to supplement our traditional military system, establish an army and a navy, require all males who attain the age of twenty—irrespective of class—to register for military service, and have them in readiness for all emergencies. Heads of communities and chiefs of villages should keep this aim in mind and they should instruct the people so that they will understand the fundamental principle of national defense.

Precepts for Soldiers and Sailors, 1882

1. The soldier and sailor should consider loyalty their essential duty. Who that is born in this land can be wanting in the spirit of grateful service to it? No soldier or sailor, especially, can be considered efficient unless this spirit be strong within him. A soldier or a sailor in whom this spirit is not strong, however skilled in art or proficient in science, is a mere puppet; and a body of soldiers or sailors wanting in loyalty, however well ordered and disciplined it may be, is in an emergency no better than a rabble. Remember that, as the protection of the state and the maintenance of its power depend upon the strength of its arms, the growth or decline of this strength must affect the nation's destiny for good or for evil; therefore neither be led astray by current opinions nor meddle in politics, but with single heart fulfil your essential duty of loyalty, and bear in mind that duty is weightier than a mountain, while death is lighter than a feather. Never by failing in moral principle fall into disgrace and bring dishonor upon your name.

[The second article concerns the respect due to superiors and consideration to be shown inferiors. The third urges bravery and a sense of duty.]

4. The soldier and the sailor should highly value faithfulness and righteousness. . . . Faithfulness implies the keeping of one's word, and righteousness the fulfilment of one's duty. If then you wish to be faithful and righteous in any thing, you must carefully consider at the outset whether you can accomplish it or not. If you thoughtlessly agree to do something that is vague in its nature and bind yourself to unwise obligations, and then try to prove yourself faithful and righteous, you may find yourself in great straits from which there is no escape. . . . Ever since ancient times there have been repeated instances of great men and heroes who, overwhelmed by misfortune, have perished and left a tarnished name to posterity, simply because in their effort to be faithful in small matters they failed to discern right and wrong with reference

to fundamental principles, or because, losing sight of the true path of public duty, they kept faith in private relations. You should, then, take serious warning by these examples.

5. The soldier and sailor should make simplicity their aim. If you do not make simplicity your aim, you will become effeminate and frivolous and acquire fondness for luxurious and extravagant ways; you will finally grow selfish and sordid and sink to the last degree of baseness, so that neither loyalty nor valor will avail to save you from the contempt of the world.

On Local Government, 1890

. . . According to what I have heard, discord between political parties has gradually extended into every aspect of community life. Hardly a person in social, business, and economic relations, and in education, has remained untouched by this situation. . . . There are some people who abandon what they should be doing and expend both time and effort in unproductive political debate, and some who, losing their sense of purpose, even run afoul of the law. These evils are spreading their influence, morally, economically, and politically, throughout the country. They will impair the people's happiness and exert a harmful effect on the prosperity of the nation. In general, if a new government, in the course of its establishment, is abused for reasons of personal interests, the results could be extremely harmful. They could affect the strength and the cohesion of the entire people and become the cause of the decline of the nation. The history of our country and that of other countries provides many such examples in every age. The people, if they wish to prevent the growth of such evil influences, must regard at all times the unified endeavor of all as their highest aim. And the responsibility of those in a position to guide the people must be to apply themselves as administrators of the government to this ideal.

His Majesty the Emperor has granted the constitutional system to his ministers and subjects for the purpose of elevating their morals and of promoting their happiness. By virtue of this constitution ministers and subjects have been enabled to gain a higher degree of freedom and to improve their lot in life so that they can stand on an equal footing with peoples of other civilized nations. But if, unfortunately, we should err—however little—in putting this constitutional system into operation, we the people will have lost our position of honor. And thus, today, the duty of a loyal subject is to cultivate true constitutional liberty and to enjoy its benefits in peace.

If men lack self-respect and self-restraint, there cannot be freedom in its true sense. One who respects himself will of necessity respect others. One who wishes others to respect his own opinions must respect the views of others. There is no logic in the position that only one's own opinions are correct. Irrespective of place, diverse opinions are inevitable when the interests of people are not the same. Thus, we must make every effort to tolerate the views of others and to resolve differences mutually. If this is not done contention will not cease. The constitutional system is an instrument for the adjustment of diverse views: the use of force and violence will not only fail to eradicate differences in viewpoints but will also aggravate them.

Political problems do not encompass the entire field of human interests. The people who might entertain different political views very frequently hold mutually identical views in religious and moral matters, and in matters of personal and social relations. It is not the way of a loyal, trustworthy man to set aside his religious, moral, personal, and social relationships in the sole interest of politics. Thus, to promote party rivalry to extremes is a human misfortune. Nay, to resort to violence and to use obstructionist methods against an opponent to promote one's political position is to permit personal passions to enslave him. It is against the principle of the observance of the law. It is against the spirit of the constitutional system.

It is especially undesirable that one abandon his occupational pursuit for the sake of a political cause. It is against his own interest as well as that of society as a whole. The economic strength of a country is dependent mainly on productive labor. Thus, it is not the way of the good citizen to indulge in needless arguments to the neglect of his calling. Not only will he thus fail to add his bit to the national wealth but he will also fail to induce others to develop industrious habits of self-reliance.

On Political Parties, 1917 (Repeating an 1898 Essay)

The parties seem smugly unconcerned over the danger to our country of having to stand alone and without support in the future among the powers of the world. The evils of partisan politics are indeed deplorable. If this trend is permitted to develop unchecked, I fear that the spirit of the Meiji Restoration will die and the splendid achievements of the late emperor will soon come to naught. The actual situation with respect to political parties in our country today indicates that when one party is excessively strong in Parliament, that party becomes reckless and arbitrary. When two parties are evenly matched, the struggle between them becomes extremely violent. Thus, to eliminate arbitrary actions and violent political struggles, it would seem advisable to divide their strength and to have them restrain each other mutually. I have faith in a plan to establish a three-party system in the Diet which would eliminate excesses and help foster moderation. If the third party is organized by men who are impartial and moderate, and possessed of intelligence and a sincere concern for the well-being of the country, it is my belief that it can make a contribution to the state toward the achievement of constitutional government, and it will set an example to others. . . . We must organize a group consisting of fair and intelligent men who will stand between the two existing parties and be partial to neither; who can check party excesses and irregularities; who can restrain the ambitions of those who seek to satisfy their avarice or their desire for political power through the instrument of the party; who can transcend the common run of politicians for whom politics is a means of livelihood; and who can go forward, resolutely and firmly, with but the one thought in mind of service to the state. Only by the conduct of a central core of such men who would not be corrupted by thoughts of personal gain or fame, and only by having as a nucleus in the Diet men who would not falter in their public devotion, can the secret of true constitutional government be achieved.

The greater the number of such representatives we can gather, the better it will be. However, the number of such men, both economically established and patriotically inclined, need not be numerous. . . . There must be several million among our population of seventy million who have fixed property and are economically secure, and who therefore are above corruption. If such men come forward to organize a solid nucleus in the Diet, the empire will be on a firm and secure foundation, and there need be no anxiety in the country. . . .

CHAPTER 26

BUSINESS VALUES IN THE INDUSTRIAL REVOLUTION

Western Europe and Japan

This chapter explores the similarities and differences between the ideas and motivations of businessmen in two of the key industrial areas of the long nineteenth century: Western Europe and Japan.

Comparing business values in Japan and Western Europe offers two angles, both central to world history from the nineteenth century onward. First is the question of what kind of business culture links to successful industrialization; the West displayed a highly functional set of business values, but so ultimately did Japan in a somewhat different fashion. Comparison helps expand our understanding of the two industrial approaches and, potentially, sets a basis for considering industrial cultures more generally. The second point involves what by the later twentieth century was being referred to as the development of a global middle class, as part of the globalization process more generally. For Japan, the later nineteenth century was the time when the key adjustments to globalization occurred. Comparing Japan and the West offers suggestions about the expansion of middle-class values ultimately on a global scale. The industrial revolution was one of the fundamental developments of modern world history, introducing powerful new technology to most branches of production, transportation, and communication, while propelling manufacturing ahead of agriculture as a source of jobs and wealth.

Amid all the facets of industrialization, the role of the business community was a crucial ingredient and an important result. Industrialization everywhere depended on business initiatives in the nineteenth century, but it also depended on new business attitudes. More traditional merchants, in places like Western Europe and Japan, did not welcome the innovations that came with industrialization. They found industrial technology messy and industrial investment too risky. They viewed industrial entrepreneurs as grubby upstarts—at least until success brought great wealth.

Yet there were new values and motivations available. In Western Europe, the Enlightenment helped provide a new belief in the value of work and the validity of increasing wealth. The same ideas of progress that could inspire political or scientific revolution could justify new economic initiatives. In some cases, Enlightenment ideals combined with religious interests to produce businessmen eager to demonstrate God's grace through economic success.

By the early nineteenth century many spokespeople proclaimed the virtues of social mobility and the acquisition of wealth. Self-help manuals urged hard work, thrift, and daring as the keys to legitimate business success. And businessmen themselves periodically wrote tracts or memoirs extolling similar values, which they viewed as fundamental to their own success and the good of society at large.

The new attributes associated with business innovation could be challenging to many societies outside the West. Japan was a case in point, after the Meiji era began under western pressure in 1868. Though Japan had a substantial merchant tradition, there were fewer preindustrial businessmen and less business wealth than had existed in the West. Japan had not experienced the scientific revolution or the Enlightenment. During the seventeenth and eighteenth centuries the hold of Confucianism had increased.

In this setting Japan developed a complex combination of imitation and adaptation, which would allow industrial development to mesh with established values. Businessmen and Confucian leaders alike wrestled with the problems of defining appropriate goals, and on the whole outright westernization was rejected. Government played a greater direct role in Japan's industrialization than had been the case in countries like Britain and France. A Ministry of Industry, set up in 1881, sponsored technological innovation, directly subsidized individual business leaders, and ran many operations in heavy industry directly. But Japan did experience a surge of new business leadership and social mobility. Talented former peasants generated most factory operations in textiles. A large middle-class sector developed around them.

Comparison with the West contributes to our understanding of why Japan was poised for rapid economic change, why it could create its own version of an energetic business class. Western and Japanese business sectors continue to interact and to differ. Distinctive approaches to middle-class goals, emerging in the early industrial periods, continue to matter in the two leading regions of industrialization today.

The following selections are from the writings of a British publicist and a Japanese reformer and from the accounts of actual industrialists in France and Japan.

Questions

1. What did Samuel Smiles mean by self-help? How did he compare the roles of business and of education in preparing the individual? What attitudes did he imply toward workers who did not manage to rise?

2. What, according to Smiles, were the rewards for work?

3. Did Narcisse Faucheur—a businessman, not a writer—show the same values that Smiles preached so widely? What were his main motivations? How did he define success? What kinds of attitudes toward his workers and toward society at large did Faucheur seem to have?

4. What is the nature of the individualism preached and practiced by members of the Western middle class in the nineteenth century?

5. How did Fukuzawa define and defend individualism? How did Shibuzawa's goals differ from Fukuzawa's prescriptions?

6. How did Confucianism affect definitions of business entrepreneurship in late-nineteenth-century Japan?

7. How did nationalism help justify business in Meiji Japan? Did early Western industrialists invoke nationalism in the same way? What might account for differences here?

8. How did Faucheur and Shibuzawa describe their own work values?

9. How would Faucheur react to Shibuzawa's statement of motives? How would Shibuzawa critique Smiles's basic approach to success?

10. What were the most important similarities between the roles and ideas of Japanese and Western business leaders?

For Further Discussion

1. How could two different sets of business values work equally well in under-girding industrialization and the rise of a new middle class?

2. How might Western and Japanese middle-class values lead to different attitudes toward the role of government in industry? How might they lead to different attitudes toward workers and worker organizations? Would the attitudes produce different reactions to aggressive worker unions and strikes—and which business group would resist protest more fiercely?

3. Were Japanese business values and political conservatism (chapter 23) opposed to each other, or did they blend together in creating a distinctive approach to modern society?

4. Did Western and Japanese business styles relate at all to earlier definitions of feudalism, in which the two regions had also overlapped and yet diverged (see chapter 8)?

5. How do different traditions of business goals continue to distinguish Japanese economic organization and behavior from their Western counterparts? Why do some Western leaders argue that certain Japanese emphases should now be imitated elsewhere?

BUSINESS IDEALS IN BRITAIN: SAMUEL SMILES

Samuel Smiles was the leading spokesperson for middle-class values of work and mobility in mid-nineteenth-century Britain. A small-town doctor, Smiles early turned to writing as his main source of income. His books, notably the classic *Self-Help* (first published in 1859), went through many editions, until interest in this up-by-the-bootstraps approach declined as business organization became more complex after 1870. Many artisans and shopkeepers read Smiles, seeking clues that would improve their own fortune. We cannot know how many people agreed with Smiles's preachments, but the evidence suggests widespread interest. Interpreting Smiles and the many similar authors throughout the early industrial West is not a totally straightforward task, for though the value system was not complex, it was new, a departure from more traditional Western social measurements.

• • •

The spirit of self-help, as exhibited in the energetic action of individuals, has in all times been a marked feature in the English character, and furnishes the true measure of our power as a nation. Rising above the heads of the mass there were always to be found a series of individuals distinguished beyond others, who commanded the public homage. But our progress has also been owing to multitudes of smaller and less known men. Though only the generals' names may be remembered in the history of any great campaign, it has been in a great measure through the individual valour and heroism of the privates that victories have been won. . . . Even the humblest person, who sets before his fellows an example of industry, sobriety, and upright honesty of purpose in life, has a present as well as a future influence upon the well-being of his country; for his life and character pass unconsciously into the lives of others, and propagate good example for all time to come.

Daily experience shows that it is energetic individualism which produces the most powerful effects upon the life and action of others, and really constitutes the best practical education. Schools, academies, and colleges, give but the merest beginnings of culture in comparison with it. Far more influential is the life-education daily given in our homes, in the streets, behind counters, in workshops, at the loom and the plough, in counting-houses and manufactories, and in the busy haunts of men. This is that finishing instruction as members of society, . . .—all that tends to discipline a man truly, and fit him for the proper performance of the duties and business of life,—a kind of education not to be learnt from books, or acquired by any amount of mere literary training. . . .

From Samuel Smiles, *Self-Help* (London, 1859), 38–39, 47–48, 115–19, 281–84.

The instances of men, in this and other countries, who, by dint of persevering application and energy, have raised themselves from the humblest ranks of industry to eminent positions of usefulness and influence in society, are indeed so numerous that they have long ceased to be regarded as exceptional. Looking at some of the more remarkable, it might almost be said that early encounter with difficulty and adverse circumstances was the necessary and indispensable condition of success. . . . [Many of our leaders are partly proud] to think that a person risen from that condition [of child labor in the factories] should be able to sit side by side, on equal terms, with the hereditary gentry of the land. . . .

Fortune has often been blamed for her blindness; but fortune is not so blind as men are. Those who look into practical life will find that fortune is usually on the side of the industrious, as the winds and waves are on the side of the best navigators. In the pursuit of even the highest branches of human inquiry the commoner qualities are found the most useful—such as common sense, attention, application, and perseverance. Genius may not be necessary, though even genius of the highest sort does not disdain the use of these ordinary qualities. The very greatest men have been among the least believers in the power of genius, and as worldly wise and persevering as successful men of the commoner sort. Some have even defined genius to be only common sense intensified . . . owing their success in a great measure, to their indefatigable industry and application. . . .

Hence, a great point to be aimed at is to get the working quality well trained. When that is done, the race will be found comparatively easy. We must repeat and again repeat; facility will come with labour. Not even the simplest art can be accomplished without it; and what difficulties it is found capable of achieving: It was by early discipline and repetition that the late Sir Robert Peel [British politician, son of a businessman] cultivated those remarkable, though still mediocre powers, which rendered him so illustrious an ornament of the British Senate. When a boy at Drayton Manor, his father was accustomed to set him up at table to practise speaking ex tempore; and he early accustomed him to repeat as much of the Sunday's sermon as he could remember. Little progress was made at first, but by steady perseverance the habit of attention became powerful, and the sermon was at length repeated almost verbatim. When afterwards replying in succession to the arguments of his parliamentary opponents—an art in which he was perhaps unrivalled—it was little surmised that the extraordinary power of accurate remembrance which he displayed on such occasions had been originally trained under the discipline of his father in the parish church of Drayton.

It is indeed marvellous what continuous application will effect in the commonest of things. . . .

To wait patiently, however, men must work cheerfully. Cheerfulness is an excellent working quality, imparting great elasticity to the character. As a bishop has said,

'Temper is nine-tenths of Christianity'; so are cheerfulness and diligence nine-tenths of practical wisdom. They are the life and soul of success, as well as of happiness: perhaps the very highest pleasure in life consisting in clear, brisk, conscious working; energy, confidence, and every other good quality mainly depending upon it. . . .

How a man uses money—makes it, saves it, and spends it—is perhaps one of the best tests of practical wisdom. Although money ought by no means to be regarded as a chief end of man's life, neither is it a trifling matter, to be held in philosophic contempt, representing as it does to so large an extent the means of physical comfort and social well-being. Indeed, some of the finest qualities of human nature are intimately related to the right use of money; such as generosity, honesty, justice, and self-sacrifice; as well as the practical virtues of economy and providence. On the other hand, there are their counterparts of avarice, fraud, injustice, and selfishness, as displayed by the inordinate lovers of gain; and the vices of thriftlessness, extravagance, and improvidence, on the part of those who misuse and abuse the means entrusted to them. . . .

Comfort in worldly circumstances is a condition which every man is justified in striving to attain by all worthy means. . . . The very effort required to be made to succeed in life with this object is of itself an education; stimulating a man's sense of self-respect, bringing out his practical qualities, and disciplining him in the exercise of patience, perseverance, and such like virtues. The provident and careful man must necessarily be a thoughtful man, for he lives not merely in the present, but with provident forecast makes arrangements for the future. He must also be a temperate man, and exercise the virtue of self-denial, than which nothing is so much calculated to give strength to the character. . . .

Hence the lesson of self-denial—the sacrificing of a present gratification for a future good—is one of the last that is learnt. Those classes which work the hardest might naturally be expected to value the most the money which they earn. Yet the readiness with which so many are accustomed to eat up and drink up their earnings as they go renders them to a great extent helpless and dependent upon the frugal. There are large numbers of persons among us who, though enjoying sufficient means of comfort and independence, are often found to be barely a day's march ahead of actual want when a time of pressure occurs; and hence a great cause of social helplessness and suffering. . . .

. . . That there should be a class of men who live by their daily labour in every state is the ordinance of God, and doubtless is a wise and righteous one; but that this class should be otherwise than frugal, contented, intelligent, and happy is not the design of Providence, but springs solely from the weakness, self-indulgence, and perverseness of man himself. The healthy spirit of self-help created amongst working people would more than any other measure serve to raise them as a class, and this, not by pulling down others, but by levelling them up to a higher and still advancing standard of religion, intelligence, and virtue.

A FRENCH BUSINESSMAN: NARCISSE FAUCHEUR

Narcisse Faucheur set up a textile factory from the 1820s onward, the early decades of French industrialization. He was not an industrial giant but a fairly average industrialist—the sort that really helped industrial firms to spread after someone else took a lead. Faucheur notes his dependence on British technological innovations, for example, which he simply imported. He was from a rather traditional small merchant family, whose habits he both utilized and transcended as he moved into the modern business context. He wrote an autobiography reviewing his career, printed in the 1880s in a limited edition for his children and grandchildren. His discussion of his activities and his self-elevation provide solid clues about his basic ideas and motivations, though he never spells these matters out directly.

• • •

. . . The idea of leaving for America again struck my fancy, but my parents were absolutely opposed to it. I yielded to their wishes rather than cause them the least unhappiness. . . . Finally, after a long and very arduous search, our friend announced that he had found a position for me with the most important wholesalers in Clermont. . . .

The friend whom I mentioned in the last chapter had found an opening for me in the firm of M. Cassan-Guyot, who was a wholesale dealer in [cloth] products. . . . This firm was, without doubt, the most important in Clermont. Unfortunately, I received a very meager salary, and because I was living with my parents I gave my mother all my earnings to help with the household expenses, which had risen sharply upon my arrival. I had rather quickly observed how poor my unfortunate parents were, so it was with real joy that at the end of each month I placed into my mother's hands the paltry sum I had earned. . . .

I soon saw, therefore, that it would be necessary for me to find another source of income in order to maintain a modest but always neat and proper wardrobe. . . .

When I became a travelling salesman for M. Delcros, I had the opportunity to talk with many other merchants and salesmen in Lille. They spoke of it as a city with a great commercial future and as an area full of opportunities for a young man such as I to establish himself by his own efforts. I was taken with the idea because I was already preoccupied with plans for the future. I wrote to my brother about it, and he encouraged me to transfer to Lille, not only because we would have the pleasure of

From Narcisse Faucheur, *Mon histoire à mes chers enfants et petit enfants* (Paris, 1886), quoted in Peter N. Stearns, ed., *The Impact of the Industrial Revolution* (Englewood Cliffs, N.J.: Prentice-Hall, 1972), 105–12. Reprinted by permission of the author.

seeing each other often, but also because it would be a step toward the realization of my goals.

Although I was well liked by my employer, the firm offered me no prospects of a partnership. It didn't have enough capital to expand its operations to the point that I might one day acquire a financial interest in it. I was condemned, therefore, to grow old as a salesman and to devote all my energies to [working for] other people. . . .

My lace business prospered for several years, but gradually a new product began to hurt it. I am speaking of tulle, which replaced lace and was much cheaper. The designs on the tulle, all of which was imported, were nearly all in very bad taste. I thought that if I embroidered on the tulle some attractive French designs, I could sell it easily and make a large profit.

I went to England to learn about this industry and to see if I could bring it into France. I took from England all the information I needed, but I decided against buying the looms used to make plain tulle, for they were too expensive and their purchase would have used funds which I needed in my other commercial ventures. Therefore, I concentrated on information dealing with embroidering tulle, an operation I hoped to start in France. I returned to Lille with some detailed designs and some patterns by which one could determine the number of stitches each design required. Since tulle embroidery work was paid according to the number of stitches in a design, these patterns made it easy for me to determine labor costs and set the final price.

In Saint-Armand I was in contact with two old spinsters who had two very intelligent nieces. The nieces were very good embroiderers but they didn't know how to work with tulle. I showed these ladies some samples of this embroidery and they assured me that if a woman skilled in the technique would give them some lessons, they could easily learn to do it themselves. They also claimed that they would be able to train many other young girls in Saint-Armand to be embroiderers, since there was no other occupation open to them in the region, no matter what their social class. We agreed that if I put my plan into practice my workshop would be in the home of the aunts, who would then be directors, and that the nieces would be foremen, all of them earning a reasonable salary.

When I was sure of being able to establish an embroidery workshop at Saint-Armand on advantageous terms, I left for Paris, where I had a good designer make a number of attractive patterns. I next arranged for an English woman from Nottingham who was very skilled in embroidery work to teach the two nieces of the ladies Dutordoir. . . .

From the start everything succeeded according to my wishes. In a short time I had a factory of more than three hundred embroiderers in the Dutordoir home. The first pieces I put up for sale gave me a profit all the more considerable since labor costs were very low. . . .

In every way possible I tried to speed up production. I was involved with every detail, for the newness of the designs determined their merit and price. But I was unable to rush production as much as I hoped and the scale of my business remained limited. . . .

. . . [My sales] trips varied from twenty-five to forty days. . . . But an ordinary salesman would have certainly doubled the time, for he would not have wanted to subject himself to all the strain that I endured. For several years I had to make two or three of these whirlwind trips, and God knows all the difficulty that they stirred up for me, no matter how necessary they were!

My yearly profits did not reflect all the work I put in, but over the long run my fortune grew slowly. The market was such that one had to make his decisions with courage. The competition was intense, the profits small, and one could lose all his customers if he set his prices higher than his competitors. . . .

In the preceding chapters I have told you of the hard work to which your mother and I diligently devoted ourselves to make our business prosper. It is now time to describe for you the order and thrift which guided our expenditures. Since our annual profits were not very large, our budget had to be rigorously kept within our income if our savings were to increase little by little. . . .

PRAISING INDIVIDUALISM: FUKUZAWA YUKICHI

The following two passages were written by a tireless Meiji westernizer. Fukuzawa (1834–1901) visited the United States and Western Europe early, in 1860. Proud of Japan and sometimes capable of defending Confucianism when he was too hard-pressed by more conservative figures (see chapter 23), Fukuzawa on the whole stood for change in a Western direction. Much of his work was devoted to educational reform, where he urged a more individualistic approach, but he also wrote on business topics directly. His views helped stimulate debate among businessmen, most of whom sought to reintroduce a more Confucian element—as the next selection suggests.

• • •

ON EDUCATION

In my interpretation of education, I try to be guided by the laws of nature and I try to co-ordinate all the physical actions of human beings by the very simple laws of

From Eichi Kiyooka, trans., *The Autobiography of Yukichi Fukuzawa* (New York: Columbia University Press, 1980), 44–47. Reprinted by permission of the publisher.

"number and reason." In spiritual or moral training, I regard the human being as the most sacred and responsible of all orders, unable in reason to do anything base. Therefore, in self-respect, a man cannot change his sense of humanity, his justice, his loyalty or anything belonging to his manhood even when driven by circumstances to do so. In short, my creed is that a man should find his faith in independence and self-respect.

From my own observations in both Occidental and Oriental civilizations, I find that each has certain strong points and weak points bound up in its moral teachings and scientific theories. But when I compare the two in a general way as to wealth, armament, and the greatest happiness for the greatest number, I have to put the Orient below the Occident. Granted that a nation's destiny depends upon the education of its people, there must be some fundamental differences in the education of Western and Eastern peoples.

In the education of the East, so often saturated with Confucian teaching, I find two things lacking; that is to say, a lack of studies in number and reason in material culture, and a lack of the idea of independence in spiritual culture. But in the West I think I see why their statesmen are successful in managing their national affairs, and the businessmen in theirs, and the people generally ardent in their patriotism and happy in their family circles.

I regret that in our country I have to acknowledge that people are not formed on these two principles, though I believe no one can escape the laws of number and reason, nor can anyone depend on anything but the doctrine of independence as long as nations are to exist and mankind is to thrive. Japan could not assert herself among the great nations of the world without full recognition and practice of these two principles. And I reasoned that Chinese philosophy as the root of education was responsible for our obvious shortcomings.

With this as the fundamental theory of education, I began and, though it was impossible to institute specialized courses because of lack of funds, I did what I could in organizing the instructions on the principles of number and reason. And I took every opportunity in public speech, in writing, and in casual conversations, to advocate my doctrine of independence. Also I tried in many ways to demonstrate the theory in my actual life. During my endeavor I came to believe less than ever in the old Chinese teachings.

ON BUSINESS

In the primitive, uncivilized world men could not benefit themselves without injuring others; therefore those who were active in mind and body and accomplished things were always thieves. This is not so in the civilized world; those who gain riches and fame always benefit others by doing so. . . .

Everyone in the country individually aims at increasing his own private wealth. . . . Desiring more and still more, they utilize all their secret skills in the competition for new things, and in this way new methods are evolved, land is reclaimed and developed, machines are invented, transportation and communications are improved, and the investment of capital is effected. . . . Private zeal is the source of national wealth.

A JAPANESE BUSINESSMAN'S VIEWS: SHIBUZAWA EIICHI

The following selections were written by a leading businessman of the Japanese reform (Meiji) era, as industrialization was getting under way. Shibuzawa Eiichi (1840–1931) ultimately presided over a hundred companies, after a period of service in government. He was from a prosperous peasant family. As an industrialist he concentrated particularly on factory textile production. He also participated actively in the growing debate over Western values as they applied to economic life.

• • •

FROM THE *AUTOBIOGRAPHY*

The business world around 1873, the year when I resigned my post at the Ministry of Finance, was one filled with inertia. That condition is hard to imagine from the standards we hold for the business world today [1927, when Shibuzawa dictated this autobiography]. There was a tradition of respecting officials and despising common people. All talented men looked to government services as the ultimate goal in their lives, and ordinary students followed the examples set by them. There was practically no one who was interested in business. When people met, they discussed only matters relating to the affairs of state and of the world. There was no such thing as practical business education.

It was said that the Meiji Restoration was to bring about equality among the four classes of people. In practice, however, those who engaged in commerce and industry were regarded as plain townspeople as before, and were despised and had to remain subservient to government officials. I knew conditions such as this should not be allowed to persist. A rigid class structure should not be tolerated. We should be able to treat each other with respect and make no differentiation between government officials and townspeople. This was essential to our national welfare, as we

Yukichi Fukuzawa, "On Business," trans. Fukuo Hyakawa, in Byron K. Marshall, *Capitalism and Nationalism in Prewar Japan* (Stanford, Califo.: Stanford University Press, 1967), 33. © 1967 by the Board of Trustees of the Leland Stanford Junior University, renewed 1995. All rights reserved. Used with permission of Stanford University Press, www.sup.org.

looked forward to strengthening the country which required wealth to back it up. We needed commerce and industry to attain the goal of becoming a rich nation. Unworthy as I was, I thought of engaging in commerce and industry to help promote the prosperity of our nation. I might not have talent to become a good politician, but I was confident that I could make a difference in the fields of commerce and industry. . . .

As to the question of development of commerce and industry, I felt that to engage in an individually managed shop would be going against the tide of the times, and it was necessary for small business firms to join their forces together. In other words, they have to incorporate, and I decided to devote my energy to this endeavor. As to the laws governing incorporation, I thought about them while studying in France. After my return from France and before my entering into government service, I organized a chamber of commerce in Shizuoka to serve as a model for incorporation in this country. Since that time, I have consistently advocated the advantages of incorporation.

In organizing a company, the most important factor one ought to consider is to obtain the services of the right person to oversee its operation. In the early years of Meiji, the government also encouraged incorporation of companies and organized commercial firms and development companies. The government actively participated in these companies' affairs and saw to it that their various needs were met fully. However, most of these companies failed because their management was poor. To state it simply, the government failed to have the right men as their managers. I had no experience in commerce and industry, but I also prided myself on the fact that I had greater potential for success in these fields than most of the nongovernmental people at that time.

I also felt that it was necessary to raise the social standing of those who engaged in commerce and industry. By way of setting an example, I began studying and practicing the teachings of the *Analects of Confucius*. It contains teachings first enunciated more than twenty-four hundred years ago. Yet it supplies the ultimate in practical ethics for all of us to follow in our daily living. It has many golden rules for businessmen. For example, there is a saying: "Wealth and respect are what men desire, but unless a right way is followed, they cannot be obtained; poverty and lowly position are what men despise, but unless a right way is found, one cannot leave that status once reaching it." It shows very clearly how a businessman must act in this world. Thus, when I entered the business world, I engaged in commerce and industry in a way consistent with the teachings of the *Analects* and practiced the doctrine of unity of knowledge and action.

From *Shibuzawa Eiichi Jijoden* [Autobiography of Shiuzawa Eiichi], in *Japan: A Documentary History*, ed. David J. Lu (Armonk, N.Y.: M. E. Sharpe, 1997) 354–56. Translation Copyright © 1997 by David J. Lu. Reprinted by permission of the publisher.

FROM "MY VIEW OF LIFE"

There are in the final analysis only two types: i.e., those who consider the existence of self objectively and those who consider it subjectively. The objective view regards society first and the self second. The ego is disregarded to the point where one sacrifices the self for the sake of society without hesitation. The subjective view, on the other hand, is selfishly aware of the existence of the ego in all situations and recognizes the existence of society only secondarily. To this extent it is willing even to sacrifice society for the sake of the self. . . .

We would end in a situation in which the appetites could only be satisfied by men looting from one another. If the human heart comes to that, then the ultimate result would be such indecent behavior as forgetting our benefactors, turning our backs on our friends, and abandoning our loved ones. . . .

FROM "INDEPENDENCE AND SELF-RELIANCE"

One must beware of the tendency of some to argue that it is through individualism or egoism [*jiko hon'i*] that the State and society can progress most rapidly. They claim that under individualism, each individual competes with the others, and progress results from this competition. But this is to see merely the advantages and ignore the disadvantages, and I cannot support such a theory. Society exists, and a State has been founded. Although people desire to rise to positions of wealth and honor, the social order and the tranquillity of the State will be disrupted if this is done egoistically. Men should not do battle in competition with their fellow men. Therefore, I believe that in order to get along together in society and serve the State, we must by all means abandon this idea of independence and self-reliance and reject egoism completely.

From Byron K. Marshall, *Capitalism and Nationalism in Prewar Japan* (Stanford, Califo.: Stanford University Press, 1967), 34–35. © 1967 by the Board of Trustees of the Leland Stanford Junior University, renewed 1995. All rights reserved. Used with permission of Stanford University Press, www.sup.org.

CHAPTER 27

WOMEN AND EDUCATION IN THE NINETEENTH CENTURY

The spread of education was one of the key developments in nineteenth-century world history. It began in the West, which already had reasonably extensive literacy and schooling. New political ideas, associated with the revolutionary era, pushed leaders to think about greater access to education in order to create opportunities for the lower classes and to produce better-informed (or more loyal) citizens. Children were increasingly cherished, particularly in middle-class ideology, and this led to the belief that they deserved the chance to learn—perhaps to learn even more than their parents had. Industrialization prompted demands for a better-trained workforce, able to do some arithmetic and capable of reading factory rules and consumer advertisements. As factories became more complex, child labor became less useful—another reason to think about schooling.

Given the Western example, which seemed to demonstrate that modern, widespread education was crucial to the operation of effective states and to economic growth, many societies began to follow suit. Japan, with a large school system already, decreed mass education in 1872 and also began to replace pure Confucianism with science and technology in the higher schools. Russia expanded its schools, and reform regimes in Latin America began to do the same.

The spread of education is already a vital topic in nineteenth-century world history. But there's an additional, important twist, which makes it a fundamental topic in women's world history as well.

For everywhere, the expansion of education involved women, despite the widespread belief that women were intellectually inferior to men. Officials realized that women might have as much use for basic reading and arithmetic skills as men, if only to hold factory jobs (in the working class) or run a household (in all classes) or raise intelligent sons. Further, women's special roles might require an additional, special kind of education, stressing domestic skills, virtue, and graceful arts such as piano playing. Some women leaders, furthermore, developed still other arguments, based on claims of equal access not just to schools but also to jobs that depended on education.

Women began to catch up with men in literacy and basic skills, at the primary level, at least. They lagged in higher schooling, but here too, by the late nineteenth century, a growing minority of middle-class women began to press into American high schools or the sex-segregated secondary schools in France. A handful even entered universities; a few were admitted to professional schools in areas such as medicine.

At the same time, different regions developed different approaches to women's educational issues. This was true within the West and certainly true when other societies, including colonies like India, are considered. It was true that the spread of Western imperialism carried certain Western ideas about women to other countries. But in many cases women were newly exploited, as colonial authorities sought cheap labor for export industries. Many colonial women seemed exotic and debased, because of the different costumes they wore; both sexual exploitation and moralistic preachments resulted, from Africa to Hawaii. But where Western influence was particularly pervasive, additional signals were sometimes conveyed.

India was an obvious case in point. Effective British economic and military dominance of much of the subcontinent was established in the eighteenth century. During the nineteenth century, the British imposed fuller political control. For the most part, the British were content to leave Indian culture alone, but inevitably some new ideas gained entrance. The British tried to outlaw the practice of suttee, wherein some Indian wives killed themselves after their husbands had died on grounds that there was nothing more to live for.

Other developments in India included efforts to set up new types of schooling, including some for women. The third section that follows, a British observer's assessment, deals with these changes. The result, as in Europe, was a confusing pattern. Real innovation did occur: some women received an education that Indian women had never before enjoyed. Western influences interacted with older traditions but also new Indian initiatives in a complex mixture. How did the resultant combination compare with the complex developments affecting women in the West?

Questions

1. How did Necker de Saussure define appropriate education for women? How fully did she accept the domesticity arguments? How did she manage to argue for additional educational goals?
2. What is the nature of Duffey's argument for women's education? How does it compare with that of Necker de Saussure? Does the comparison suggest any pattern of similarities and differences in nineteenth-century situations for women in France and the United States? Do the different ideas about education relate to different family ideals in France and the United States?
3. How does Stanton's educational experience demonstrate the special limitations on women? How does it also demonstrate new opportunities?

4. Stanton was obviously an unusual woman, from an unusual family: did she reflect the more standard assumptions and situations at all? How does her actual educational experience compare with Duffey's arguments about women's education?

5. How does Stanton's experience help explain her leadership in American feminism?

6. What changes occurred in Indian education the later nineteenth century? Why did the changes occur? What were the limitations on educational goals?

7. How did Indian educational change and constraint compare with patterns in women's educational goals and experiences in the West?

8. How did many nineteenth-century women in France, India, and the United States accept and even encourage ideas and institutions that other women, at that time and since, have found unjust? Why did these accommodations occur?

For Further Discussion

1. Why, given various prejudices against women, did women's education advance at all in the nineteenth century? How did educational gains relate to other changes and continuities in the lives of adult women—did education change more or less than other aspects of life?

2. Considering education and family trends, do France and the United States fall within a common Western pattern with regard to nineteenth-century women, or do the differences suggest that the United States was a distinctive civilization?

3. Is westernization a useful concept in describing educational changes for upper-caste women in India? Or were special Indian features still predominant even amid change?

4. How do educational changes and ideas about women's education help explain the rise of feminism in the nineteenth century? Why was feminism stronger in the United States than in France, and in the West generally, than in India?

5. How have twentieth-century women's patterns in the West and in India altered nineteenth-century developments? To what extent do they still reflect nineteenth-century issues?

FRANCE

This selection was written in 1838 by Albertine-Adrienne Necker de Saussure. Necker de Saussure was a Protestant of Swiss origin, but she was widely known

From Albertine-Adrienne Necker de Saussure, *The Study of the Life of Woman* (Philadelphia, 1844), 27–29, 71, 74–75.

in France. She had earlier written on more general educational issues. Her later book, from which this passage is taken, argued for a domestic education, granting women's special roles in marriage while pushing for a wider educational range.

• • •

The same gospel which says "Women, submit yourselves to your own husbands," teaches [them] also that there is no inequality among human beings in the sight of God. "Ye are all the children of God by faith in Jesus Christ." "There is neither bond nor free, there is neither male nor female, for ye are all one in Christ Jesus."

But this part of our celestial nature which education should constantly seek to bring out, man has scarcely taken into account. He has had this life only in view, and has shut his eyes upon whatever limited his rights here. He has seen only the wife in the woman—in the young girl only the future wife. All the faculties, the qualities which have no immediate relation to his interests, have seemed to him worthless. Yet there are many of the gifts bestowed upon woman that have no relation to the state of a wife. This state, although natural, is not necessary—perhaps half the women who now exist, have not been, or are no longer, married. In the indigent classes, the girl who is able to maintain herself, quits her parents, and supports herself by her industry for a long time, perhaps for life, without requiring aid from man. No social arrangements oblige her to become dependent. It is therefore important, that education should unfold in the young girl the qualities which give the surest promise of wisdom, happiness, usefulness, and dignity, whatever may be her lot. . . .

If we would have the selfishness of men plainly exhibited, let us listen to Rousseau.

"All the education of women should bear a relation to men—to please, to be useful to them—to possess their love and esteem, to educate them in childhood, to nurse them when grown up, to counsel, to console, to make their lives pleasant and sweet; such are the duties of women and should be taught to them from infancy."

If Rousseau had said that the education of women should bear a relation to what surrounds them, to the beings with whom nature or love had entwined their fate, we would applaud this language. Why particularly designate men? Why teach young girls to consider their own sex as nothing? and why give to the necessity of loving the most dangerous tendency? . . .

. . . Sisters brought up with their brothers would be subject to the same rules and duties, justice and truth being the only means employed to guide them. In this common education, there must be more firmness, less flattery; the promises and menaces of opinion, to which boys are comparatively insensible, are rarely employed. The motives proposed to all the children are those of goodness, reason, and true moral philosophy, adapted to their comprehension.

Since the comparative weakness of girls is rarely manifested before the age of ten years, why should they be freed from the laws of natural equality? Why led to calculate upon accommodations and consideration from the other sex? Many sad disappointments are thus prepared for them. . . .

Obedience is so important an element in education, it is so truly the first duty of childhood, and the way to observe every other, that in this respect no difference can be made in the education of the two sexes. However, docility, that internal disposition which naturally leads to the fulfillment of this duty, may well be the object of peculiar cultivation in young girls. Whenever boys are placed under public instruction, they are rather governed by general rules than by the will of individuals. Women, on the contrary, are called to bear, very often, and perhaps throughout their lives, the yoke of personal obedience. Since such is their fate, it is well to accustom them to it; they must learn to yield without even an internal murmur. Their gayety, their health, their equality of temper, will all gain by a prompt and cordial docility. . . .

Hence we would exhort mothers always to exercise fearlessly the authority with which God has entrusted them, since this also is sacred authority. Even though they might obtain the accomplishment of their plans in some other way, it would be important to accustom their daughters to submission. We would suggest that long expositions of motives invite objections, and seem to show that resistance is expected. It is with little girls especially that it is important to prevent rejoinders, the habit of contradicting and of arguing on all occasions. . . .

In cherishing this sentiment you will also cultivate in your daughter other qualities: you will endow her with patience, resignation, and all the gentle virtues that a woman is infallibly called to exercise. To the caprices of fortune will be added, for her discipline, those of mankind. A multitude of illusive hopes and disappointed expectations form a part of her fate. Her best plans will be overturned: her occupations interrupted, she will have to suffer in silence humiliations and distresses still more poignant. But when, gentle and patient, she shall have supported all such trials, a high degree of virtue will be developed within her.

[Here is Necker de Saussure's schedule for organizing the hours in a young girl's day.]

Religious duties: worship and various exercises, 1

Literary and scientific studies—intellectual cultivation: elements of calculation and physical science, languages, history and geography, exercises of memory, 4 [total]

Fine arts: music and drawing, 1.5

Material duties and occupations: physical exercise, 1.5; female work and domestic care, 1.5; liberty, meals, and family circle, 4.5

On looking over the above plan, we see at once that the larger portion of the time is appropriated to recreations or duties purely material, and the smaller portion to study. It seems to us, therefore, that we cannot be accused of requiring too much mental application from young girls. But we can never approve of any diminution of the time claimed for purely intellectual education. If, then, we wish to preserve intact the four previous hours employed to develop the magnificent gift of intelligence, it is essential to lose not a moment; long preparations, idle words, must be prohibited, and this alone would be a valuable habit. The power of promptly fixing the attention forms what is called presence of mind, and also gives nerve to the character. . . .

The United States

The following two selections come from a proponent not only of women's education but also of coeducation, Eliza Duffey (d. 1898), and from the reminiscences of the tireless nineteenth-century feminist Elizabeth Cady Stanton (1815–1902). Duffey, writing in 1874, argued vigorously against limitations on women. Her work was part of the growing movement for more rounded education, including higher education and exercise—a movement that produced a growing number of women's colleges; it also resulted in women's gradual entry into high schools and coeducational colleges. Stanton, who married and had several children, was one of the distinctive personalities of nineteenth-century American history and a person of tremendous energy and persistence. By the late nineteenth century, along with a few other leaders, she helped shape the movement that would soon lead to the granting of the vote to women (in 1920; women's suffrage in France did not arrive until 1945).

• • •

ELIZA DUFFEY

As infancy begins to give place to childhood, then the distinctive training commences in earnest. The boy is allowed to be natural, the girl is forced to be artificial. Some girls break through all restraints and romp, but they are not the model girls whom mothers delight in and visitors praise for being "lady-like." Boy and girl as they are, with the same life pulsing in their veins and drawing its sustenance in precisely the same manner, with the same physical and mental needs, nature calls imperatively for an equally active life for both. They both want the air and the sunshine. They need equally to be hardened by the storms, tanned by the winds and have limbs strengthened by unrestrained exercise. But instead of this equality, while boys have their liberty more or less freely granted them, girls must stay at home and sew and read, and play prettily and quietly, and take demure walks. I am not speaking of girls in a single

From Eliza Duffey, *No Sex in Education; or, An Equal Chance for Both Girls and Boys* (Philadelphia, 1874), 40, 43, 100, 101.

stratum of society, but of girls everywhere, from the highest down almost to the lowest, wherever the word "lady" is sufficiently reverenced and misunderstood. . . .

Girls, whose energies are still the most powerful, have no opportunity for working off their surplus vitality in rude and boisterous ways, for the restraint is never lifted from them. So they enter with the whole force of their natures into their studies, and, as every teacher will bear testimony, soon far outstrip their brothers. To be at the head of their class, to receive the highest mark of merit, is their ruling ambition. Their minds are prematurely developed at the expense of their bodies. This does not result because they are educated as boys, but because *both* are educated wrongly, and the girl far more wrongly than the boy, inasmuch and just so far as her education in the general discipline of her life differs from that of the boy. . . .

When we still further admit that in matters of fresh air, exercise and dress girls almost invariably labor under disadvantages which boys do not feel, I think there has been sufficient admitted to account for all failures (supposing there to be any) of girls in keeping healthful as well as mental pace with boys. It is pernicious habits in these respects which need looking after and correcting—these and the further and to my mind still more important fact that at the close of her school-days is removed a girl's mental stimulus, and she is left to collapse. Set these things right, and let girls find a "career" open to them, and education will take care of itself.

If there is really a radical mental difference in men and women founded upon sex, you *cannot* educate them alike, however much you try. If women *cannot* study unremittingly, why then they *will* not, and you *cannot make them*. But because they do, because they choose so to do, because they will do so in spite of you, should be accepted as evidence that they can, and, all other things being equal, can with impunity. Instead of our race dying out through these women, they are the hope of the country—the women with broad chests, large limbs and full veins, perfect muscular and digestive systems and harmonious sexual organs, who will keep pace with men either in a foot or an intellectual race, who know perfectly their own powers and are not afraid to tax them to their utmost, knowing as they do that action generates force. These are the mothers of the coming race. . . . The result will be truly "the survival of the fittest."

ELIZABETH CADY STANTON

When I was eleven years old, two events occurred which changed considerably the current of my life. My only brother, who had just graduated from Union College, came home to die. A young man of great talent and promise, he was the pride of my father's heart. We early felt that this son filled a larger place in our father's affections

From Elizabeth Cady Stanton, *Eighty Years and More: Reminiscence, 1815–1897* (Boston: Northeastern University Press, 1993), 10–23.

and future plans than the five daughters together. Well do I remember how tenderly he watched my brother in his last illness, the sighs and tears he gave vent to as he slowly walked up and down the hall, and, when the last sad moment came, and we were all assembled to say farewell in the silent chamber of death, how broken were his utterances as he knelt and prayed for comfort and support. . . . As he took no notice of me, after standing a long while, I climbed upon his knee, when he mechanically put his arm about me and, with my head resting against his beating heart, we both sat in silence, he thinking of the wreck of all his hopes in the loss of a dear son, and I wondering what could be said or done to fill the void in his breast. At length he heaved a deep sigh and said: "Oh, my daughter, I wish you were a boy!" Throwing my arms about his neck, I replied: "I will try to be all my brother was."

Then and there I resolved that I would not give so much time as heretofore to play, but would study and strive to be at the head of all my classes and thus delight my father's heart. All that day and far into the night I pondered the problem of boyhood. I thought that the chief thing to be done in order to equal boys was to be learned and courageous. So I decided to study Greek and learn to manage a horse. Having formed this conclusion I fell asleep. My resolutions, unlike many such made at night, did not vanish with the coming light. I arose early and hastened to put them into execution. They were resolutions never to be forgotten—destined to mold my character anew. As soon as I was dressed I hastened to our good pastor, Rev. Simon Hosack, who was always early at work in his garden.

"Doctor," said I, "which do you like best, boys or girls?"

"Why, girls, to be sure; I would not give you for all the boys in Christendom."

"My father," I replied, "prefers boys; he wishes I was one, and I intend to be as near like one as possible. I am going to ride on horseback and study Greek. Will you give me a Greek lesson now, doctor? I want to begin at once."

"Yes, child," said he, throwing down his hoe, "come into my library and we will begin without delay." . . .

During all this time I kept up my lessons at the parsonage and made rapid progress. I surprised even my teacher, who thought me capable of doing anything. I learned to drive, and to leap a fence and ditch on horseback. I taxed every power, hoping some day to hear my father say: "Well, a girl is as good as a boy, after all." But he never said it. When the doctor came over to spend the evening with us, I would whisper in his ear: "Tell my father how fast I get on," and he would tell him, and was lavish in his praises. But my father only paced the room, sighed, and showed that he wished I were a boy; and I, not knowing why he felt thus, would hide my tears of vexation on the doctor's shoulder.

Soon after this I began to study Latin, Greek, and mathematics with a class of boys in the Academy, many of whom were much older than I. For three years one boy kept his place at the head of the class, and I always stood next. Two prizes were offered in Greek. I strove for one and took the second. How well I remember my joy in receiving that prize. There was no sentiment of ambition, rivalry, or triumph over my companions, nor feeling of satisfaction in receiving this honor in the presence of those assembled on the day of the exhibition. One thought alone filled my mind. "Now," said I, "my father will be satisfied with me." So, as soon as we were dismissed, I ran down the hill, rushed breathless into his office, laid the new Greek Testament, which was my prize, on his table and exclaimed: "There, I got it!" He took up the book, asked me some questions about the class, the teachers, the spectators, and, evidently pleased, handed it back to me. Then, while I stood looking and waiting for him to say something which would show that he recognized the equality of the daughter with the son, he kissed me on the forehead and exclaimed, with a sigh, "Ah, you should have been a boy!"

INDIA

The following selection, written around 1905, comes from a book by a British educational authority from a women's college in Oxford University, Minna G. Cowan. The report raises obvious questions about possible bias: what other kinds of data would help in assessing educational developments in India during the period? How did the directions of change, and the levels of female educational access, compare to Western patterns? Why did any change occur at all?

• • •

The Calcutta School Society ascertained in 1818 that no provision of any kind existed for the education of women, and an attempted estimate of their general literacy places the figure at one in a hundred thousand. The old ideal had so utterly vanished, that it needed the touch of Western civilization to revive even the conception of its former existence. This existence, shadowy and faint though it may appear in our eyes, is an enormous asset to the new movement in a country where everything Aryan and Vedic counts for much in the endeavor to create a national consciousness.

The modern epoch is thus in part a Renaissance, in part the introduction once more of the ideal of another faith. It will occupy our attention in detail and falls naturally into three periods. The first dates from 1819, when the Baptist Mission in Calcutta started its first school for girls till 1854, during which time the influence was almost entirely that of the women missionaries; the second, from the famous Educational Despatch of 1854 til 1884, is characterized by the [colonial] Government policy of "grants-in-aid" to voluntary associations, by the first tentative beginnings of direct Government effort, and by the expansion of Secondary education under missionary

From Minna G. Cowan, *The Education of Women in India* (New York: Fleming II. Revell, 1912), 34–35, 36–37, 38–41, 44–45, 47–50, 51–52, 53.

auspices; in the modern period dating from the presentation of the report of Sir William Hunter's Commission in 1884, the Government share in girls' education is much more direct, the spontaneous Indian element enters more strongly, and for the first time the question of a differentiation in the curriculum arises. . . .

The education given by the women missionaries consisted of such mere rudiments as were possible under the conditions and for the short period during which their pupils were available. In 1852 a second stage of missionary education was reached by the establishment in Calcutta of a Normal School for the training of Christian female teachers under the auspices of the society known later as the Zenana Bible and Medical Mission.

By the great educational charter of 1854, the Government adopted the policy of fostering and encouraging private effort by a system of grants-in-aid to all institutions which could comply with certain stipulations as to buildings, number of teachers, textbooks and type of instruction given. Religious instruction might be given but did not come within the purview of the Government officials. Departments of Public Instruction were formed, Inspectors appointed, and the well known scheme of examinations inaugurated. It is stated in the Despatch that female education shall be given "frank and cordial support."

"The importance of female education in India cannot be over-rated, and we have observed with pleasure the evidence which is now afforded of an increased desire on the part of many of the natives of India to give a good education to their daughters. By these means a far greater proportional impulse is imparted to the educational and moral tone of the people than by the education of men."

The Agra experiment was the response of Government to spontaneous Indian effort, and as the world of the Hindu pioneer who was its originator is little known, the following account may be quoted.

[From an 1860 colonial government report:] "Even in our Asiatic Provinces, before the breaking out of the troubles, a desire had sprung up among the natives to extend the blessings of education to women. Gopal Singh, a Hindu gentleman, holding under Government the post of district Inspector of native schools, had succeeded, through his own exertions, in establishing upwards of two hundred seminaries for young ladies in the Province of Agra which were attended by 3800 girls of the best families. By many of our countrymen in India, this is regarded rather as a social revolution than as an educational movement. As a rule, the natives look with suspicion on everything which comes from a foreigner, for which reason the great efforts made by the English have not produced corresponding results. 'The establishment of a little school,' observes the local ruler, 'which my own daughters and those of my immediate friends and relations attend at first like a charm, dispelled in a great measure the prejudices of my neighbours, and induced many to send their girls also. This example and my constant persuasion and reasoning have at last succeeded in inducing many respectable inhabitants of other villages to yield.' And so the movement bids fair to become national. The pupils are nearly all Hindus belonging to the more respectable classes. The teachers are all men."

The curriculum seems to have been somewhat different from that of the boys' schools, and the leader notes with satisfaction: "Girls are possessed of better memories and less selfishness than boys." The success and extent of the movement seems however to have been due to the personal influence of this one man, and with the passing of his generation the schools degenerated in type. The rapid extension of this work under Government into other districts necessitated the employment once more of men teachers. Four female Normal schools were established which appear to have been such only in name. Two British Inspectresses were appointed whose reports indicate the same problems as those of a more modern date. "The villages are not opposed to the school but they value them chiefly as a means of support for Brahmans [priests] and relatives." They could not believe that the Government were in earnest on the subject, when the girls school was accommodated in a place not more attractive than a cow-shed and the boys' in a handsome building. In 1876, a drastic reduction of 212 schools took place and the question of female education dropped into abeyance for a period. The official comment thereon was that the State had incurred much expense in founding and maintaining these schools and that the results had been painfully disappointing. Historically, the experiment indicates the danger of extending girls' schools beyond the desire of the community and beyond the possibility of constant supervision on the part of British Inspectresses. The solution of the ever present problem of a supply of teachers was only a temporary one, and the failure of the Normal schools was attributed largely to the lack of a British superintendent.

The activity of Christian missions during this period seems extraordinary, when the difficulties which hampered Government efforts are considered. Moreover, all their educational work was handicapped, so far as numbers were concerned, by the frank and open avowal of the desire to win their pupils ultimately for Christianity. The missionaries had, however, at their command the one essential asset—Western women who were willing to give themselves heart and soul to the work. Eight new women's societies, both British and American, entered India between 1860 and 1870, and educational work was their most effective means of contact with the people. Their pupils in the Primary stages were drawn both from the non-Christian population and from the orphans and converts in connection with the missions. As it was possible to retain the Christian girls, and even some of the others for longer than the usual period, owing to the exclusion of men teachers from the mission schools, a Secondary system on identical lines with that for boys began to be slowly built up.

Of the [government] aided schools there is no separate official classification to show what proportion are managed by Indian committees, and what by missionary agencies. Where possible this has been indicated from local information in the chapters on the separate provinces. The Indian spontaneous element has become however much stronger during this modern period, . . . while probably the most remarkable feature in the Indian government is the establishment of girls' schools under committees of Indian gentlemen representing different faiths. This indigenous movement is due in part to a desire to provide a good education without direct interference with the religion of the pupils, and in part to a reaction from the extreme secularism and the Westernizing influences of the Government schools.

In spite of the recent rapid increase and the steady progress of the last twenty years, the percentage of girls of school age attending school is only 4.6, and the desire for education has still in many places to be created.

This small proportion indicates, apart from the social and religious customs which cause it, a lack of balance in the whole system. Are the circumstances under which higher education is given not such as commend themselves to the Indian mind? Or is the course of studies pursued not of sufficiently practical and educational value to prove attractive to Indian women? Is there any foundation for the popular belief that the physique of Indian girls is not strong enough for a prolonged school course?

The problem of the curriculum is a very subtle one. In the early days of the reform of girls' education in Great Britian, about 1862, the greatest need seemed to be the adoption of an adequate test of knowledge, and that test one already recognized, so that there might seem to be no lower requirement to suit the supposed lower capacity of the feminine mind. The same principle worked in the early days of girls' education in India and preparation for Matriculation seemed the only means by which the standard could be raised. Whereas in Great Britain the leading girls' High schools have developed a flexibility and variety of curriculum wherein many a "womanly woman" has found her training, even if she did not prefer to seek her education in one of the numerous excellent private schools, the girls' curriculum for Indian girls has been stereotyped on masculine lines. If we assume that education should prepare for future life, it seems clearly wrong that the preparation for spheres so totally different as those of Indian men and women should be identical. . . .

PART V

The Contemporary Period, 1914–Present

THE TWENTIETH AND EARLY TWENTY-FIRST CENTURIES have
been so rich in events that their status as the opening of a new world history period must seem assured. Two world wars followed by a long Cold War (followed
by its end, in turn, in 1989); major revolutions in Russia, China, Mexico, and Iran
and many smaller upheavals elsewhere; the advent of the nuclear age; unprecedented population growth, which, along with intensifying global industrialization, helped significantly to alter the environment; the advent of airplanes,
television, computers—the list seems almost endless. Of course, many centuries
seem more full of change at the time than they turn out to be in retrospect; but
recent decades unquestionably claim a place at the top of any list. The problem
is to sort out the main lines of development.

Several major themes defined the contemporary period, from World War I
onward, as a new period in world history; each of the themes carries important
challenges for comparative analysis.

First, most societies had to reconsider established political, cultural, and social systems and replace them with new alternatives. Monarchy, empire, and aristocracy all declined. Some societies indeed introduced a series of innovations. By
the 1990s, few civilizations outside the West had the same political system that
they had had in 1900. The end of colonialism and many revolutions required
innovation. Population growth, particularly outside the industrialized centers,
provided a massive prod for social, cultural and political change. Older belief systems, ranging from adherence to one of the major religions to the deeply rooted
polytheism of areas such as sub-Saharan Africa, faced new rivals in movements
such as nationalism and Communism and in popular cultural exports from the
West. Increasing capacity for global transportation and communication, from radio to the internet, set the technological basis for dramatic new relationships.

Comparison category number one, then, involves juxtaposing the nature of
change and innovation in two or more societies. Was the widespread movement
toward authoritarian nationalism—called fascism in its most extreme form—the
same in its major European centers of power and elsewhere? How much did the
leading Communist regimes have in common? How did different societies handle
new activities by religious missionaries plus strong influences from Western

consumer culture? How did societies with different traditions about families and conditions for women respond to the huge surge in the population growth rate? The list of comparative responses to common processes, in a period of great innovation, is a long one.

International contacts. This was not a brand new development, for the pattern had been installed at least a thousand years before. But new levels of communication and trade unquestionably produced a substantive change in the rates and impacts of exchange. By the end of the century over a quarter of the world's population might watch a single sporting event on television, World Cup soccer heading the list. Meetings of scientists drew experts from every corner of the globe who shared common methods and assumptions, whatever their specific cultural backgrounds—another first in world history. Several societies, like Russia and China, that attempted considerable isolation for part of the twentieth century, decided to embrace greater globalization by the 1980s, mainly in the interest of greater economic prosperity.

The broad question for comparison category number two is, How did different societies respond to the new levels of contact? What kind of international interaction was responsible for the striking spread of political democracy at the century's end? How, on the other hand, might some societies try to insulate themselves from too much challenging contact?

Third, the relative power of the West declined. This change reversed five centuries of Western ascendancy, but it showed clearly in the declining military and political dominance of the West, even with the United States included. Moscow's decolonization was a key development; so, by 2000, was rapid economic growth in East Asia, India, and elsewhere. Yet—partly because of the growing role of the United States in world affairs—Western influence remained high, and its cultural impact on other parts of the world may have exceeded developments in previous centuries. Western countries could no longer retain their colonies, but they could distribute new styles of clothing, like blue jeans; new youth music; new kinds of restaurants, like McDonald's; new films and TV shows (*Baywatch* became for a time the world's most widely viewed television series); scientific discoveries; and even "international" artistic styles.

For comparative category number three, we examine the complex balance between new opportunities for global diversity, as the West's power declined, and new signs of looking to the West for models. Nationalism spread widely around the world and allowed many countries to praise distinctive features of their traditions; but the desire for national strength and respectability could lead to further borrowings from the West. Along with all the new events of this busy period, the new-old patterns of interaction with the West constitute perhaps the most obvious sign of a time of transition to which different societies responded differently, with responses sometimes changing as the century wore on.

It was not clear, by the early twenty-first century, that any single civilization center was poised to replace the West as the dominant world civilization. Perhaps, for a time at least, there might be none. It is important to remember that the twentieth century as the opening of a new period was just that, an opening; all sorts of clarifications might follow in subsequent decades, as has been the case in world history transitions previously. In the meantime, societies outside the West, aware of lingering Western power and the siren call of claims to cultural leadership, had to make their own adjustments to continuing, sometimes novel forms of Western influence.

For, as in earlier periods of world history, novel forces elicited somewhat different responses depending on the civilization. Some societies were more open to international contacts than others. Some responded to the need for political change with democracy—India is a case in point—while others, such as China, innovated while explicitly rejecting pluralist democracy. As in previous eras, world history continued to involve comparing reactions to some common trends and impulses. The relative decline of the West, intensifying international contacts, and the need to reconsider traditional political, social, and cultural patterns affected virtually all regions; but the results varied, because of particular twentieth-century settings and diverse prior traditions. Careful comparison remains essential, even among the societies that seemed most eagerly to embrace "international" trends.

The chapters that follow tackle issues of political change by discussing both new forms of authoritarian government and the rise of democracy in additional areas of the world, as well as outright revolution. They deal with world power balance in discussing the atomic bomb and terrorism. They deal with cultural innovations through nationalism, changes in religious balance, and the pressure of consumer values. Shifts in women's expectations and related changes in population behaviors and policies form another vital category. In all these areas, the mixture of innovation with defense of older identities, the pressure of new global contacts, and changes in world power balance, along with the continuing prestige of the West, shaped the framework in which particular societies developed patterns that can best be assessed through comparison.

CHAPTER 28

TWENTIETH-CENTURY REVOLUTIONS

The second decade of the twentieth century witnessed the early stages of three of the most important revolutions that ever occurred in world history: the Mexican, the Chinese, and the Russian. These revolutions helped set the stage for later uprisings, particularly in the 1950s–1970s decades, in various parts of Latin America, including Cuba, in Vietnam, and elsewhere. The Iranian Revolution of 1979 must be added to the list, though it had rather different bases.

Revolutions helped spur many of the key changes of the twentieth century, including the decline of monarchy and the fading of the aristocracy. They resulted in new cultural efforts, including expansion of education. They affected global politics, setting up new divisions between revolutionary and conservative powers. The tide of revolution may have ebbed by the 1990s, with the collapse of many Communist systems, but even if this proves true, revolution had been involved in many of the most important developments in contemporary world history thus far.

Revolutions obviously invite comparison. Each has a distinctive flavor and cast of characters. But revolutions also share some common dynamics and, in the twentieth century, some common causes. Comparison must also extend to impact: what were the durable political and social results in each case? What were the effects on the rest of the world?

Mexico's revolution broke out in 1910, against the aging dictatorship of Porfirio Diaz. Various components in the revolution included liberal elements and peasant protesters. From 1920 onward, after a decade of unrest, the revolution began to consolidate a new political system. While the Mexican Revolution did not produce immediate contagion elsewhere, its example helped spur social protests later, in other parts of Latin America.

Chinese revolutionaries toppled the ancient empire in 1911–1912, aided by the presence of a boy as latest official emperor. Sun Yat-sen was the leading revolutionary spokesperson. Efforts to construct a durable new system faltered, however, amid provincial disunity and, by the 1930s, Japanese invasion. Only after World War II did a Communist regime win out, ending the explicitly revolutionary period.

Russia had a preliminary revolution in 1905, which did not, however, induce the tsar to introduce significant reforms, particularly in the political arena. The hardships of World War I combined with more basic unrest to generate a major revolution in 1917, quickly captured by Vladimir Lenin and his Bolshevik wing of the Communist party. Roughly six years of conflict followed before the Communists were able to begin consolidating their rule. Lenin's interpretation of Marxism, and the success of the revolution, had wide impact on many other parts of the world, through the Cold War and until the collapse of the Bolshevik regime in 1989–1891.

Questions

1. How did the goals of the Mexican and Russian Revolutions compare? What were the major similarities and differences?
2. Is Sun Yat-sen best viewed as a modem interpreter of Chinese tradition or as a revolutionary westernizer?
3. How did Sun Yat-sen's approach compare with those of revolutionaries in Mexico and Russia?
4. How did Sun Yat-sen and Lenin compare in their views of how to organize a revolution?
5. Why and how did peasant concerns loom large in twentieth-century revolutions?
6. How did the Communist approach to peasant issues compare with reform approaches in Mexico and China? What was the relationship between the Communist approach and peasant grievances and aspirations?
7. What was the interaction between political and social goals in the three revolutions?
8. Do the documents suggest any causes of the differences among the three revolutions? What other kind of material would help to deal with this issue?

For Further Discussion

1. Do these documents suggest why these three revolutions would have different outcomes? Or why they would have different types and levels of impact in other parts of the world?
2. How do twentieth-century revolutions, in goals, organizations, and results, compare with the Atlantic revolutions of the 1770s–1820 period?
3. How would Western governments, including the United States, react to these three revolutions?
4. Is the contemporary age of revolution over? What has happened to the causes and ideals of these revolutions a century later?

MEXICO

FRANCISCO MADERO: THE PLAN OF SAN LUIS POTOSI, NOVEMBER 20, 1910

Madero was a middle-class, liberal politician who took charge of the early phase of the Mexican revolution, in direct opposition to the previous, authoritarian regime of Porfirio Diaz. He issued the Plan of San Luis Potosi after Diaz stole the Mexican election of 1910 by having Madero arrested and imprisoned. Madero fled to San Antonio and issued the Plan of San Luis Potosi calling for the nullification of the elections and upon Mexicans to take up arms against the government. The date of its issue marks the beginning of the Mexican Revolution.

• • •

Peoples, in their constant efforts for the triumph of the ideal of liberty and justice, are forced, at precise historical moments, to make their greatest sacrifices.

Our beloved country has reached one of those moments. A force of tyranny which we Mexicans were not accustomed to suffer after we won our independence oppresses us in such a manner that it has become intolerable. . . .

The legislative and judicial powers are completely subordinated to the executive, the division of powers, the sovereignty of the states, the liberty of the common councils, and the rights of the citizens exist only in writing in our great charter; but, as a fact, it may almost be said that martial law constantly exists in Mexico; the administration of justice, instead of imparting protection to the weak, merely serves to legalize the plunderings committed by the strong; the judges instead of being the representatives of justice, are the agents of the executive, whose interests they faithfully serve; the chambers of the union have no other will than that of the dictator; the governors of the States are designated by him and they in their turn designate and impose in like manner the municipal authorities. From this it results that the whole administrative, judicial, and legislative machinery obeys a single will, the caprice of General Porfirio Diaz, who during this long administration has shown that the principle motive that guides him is to maintain himself in power and at any cost. . . .

In Mexico, as a democratic Republic, the public power can have no other origin nor other basis than the will of the people, and the latter can not be subordinated to formulas to be executed in a fraudulent manner. . . .

For this reason the Mexican people have protested against the illegality of the last election and, desiring to use successively all the recourses offered by the laws of the Republic, in due form asked for the nullification of the election by the Chamber of Deputies, notwithstanding they recognized no legal origin in said body and knew beforehand that, as its members were not the representatives of the people, they would carry out the will of General Diaz, to whom exclusively they owe their investiture. In such a state of affairs the people, who are the only sovereign, also protested energetically against the election in imposing manifestations in different parts of the Republic. . . .

But such conduct was indispensable to show to the whole world that the Mexican people are fit for democracy, that they are thirsty for liberty, and that their present rulers do not measure up to their aspirations.

Besides, the attitude of the people before and during the election, as well as afterwards, shows clearly that they reject the energy of the Government of General Diaz and that, if those electoral rights had been respected, I would have been elected for President of the Republic.

Therefore, and in echo of the national will, I declare the late election illegal and, the Republic being accordingly without rulers, provisionally assume the Presidency of the Republic until the people designate their rulers pursuant to the law. In order to attain this end, it is necessary to eject from power the audacious usurpers whose only title of legality involves a scandalous and immoral fraud.

With all honesty I declare that it would be a weakness on my part and treason to the people, who have placed their confidence in me, not to put myself at the front of my fellow citizens, who anxiously call me from all parts of the country, to compel General Diaz by force of arms, to respect the national will.

THE PLAN OF AYALA

This document was issued by the radical peasant leader Emiliano Zapata, in 1911. Zapata never managed to seize power, but his economic demands, and his ability to rouse the peasantry in several key regions, affected Mexican social and political development for many decades.

• • •

[We hereby proclaim] the liberating plan of the sons of the State of Morelos, affiliated with the Insurgent Army which defends the fulfillment of the Plan of San Luis Potosi, with the reforms which they have believed necessary to add for the benefit of the Mexican Fatherland.

We, the subscribers [to this Plan], constituted in a Revolutionary Council . . . declare solemnly before the countenance of the civilized world which judges us and before the Nation to which we belong and love, the principles which we have formulated to terminate the tyranny which oppresses us and redeem the Fatherland from the dictatorships which are imposed on us, which are determined in the following plan:

Justicia y ley. [Justice and Law.] Ayala, 28 November, 1911. From Emiliano Zapata, *The Plan of Ayala* (29 November, 1911), translated by Erick Langer.

1. [Accuses Francisco I. Madero, the leader of the 1910 revolution and president of Mexico, of betraying the revolution and allying himself with the oppressive old guard in the State of Morelos.]

2. Francisco I. Madero is disavowed as Chief of the Revolution and as President of the Republic, for the above reasons, [and we will] endeavor to overthrow this official.

3. The illustrious General Pascual Orozco, second of the *caudillo* Don Francisco I. Madero, is recognized as Chief of the Liberating Revolution, and in case he does not accept this delicate post, General Emiliano Zapata is recognized Chief of the Revolution.

4. The Revolutionary Junta of the Sate of Morelos manifest the following formal points . . . and will make itself the defender of the principles that it will defend until victory or death.

5. The Revolutionary Junta of the State of Morelos will not admit transactions or political compromises until the overthrow of the dictatorial elements of Porfirio Diaz and Francisco I. Madero, since the Nation is tired of false men and traitors who make promises as liberators but once in power, forget them and become tyrants.

6. As an additional part of the Plan which we invoke, we assert that: the fields, woodlands, and water which the haciendados [landlords], *cientificos* or bosses in the shadow of tyranny and venal justice have usurped, will revert to the possession of the towns or citizens who have their corresponding titles to these properties. [These properties] have been usurped through the bad faith of our oppressors, who maintained all along with arms in hand the above mentioned possession. The usurpers who feel they have the right [to ownership], will demonstrate this before special tribunals which will be established when the Revolution triumphs.

7. In virtue of the fact that the immense majority of the towns and Mexican citizens are not masters of the soil they step upon, suffering horrors of misery without being able to better their social condition at all nor dedicate themselves to industry or agriculture because of the monopoly in a few hands of the land, woodlands, and waters, for this reason [the lands] will be expropriated, with indemnity of the third part of these monopolies to their powerful owners, so that the towns and citizens of Mexico can obtain common lands *[ejidos]*, colonies, and legitimate resources for towns or agricultural fields and that above all the lack of prosperity and well-being of the Mexican people is improved.

8. The haciendados, *cientificos* or bosses who oppose directly or indirectly the present plan, will have their possessions nationalized and two thirds of what they own will be destined for war indemnities, [and] pensions for the widows and orphans of the victims who succumb in the fight for this plan.

9. To regulate the procedures in regard to the items mentioned above, the laws of disentailment and nationalization will be applied as is appropriate. [The laws] put into effect by the immortal Juarez regarding Church lands will serve as a guide and example, which set a severe example to the despots and conservatives who at all times have tried to impose the ignominious yoke of oppression and backwardness.

10. The insurgent military chiefs of the Republic, who rose up in armed revolt at the behest of Francisco I. Madero to defend the plan of San Luis Potosí and who now oppose by force the present Plan, are to be judged traitors to the cause they defended and to the Fatherland, given the fact that in actuality many of them to please the tyrants for a handful of coins, or for bribes, are spilling the blood of their brethren who demand the fulfillment of the promises which don Francisco I. Madero made to the Nation.

11–14. [Details the payment of the expenses of war and the administration of the country after the Plan's success, and bids Madero to step down voluntarily.]

15. Mexicans: Consider that the cleverness and the bad faith of one man is spilling blood in a scandalous manner because of his inability to govern; consider that his system of government is putting the Fatherland in chains and by brute force of bayonets trampling under foot our institutions; and as we raised our arms to elevate him to power, today we turn them against him for having gone back on his agreements with the Mexican people and having betrayed the Revolution he initiated; we are not personalists, we are believers in principles, not in men. People of Mexico: Support with your arms in hand this Plan and you will create prosperity and happiness for the Fatherland.

CHINA

China's initial risings in 1911 led to the formal ending to the empire, in 1912, with a document that expressed new political goals while concealing the actual machinations that pushed the boy emperor to this point. This is followed by a fuller statement by the would-be reform leader of the new regime, the Western-educated Sun Yat-sen (1866–1925), who formed a new Nationalist Party but was unsuccessful in wresting power from regional warlords during the early 1920s.

• • •

PROCLAMATION OF THE ABDICATION OF THE MANCHUS, 1912

"The Whole Country is tending towards a republican form of government. It is the Will of Heaven, and it is certain that we could not reject the people's desire for the sake of one family's honor and glory."

"We, the Emperor, hand over the sovereignty to the people. We decide the form of government to be a constitutional republic."

"In this time of transition, in order to unite the South and the North, We appoint Yuan Shi-kai to organize a provisional government, consulting the people's army

From Eva March Tappan, ed., *China, Japan, and the Island of the Pacific*, Vol. I of *The World's Story: A History of the World in Story, Song, and Art* (Boston: Houghton Mifflin, 1914), 261.

regarding the union of the five peoples, Manuchus, Chinese, Mongolians, Mohammedans, and Tibetans. These peoples jointly constitute the great State of Chung Hwa Ming-Kus [a republic of China].

"We retire to a peaceful life and will enjoy the respectful treatment of the nation."

This was signed by the Emperor; by Yuan Shi-kai as Prime Minister; and also by the other Ministers.

SUN YAT-SEN: FUNDAMENTALS OF NATIONAL RECONSTRUCTION (1923 C.E.)

I Principles of Revolution

The term Kemin, or *revolution,* was first used by Confucius. Incidents of a revolutionary nature repeatedly happened in Chinese history after Tang (founder of the Shang Dynasty, 1766 B.C.E.) and Wu (founder of the Zhou Dynasty, 1122 B.C.E.). In Europe revolutionary tides surged in the seventeenth and eighteenth centuries and they have since spread over the whole world. In due course they created republics, and they conferred constitutions on monarchies. The principles that I have held in promoting the Chinese revolution were in some cases copied from our traditional ideals, in other cases modeled on European theory and experience, and in still others formulated according to original and self- developed theories. They are described as follows:

1. PRINCIPLE OF NATIONALISM

Revelations of Chinese history prove that the Chinese as a people are independent in spirit and in conduct. Coerced into touch with other people, they could at times live in peace with them by maintaining friendly relations and at others assimilate them as the result of propinquity. During the periods when their political and military prowess declined, they could not escape for the time from the fate of a conquered nation, but they could eventually vigorously reassert themselves. Nationalistic ideas in China did not come from a foreign source; they were inherited from our remote forefathers. Upon this legacy is based my principle of nationalism, and where necessary, I have developed it and amplified and improved upon it. No vengeance has been inflicted on the Manchus and we have endeavored to live side by side with them on an equal footing. This is our nationalistic policy toward races within our national boundaries. Externally, we should strive to maintain independence in the family of nations, and to spread our indigenous civilization as well as to enrich it by absorbing what is best in world civilization, with the hope that we may forge ahead with other nations towards the goal of ideal brotherhood.

2. PRINCIPLE OF DEMOCRACY

In ancient China we had the Emporer Yao (2357–2258 B.C.E.) and Emperor Shun (2258–2206 B.C.E) who departed from the hereditary system and chose their successors. We also had Tang and Wu who over threw kingdoms by revolution. Preserved in our books are such sayings as: "Heaven sees as the people see; Heaven hears as the people hear." "We have heard of a person name Zhou having been slain, we have not heard of a monarch having been murdered." "The people are most important, while the king is of the least importance." All these sayings ring with democratic sentiments. Since we have had only ideas about popular rights, and no democratic system has been evolved, we have to go to Europe and America for a republican form of government. . . .

All through my revolutionary career I have held the view that China must be made a republic. There are three reasons. First, from a theoretical point of view, there is no ground for preserving a monarchical form of government, since it is widely recognized that the people constitute the foundation of a nation and they are all equal in their own country. In the second place, under Manchu occupation the Chinese were forced into the position of the vanquished, and suffered oppression for more than two hundred and sixty years. While a constitutional monarchy may not arouse deep resentment in other countries and can maintain itself for the time being, it will be an impossibility in China. This is from a historical point of view. A third reason may be advanced with an eye on the future of the nation. That in China prolonged periods of disorder usually followed a revolution was due to the desire of every insurgent to be a king and to his subsequent contention for the throne. If a republican government is adopted, there will be no contention. For these three reasons, I have decided for the republican form of government in order to realize the principle of democracy.

My second decision is that a constitution must be adopted to ensure good government. The true meaning of constitutionalism was discovered by Montesquieu. The threefold separation of the legislative, judicial, and executive powers as advocated by him was accepted in every constitutional country in Europe.

3. PRINCIPLE OF LIVELIHOOD

With the invention of modern machines, the phenomenon of uneven distribution of wealth in the West has become all the more marked. Intensified by crosscurrents, economic revolution was flaring up more ferociously than political revolution. This situation was scarcely noticed by our fellow-countrymen thirty years ago. On my tour of Europe and America, I saw with my own eyes the instability of their economic structure and the deep concern of their leaders in groping for a solution. I felt that, although the disparity of wealth under our economic organization is not so great as in the West, the difference is only in degree, not in character. The situation will become more acute when the West extends its economic influence to China. We must form plans beforehand in order to cope with the situation. After comparing various schools of economic thought, I have come to the realization that the principle of state ownership is most profound, reliable and practical. Moreover, it will forestall in China difficulties which have already caused much anxiety in the West. I have therefore decided to enforce the principle of the people's livelihood simultaneously with the principles of nationalism and democracy, with the hope to achieve our political objective and nip economic unrest in the bud.

II Fundamentals of Revolution

According to my plan, the progress of our revolution should be regulated and divided into three stages: First, military rule; second, political tutelage; third, constitutional government. The first stage is a period of destruction, during which military rule is installed. The revolutionary army is to break down (as it did) Manchu despotism, sweep away official corruption, and reform vicious customs.

RUSSIA

This famous pamphlet was published in 1902, when Lenin's Bolshevik wing of the Communist movement was under police attack and very much out of power. It suggests both the goals and the methods Lenin and his colleagues would use when revolution came.

When Lenin tried to organize a Marxist revolutionary party in Russia, he faced a dilemma. The ultimate goal was a disciplined party. He was irritated by the dissent and controversy that raged in revolutionary circles. In this famous treatise he outlined his ideas on freedom in powerful words that to later generations read like a denunciation of freedom as it is normally understood. Implemented by Lenin himself after the 1917 revolution and exacerbated by Stalin, they transformed Marx's dream of a "dictatorship of the proletariat" (absolute rule by the people, depriving the old ruling class of its power) into its opposite, a dictatorship over the proletariat. In later decades, the rationale for repression outlined here was advanced again and again by dictatorial Communist governments as they argued that the small "vanguard" of the proletariat was capable of leading the masses for their own good, even in opposition to their express will. Why does he argue no criticism can be made of socialist ideology?

• • •

V. I. LENIN, WHAT IS TO BE DONE

"Freedom"—it's a great word, but under the flag of "freedom of industry" the most rapacious of wars were conducted. Under the banner of "freedom of labor" workers have been robbed. The very same internal hypocrisy is contained in the contemporary phrase "freedom to criticize." People who are truly convinced that they have advanced the frontier of science would not demand freedom for new ideas to coexist next to old, but to replace them. . . .

We are walking in a small, tight group along a steep and difficult path, firmly joining hands. We are surrounded by enemies, and must continue almost always under their fire. We have freely and consciously decided to unite to fight the enemy. . . .

We said that Social-Democratic consciousness could not exist among the workers. But it could be brought to them from without. The history of all countries testifies that workers left exclusively to their own strength can cultivate only a trade union consciousness—that is the belief in the need to unite into a union, struggle against the bosses, press the government to pass needed labor legislation, etc. The doctrine of Socialism grew out of philosophic, historical, and economic theories which were worked out by the educated representatives of the propertied class, the intelligentsia. The founders of modern scientific socialism, Marx and Engels belonged themselves to the bourgeois intelligentsia. Just as in Russia, the theoretical doctrine of Social-Democracy arose quite independently from spontaneous growth of a workers movement, but arose rather as a natural and inevitable result of the development of ideas among the revolutionary socialist intelligentsia. . . .

Since there can be no talk of an independent ideology developed by the working masses in the process of their movement, the only choice is: bourgeois or socialist ideology. There is no middle way (for mankind has not developed any "third" ideology), and generally speaking, in a society torn by class opposition there could never be a non-class or an above-class ideology. Therefore any belittlement of socialist ideology, any dismissal of it signified the strengthening of bourgeois ideology.

A small, tight, solid nucleus of the most dependable, experienced and hardened workers having trustworthy representatives in the main regions and connected by all the rules of secrecy with the organization of revolutionaries can quite capably, with the widest support of the masses and without any formal organization, fulfill all functions of a professional organization, in a manner desirable to a Social-Democratic movement.

LENIN'S CALL TO POWER, OCTOBER 24, 1917

When revolution broke out in Russia, Lenin was in exile in Switzerland. But the German government facilitated his travel to Russia, hoping his agitation would weaken the Russian war effort in World War I (an effort the first revolutionary

government, under the liberal Kerensky, attempted to continue). Lenin's statement accurately reflected the forceful moves he and the revolutionary workers' soviets would adopt in toppling the liberal regime and replacing it with Communist leadership.

· · ·

The situation is critical in the extreme. In fact, it is now absolutely clear that to delay the uprising would be fatal. With all my might I urge comrades to realize that everything now hangs by a thread; that we are confronted by problems which are not to be solved by conferences or congresses (even congresses of Soviets), but exclusively by peoples, by the masses, by the struggle of the armed people. . . .

All districts, all regiments, all forces must be mobilized at once and must immediately send their delegations to the Revolutionary Military Committee and to the Central Committee of the Bolsheviks with the insistent demand that under no circumstances should power be left in the hands of Kerensky and Co. . . .

. . . It would be an infinite crime on the part of the revolutionaries were they to let the chance slip, knowing that the salvation of the revolution, the offer of peace, the salvation of Petrograd [St. Petersburg], salvation from famine, the transfer of the land to the peasants depend upon them.

The government is tottering. It must be given the death-blow at all costs.

THE FUNDAMENTAL LAW OF LAND SOCIALIZATION

This decree was one of the early moves of the new Bolshevik regime, ushering in a huge social and economic change but also setting up a radical new system of agricultural organization that would antagonize many peasants.

· · ·

Decree of the Central Executive Committee, February 19, 1918

PART I. GENERAL PROVISIONS

Article 1. All private ownership of land, minerals, waters, forests, and natural resources within the boundaries of the Russian Federated Soviet Republic is abolished forever.

Article 2. Henceforth all the land is handed over without compensation (open or secret) to the toiling masses for their use.

Article 3. With the exceptions indicated in this decree the right to the use of the land belongs to him who cultivates it with his own labor.

Article 4. The right to use of the land cannot be limited on account of sex, religion, nationality, or citizenship.

Article 5. All minerals, forests, water, and other live forces of nature (depending on their importance) are placed at the disposition of the uzed, gubernia, regional, or federal Soviets to be controlled by them. The methods of utilizing and managing the above resources will be determined by special decree.

Article 6. All privately owned live stock, agriculture implements, and buildings of estates that are worked by hired labor shall be taken over by the land departments of the [local and Soviet governments] without compensation. . . .

Article 11. In addition to effecting an equitable distribution of the agricultural land among the toiling agricultural population and a more efficient utilization of the national resources, the local and federal land departments have also the following duties: (a) to create conditions favorable to the development of the productive forces of the country by increasing the productivity of the soil, to develop scientific farming, and to raise the general level of agricultural knowledge among the land toilers; (b) to create a reserve of agricultural land; (c) to develop agricultural enterprises such as horticulture, apiculture, market-gardening, stock raising, dairying, etc.; (d) to hasten in certain areas the transition from a less productive to a more productive system of land cultivation by effecting a better distribution of the agricultural population; (e) to encourage the collective system of agriculture at the expense of individual farming, the former being more economical and leading to socialistic economy.

CHAPTER 29

AUTHORITARIANISM ON THE RIGHT

Italian Fascism, German Nazism, And Argentine Peronism

A new kind of authoritarianism was born in Europe at the end of the nineteenth century. It built on strong nationalism but added a greater hostility to liberal ideas and institutions. Authoritarians resented the divisions and bickering of parliamentary systems. They disliked individualism and the consumer society, believing that people should find a higher purpose in the nation and its state. Most feared the rise of socialism, seeking to cure social ills by other, state-sponsored means. Authoritarianism was a noisy but also a small force in Europe until the huge disruptions of World War I. Then additional nationalist discontents, the fear of Communism in Russia, and sheer confusion gave the authoritarian movements additional support. First in Italy, then in other countries, the movements were able to gain power, usually by legal means, though none ever obtained an outright majority in any free election.

Authoritarianism also grew outside Europe. In Latin America many authoritarian dictators had flourished at times during the nineteenth century; they were called *caudillos,* the Spanish word for *leader*. Most authoritarians defended existing institutions—property owners, the army, the church. They gained power because of the difficulty of establishing stable governments after the independence wars earlier in the century. Some caudillos added a populist twist, wooing elements of the common people by programs of public works and state jobs. Authoritarianism continued in the twentieth century, off and on, and it picked up some of the trappings of European fascism, from grandiose principles of state power and nationalism to the uniformed movements, whose members were taught to march in military style, a tactic designed to whip up loyalty and discipline. Authoritarian leaders sprang up in Africa, the Middle East, and parts of Asia after World War II, again in part because some newly independent states found it hard to generate effective political institutions in any other way. Some of these leaders, too, took on certain fascist overtones.

A comparison of European fascism and a significant adaptation of authoritarianism in Latin America allows consideration of one of the vital political currents of the twentieth century. Authoritarian movements, after the fascist example, undoubtedly shared certain features and imitated each other, but they were not all alike. Ideas varied, and contexts varied as well; a full Nazi-style state was possible only in an industrialized society, for example. Even in Europe, Italian fascism and German Nazism clearly differed, despite some shared causes and shared impulses.

Mussolini's movement came first, among the modern versions of authoritarianism; Mussolini came into power in 1923. A former socialist, Mussolini developed a fascist ideology amid the social strife and disappointed nationalism of post–World War I Italy. Italian liberal democracy was a rather new creation, and it was not functioning well.

Hitler, an ardent nationalist and anti-Semite and a disgruntled war veteran, struggled through the 1920s. Many Germans deeply resented their loss in World War I and the harsh peace imposed on their country. But Hitler got his chance only when economic depression, in 1929, fueled the discontent; he came to power in 1933.

But by the late nineteenth century some Latin American Caudillos were embellishing their dictatorships by working for greater economic development and reaching out for more active popular support. Juan Peron was in this newer tradition. When he came to power in 1946, he also had the example of European fascism before him—Argentina was one of the more Europeanized Latin American countries, with a large minority of Italian origin.

A key analytical problem, as sources from fascism, Nazism, and Peronism readily attest, is that leaders of those movements were not interested in careful statements of principle or even in complete consistency. They talked of subordinating the individual to higher purposes, but they also praised human freedom. They were hostile to Marxism, but they often talked about social justice and sometimes (as with Peron) established themselves as friends of the working class in order to gain extensive working-class support.

A final question must be applied to Mussolini, to Hitler, and to Peron alike: why did they gain so much popularity? Do their ideas help explain the appeal of authoritarian movements in many different countries from the 1920s onward?

Questions

1. Why was fascism opposed to socialism? to democracy? to liberalism? What was the fascist alternative, according to Mussolini? What were the principles and goals of a fascist state?
2. How did the fascist state contrast with the liberal idea of the state? What was the fascist alternative to individualism?
3. What was Hitler's definition of a folkish state? How do Hitler's ideas show the bases of the launching of World War II and the Holocaust?

4. What ideas did Mussolini and Hitler share concerning methods for their movements? Did they have similar ideas about the state? Did Mussolini anticipate Hitler's ideas of a folkish state?

5. Why did Hitler, Mussolini, and Peron all claim to be revolutionary?

6. How do Mussolini, Hitler, and Peron suggest some of the political and social problems that gave rise to their movements?

7. How did Peron learn what not to say, from the fates and international reputations of Italian and German fascism?

8. How did Peron's ideas of the nation compare with Hitler's? How did his idea of individualism compare with the fascist approach? Judging by his stated goals, is it useful to think of Peron as a fascist? as a Nazi?

9. How did Peron distinguish himself from traditional Latin American caudillos?

10. If Peron should not be called a fascist, how are his political movement and beliefs best described?

For Further Discussion

1. Why might elements of European fascism prove attractive in the Latin American political context after World War II?

2. Why was it unlikely that a leader like Peron could set up a full Nazi state?

3. What was the relationship between fascistlike movements and nationalism? What kinds of nationalism avoided some kind of fascist outgrowth, and why?

4. Do conditions for fascism still exist in the world today? What societies, currently, would seem the most likely potential centers of serious fascist movements?

ITALIAN FASCISM: MUSSOLINI

Mussolini (1883–1945) came to power in 1923, following a famous "march on Rome" when armed bands (*Squadriste*), which had been violently disrupting democratic political meetings, mounted a largely peaceful, symbolic protest surge on the national capital. Mussolini spelled out his fascist doctrine (the name fascist came from the movement's symbol, a bundle or *fascio*) at various points in his career. The following selection comes from a 1932 article, "Doctrine of Fascism," written at a time when he was already well established as dictator. During the 1920s Mussolini had suppressed political opposition and had developed

From Benito Mussolini, *The Political and Social Doctrine of Fascism,* trans. Jane Soames (London: Hogarth Press, 1933), 8–14, 16–26.

extensive public works projects, while dismantling the previous liberal state and turning parliament into a rubber stamp. Mussolini was toppled by the allied invasion of Italy during World War II and killed by resistance fighters.

• • •

Fascism was not the nursling of a doctrine worked out beforehand with detailed elaboration; it was born of the need for action and was itself from the beginning practical rather than theoretical; it was not merely another political party but, even in the first two years, in opposition to all political parties as such, and itself a living movement. The name which I then (1919) gave the organization fixed its character. And yet, if one were to re-read, in the now dusty columns of that date, the report of the meeting in which the *Fasci Italiani di combattimento* were constituted, one would there find no ordered expression of doctrine, but a series of aphorisms, anticipations and aspirations which, when refined by time from the original ore, were destined after some years to develop into an ordered series of doctrinal concepts, forming the Fascist political doctrine—different from all others either of the past or the present day. . . .

The years which preceded the march to Rome were years of great difficulty, during which the necessity for action did not permit of research or any complete elaboration of doctrine. The battle had to be fought in the towns and villages. There was much discussion, but—what was more important and more sacred—men died. They knew how to die. Doctrine, beautifully defined and carefully elucidated . . . might be lacking; but there was to take its place something more decisive—Faith. Even so, anyone . . . will find that the fundamentals of doctrine were cast during the years of conflict. It was precisely in those years that Fascist thought armed itself, was refined, and began the great task of organization. The problem of the relation between the individual citizen and the State; the allied problems of authority and liberty; political and social problems as well as those specifically national—a solution was being sought for all these while at the same time the struggle against Liberalism, Democracy, Socialism and the Masonic bodies was being carried on. . . .

And above all, Fascism . . . believes neither in the possibility nor the utility of perpetual peace. It thus repudiates the doctrine of Pacifism—born of a renunciation of the struggle and an act of cowardice in the face of sacrifice. War alone brings up to its highest tension all human energy and puts the stamp of nobility upon the peoples who have the courage to meet it. . . . This anti-Pacifist spirit is carried by Fascism even into the life of the individual; the proud motto of the *Squadrista, "Me ne frego"* ["We don't give a damn"] . . . is an act of philosophy not only stoic, the summary of a doctrine not only political—it is the education to combat, the acceptation of the risks which combat implies, and a new way of life for Italy. Thus the Fascist accepts life and loves it, knowing nothing of and despising suicide: he rather conceives of life as a duty and struggle and conquest, life which should be high and full, lived for oneself, but above all for others. . . .

Such a conception of life makes Fascism the complete opposition of that doctrine, the base of so-called scientific and Marxian Socialism, the materialist conception of history; according to which the history of human civilization can be explained simply through the conflict of interests among the various social groups and by the change and development in the means and instruments of production. . . . Fascism, now and always, believes in holiness and in heroism; that is to say, in actions influenced by no economic motive, direct or indirect. . . . It follows that the existence of an unchangeable and unchanging class-war is also denied—the natural progeny of the economic conception of history. And above all Fascism denies that classwar can be the preponderant force in the transformation of society. These two fundamental concepts of Socialism being thus refuted, nothing is left of it but the sentimental aspiration . . . towards a social convention in which the sorrows and sufferings of the humblest shall be alleviated. . . . Fascism denies the validity of the equation, well-being=happiness, which would reduce men to the level of animals, caring for one thing only—to be fat and well-fed—and would thus degrade humanity to a purely physical existence.

After Socialism, Fascism combats the whole complex system of democratic ideology, and repudiates it, whether in its theoretical premises or in its practical application. Fascism denies that the majority, by the simple fact that it is a majority, can direct human society; it denies that numbers alone can govern by means of a periodical consultation, and it affirms the immutable, beneficial and fruitful inequality of mankind, which can never be permanently leveled through the mere operation of a mechanical process such as universal suffrage. The democratic regime may be defined as from time to time giving the people the illusion of sovereignty, while the real effective sovereignty lies in the hands of other concealed and irresponsible forces. . . .

Fascism has taken up an attitude of complete opposition to the doctrines of Liberalism, both in the political field and the field of economics. . . . Liberalism only flourished for half a century. . . .

The foundation of Fascism is the conception of the State, its character, its duty, and its aim. Fascism conceives of the State as an absolute, in comparison with which all individuals or groups are relative, only to be conceived of in their relation to the State. The conception of the Liberal State is not that of a directing force, guiding the play and development, both material and spiritual, of a collective body, but merely a force limited to the function of recording results: on the other hand, the Fascist State is itself conscious, and has itself a will and a personality—thus it may be called the "ethic" State. In 1929 . . . I said:

"For us Fascists, the State is not merely a guardian . . . nor is it an organization with purely material aims. . . . Nor is it a purely political creation. . . . The State, as conceived of and as created by Fascism, is a spiritual and moral fact in itself, since its political, juridical and economic organization of the nation is a concrete thing; and such an organization must be in its origins and development a manifestation of the spirit. The State is the guarantor of security both internal and external, but it is also the custodian and transmitter of the spirit of the people, as it has grown up through the centuries in language, in customs and in faith. And the State is not only a living reality of the present, it is also linked with the past and above all with the future, and thus transcending the brief limits of individual life, it represents the immanent spirit of the nation. . . ."

From 1929 until today [1932], evolution, both political and economic, has everywhere gone to prove the validity of these doctrinal premises. Of such gigantic importance is the State. It is the force which alone can provide a solution to the dramatic contradictions of capitalism, and that state of affairs which we call the crisis can only be dealt with by the State, as between other States. . . . Yet the Fascist State is unique, and an original creation. It is not reactionary, but revolutionary, in that it anticipates the solution of the universal political problems which elsewhere have to be settled in the political field by the rivalry of parties, the excessive power of the Parliamentary regime and the irresponsibility of political assemblies; while it meets the problems of the economic field by a system of syndicalism* which is continually increasing in importance, as much in the sphere of labour as of industry: and in the moral field enforces order, discipline, and obedience to that which is the determined moral code of the country. Fascism desires the State to be a strong and organic body, at the same time reposing upon broad and popular support. The Fascist State has drawn into itself even the economic activities of the nation, and, through the corporative social and educational institutions created by it, its influence reaches every aspect of the national life and includes, framed in their respective organizations, all the political, economic and spiritual forces of the nation. A State which reposes upon the support of millions of individuals who recognize its authority, are continually conscious of its power and are ready at once to serve it, is not the old tyrannical State. . . . The individual in the Fascist State is not annulled but rather multiplied, just in the same way that a soldier in a regiment is not diminished but rather increased by the number of his comrades. The Fascist State organizes the nation, but leaves a sufficient margin of liberty to the individual; the latter is deprived of all useless and possibly harmful freedom, but retains what is essential; the deciding power in the question cannot be the individual, but the State alone. . . .

According to Fascism, government is not so much a thing to be expressed in territorial or military terms as in terms of morality and the spirit. It must be thought of as an Empire—that is to say, a nation which directly or indirectly rules other nations, without the need for conquering a single square yard of territory. For Fascism, the growth of Empire, that is to say the expansion of the nation, is an essential manifestation of vitality, and its opposite a sign of decadence. Peoples which are rising, or rising again after a period of decadence, are always imperialist; any renunciation is a sign of

---

*Mussolini meant this as an alternative to class-based unions. He installed state-dominated employer-worker boards, outlawing other unions and strikes.

decay and death. Fascism is the doctrine best adapted to represent the tendencies and the aspirations of a people, like the people of Italy, who are rising again after many centuries of abasement and foreign servitude. But Empire demands discipline, the co-ordination of all forces and a deeply-felt sense of duty and sacrifice: this fact explains . . . the necessarily severe measures which must be taken against those who would oppose this spontaneous and inevitable movement of Italy in the twentieth century.

German Nazism: Hitler

The following passage comes from Hitler's *Mein Kampf*, which outlined his goals for a Nazi state with suprising frankness. Hitler wrote the book after he was jailed for an attempted revolt in a Munich beer hall in 1923. He was released in less than a year and resumed his propaganda activities, though his movement was foundering until the Depression hit Germany at the end of the decade. Then, votes for Nazism began to soar, reaching more than a third of the total in a 1932 election. Once he was in power in 1933, Hitler constructed a dictatorship; actively promoted economic development, particularly toward building up German armaments; attacked and ultimately killed most Jews in Germany and Europe (the Holocaust); and launched a series of aggressive moves that led to World War II, committing suicide in 1945 as Soviet armies invaded Berlin.

. . .

For the realization of philosophical ideals and of the demands derived from them no more occurs through men's pure feeling or inner will in themselves than the achievement of freedom through the general longing for it. No, only when the ideal urge for independence gets a fighting organization in the form of military instruments of power can the pressing desire of a people be transformed into glorious reality.

Every philosophy of life, even if it is a thousand times correct and of highest benefit to humanity, will remain without significance for the practical shaping of a people's life, as long as its principles have not become the banner of a fighting movement which for its part in turn will be a party as long as its activity has not found completion in the victory of its ideas and its party dogmas have not become the new state principles of a people's community. . . .

This transformation of a general, philosophical, ideal conception of the highest truth into a definitely delimited, tightly organized political community of faith and struggle, unified in spirit and will, is the most significant achievement, since on its

From Adolf Hitler, *Mein Kampf*, trans. Ralph Manheim (Boston: Houghton Mifflin, 1971), 380, 390–95. Reprinted by permission of the publisher.

happy solution alone the possibility of the victory of an idea depends. From the army of often millions of men, who as individuals more or less clearly and definitely sense these truths, and in part perhaps comprehend them, *one* man must step forward who with apodictic force will form granite principles from the wavering idea-world of the broad masses and take up the struggle for their sole correctness, until from the shifting waves of a free thought-world there will arise a brazen cliff of solid unity in faith and will.

The general right for such an activity is based on necessity, the personal right on success. . . .

What has been profitably Germanized in history is the soil which our ancestors acquired by the sword and settled with German peasants. In so far as they directed foreign blood into our national body in this process, they contributed to that catastrophic splintering of our inner being which is expressed in German super-individualism—a phenomenon, I am sorry to say, which is praised in many quarters. . . .

. . . [T]he state must, therefore, in the light of reason, regard its highest task as the preservation and intensification of the race, this fundamental condition of all human cultural development.

It was the Jew, Karl Marx, who was able to draw the extreme inference from those false conceptions and views concerning the nature and purpose of a state: by detaching the state concept from racial obligations without being able to arrive at any other equally acknowledged formulation, the bourgeois world even paved the way for a doctrine which denies the state as such. . . .

It is, therefore, the first obligation of a new movement, standing on the ground of a folkish world view, to make sure that its conception of the nature and purpose of the state attains a uniform and clear character.

Thus the basic realization is: *that the state represents no end, but a means. It is, to be sure, the premise for the formation of a higher human culture, but not its cause, which lies exclusively in the existence of a race capable of culture.* Hundreds of exemplary states might exist on earth, but if the Aryan* culture-bearer died out, there would be no culture corresponding to the spiritual level of the highest peoples of today. We can go even farther and say that the fact of human state formation would not in the least exclude the possibility of the destruction of the human race, provided that superior intellectual ability and elasticity would be lost due to the absence of their racial bearers. . . .

The *state* in itself does not create a specific cultural level; it can only preserve the race which conditions this level. Otherwise the state as such may continue to exist unchanged for centuries while, in consequence of a racial mixture which it has not prevented, the cultural capacity of a people and the general aspect of its life conditioned

*Hitler used the term Aryan to designate the Germanic "race."

by it have long since suffered a profound change. The present-day state, for example, may very well simulate its existence as a formal mechanism for a certain length of time, but the racial poisoning of our national body creates a cultural decline which even now is terrifyingly manifest.

Thus, the precondition for the existence of a higher humanity is not the state, but the nation possessing the necessary ability. . . .

The state is a means to an end. Its end lies in the preservation and advancement of a community of physically and psychically homogeneous creatures. This preservation itself comprises first of all existence as a race and thereby permits the free development of all the forces dormant in this race. Of them a part will always primarily serve the preservation of physical life, and only the remaining part the promotion of a further spiritual development. Actually the one always creates the precondition for the other.

States which do not serve this purpose are misbegotten, monstrosities in fact. The fact of their existence changes this no more than the success of a gang of bandits can justify robbery.

We National Socialists as champions of a new philosophy of life must never base ourselves on so-called 'accepted facts'—and false ones at that. If we did, we would not be the champions of a new great idea, but the coolies of the present-day lie. We must distinguish in the sharpest way between the state as a vessel and the race as its content. This vessel has meaning only if it can preserve and protect the content; otherwise it is useless.

Thus, the highest purpose of a folkish state is concern for the preservation of those original racial elements which bestow culture and create the beauty and dignity of a higher mankind. We, as Aryans, can conceive of the state only as the living organism of a nationality which not only assures the preservation of this nationality, but by the development of its spiritual and ideal abilities leads it to the highest freedom.

But what they try to palm off on us as a state today is usually nothing but a monstrosity born of deepest human error, with untold misery as a consequence.

We National Socialists know that with this conception we stand as revolutionaries in the world of today and are also branded as such. But our thoughts and actions must in no way be determined by the approval or disapproval of our time, but by the binding obligation to a truth which we have recognized. Then we may be convinced that the higher insight of posterity will not only understand our actions of today, but will also confirm their correctness and exalt them. . . .

A state can be designated as exemplary if it is not only compatible with the living conditions of the nationality it is intended to represent, but if in practice it keeps this nationality alive by its own very existence—quite regardless of the importance of this state formation within the framework of the outside world. For the function of the state is not to create abilities, but only to open the road for those forces which are present. *Thus, conversely, a state can be designated as bad if, despite a high cultural level, it dooms the bearer of this culture in his racial composition. For thus it destroys to all* intents and purposes the premise for the survival of this culture which it did not create, but which is the fruit of a culture-creating nationality safeguarded by a living integration through the state. The state does not represent the content, but a form. *A people's cultural level at any time does not, therefore, provide a standard for measuring the quality of the state* in which it lives. It is easily understandable that a people highly endowed with culture offers a more valuable picture than a Negro tribe; nevertheless, the state organism of the former, viewed according to its fulfillment of purpose, can be inferior to that of the Negro. Though the best state and the best state form are not able to extract from a people abilities which are simply lacking and never did exist, a bad state is assuredly able to kill originally existing abilities by permitting or even promoting the destruction of the racial culture-bearer.

Hence our judgment concerning the quality of a state can primarily be determined only by the relative utility it possesses for a definite nationality, and in no event by the intrinsic importance attributable to it in the world. . . .

If, therefore, we speak of a higher mission of the state, we must not forget that the higher mission lies essentially in the nationality whose free development the state must merely make possible by the organic force of its being.

ARGENTINA: PERONISM

The following materials are excerpts from speeches given by the Argentine dictator between 1946 and 1949, when he was head of state. Peron (1896–1973) entered the Argentine government as a result of a coup in 1943 and became president in 1946. Developing an ardent following, particularly among urban workers, he launched extensive building projects and welfare programs. He was ousted in 1956, returning briefly thereafter, but a Peronist political movement remained an important force in Argentine politics for some time.

• • •

1. 1946

The Argentine Republic was born as a country of peace and work, endowed by nature with everything people may hope for to live happily and in peace; on this fact our international policy is based, we are inevitably heading for prosperity and greatness achieved partly by reason of our geographical situation and by our historical destiny.

There is nothing we can envy others, since God gave us whatever we may wish for. Our policy is born of this aspect of our own natural greatness. We can never seek

From Juan Peron, *The Voice of Peron* (Buenos Aires: Argentine Government, 1950), 22, 36–37, 59, 64, 69–70, 71, 94, 110–11.

to take something from someone since we are surrounded on this earth by countries less fortunate than ours. For this reason, our international policy is a policy of peace, friendship, and the desire to trade honestly and freely, whenever we are offered the same freedom we grant, for in a world where absolute freedom of trade does not exist, it would be suicidal to profess this absolute liberty.

2. 1946

Social conscience has banished for ever the selfish individualism that looked only for personal advantages, to seek the welfare of all through the collective action of unions. Without that social conscience modern peoples are driven to struggle and despair dragging their country to misery, war and distress.

This magnificent spectacle of the awakening of a social conscience is condemned by men maintaining old standards, but they must not be blamed for they are the product of an unhappy era already surpassed by the Argentine Republic. They are the product of that individualistic and selfish age. They were born when gold was the only thing that mattered, when gold was handled without consulting the heart and therefore without understanding and realising that gold is not everything on this earth, that dividends are not of paramount importance.

3. 1946

The Five-Year Plan, as we have drawn it up, is simply the result of a careful study of all the Argentine problems, in the institutional order, in the field of national defence, and also in the field of national economy. We have considered each of these Argentine problems in detail, trying to discover their roots in order to find an adequate solution.

Only a plan of vast proportions is in keeping with a great nation such as the Argentine Republic. The mediocre, those who lack courage and faith, always prefer small plans. Great nations, such as our own, with lofty ambitions and aspirations, must also envisage great plans. Nothing valuable can be achieved by planning trivialities.

4. 1946

Nowadays policy has changed: each person is at his post, working for the common patrimony. When something is achieved, it must benefit everyone; when suffering awaits us, all must share the sorrow. But let us advise those who still uphold ideas of the old politicians that today, Argentine men and Argentine women are aware of the existence of a movement supported by the whole country; that we all work and struggle for this joint movement; therefore, that any personal or group policy will be destroyed by us and also that our policy originates in this movement of union.

5. 1947

Encouraged by an overwhelming spirit of patriotism and steadily following the principles and standards of conduct set by precedent, an officer must apply all his strength of character and bring into play all his stalwart personality so that whatever may be the circumstances in which they find themselves, the Armed Forces will never cease to be an orderly and disciplined institution at the exclusive service of the Nation. He must be sure that they are never transformed into a constant danger which undervalues and hampers the will of a sovereign people.

6. 1948

To guide the masses one must first instruct and educate them, which can be done at meetings or at lectures on politics, to be given in our centres, not to tell them to vote for us, or that they must do this or that so that Peter or James will be elected to represent them. No, we must speak to them of what are their obligations, because in our country there is much talk of rights and little of moral obligations. We must talk somewhat more about the obligations of each citizen towards his country and towards his fellow countrymen, and forget for a time their rights since we have mentioned them often enough.

7. 1949

The Peronistic doctrine has to go forward with its fundamental idea; to free the people to prepare them to make the right use of this freedom. Neither can any Argentine, and still less a Peronist, use unfairly the individual freedom which the Magna Charter of the Republic offers him as a man of honour and not as a criminal. A Peronist must be a slave to the law because that is the only way in which he can eventually obtain his freedom. But it is not enough for a Peronist to be a slave of the law. He must also observe the Peronist code of ethics, because those who break laws are not the only criminals, those who abuse their freedom and who break the community laws of the land they live in to the detriment of their fellow beings, are also guilty.

8. 1949

Liberal Democracy, flexible in matters of political or economic retrocession, or apparent discretion, was not equally flexible where social problems were concerned. And the bourgeoisie after breaking their lines, have presented the spectacle of peoples who all rise at once so as to measure the might of their presence, the volume of their clamour, and the fairness of their claims. Popular expectation is followed by discontent. Hope placed in the power of law is transformed into resentment if these laws tolerate injustice. The State looks on impotently at a growing loss of prestige. Its institutions prevent it from taking adequate measures and there are signs of a divorce between its interpretation and that of the nation which it professes to represent. Having lost prestige it becomes ineffectual, and is threatened by rebellion, because if society does not find in the ruling powers the instrument with which to achieve its happiness it will devise in its unprotected state, the instrument with which to overthrow them.

9. 1949

The ambition for social progress has nothing to do with its noisy partisan exploitation, neither can it be achieved by reviling and lowering the different types of men. Mankind needs faith in his destiny and in what he is doing and to possess sufficient insight to realise that the transition from the "I" to the "we" does not take place in a flash as the extermination of the individual, but as a renewed avowal of the existence of the individual functioning in the community. In that way the phenomenon is orderly and takes place during the years in the form of a necessary evolution which is more in the nature of "coming of age" than that of a mutiny.

11. 1949

The "caudillo" [name given to South American autocratic political leaders] improvises while the statesman makes plans and carries them out. The "caudillo" has no initiative, the statesman is creative. The "caudillo" is only concerned with measures which are applicable to the reigning circumstances whereas the statesman plans for all time; the deeds of the "caudillo" die with him, but the statesman lives on in his handiwork. For that reason the "caudillo" has no guiding principles or clear-cut plan while the statesman works methodically, defeating time and perpetuating himself in his own creations. "Caudillismo" is a trade, but statecraft is an art.

12. 1949

The politician of the old school made posts and favouritism a question of politics, because as he achieved nothing of general usefulness, he had at least to win the good will of those who would support him in the field of politics. The natural consequences of this nepotism were political cliques; one politician dominated one clique and another a different one. They fought among themselves until one of the cliques came out on top and from them emerged the general staff bent not on fulfilling their public office with self-denial and sacrifice, but on making the most of their position to use the Nation as a huge body at the service of their own interests and to throw away the wealth of the country with [no] sense of order and the fitness of things. . . .

13. 1949

The revolutionary idea would not have been able to materialise along constitutional lines if it had not been able to withstand the criticism, the violent attacks and even the strain on principles when they run up against the rocks which appear, every day, in the path of a ruler. The principles of the revolution would not have been able to be upheld if they had not been the true reflection of Argentine sentiments.

The guiding principles of our movement must have made a very deep impression on the national conscience for the people in the last elections to have consecrated them by giving us full power to make reforms.

CHAPTER 30

DROPPING THE ATOMIC BOMB ON JAPAN

On August 6, 1945, the United States dropped an atomic bomb on Hiroshima, killing eighty thousand people and injuring and sickening many more; three days later it unleashed another, on Nagasaki, which killed ninety thousand (including later deaths from radiation sickness). Japan surrendered the next day.

This chapter deals with issues surrounding the atomic bomb. Bombing Japan not only hastened the end of World War II. It also opened a new age of military technology, which would steadily escalate during the Cold War. The threats and fears associated with atomic weaponry have been part of world experience ever since 1945. In the selections that follow, two sets of comparisons are offered: first, a comparison of the tenor of the American decision to drop the bomb with Japanese reactions; second, a comparison of historical memory, of how groups in the United States and Japan still disputed the interpretation of what happened, fifty years after the event. The second comparison is based on a summary of a bitter dispute about historical presentation in the United States, at the national museum complex, the Smithsonian.

American scientists were not unanimous in recommending dropping the bomb: some urged a demonstration first to give Japan a chance to surrender. But there were few bombs available, and the decision to act directly reflected an eagerness to end the war, the desire to punish Japanese intransigence, and a new concern about Russian intervention in the area. The first two documents suggest American attitudes—first, those of President Truman, who made the decision, and second, those revealed in the description of the Hiroshima mission by the pilot of the decisive plane, the super fortress *Enola Gay*. What kinds of attitudes are suggested about the bomb itself and about the Japanese? How did these two Americans relate themselves to one of the great events of contemporary history? A third passage, by a doctor in Nagasaki, recounts the experience of being bombed. Needless to say, from a comparative standpoint, the three documents together show the huge differences in perspective between people who do the bombing and people on the receiving end of an unprecedented technological experience. (This comparison deserves consideration in terms of another event-based, two-sided comparison, the one that deals with the Opium War, in chapter 20.)

Following World War II, of course, the United States developed its nuclear weaponry further, as fears of the Soviet Union increased and several other powers joined the nuclear arms race. Japan, under American occupation but also profoundly affected by the war itself, abandoned significant military activity and did not participate in the weapons buildup.

The second set of comparative issues requires more subtle analysis. An article by an American scholar recounts the bitter divisions that arose in the United States in 1995 over a proposed Smithsonian Institution commemoration of the bomb's anniversary. The planned *Enola Gay* exhibit presented American historians' current understanding of the complexity of the event, in light of what was known by then about motives and alternatives. This complex rendering (with which the author of the article clearly agrees) aroused massive hostility from veterans' groups and a growing conservative-nationalist sentiment in Congress at the time. The exhibit was replaced with a simpler narrative, about the *Enola Gay* itself. Japan protested this version because it clashed with its own complex memories. Historical memory is an active ingredient in the life of any society, and it is almost always composed of a mixture of selected facts and myths. After World War II most Americans were eager to see former opponents confront their "real" war history. The Germans should teach about the evils of Nazism; the Japanese should teach about their wartime atrocities, including mistreatment of many prisoners. Neither nation moved as far along as some observers thought they should, because nationalist traditions and the task of rebuilding an undeniably different political structure made confronting too much pain too difficult. But some Japanese, even in official life, did acknowledge some of the wartime responsibilities. The United States has its own set of historical memory issues (not just concerning the war) as it teaches its national history. Is the dropping of the atomic bomb something Americans should probe more deeply, in order to understand themselves?

Questions

1. What were President Truman's motives in deciding to use the bomb? Did he understand its potential? How did Truman's note suggest he was justifying his decision to himself?
2. What kinds of attitudes does the Tibbets note suggest? What were Tibbets's feelings about his unprecedented mission and its results? Would he and Truman have agreed about the way to approach the use of the bomb? What are the best arguments today for defending Truman's policy and Tibbets's participation? What are the leading questions about the policy?
3. How do Tibbets's and Akizuki's descriptions of the bomb's impact compare? How do the two accounts prepare for the different (American and Japanese) historical memories John Dower describes?

4. Do you think the Smithsonian was right to withdraw the original exhibit?
5. What kind of historical memory did John Dower think we should have? Why did he feel that rosy memories about World War II remain so important in the United States?
6. What attitudes toward Japan were involved in dropping the bomb? Are any remnants of those feelings still active now in the United States?
7. What kind of historical memory of the bomb do most Japanese seek? Why did they protest the simpler Smithsonian exhibit that replaced the controversial display?
8. What are the main disputes over how to remember the bombing, within each country (United States and Japan) and between them?

For Further Discussion

1. Was dropping the bomb a "war crime"?
2. Did the atomic bomb change the nature of modern war and diplomacy?
3. Why did the bomb experience have such different impacts in the United States and Japan?
4. Why both the American and the Japanese versions of remembering the bomb seem so important to citizens of the two nations, so long after the fact?
5. What kind of bomb "memory" works for you, and why?

DROPPING THE BOMB: TRUMAN, TIBBETS, AND AKIZUKI

The following three selections surround the immediate experience of the bomb, in 1945. Harry Truman was the thirty-third president of the United States, assuming office after the death of Franklin Roosevelt in April 1945. When he took office, Truman was immediately confronted with basic military and foreign policy issues as World War II drew to a close. Decisions about the bomb, developed after five years of crash research, were paramount among these issues. Truman here writes at the Potsdam Conference—the last conference among the allies, including Stalin of the Soviet Union and Churchill of Britain—which dealt with conditions of the postwar world. Tensions between Stalin and the Western powers ran high at Potsdam.

Col. Paul Tibbets was an experienced pilot in the U.S. Army Air Force (the Air Force had not yet become a separate military branch). He was twenty-nine when he piloted the *Enola Gay*. Later, he frequently defended his action and refuted rumors that he had suffered mental illness as a result of remorse. In 1995 he argued that he had never had any doubts about his action and that it had saved lives by hastening the end of the war. Earlier, in 1976, he had caused controversy by recreating the attack in a Texas airshow complete with mushroom cloud; Japanese bomb survivors protested this act as callous.

Dr. Tatsuichiro Akizuki practiced medicine in Nagasaki. He described his experiences after learning about the earlier bomb in Hiroshima and then after the second bomb was dropped on his own city. His recollections were extremely unusual because there were so few survivors, though the doctor himself lived a number of years after the attack.

• • •

HARRY TRUMAN

Diary: Potsdam 25 July 1945

We met at eleven today. That is Stalin, Churchill, and the US President. But I had a most important session with Lord Mountbatten and General Marshall before that. We have discovered the most terrible bomb in the history of the world. It may be the fire destruction prophesied in the Euphrates Valley Era, after Noah and his fabulous Ark.

Anyway we 'think' we have found the way to cause a disintegration of the atom. An experiment in the New Mexican desert was startling—to put it mildly. Thirteen pounds of the explosive caused the complete disintegration of a steel tower 60 feet high, created a crater 6 feet deep and 1,200 feet in diameter, knocked over a steel tower 1⁄2 mile away and knocked men down 10,000 yards away. The explosion was visible for more than 200 miles and audible for 40 miles and more.

This weapon is to be used against Japan between now and August 10th. I have told the Sec. of War, Mr Stimson, to use it so that military objectives and soldiers and sailors are the target and not women and children. Even if the Japs are savages, ruthless, merciless and fanatic, we as the leader of the world for the common welfare cannot drop this terrible bomb on the old capital or the new.

He and I are in accord. The target will be a purely military one and we will issue a warning statement asking the Japs to surrender and save lives. I'm sure they will not do that, but we will have given them the chance. It is certainly a good thing for the world that Hitler's crowd or Stalin's did not discover this atomic bomb. It seems to be the most terrible thing ever discovered, but it can be made the most useful.

[The following day, 26 July, the Allies called upon Japan to surrender. The alternative they said was 'prompt and utter destruction.' Japan did not surrender.]

From Harry S. Truman, *Off the Record: The Private Papers of Harry S. Truman* (New York: Harper and Row, 1986), 55–56. Reprinted by permission of Ann Elmo Agency, Inc. West.

COL. PAUL TIBBETS, USAAF PILOT OF THE BOMB-CARRYING PLANE

Up to this point it was common practice in any theatre of war to fly straight ahead, fly level, drop your bombs, and keep right on going, because you could bomb several thousands of feet in the air and you could cross the top of the place that you had bombed with no concern whatsoever. But it was determined by the scientists that, in order to escape and maintain the integrity of the aircraft and the crew, that this aeroplane could not fly forward after it had dropped the bomb. It had to turn around and get away from that bomb as fast as it could. If you placed this aeroplane in a very steep angle of bank to make this turn, if you turned 158 degrees from the direction that you were going, you would then begin to place distance between yourself and that point of explosion as quickly as possible. You had to get away from the shock wave that would be coming back from the ground in the form of an ever expanding circle as it came upwards. It's necessary to make this turn to get yourself as far as possible from an expanding ring and 158 degrees happened to be the turn for that particular circle. It was difficult. It was something that was not done with a big bomber aeroplane. You didn't make this kind of a steep turn—you might almost call it an acrobatic manoeuvre—and the big aircraft didn't do these things. However, we refined it, we learned how to do it. It had been decided earlier that there was a possibility that an accident could occur on take-off, and so therefore we would not arm this weapon until we had left the runway and were out to sea. This of course meant that had there been an accident there would have been an explosion from normal powder charges but there would not have been a nuclear explosion. As I said this worried more people than it worried me because I had plenty of faith in my aeroplane. I knew my engines were good. We started our take-off on time which was somewhere about two-forty-five I think, and the aeroplane went on down the runway. It was loaded quite heavily but it responded exactly like I had anticipated it would. I had flown this aeroplane the same way before and there was no problem and there was nothing different this night in the way we went. We arrived over the initial point and started in on the bomb run which had about eleven minutes to go, rather a long type of run for a bomb but on the other hand we felt we needed this extra time in straight and level flight to stabilize the air speed of the aeroplane, to get everything right down to the last-minute detail. As I indicated earlier the problem after the release of the bomb is not to proceed forward but to turn away. As soon as the weight had left the aeroplane I immediately went into this steep turn and we tried then to place distance between ourselves and the point of impact. In this particular case that bomb took fifty-three seconds from the time it left the aeroplane until it exploded and this gave us adequate time of course to make the turn. We had just made the turn and rolled out on level flight when it seemed like

From Mark Arnold Foster, *The World of War* (London: William Collins and Sons, Thomas Television Ltd. 1973), 348–49.

somebody had grabbed a hold of my aeroplane and gave it a real hard shaking because this was the shock wave that had come up. Now after we had been hit by a second shock wave not quite so strong as the first one I decided we'll turn around and go back and take a look. The day was clear when we dropped that bomb, it was a clear sunshiny day and the visibility was unrestricted. As we came back around again facing the direction of Hiroshima we saw this cloud coming up. The cloud by this time, now two minutes old, was up at our altitude. We were 33,000 feet at this time and the cloud was up there and continuing to go right on up in a boiling fashion, as if it was rolling and boiling. The surface was nothing but a black boiling, like a barrel of tar. Where before there had been a city with distinctive houses, buildings and everything that you could see from our altitude, now you couldn't see anything except a black boiling debris down below.

DR. TATSUICHIRO AKIZUKI

During the morning Mr Yokota turned up to see his daughter, who was one of our in-patients. He lived at the foot of Motohara Hill, and was an engineer in the research department of the Mitsubishi Ordnance Factory, then one of the centres of armament manufacture in Japan. The torpedoes used in the attack on Pearl Harbor had been made there. Mr Yokota always had something interesting to say. He used to visit me now and again, often passing on some new piece of scientific information.

He said: 'I hear Hiroshima was very badly damaged on the sixth.'

Together we despaired over the destiny of Japan, he as an engineer, I as a doctor.

Then he said gloomily: 'I don't think the explosion was caused by any form of chemical energy.'

'What then?' I inquired, eager to know about the cause of the explosion, even though my patients were waiting for me.

He said: 'The power of the bomb dropped on Hiroshima is far stronger than any accumulation of chemical energy produced by the dissolution of a nitrogen compound, such as nitro-glycerine. It was an *atomic* bomb, produced by atomic fission.'

'Good heavens! At last we have atomic fission!' I said, though somewhat doubtfully.

Just then the long continuous wail of a siren arose.

'Listen. . . . Here comes the regular air-raid.'

'The first warning. . . . The enemy are on their way.' . . .

About thirty minutes later the all-clear sounded. I said to myself: In Nagasaki everything is still all right. . . .

From Tatsuichiro Akizuki, *Nagasaki 1945*, trans. Keiichi Nagata (New York: Quartet Books, 1981), 23–24, 25, 26–27, 29–31, 33. © 1981 Tatsuichiro Akizuki & Keiichi Nagata. Reprinted by permission of the Peters Fraser and Dunlop Group Limited.

I went down to the consulting room, humming cheerfully. . . .

I stuck the pneumo-thorax needle into the side of the chest of the patient lying on the bed. It was just after eleven a.m.

I heard a low droning sound, like that of distant aeroplane engines.

'What's that?' I said. 'The all-clear has gone, hasn't it?'

At the same time the sound of the plane's engines, growing louder and louder, seemed to swoop down over the hospital.

I shouted: 'It's an enemy plane! Look out—take cover!'

As I said so, I pulled the needle out of the patient and threw myself beside the bed.

There was a blinding white flash of light, and the next moment—*Bang! Crack!* A huge impact like a gigantic blow smote down upon our bodies, our heads and our hospital. I lay flat—I didn't know whether or not of my own volition. Then down came piles of debris, slamming into my back.

The hospital has been hit, I thought. I grew dizzy, and my ears sang.

Some minutes or so must have passed before I staggered to my feet and looked around. The air was heavy with yellow smoke; white flakes of powder drifted about; it was strangely dark.

Thank God, I thought—I'm not hurt! But what about the patients? . . .

No one knew what had happened. A huge force had been released above our heads. What it was, nobody knew. Had it been several tons of bombs, or the suicidal destruction of a plane carrying a heavy bomb-load?

Dazed, I retreated into the consulting room, in which the only upright object on the rubbish-strewn floor was my desk. I went and sat on it and looked out of the window at the yard and the outside world. There was not a single pane of glass in the window, not even a frame—all had been completely blown away. Out in the yard dun-colored smoke or dust cleared little by little. I saw figures running. Then, looking to the south-west, I was stunned. The sky was as dark as pitch, covered with dense clouds of smoke; under that blackness, over the earth, hung a yellow-brown fog. Gradually the veiled ground became visible, and the view beyond rooted me to the spot with horror.

All the buildings I could see were on fire: large ones and small ones and those with straw-thatched roofs. Further off along the valley, Urakami Church, the largest Catholic church in the east, was ablaze. The technical school, a large two-storeyed wooden building, was on fire, as were many houses and the distant ordnance factory. Electricity poles were wrapped in flame like so many pieces of kindling. Trees on the nearby hills were smoking, as were the leaves of sweet potatoes in the fields. To say that everything burned is not enough. It seemed as if the earth itself emitted fire and smoke, flames that writhed up and erupted from underground. The sky was dark, the ground was scarlet, and in between hung clouds of yellowish smoke. Three kinds of colour—black, yellow and scarlet—loomed ominously over the people, who ran about like so many ants seeking to escape. What had happened? Urakami Hospital had not been bombed—I understood that much. But that ocean of fire, that sky of smoke! It seemed like the end of the world. . . .

About ten minutes after the explosion, a big man, half-naked, holding his head between his hands, came into the yard towards me, making sounds that seemed to be dragged from the pit of his stomach.

'Got hurt, sir,' he groaned; he shivered as if he were cold. 'I'm hurt.'

I stared at him, at the strange-looking man. Then I saw it was Mr Zenjiro Tsujimoto, a market-gardener and a friendly neighbour to me and the hospital. I wondered what had happened to the robust Zenjiro.

'What's the matter with you, Tsujimoto?' I asked him, holding him in my arms.

'In the pumpkin field over there—getting pumpkins for the patients—got hurt . . .' he said, speaking brokenly and breathing feebly.

It was all he could do to keep standing. Yet it didn't occur to me that he had been seriously injured.

'Come along now,' I said. 'You are perfectly all right, I assure you. Where's your shirt? Lie down and rest somewhere where it's cool. I'll be with you in a moment.'

His head and his face were whitish; his hair was singed. It was because his eyelashes had been scorched away that he seemed so bleary-eyed. He was half-naked because his shirt had been burned from his back in a single flash. But I wasn't aware of such facts. I gazed at him as he reeled about with his head between his hands. What a change had come over this man who was stronger than a horse, whom I had last seen earlier that morning. It's as if he's been struck by lightning, I thought.

After Mr Tsujimoto came staggering up to me, another person who looked just like him wandered into the yard. Who he was and where he had come from I had no idea. 'Help me,' he said, groaning, half-naked, holding his head between his hands. He sat down, exhausted. 'Water . . . Water . . .' he whispered.

'What's the trouble? What's wrong with you? What's become of your shirt?' I demanded.

'Hot-*hot* . . . Water . . . I'm burning.' They were the only words that were articulate.

As time passed, more and more people in a similar plight came up to the hospital—ten minutes, twenty minutes, an hour after the explosion. All were of the same appearance, sounded the same. 'I'm hurt, *hurt!* I'm burning! Water!' They all moaned the same lament. I shuddered. Half-naked or stark naked, they walked with strange, slow steps, groaning from deep inside themselves as if they had travelled from the depths of hell. They looked whitish; their faces were like masks. I felt as if I were dreaming, watching pallid ghosts processing slowly in one direction—as in a dream I had once dreamt in my childhood.

These ghosts came on foot uphill towards the hospital, from the direction of the burning city and from the more easterly ordnance factory. Worker or student, girl or man, they all walked slowly and had the same mask-like face. Each one groaned and

339

cried for help. Their cries grew in strength as the people increased in number, sounding like something from the Buddhist scriptures, re-echoing everywhere, as if the earth itself were in pain.

One victim who managed to reach the hospital yard asked me, 'Is this a hospital?' before suddenly collapsing on the ground. There were those who lay stiffly where they fell by the roadside in front of the hospital; others lay in the sweet-potato fields. Many went down to the steep valley below the hospital where a stream ran down between the hill of Motohara and the next hill. 'Water, water,' they cried. They went instinctively down to the banks of the stream, because their bodies had been scorched and their throats were parched and inflamed; they were thirsty. I didn't realize then that these were the symptoms of 'flash-burn.' . . .

In the afternoon a change was noticeable in the appearance of the injured people who came up to the hospital. The crowd of ghosts which had looked whitish in the morning were now burned black. Their hair was burnt; their skin, which was charred and blackened, blistered and peeled. Such were those who now came toiling up to the hospital yard and fell there weakly.

'Are you a doctor? Please, if you wouldn't mind, could you examine me?' So said a young man.

'Cheer up!' I said. It was all I could say.

He died in the night. He must have been one of the many medical students who were injured down at the medical college. His politeness and then his poor blackened body lying dead on the concrete are things I shall never forget.

The Controversy over Memory: John Dower

This account was written by a historian specializing in international relations and Japan. It describes the controversy that arose over the proposed Smithsonian commemoration of the fiftieth anniversary of the bomb in 1995. A host of groups, spearheaded by several veterans' organizations, attacked the original plans, which had been prepared by a variety of historians and other experts. The opposition, echoed in a Congress dominated by conservatives, prompted the museum to back down and offer a minimal display centered around the airplane *Enola Gay* itself. This decision brought another set of protests, including criticisms from Japanese authorities who felt that the United States was adopting a double standard: real confrontation with historical issues for others, congratulatory history for itself.

• • •

From John W. Dower, "Triumphal and Tragic Narratives of the War in Asia," *Journal of American History* (December 1995): 1124–34.

REMEMBERING THE BOMB

Fiftieth anniversaries are unlike other commemorative occasions, especially when they are anniversaries of war. Participants in the events of a half century ago are still alive to tell their emotional personal tales. Their oral histories confront the skepticism and detachment of younger generations who have no memories of the war. Historians with access to materials that were previously inaccessible (or simply ignored) develop new perspectives on the dynamics and significance of what took place. Politicians milk the still palpable human connection between past and present for every possible drop of ideological elixir. History, memory, scholarship, and politics become entangled in intricate ways. . . .

It is a measure of the impoverishment of our present-day political climate in the United States that Americans have been denied a rare opportunity to use the fiftieth anniversary of Hiroshima and Nagasaki to reflect more deeply about these developments that changed our world forever. That opportunity was lost early this year when the Smithsonian Institution, bowing to political pressure (including unanimous condemnation by the United States Senate), agreed to scale back drastically a proposed major exhibition on the atomic bombs and the end of the war against Japan in its Air and Space Museum in Washington.

The exhibition initially envisioned by the Smithsonian's curators would have taken viewers through a succession of rooms that introduced, in turn, the ferocity of the last year of the war in Asia, the Manhattan Project and the unfolding imperatives behind the United States decision to use the bombs against Japan, the training and preparation of the *Enola Gay* mission that dropped the first bomb on Hiroshima (with the fuselage of the *Enola Gay* as the centerpiece of the exhibition), the human consequences of the bombs in the two target cities, and the nuclear legacy to the postwar world. The draft script included occasional placards that concisely summarized the "historical controversies" that have emerged in scholarship and public discourse.

This ambitious proposal proved to be politically unacceptable. The Senate denounced the draft script as being "revisionist and offensive to many World War II veterans." Critics accused curators responsible for the draft of being "politically correct" leftists and rarely hesitated to brand as "anti-American" anyone who questioned the use of the bombs. Confronted by such criticism, and by a conservative Congress threatening to cut off federal funding to "liberal" projects in general, the Smithsonian—like Japan fifty years earlier—surrendered unconditionally. Visitors to the Air and Space Museum eventually were offered only a minimalist exhibition featuring the refurbished fuselage of the *Enola Gay* and a brief tape and text explaining that this was the plane that dropped the first atomic bomb, following which, nine days later, Japan surrendered. The artifact, supporters of this bare presentation declare, speaks for itself.

Artifacts do not in fact speak for themselves. Essentially the United States government has chosen to commemorate the end of World War II in Asia by affirming that only one orthodox view is politically permissible. This orthodoxy amounts to a "heroic" narrative, and its contours are simple: The war in Asia was a brutal struggle against a fanatic, expansionist foe (which is true, albeit cavalier about European and American colonial and neocolonial control in Asia up to 1941). That righteous war against Japanese aggression was ended by the dropping of the atomic bombs, which saved the enormous numbers of American lives that would have been sacrificed in invading Japan. As the Senate's condemnation of the Smithsonian's plans put it, the atomic bombs brought the war to a "merciful" end.

. . . The triumphal American narrative offers an entirely understandable view of World War II—emphasizing the enormity of German and Japanese behavior, eulogizing American "valor and sacrificial service" (in the words of the Senate resolution), and applauding the bombs for forcing Japan's surrender and saving American lives.

But what does this heroic narrative leave out? What are the "historical controversies" the Smithsonian's curators thought worth making known to the public? What might we have learned from a truly serious commemorative engagement with the end of the war in Asia?

There are many answers. To begin, the argument that the bombs were used simply to end the war quickly and thereby save untold lives neglects complicating facts, converging motives and imperatives, and possible alternative policies for ending the war. Such considerations can do more than deepen our retrospective understanding of the decision to use the bombs. They also can help us better appreciate the complexities of crisis policy making in general.

If, moreover, we are willing to look beyond the usual end point in the conventional heroic narrative—beyond (or beneath) the sparkling *Enola Gay* and the almost abstract mushroom cloud—we can encounter the human face of World War II. Humanizing the civilians killed and injured by the bombs, and, indeed, humanizing the Japanese enemy generally, is difficult and distasteful for most Americans. If this is done honestly in the context of Hiroshima and Nagasaki, it becomes apparent that we confront something more than the human consequences of nuclear war. We are forced to ask painful questions about the morality of modern war itself—specifically, the transformation of moral consciousness that, well before the atomic bombs were dropped, had led *all* combatants to identify civilian men, women, and children as a legitimate target of "total war."

To engage the war at this level is to enter the realm of tragic, rather than triumphal, narratives. As the Smithsonian controversy revealed, however, even after the passage of a half century there is little tolerance of such reflection in the United States, and now virtually none at all at the level of public institutions. We have engaged in self-censorship and are the poorer for it.

. . . Critics of the Air and Space Museum's early scripts emphasized what was missing in them—most notably, a vivid sense of the fanaticism, ferocity, and atrocious war conduct of the Japanese enemy. This was a fair criticism. Using the same criteria, it also is fair to ask what the heroic American narrative of the end of the war neglects.

At the simplest level, the popular triumphal narrative tends to neglect events and developments that are deemed important in the scholarly literature on the bombs. The entry of the Soviet Union into the war against Japan on August 8, two days after the bombing of Hiroshima, for example, tends to be downplayed or entirely ignored—and with it the fact that the American leadership had solicited the Soviet entry from an early date, knew it was imminent, and knew the Japanese were terrified by the prospect. Why the haste to drop the bombs before the effect of the Soviet entry could be gauged?

The nuclear devastation of Nagasaki on August 9 is similarly marginalized in the orthodox narrative. What are we to make of this second bomb? Why was it dropped before Japan's high command had a chance to assess Hiroshima and the Soviet entry? How should we respond to the position taken by some Japanese—namely, that the bombing of Hiroshima may have been necessary to crack the no-surrender policy of the militarists, but the bombing of Nagasaki was plainly and simply a war crime. . . .

Shortly after the end of the war, United States intelligence experts themselves publicly concluded that Japan was already at the end of its tether when the bombs were dropped. . . . [This raises] pertinent questions about the nature and shortcoming of wartime Allied intelligence evaluations of the enemy.

It also became known after Japan's surrender that alternatives to using the bombs on civilian targets had been broached in American official circles. Navy planners believed that Japan could be brought to its knees by intensified economic strangulation (the country's merchant marine and most of its navy had been sunk by 1945). Within the Manhattan Project, the possibility of dropping the bomb on a noncombat "demonstration" target, with Japanese observers present, had been broached but rejected. Conservative officials such as Acting Secretary of State Joseph Grew, the former ambassador to Japan, argued that the Japanese could be persuaded to surrender if the United States abandoned its policy of "unconditional surrender" and guaranteed the future existence of the emperor system. . . .

These developments complicate the simple story line of the heroic narrative. Greater complication, however, arises from the fact that declassification of the archival record has made historians aware of how many different considerations officials in Washington had in mind when they formulated nuclear policy in the summer of 1945. No one denies that these policy makers desired to hasten the war's end and to save American lives, but no serious historian regards those as the sole considerations driving the use of the bombs on Japanese cities.

Although the initial Anglo-American commitment to build nuclear weapons was motivated by fear that Nazi Germany might be engaged in such a project, it is now known that by 1943, . . . United States planners had identified Japan as the prime target for such a weapon. . . .

Sheer visceral hatred abetted this early targeting of Japan for nuclear destruction. Although critics of the Smithsonian's original script took umbrage at a passing statement that called attention to the element of vengeance in the American haste to use the bombs, few historians (or honest participants) would discount this. "Remember Pearl Harbor—Keep 'em Dying" was a popular military slogan from the outset of the war, and among commentators and war correspondents at the time, it was a commonplace that the Japanese were vastly more despised than the Germans. As we know all too well from our vantage place fifty years later, race and ethnicity are hardly negligible factors in the killing game. . . .

. . . In Japan, as might be expected, popular memory of the atomic bombs tends to begin where the American narrative leaves off. In the heroic narrative, one rides with the crew of the *Enola Gay*, cuts away from the scene the moment the Little Boy bomb is released, gazes back from a great distance (over eleven miles) at a towering, iridescent mushroom cloud. If by chance one does glance beneath the cloud, it is the bomb's awesome physical destructiveness that usually is emphasized. Rubble everywhere. A silent, shattered cityscape. In this regard, the heroic narrative differs little from a Hollywood script.

By contrast, conventional Japanese accounts begin with the solitary bomber and its two escort planes in the azure sky above Hiroshima, with the blinding flash (*pika*) and tremendous blast (*don*) of the nuclear explosion, with the great pillar of smoke—and then move directly to ground zero. They dwell with excruciating detail on the great and macabre human suffering the new weapon caused, which continues to the present day for some survivors.

This Japanese perception of the significance of Hiroshima and Nagasaki can become maudlin and nationalistic. The nuclear destruction of the two cities is easily turned into a "victimization" narrative, in which the bombs fall from the heavens without historical context—as if the war began on August 6, 1945, and innocent Japan bore the cross of bearing witness to the horrendous birth of the nuclear age. In this subjective narrative, the bombs become the symbolic stigmata of unique Japanese suffering.

It is virtually a mantra in the United States media that what the Japanese really suffer from is historical amnesia. They cannot honestly confront their World War II past, it is said, and there are indeed numerous concrete illustrations of this beyond fixation on the misery caused by the atomic bombs. These range from sanitized textbooks to virtually routinized public denials of Japanese aggression and atrocity by conservative politicians (usually associated with the Liberal Democratic party, the United States government's longtime protégé) to the government's failure, until very recently, to offer an unequivocal apology to Asian and Allied victims of imperial Japan's wartime conduct.

In actuality, however, popular Japanese discourse concerning both war responsibility and the experience of the atomic bomb is more diversified than usually is appreciated

outside Japan. Since the early 1970s, when Japan belatedly established relations with the People's Republic of China, the Japanese media have devoted conspicuous attention not only to exposing Japanese war crimes in Asia but also to wrestling with the complex idea that victims (*bigaisha*) can simultaneously be victimizers (*kagaisha*). . . .

Other Japanese have introduced other moral considerations in attempting to come to grips with the meaning of Hiroshima and Nagasaki. Some see the bombs as a plain atrocity—an American war crime, as it were, that cancels out, or at least mitigates, the enormity of Japan's own wartime transgressions. More typically, however—and this was true even in the immediate aftermath of the bombings—anti-American sentiment per se is surprisingly muted. The focus instead has been on using the bomb experience to bring an antinuclear message to the world. . . .

Moral reflections of this sort—by Japanese or by critics of the use of the bombs in general—usually are given short shrift by American upholders of the heroic narrative. In their view, war is hell, the Japanese brought the terrible denouement of the bombs upon themselves, and the only morality worth emphasizing is the moral superiority of the Allied cause in World War II. Indeed, one of the formulaic terms that emerged among critics of the Air and Space Museum's original plans (alongside the "merciful" nature of the use of the bombs) labeled the nuclear destruction of the two Japanese cities "morally unambiguous."

It was not, and it may well be that the most enduring legacy of the Smithsonian controversy will be its graphic exposure of the moral ambiguity of the use of the bombs—and of Allied strategic bombing policy more generally. Here is where the triumphal story line gives way to a tragic narrative. The "good war" against Axis aggression and atrocity was brought to an end by a policy that the United States, Great Britain, and the League of Nations all had condemned only a few years previous, when first practiced by Japan and Germany, as "barbarous" and "in violation of those standards of humane conduct which have been developed as an essential part of modern civilization." That policy was the identification of civilian men, women, and children as legitimate targets of aerial bombardment. The United States, President Franklin D. Roosevelt typically declared in 1940, could be proud that it "consistently has taken the lead in urging that this inhuman practice be prohibited." Five years later, well before Hiroshima and Nagasaki, this inhuman practice was standard United States operating procedure. . . .

Nothing brought this to life more succinctly than the juxtaposition of the Superfortress and the lunch box.

Among artifacts the Smithsonian's curators proposed bringing to Washington from the Peace Memorial Museum in Hiroshima was a seventh-grade schoolgirl's charred lunch box, containing carbonized rice and peas, that had been recovered from the ashes. The girl herself had disappeared. In the Japanese milieu, this is a typical, intensely human atomic bomb icon; and to American visitors to an exhibition, it would be intensely human too. This pathetic artifact (and other items like it) obsessed and

alarmed critics of the proposed exhibition, and for obvious reasons: for the little lunch box far outweighed the glistening Superfortress in the preceding room. It would linger longer in most visitors' memories. Inevitably, it would force them to try imagining an incinerated child. Museum visitors who could gaze on this plain, intimate item and still maintain that the use of the bombs was "morally unambiguous" would be a distinct minority.

This sense of the tragedy of the war, even of the "good war" against an atrocious Axis enemy, became lost in the polemics that engulfed the Smithsonian. Yet it is not an original perception, certainly not new to the more civilized discourse on the bombs that has taken place in previous years. Indeed, in oblique ways even President Harry S Truman, a hero of the triumphal narrative, showed himself sensitive to the tragic dimensions of his decision to use the bombs. The day after Nagasaki was bombed, he expressed qualms about killing "all those kids."

CHAPTER 31

THE SPREAD OF DEMOCRACY AT THE END
OF THE CENTURY

China, Africa, and the Middle East

During the decades after World War II, political systems in the world seemed divided among multiparty democracies (the West, India, Japan), Communist systems, and authoritarian regimes (see chapter 26). Many new nations, in Africa and elsewhere, initially tried democracy but then turned to military or one-man rule, if only because of huge internal divisions within their countries. Democratic ideals remained lively in areas such as Latin America and Africa, but their prospects often seemed bleak.

Beginning in the late 1970s, democracy began to spread. Western encouragement combined with a sense that democracy might be the best system to foster economic growth, an alternative to heavy-handed state planning. Democratic systems gained throughout Latin America and then in the former Communist zone of Eastern Europe. The Soviet Union sponsored more open political activity in 1985, and the collapse of the Soviet empire after 1989 brought democratic systems to most of the East European states. In several non-Communist Asian states, such as South Korea and the Philippines, authoritarian regimes were replaced by more democratic governments. By the early 1990s democratic reforms were spreading in Africa, though still as a minority current. The establishment of democracy in South Africa, where the black majority had previously been excluded from voting as part of the racist apartheid system, was a huge achievement. In 1994 Nelson Mandela became that nation's first democratically elected president.

The late-twentieth-century spread of democracy thus involved both situations in which the majority of the people obtained the vote for the first time—the South African case—and situations where free elections, with open political discussion and choices among parties, replaced controlled voting systems—the more common ex-authoritarian or ex-Communist case.

Comparing democratic movements in areas where full democracy had not previously prevailed raises a number of analytical issues. The first involves causation: why, in places otherwise so different, did democracy begin to provide a

more popular, acceptable political vocabulary? Do statements about democracy help get at the general, global conditions that gave this particular political system an edge in the final decades of the century?

Comparison also involves the usual, essential task of close analysis. Not all democratic movements were necessarily the same. Some doubtless reflected different contexts and traditions. Some may have been primarily for show, to win international approval and support without real commitment.

Comparison is even more obviously essential in dealing with global exceptions to the democratic current. Democratic sentiment increased in China during this period, but the regime vowed to maintain a single-party, politically Communist system.

The Middle East was another region where the surge toward democracy was halting. Israel was a well-established democracy, though with a long history of repressing the large Palestinian (Arab) minority. Turkey and a few other Muslim nations were democratic or made new gestures toward democracy, but in general Islam and democracy did not readily coincide at this point. Royal, military, or one-party rule was more common. Yet there were reasons for some new bows to democracy in this context, given the larger global patterns. The collapse of European Communism, and the U.S. invasion of Iraq at the end of the Cold War, made the West a more important player in Middle Eastern affairs, a fact that could generate more democratic influence.

The selections in this chapter come from three specific cases, all involving advances of democratic sentiment. Two of the cases—China and the Middle East—also involve some of the more resistant contexts. Comparison can thus highlight (1) assessment of the democratic phenomenon in general at this time period, (2) the search for general factors of causation, and (3) a juxtaposition of cases in which democracy surged forward (South Africa), gained ground amid inconclusive results (the Middle East), or had to yield to overwhelming repression even as economic conditions and the informal political climate changed rapidly (China).

China had no deep democratic tradition. Confucianism, its dominant political culture, was strongly hierarchical. The Chinese revolution of 1911 was led by Western-style reformers who hoped to install a democratic system, though their own movement, pressed by internal disarray and Japanese attack, turned increasingly authoritarian. Chinese Communists themselves moved to reform in 1978, but mainly in the economic sphere. A democratic surge crested in 1989, however, with a series of demonstrations in major cities, including the capital, Beijing. The state cracked down, dispersing the demonstrators and arresting or exiling key leaders.

The African National Congress struggled against South Africa's rigid racial inequality, the apartheid system. By the 1980s international opposition to the South African regime was growing, as was internal resistance, punctuated by periodic riots and other acts of disobedience. Government repression stiffened in

the 1980s, with many arrests, but in 1990 a new white leadership began to offer concessions. Nelson Mandela, who headed negotiations for the black majority, had himself been a political prisoner for many years.

Israel gained independence as a Jewish state in 1948. For decades Jewish settlers, many of them nationalists, had been entering this historic territory, which was dominated by Arab settlers and held as a mandate territory (essentially, a colony) by Britain. Arab guerrilla action continued in subsequent years, amid Arabs who remained in Israel as well as those in neighboring states. In 1964 the dissident Arabs formed the Palestinian Liberation Organization. The PLO continually vowed to destroy Israel and emphasized terrorist attacks. But there were other tactics as well, and in the late 1980s efforts to appeal to world opinion helped prompt PLO leaders to deemphasize terrorism in favor of broader political claims—including attacks on the Israeli state as fascist. By the mid-1990s negotiations with Israel, strongly backed by the United States and West European powers, led to some compromise. Autonomous (but not independent) Palestinian territories were established within Israel, and the PLO took over their government with a pledge to set up a democracy.

Questions

1. What were the main arguments of the Chinese democrats? Why did some advocates anticipate difficulties in meshing democracy with Chinese traditions and current conditions?
2. Why did democracy provide a useful vocabulary in attacks on South Africa's racist regime?
3. Do the African and Chinese statements display the same basic definition of democracy? What factors might explain any differences?
4. Is the PLO declaration democratic? What factors might explain some PLO hesitation about full commitment to democracy? Are actual democratic procedures suggested?
5. What causes for increased global interest in democracy do the selections collectively suggest?
6. What differences were there in the definition and precision of democratic commitment among the Chinese students, Nelson Mandela, and the PLO?
7. What different world patterns favored or impeded democracy at the end of the twentieth century?

For Further Discussion

1. What is a viable definition of democracy that fits global, and not just Western, conditions?

2. Is democracy an easy system to establish in areas that lack explicit democratic precedents? What kinds of conditions in the late twentieth century most favor the installation of new democracies?
3. Why, by the late 1980s and the 1990s, was Africa more friendly to the installation of new democracies than China or the Middle East?
4. Did Palestinian ideas about democracy reflect Muslim political traditions (see chapter 7), or was this a more purely secular movement?
5. Do you think democracy will spread further—for example, to China?

CHINESE DEMOCRATIC DISSIDENTS: HAN MINZHU

The following passages were collected and issued by an anonymous 1989 dissident who used the Chinese words for "Han democracy" as his pseudonym (Han being China's dominant ethnic group). After the government crackdown, publishing prodemocratic materials was extremely dangerous, though there was a postrepression flurry of such writings; some activists, including dissidents now in exile, have continued such efforts.

• • •

From a 1989 Poster at the People's University

. . . The government is facing bankruptcy. It has no money for education, no money for national defense, no money for energy, no money for transportation. It does not even have enough money to keep the living standard of ordinary state employees up to previous levels. Where has all the money gone? It has gone into the pockets of the corrupt officials, into the banking accounts of those big and small leaders who enjoy authority. The small amount of capital people have toiled to create has turned into Mercedes Benzes and Cadillacs—cars on the streets—and into hotels and restaurants [where these big and small leaders dine, stay, and entertain their relatives and friends for free]. . . .

Political corruption is the key problem [facing China]. The only weapon for smashing dictatorship and autocracy and ending all types of corruption that plague China is democracy. The power [presently] concentrated in individuals and a small portion of the people must be restricted; there must be some mechanism of checks and balances. The most basic meaning of democracy is that people themselves administer matters. In modern countries, direct democracy is not easy to implement; therefore, it is transformed into indirect democracy, that is, people entrust part of their

From Han Minzhu, ed., *Cries for Democracy: Writings and Speeches from the 1989 Chinese Democracy Movement* (Princeton, N.J.: Princeton University Press, 1989), 33–35, 72, 291–93. Copyright © 1990 Princeton University Press. Reprinted by permission of the publisher.

power to others, and these people so entrusted are selected by the people. Since people are concerned that the people entrusted by them may abuse their power, they establish several institutions that counterbalance each other, and each institution is independently responsible to the people. This is the basic principle of democracy.

What does China have? Nothing. On hearing [calls] for democracy, the government says that the level of the people is too low for the implementation of democracy. But they have forgotten that when Chiang Kai-shek [the head of the Nationalist Party] ran the country under a dictatorship, one of his rationales was that the people were unenlightened and that they needed "instructive politics." When the Communist Party was fighting Chiang Kai-shek and the Nationalist Party, the Party was eager to demand democracy. How can it be that the Chinese people are, after forty years of communist leadership, still in the same ignorant condition as they were under Chiang Kai-shek's regime? If some old people over the age of fifty are unenlightened, this can be blamed on Chiang Kai-shek. But people under the age of fifty were all born "under the red flag and raised under the red flag"! How can it be that forty years of communist rule have produced a citizenship that is not even fit for a democratic society? Is this self-contradictory? On the one hand, the party boasts in its propaganda of forty years of achievements. On the other hand, it denies those achievements [by denying that the people are ready for democracy]. What kind of logic is this? There is no way out for China if we do not have democracy now.

Of course, we do not expect to achieve a perfect and beautiful democratic society at once; after all, the Chinese people have not had a single day of a free life. The dictatorship of thousands of years, particularly that of the last several decades, has made most people unable to adjust quickly to a democratic society. But this is no excuse for not having a democracy. Certainly, at least urban citizens, intellectuals, and Communist Party members are as ready for democracy as any of the citizens who already live in democratic societies. Thus, we should at least implement complete democracy within the Communist Party and within the urban areas. Furthermore, during the process of urbanization, we should see that people in those [rapidly developing] rural areas become acquainted with democracy. . . .

. . . Chinese intellectuals still possess aristocratic airs: even in the revolutions for freedom and equality, they always give the impression of belonging to a class superior to others. Everyone is born equal; this issue was resolved during the Enlightenment. People's level of education may be high or low, and their contributions to society large or small, but they are all born as people and deserve the same respect. They all have the same right to pursue a good life. Intellectuals should not separate themselves from other classes and cannot claim special rights and interests. Intellectuals should be the spokesmen for the entire nation and the vanguard of social justice. The achievements of this movement that has been initiated by intellectuals will in the end be measured by the influence it has on the people. We should put our efforts into thinking about the future of the Chinese people. We should only be responsible to the people.

Democracy and equality are like Siamese twins; one cannot have one without the other.

China's future rests on the shoulders of her one billion people. Only if we implement widespread democracy and more flexible economic policies will China have a way out. Democracy will check the hereditary system [that breeds corruption]; limited privatization will accelerate the development of the economy; freedom of speech and freedom of the press will provide effective supervision over the government; and equality will unite people into a greater force. But none of this will come to us: we must reach out and struggle for it.

Essay on a Banner in Tiananmen Square, Beijing, 1989

. . . We have never cast off the specter of authoritarianism which, either in the form of naked tyranny or in the cloak of idealism, never ceases to hover above our heads, sucking away the vitality of our nation and leaving our creativity sucked dry. Under the authoritarian system, the leaden weights of totalitarian politics and an unfree economy have suppressed the talents and wisdom of this most gifted people in the world. Mired in this stagnation, our nation becomes poorer and more backward with each passing day. China can be saved only if our political system is fundamentally transformed. Only democracy can save China. Our ancestors missed many opportunities for cultural regeneration. We cannot afford to miss another such opportunity. . . .

"There is never such a thing as a Savior." Let those who think themselves intelligent for advocating "old" authoritarianism or "new" authoritarianism [realize the impotence of their schemes] in the face of the people's immense power, and crawl off to console themselves. The realization of democracy cannot be dependent upon the benevolence of any person, as no dictator has ever shown a benevolent heart. Receiving alms while sitting locked in a cage is not democracy. Democracy can only be obtained by the struggle of the people themselves. It's nonsense to say that "the people would not know how to exercise democratic rights" or "democracy is not suited to the national conditions." Democracy has always been given to the government by the people, and *not* the other way round.

Democracy is not a mystical concept; it is a concrete way of conducting your life. It means that you can choose your own path in life. It means that you have the right to improve your government, the right to express your thoughts freely, and the right to write books and spread your beliefs. It means that every single person must abide by the law, while at the same time each may use your intelligence to the fullest to have a [bad] law rescinded. Under democracy, you can be free from the terror of a government which acts without the least regard for human life. In other words, if democracy is trampled upon, then the dark shadows of authoritarianism will be cast into the life of every individual. In China, it has always been the case that the officials are allowed to get away with arson while the people may not even light their lamps. In China, no one has ever valued the individual—"a human life isn't worth a cent." In China, no one has ever heeded the groans of the common people. It's about time, my fellow Chinese! We do not want to live our lives in this manner any more! . . .

It's about time, my fellow Chinese. Let us break our chains and become free human beings. Let us rise and free our country from the vicious cycle of its history.

With the blood of our devotion let us light the torch of truth, and let it illuminate this dark wilderness at this last moment before daybreak. The power of democracy is like a spring tide bursting through a tiny opening—once it starts coming there is no way to counter its force. This is where the hearts of the people lie. This is the march of history. How then can we let this hope be stifled?

SOUTH AFRICA: NELSON MANDELA'S ADDRESS

This speech occurred on Nelson Mandela's release from prison, February 11, 1990.

• • •

Friends, comrades and fellow South Africans.

I greet you all in the name of peace, democracy and freedom for all.

I stand here before you not as a prophet but as a humble servant of you, the people. Your tireless and heroic sacrifices have made it possible for me to be here today. I therefore place the remaining years of my life in your hands.

On this day of my release, I extend my sincere and warmest gratitude to the millions of my compatriots and those in every corner of the globe who have campaigned tirelessly for my release. . . .

I salute the African National Congress. It has fulfilled our every expectation in its role as leader of the great march to freedom. . . .

I greet the traditional leaders of our country—many of you continue to walk in the footsteaps of great heroes like Hintsa and Sekhukune.

I pay tribute to the endless heroism of youth, you, the young lions. You, the young lions, have energized our entire struggle.

I pay tribute ot he mothers and wives and sisters of our nation. You are the rock-hard foundation of our struggle. Apartheid has inflicted more pain on you than on anyone else.

On this occasion, we thank the world community for their great contribution to the anti-apartheid struggle. Without your support our struggle would not have reached this advanced stage. The sacrifice of the frontline states will be remembered by South Africans forever. . . .

From AWC Historical documents, http://www.awc.org.2a/ancdocs/hisotry/mandela/1191/sp91122a.html.

Today the majority of South Africans, black and white, recognize that apartheid has no future. It has to be ended by our own decisive mass action in order to build peace and security. The mass campaign of defiance and other actions of our organization and people can only culminate in the establishment of democracy. The destruction caused by apartheid on our subcontinent is incalculable. The fabric of family life of millions of my people has been shattered. Millions are homeless and unemployed. Our economy lies in ruins and our people are embroiled in political strife. Our resort to the armed struggle in 1960 with the formation of the military wing of the ANC, Umkhonto we Sizwe, was a purely defensive action against the violence of apartheid. The factors which necessitated the armed struggle still exist today. We have no option but to continue. We express the hope that a climate conducive to a negotiated settlement will be created soon so that there may no longer be the need for the armed struggle. . . .

There are further steps that have to be met before negotiations on the basic demands of our people can begin. I reiterate our call for, inter alia, the immediate ending of the State of Emergency and the freeing of all, and not only some, political prisoners. Only such a normalized situation, which allows for free political activity, can allow us to consult our people in order to obtain a mandate.

The people need to be consulted on who will negotiate and on the content of such negotiations. Negotiations cannot take place above the heads or behind the backs of our people. It is our belief that the future of our country can only be determined by a body which is democratically elected on a non-racial basis. Negotiations on the dismantling of apartheid will have to address the overwhelming demand of our people for a democratic, non-racial and unitary South Africa. These also must be political and economic systems to ensure that the inequalities of apartheid are addressed and our society thoroughly democratized. . . .

Our struggle has reached a decisive moment. We call on our people to seize this moment so that the process towards democracy is rapid and uninterrupted. We have waited too long for our freedom. We can no longer wait. Now is the time to intensify the struggle on all fronts. To relax our efforts now would be a mistake which generations to come will not be able to forgive. The sight of freedom looming on the horizon should encourage us to redouble our efforts.

It is only through disciplined mass action that our victory can be assured. We call on our white compatriots to join us in the shaping of a new South Africa. The freedom movement is a political home for you too. We call on the international community to continue the campaign to isolate the apartheid regime. To lift sanctions now would be to run the risk of aborting the process towards the complete eradication of apartheid.

Our march to freedom is irreversible. We must not allow fear to stand in our way. Universal suffrage on a common voters' role in a united democratic and non-racial South Africa is the only way to peace and racial harmony.

THE PALESTINE LIBERATION ORGANIZATION:
PROCLAMATION, 1988

The 1988 declaration was part of an internal reshuffling within this organization, operating from headquarters in exile and vigorously opposing Israeli policy. Using democratic language, PLO leaders hailed negotiations with leading (authoritarian) Arab states like Syria and also insisted on purging certain leaders assigned to regional responsibilities in the Gaza area (one of the areas heavily populated by Palestinians that is now part of the Palestinian autonomy territory). The PLO also refers to renewed agitation against Israel in its United National Command and seeks to raise support among ordinary Palestinians.

• • •

O masses of our people

Forty years have passed since the expulsion of our people from its homeland and the attempt to liquidate its existence and its national existence, but our valiant people is stronger than the expulsion and the efforts to suppress its identity. Its national revolution has succeeded, through the continuous processions of martyrs and victims, in thwarting those attempts and in gaining international recognition for its legitimate national rights [and] for its exclusive representation by the PLO. In the forefront of these rights is the right of return, self-determination, and the establishment of an independent national state under the leadership of the PLO.

The achievements of the Palestinian revolution, the glory of the magnificent uprising which is entering its sixth month, are continuing tirelessly and relentlessly. When our people declared the uprising, it understood the scale of the sacrifices that would be required for liberation and independence.

Our people, who declared the uprising, is aware of the dimensions of the sacrifice that will be demanded of it on the road to national liberation. The people consciously pay the price for its aspirations in the form of victims, wounded, detainees, and deportees. [It] grasps the nature of the enemy with whom it is locked in struggle, his barbarism and the actions of his fascist forces, such as the use of poison gas, bullets, house demolitions, and a criminal war of starvation. Despite this, our people has chosen the road of struggle and sacrifice as the only road through which to achieve its national rights.

Just as our people grasps the essence of the enemy, so it is also aware of the character of the war it is waging. Our war is a lengthy one. It is a war of attrition in which each passing day raises the economic and political price paid by the occupier [Israel], intensifies his international isolation, exposes the ugly truth about the occupation, and

From Shaul Mishal and Reuben Aharoni, *Speaking Stones: Communiqués from the Intifada Underground* (Syracuse, N.Y.: Syracuse University Press, 1994), 93–95. Reprinted by permission of the publisher.

shatters the illusion of coexistence that the enemy has tried to foster. Moreover, it re-inforces our legitimate national rights.

The glorious December uprising was launched to demonstrate the solid strength of the fighting army and to raise the [people's] struggle and its national cause to a new level of which the axis is the continuation of the struggle and the resistance and esca-lation of the confrontation toward civil disobedience.

The United National Command of the Uprising, as it pursues the struggle with you and through you, under the banners of our sole legitimate representative, the PLO, reaffirms our people's readiness for great sacrifices and devotion, to move to-ward civil disobedience, meaning primarily the liberation of our masses from the occupation and all that this entails: sacrifices and belt-tightening, storing basic food-stuffs, storing medicines, suffering for the sake of the homeland, and relentless and tireless forbearance and determination. The United Command stresses the determina-tion of the uprising masses to remove all the obstacles on the road to civil disobedi-ence, involving especially the resignation of all [the personnel in] the mechanisms of the occupation such as the tax apparatus, the police, and the appointed municipalities.

O our glorious masses,

1. The United National Command welcomes the removal of the obstacles on the road to normalization of Palestinian-Syrian relations and on the road to perfection of Palestinian national unity through a constructive democratic dialogue. Marginal dis-putes must not be encouraged. We must turn to democratic dialogue as the only means for settling internal disputes. [The United Command] condemns those who deviate from the unity of our people and are splitting its ranks. . . .

2. The immediate resignation must be effected of department directors in the Civil Administration in Gaza. . . . Let there be no mistake: the masses of the uprising and the shock squads will punish those who deviate from the will of the people and the decisions of its Command when they see fit.

3. Establishment of the popular committees and their dispersal in all areas must be completed. There must be no delay in executing this struggle mission. The other functional popular committees have the task of organizing the inhabitants' lives and ensuring proper services—food supplies, medicine, education, and security. For the popular committees are the government of the people and the uprising, a substitute for the collapsing occupation mechanisms, and a political tool for introducing civil disobedience and making it succeed.

4. Beat vigorously policemen, collaborators, and members of appointed municipal councils who, by not resigning from the service of the enemy, deviate from the na-tional consensus.

CHAPTER 32

ISSUES OF CULTURAL IDENTITY

Africa and Latin America

This chapter focuses on efforts by intellectuals to define the position of their cultures—one Nigerian, one Mexican—in a period of rapid cultural change. Both areas had witnessed important cultural impositions by other societies, including Western Europe and the United States. Both, however, retained prior cultural traditions and an active desire to assert a distinctive identity. Identity issues ride high on the contemporary global agenda. How can societies handle new cultural forms, often brought through outside influences, and still retain a link to their cultural roots?

The past hundred years have been a period of major cultural change, almost literally worldwide. No culture retained all of the key assumptions and values that had predominated in 1900. Yet the patterns of change were complex. In a number of societies, the strength of traditional religion weakened as it faced competition from new beliefs such as nationalism, consumer materialism, or Marxism. But in certain cases new religious enthusiasms spread. Thus, in sub-Saharan Africa there were many conversions to Islam and Christianity: where 80 percent of the population was committed to some form of polytheism in 1900, only 20 percent retained primary commitment to polytheistic beliefs by the 1990s. Latin America, converted earlier to Catholicism (though often in combination with older American Indian or African beliefs), saw a wave of enthusiasm for fundamentalist Protestantism toward the end of the twentieth century. Several societies, finally, including Hindu-dominated India and the Islamic Middle East, experienced a surge of religious revival from the 1970s onward. Cultural change was the order of the day, but the overall directions were far from clear.

One issue loomed large, though it was handled differently depending on current beliefs and past traditions: the influence of Western culture was a formidable force for change. From the West many societies incorporated new political beliefs, including aspects of representative democracy and, of course, nationalism. But the most important pressures from the West involved the power of modern science and the seductions of material acquisition (consumerism) and individual advancement.

Latin America and Africa faced particular pressures from outside cultural forces. Many Latin Americans had long looked to Western Europe for cultural models, beginning with Catholicism. Africa had more recently undergone Western imperialism, leading to new systems of education, missionary activity, and the general force of consumerism. Neither society was culturally fully Western, because of the diverse cultural groups that remained active and because of powerful prior traditions; yet neither could easily rely on traditional values to define personal beliefs or larger identities.

Not surprisingly, intellectuals in twentieth-century Africa and Latin America worried extensively about identity, particularly in relationship to Europe and the United States. African writers, usually educated in Western schools and writing in English or French, tried to deal with the need for a definable culture that would be something more than derivative. Latin American thinkers, with a longer tradition of encountering Western influence but equally preoccupied with defining values that were both distinctive and appropriate to the modern world, used history and comparison to try to define the flavor of their cultures.

This chapter features selections from two novels by the leading Nigerian novelist, Chinua Achebe, where he discusses successive phases of Western influence on Africa, first Christian, then urban-consumer. Writing from the 1950s onward, Achebe was fascinated by the process of change, which he felt undermined a coherent traditional culture but brought some undeniable benefits. The titles of his novels, *Things Fall Apart* and *No Longer at Ease,* suggest the confusions he believed change had created, as Africans renounced older belief patterns without fully clear or valid substitutes. Achebe's characterizations should be considered along with African nationalist views (chapter 25) and the views of African women (chapter 29), to widen the picture of African culture in a century of varied change.

A second set of selections comes from an essay collection by the prize-winning Mexican novelist and essayist, Octavio Paz, written initially in the 1950s and supplemented in a 1970s edition. Paz attempts to define essential features of Mexican culture, while comparing it with what he sees as the culture of the United States, Mexico's powerful neighbor, and the more general forces of modern economic life. His impressions of cultural change differ from those of Achebe, but he grapples with some of the same issues of distinctive identity.

The passages below flow from the pens of intellectuals. They do not necessarily represent popular cultural beliefs, though they try to fathom popular values. Interpreting the significance of the passages has to involve some thinking about the role of intellectuals in modern life, in civilizations generally, and in Africa and Latin America in particular. Are the concerns of intellectuals particularly significant or revealing? Comparisons remain important as well. Africa and Latin America faced the same cultural and identity issues. What are the most important differences?

Questions

1. What forces of change does Achebe deal with in his successive novelistic treatments of Nigeria? How do the shifts under Christian missionary influence, around 1900, compare with those of urban Nigeria in the 1920s, still under British rule?

2. What kinds of people were most open to Western-inspired cultures? What kinds resisted most firmly? Does Achebe believe that a coherent new culture emerged?

3. Does Achebe believe that it would be better for Africa if traditional values could be restored?

4. Why does Paz argue that Mexicans seek a certain kind of solitude? How does he define the major strengths of Mexican culture?

5. Does Paz believe that Mexican culture can accommodate to modern economic and political life? On what basis does he criticize Western values?

6. Do Paz and Achebe define Western values in similar ways?

7. What kinds of history have shaped Mexico, according to Paz? Does he have the same view of historical disruptions that Achebe highlights? Is his sense of the problem of modern identity the same?

8. Which author, Paz or Achebe, is more hostile to Western values? Which believes that Western values are more threatening to established cultural traditions?

9. How does Paz's characterization of modern worker culture, in its relationship to prior Mexican values, compare with Achebe's description of urban standards in relation to earlier village beliefs?

For Further Discussion

1. Is Achebe an African nationalist? How might Mexican nationalists disagree with Paz?

2. Did intellectuals such as Achebe and Paz represent widespread popular concerns in their respective societies? Did their views relate at all to the concerns expressed by African and Mexican women (see chapter 29)?

3. Why were many twentieth-century African and Latin American intellectuals particularly preoccupied with issues of cultural identity?

4. Will Latin American and African cultures become increasingly westernized in the next few decades (and how do you define cultural westernization)?

NIGERIA: CHINUA ACHEBE

Chinua Achebe, born in 1930, wrote a series of novels on the impact of the West on his native Nigeria, titling the first one *Things Fall Apart* (1958). This novel was set in the Ibo section of Nigeria around 1900, when Western missionary activity was increasing under the protection of British colonial rule. The passage describes the various reasons different Africans were drawn to Christianity or resisted it. Achebe is fascinated by the divisions among Africans in response to Western values and colonial controls.

The second selection comes from Achebe's novel *No Longer at Ease;* one of the characters is a descendant of the same Okonkwo family, from the same village, who had moved to Lagos (Nigeria's capital) in the 1920s. Here the impact of Western-style urban culture is explored, as it further jeopardized traditional values and behaviors. Obi Okonkwo was the first village member to have received higher education in British-run schools, and he later obtained a civil-service job.

• • •

THINGS FALL APART

The missionaries spent their first four or five nights in the marketplace, and went into the village in the morning to preach the gospel. They asked who the king of the village was, but the villagers told them that there was no king. "We have men of high title and the chief priests and the elders," they said.

It was not very easy getting the men of high title and the elders together after the excitement of the first day. But the missionaries persevered, and in the end they were received by the rulers of Mbanta. They asked for a plot of land to build their church.

Every clan and village had its "evil forest." In it were buried all those who died of the really evil diseases, like leprosy and smallpox. It was also the dumping ground for the potent fetishes of great medicine men when they died. An "evil forest" was, therefore, alive with sinister forces and powers of darkness. It was such a forest that the rulers of Mbanta gave to the missionaries. They did not really want them in their clan, and so they made them that offer which nobody in his right sense would accept.

"They want a piece of land to build their shrine," said Uchendu to his peers when they consulted among themselves. "We shall give them a piece of land." He paused, and there was a murmur of surprise and disagreement. "Let us give them a portion of the Evil Forest. They boast about victory over death. Let us give them a real battlefield in which to show their victory." They laughed and agreed, and sent for the missionaries, whom they had asked to leave them for a while so that they might "whisper together." They offered them as much as the Evil Forest as they cared to take. And to their greatest amazement the missionaries thanked them and burst into song.

From Chinua Achebe, *Things Fall Apart* (London: William Heinemann, 1959), 138–41, 162, 163, 166–67, 186–88. Copyright © 1959 by Chinua Achebe. Reprinted by permission of William Heinemann Limited.

"They do not understand," said some of the elders. "But they will understand when they go to their plot of land tomorrow morning." And they dispersed.

The next morning the crazy men actually began to clear a part of the forest and to build their house. The inhabitants of Mbanta expected them all to be dead within four days. The first day passed and the second and third and fourth, and none of them died. Everyone was puzzled. And then it became known that the white man's fetish had unbelievable power. It was said that he wore glasses on his eyes so that he could see and talk to evil spirits. Not long after, he won his first three converts.

Although Nwoye had been attracted to the new faith from the very first day, he kept it secret. He dared not go too near the missionaries for fear of his father. But whenever they came to preach in the open marketplace or the village playground, Nwoye was there. And he was already beginning to know some of the simple stories they told.

"We have now built a church," said Mr. Kiaga, the interpreter, who was now in charge of the infant congregation. The white man had gone back to Umuofia, where he built his headquarters and from where he paid regular visits to Mr. Kiaga's congregation at Mbanta.

"We have now built a church," said Mr. Kiaga, "and we want you all to come in every seventh day to worship the true God."

On the following Sunday, Nwoye passed and repassed the little red-earth and thatch building without summoning enough courage to enter. He heard the voice of singing and although it came from a handful of men it was loud and confident. Their church stood on a circular clearing that looked like the open mouth of the Evil Forest. Was it waiting to snap its teeth together? After passing and re-passing by the church, Nwoye returned home.

It was well known among the people of Mbanta that their gods and ancestors were sometimes long-suffering and would deliberately allow a man to go on defying them. But even in such cases they set their limit at seven market weeks or twenty-eight days. Beyond that limit no man was suffered to go. And so excitement mounted in the village as the seventh week approached since the impudent missionaries built their church in the Evil Forest. The villagers were so certain about the doom that awaited these men that one or two converts thought it wise to suspend their allegiance to the new faith.

At last the day came by which all the missionaries should have died. But they were still alive, building a new red-earth and thatch house for their teacher, Mr. Kiaga. That week they won a handful more converts. And for the first time they had a woman. Her name was Nneka, the wife of Amadi, who was a prosperous farmer. She was very heavy with child.

Nneka had had four previous pregnancies and childbirths. But each time she had borne twins, and they had been immediately thrown away. Her husband and his family were already becoming highly critical of such a woman and were not unduly perturbed when they found she had fled to join the Christians. It was a good riddance. . . .

"Does the white man understand our custom about land?"

"How can he when he does not even speak our tongue? But he says that our customs are bad; and our own brothers who have taken up his religion also say that our customs are bad. How do you think we can fight when our own brothers have turned against us? The white man is very clever. He came quietly and peaceably with his religion. We were amused at his foolishness and allowed him to stay. Now he has won our brothers, and our clan can no longer act like one. He has put a knife on the things that held us together and we have fallen apart." . . .

There were many men and women in Umuofia who did not feel as strongly as Okonkwo a traditionalist leader about the new dispensation. The white man had indeed brought a lunatic religion, but he had also built a trading store and for the first time palm-oil and kernel became things of great price, and much money flowed into Umuofia. . . .

Mr. Brown [the missionary to the Ibo village] learned a good deal about the religion of the clan and he came to the conclusion that a frontal attack on it would not succeed. And so he built a school and a little hospital in Umuofia. He went from family to family begging people to send their children to his school. But at first they only sent their slaves or sometimes their lazy children. Mr. Brown begged and argued and prophesied. He said that the leaders of the land in the future would be men and women who had learned to read and write. If Umuofia failed to send her children to the school, strangers would come from other places to rule them. They could already see that happening in the Native Court, where the D.C. was surrounded by strangers who spoke his tongue. Most of these strangers came from the distant town of Umuru on the bank of the Great River where the white man first went.

In the end Mr. Brown's arguments began to have an effect. More people came to learn in his school, and he encouraged them with gifts of singlets and towels. They were not all young, these people who came to learn. Some of them were thirty years old or more. They worked on their farms in the morning and went to school in the afternoon. And it was not long before the people began to say that the white man's medicine was quick in working. Mr. Brown's school produced quick results. A few months in it were enough to make one a court messenger or even a court clerk. Those who stayed longer became teachers; and from Umuofia laborers went forth into the Lord's vineyard. New churches were established in the surrounding villages and a few schools with them. From the very beginning religion and education went hand in hand. . . .

"You all know why we are here, when we ought to be building our barns or mending our huts, when we should be putting our compounds in order. My father used to say to me: 'Whenever you see a toad jumping in broad daylight, then know that something is after its life.' When I saw you all pouring into this meeting from all the quarters of our clan so early in the morning, I knew that something was after our life." He paused for a brief moment and then began again:

"All our gods are weeping. Idemili is weeping, Ogwugwu is weeping, Agbala is weeping, and all the others. Our dead fathers are weeping because of the shameful sacrilege they are suffering and the abomination we have all seen with our eyes." He stopped again to steady his trembling voice.

"This is a great gathering. No clan can boast of greater numbers or greater valor. But are we all here? I ask you: Are all the sons of Umuofia with us here?" A deep murmur swept through the crowd.

"They are not," he said. "They have broken the clan and gone their several ways. We who are here this morning have remained true to our fathers, but our brothers have deserted us and joined a stranger to soil their fatherland. If we fight the stranger we shall hit our brothers and perhaps shed the blood of a clansman. But we must do it. Our fathers never dreamed of such a thing, they never killed their brothers. But a white man never came to them. So we must do what our fathers would never have done. Eneke the bird was asked why he was always on the wing and he replied: 'Men have learned to shoot without missing their mark and I have learned to fly without perching on a twig.' We must root out this evil. And if our brothers take the side of evil we must root them out too. And we must do it *now*. We must bale this water now that it is only ankle-deep. . . ."

At this point there was a sudden stir in the crowd and every eye was turned in one direction. There was a sharp bend in the road that led from the marketplace to the white man's court, and to the stream beyond it. And so no one had seen the approach of the five court messengers sent by English colonial leaders until they had come round the bend, a few paces from the edge of the crowd. Okonkwo was sitting at the edge. . . .

"What do you want here?"

"The white man whose power you know too well has ordered this meeting to stop."

In a flash Okonkwo drew his machete. The messenger crouched to avoid the blow. It was useless. Okonkwo's machete descended twice and the man's head lay beside his uniformed body.

The waiting backcloth jumped into tumultuous life and the meeting was stopped. Okonkwo stood looking at the dead man. He knew that Umuofia would not go to war. He knew because they had let the other messengers escape. They had broken into tumult instead of action. He discerned fright in that tumult. He heard voices asking: "Why did he do it?"

He wiped his machete on the sand and went away.

NO LONGER AT EASE

As a boy in the village of Umuofia he had heard his first stories about Lagos from a soldier home on leave from the war. Those soldiers were heroes who had seen the great world. They spoke of Abyssinia, Egypt, Palestine, Burma and so on. Some of them had been village ne'er-do-wells, but now they were heroes. They had bags and bags of money, and the villagers sat at their feet to listen to their stories. One of them went regularly to a market in the neighboring village and helped himself to whatever he liked. He went in full uniform, breaking the earth with his boots, and no one dared touch him. It was said that if you touched a soldier, Government would deal with you. Besides, soldiers were as strong as lions because of the injections they were given in the army. It was from one of these soldiers that Obi had his first picture of Lagos.

"There is no darkness there," he told his admiring listeners, "because at night the electric shines like the sun, and people are always walking about, that is, those who want to walk. If you don't want to walk you only have to wave your hand and a plea-sure car stops for you." His audience made sounds of wonderment. Then by way of digression he said: "If you see a white man, take off your hat for him. The only thing he cannot do is mold a human being."

For many years afterwards, Lagos was always associated with electric lights and motorcars in Obi's mind. Even after he had at last visited the city and spent a few days there before flying to the United Kingdom his views did not change very much. Of course, he did not really see much of Lagos then. His mind was, as it were, on higher things. He spent the few days with his "countryman," Joseph Okeke, a clerk in the Survey Department. Obi and Joseph had been classmates at the Umuofia C.M.S. Central School. But Joseph had not gone on to a secondary school because he was too old and his parents were poor. He had joined the Education Corps of the 82nd Division and, when the war ended, the clerical service of the Nigerian Government.

Joseph was at Lagos Motor Park to meet his lucky friend who was passing through Lagos to the United Kingdom. He took him to his lodgings in Obalende. It was only one room. A curtain of light-blue cloth ran the full breadth of the room sep-arating the Holy of Holies (as he called his double spring bed) from the sitting area. His cooking utensils, boxes, and other personal effects were hidden away under the Holy of Holies. The sitting area was taken up with two armchairs, a settee (otherwise called "me and my girl"), and a round table on which he displayed his photo album. At night, his houseboy moved away the round table and spread his mat on the floor.

Joseph had so much to tell Obi on his first night in Lagos that it was past three when they slept. He told him about the cinema and the dance halls and about politi-cal meetings.

"Dancing is very important nowadays. No girl will look at you if you can't dance. I first met Joy at the dancing school." "Who is Joy?" asked Obi, who was fascinated by what he was learning of this strange and sinful new world. "She was my girl friend for—let's see . . ."—he counted off his fingers—". . . March, April, May, June, July—for five months. She made these pillowcases for me."

Obi raised himself instinctively to look at the pillow he was lying on. He had taken particular notice of it earlier in the day. It had the strange word *osculate* sewn on it, each letter in a different color.

"She was a nice girl but sometimes very foolish. Sometimes, though, I wish we hadn't broken up. She was simply mad about me; and she was a virgin when I met her, which is very rare here."

Joseph talked and talked and finally became less and less coherent. Then without any pause at all his talk was transformed into a deep snore, which continued until the morning.

The very next day Obi found himself taking a compulsory walk down Lewis Street. Joseph had brought a woman home and it was quite clear that Obi's presence in the room was not desirable; so he went out to have a look round. The girl was one of Joseph's new finds, as he told him later. She was dark and tall with an enormous pneumatic bosom under a tight-fitting red and yellow dress. Her lips and long fingernails were a brilliant red, and her eyebrows were fine black lines. She looked not unlike those wooden masks made in Ikot Ekpene. Altogether she left a nasty taste in Obi's mouth, like the multicolored word *osculate* on the pillowcase. . . .

On top of it all came his mother's death. He sent all he could find for her funeral, but it was already being said to his eternal shame that a woman who had borne so many children, one of whom was in a European post, deserved a better funeral than she got. One Umuofia man who had been on leave at home when she died brought the news to Lagos to the meeting of the Umuofia Progressive Union.

"It was a thing of shame," he said. Someone else wanted to know, by the way, why that beast (meaning Obi) had not obtained permission to go home. "That is what Lagos can do to a young man. He runs after sweet things, dances breast to breast with women and forgets his home and his people. Do you know what medicine that *osu* woman may have put into his soup to turn his eyes and ears away from his people?" . . .

"Everything you have said is true. But there is one thing I want you to learn. Whatever happens in this world has a meaning. As our people say: 'Wherever something stands, another thing stands beside it.' You see this thing called blood. There is nothing like it. That is why when you plant a yam it produces another yam, and if you plant an orange it bears oranges. I have seen many things in my life, but I have never yet seen a banana tree yield a coco yam. Why do I say this? You young men here, I want you to listen because it is from listening to old men that you learn wisdom. I know that when I return to Umuofia I cannot claim to be an old man. But here in this

Lagos I am an old man to the rest of you." He paused for effect. "This boy that we are all talking about, what has he done? He was told that his mother died and he did not care. It is a strange and surprising thing."

Mexico: Octavio Paz

Octavio Paz was born in 1914 in Mexico City. He enjoyed an outstanding career in poetry and criticism, founding a number of literary reviews. He served in the Mexican diplomatic corps, though he often protested government repression of political dissent. Paz frequently taught in the United States and wrote in English as well as Spanish; he also developed extensive contacts with intellectual circles in Europe. *Labyrinth of Solitude,* his most famous single work (published in 1962), is an exploration of Mexican character as it was shaped historically and as it compares to the characteristics of other nations in Latin America and the West. Paz won the Nobel Prize in literature in 1990. He died in 1998.

• • •

THE LABYRINTH OF SOLITUDE

Our [Mexican] sense of inferiority—real or imagined—might be explained at least partly by the reserve with which the Mexican faces other people and the unpredictable violence with which his repressed emotions break through his mask of impassivity. But his solitude is vaster and profounder than his sense of inferiority. It is impossible to equate these two attitudes: when you sense that you are alone, it does not mean that you feel inferior, but rather that you feel you are different. Also, a sense of inferiority may sometimes be an illusion, but solitude is a hard fact. We are truly different. And we are truly alone. . . .

Man is alone everywhere. But the solitude of the Mexican, under the great stone night of the high plateau that is still inhabited by insatiable gods, is very different from that of the North American, who wanders in an abstract world of machines, fellow citizens and moral precepts. In the Valley of Mexico man feels himself suspended between heaven and earth, and he oscillates between contrary powers and forces, and petrified eyes, and devouring mouths. Reality—that is, the world that surrounds us—exists by itself here, has a life of its own, and was not invented by man as it was in the United States. The Mexican feels himself to have been torn from the womb of this reality, which is both creative and destructive, both Mother and Tomb.

From Octavio Paz, *The Labyrinth of Solitude, and Other Essays,* trans. Lysander Kemp, Yara Milos, and R. P. Belash (New York: Grove Press, 1985), 19, 20, 29–30, 37, 66–67, 362, 372–73, 374. Reprinted by permission of the publisher.

He has forgotten the word that ties him to all those forces through which life manifests itself. Therefore he shouts or keeps silent, stabs or prays, or falls asleep for a hundred years.

The history of Mexico is the history of a man seeking his parentage, his origins. He has been influenced at one time or another by France, Spain, the United States and the militant indigenists of his own country, and he crosses history like a jade comet, now and then giving off flashes of lightning. What is he pursuing in his eccentric course? He wants to go back beyond the catastrophe he suffered: he wants to be a sun again, to return to the center of that life from which he was separated one day. (Was that day the Conquest? Independence?) Our solitude has the same roots as religious feelings. It is a form of orphanhood, an obscure awareness that we have been torn from the All, and an ardent search: a flight and a return, an effort to re-establish the bonds that unite us with the universe. . . .

. . . The Mexican is always remote, from the world and from other people. And also from himself.

The speech of our people reflects the extent to which we protect ourselves from the outside world: the ideal of manliness is never to "crack," never to back down. Those who "open themselves up" are cowards. Unlike other people, we believe that opening oneself up is a weakness or a betrayal. The Mexican can bend, can bow humbly, can even stoop, but he cannot back down, that is, he cannot allow the outside world to penetrate his privacy. The man who backs down is not to be trusted, is a traitor or a person of doubtful loyalty; he babbles secrets and is incapable of confronting a dangerous situation. Women are inferior beings because, in submitting, they open themselves up. Their inferiority is constitutional and resides in their sex, their submissiveness, which is a wound that never heals.

Hermeticism is one of the several recourses of our suspicion and distrust. It shows that we instinctively regard the world around us to be dangerous. This reaction is justifiable if one considers what our history has been and the kind of society we have created. The harshness and hostility of our environment and the hidden, indefinable threat that is always afloat in the air, oblige us to close ourselves in, like those plants that survive by storing up liquid within their spiny exteriors. . . .

. . . The Mexican, heir to the great pre-Columbian religions based on nature, is a good deal more pagan than the Spaniard, and does not condemn the natural world. Sexual love is not tinged with grief and horror in Mexico as it is in Spain. Instincts themselves are not dangerous; the danger lies in any personal, individual expression of them. . . . It is noteworthy that our images of the working class are not colored with similar feelings, even though the worker also lives apart from the center of society, physically as well as otherwise, in districts and special communities. When a contemporary novelist introduces a character who symbolizes health or destruction, fertility or death, he rarely chooses a worker, despite the fact that the worker represents the death of an old society and the birth of a new. . . .

The modern worker lacks individuality. The class is stronger than the individual and his personality dissolves in the generic. That is the first and gravest mutilation a man suffers when he transforms himself into an industrial wage earner. Capitalism deprives him of his human nature (this does not happen to the servant) by reducing him to an element in the work process, *i.e.,* to an object. And like any object in the business world, he can be bought and sold. Because of his social condition he quickly loses any concrete and human relationship to the world. The machines he operates are not his and neither are the things he produces. Actually he is not a worker at all, because he does not create individual works or is so occupied with one aspect of production that he is not conscious of those he does create. He is a laborer, which is an abstract noun designating a mere function rather than a specific job. . . .

. . . Not only the popular religion of Mexico but the Mexicans' entire life is steeped in Indian culture—the family, love, friendship, attitudes toward one's father and mother, popular legends, the forms of civility and life in common, the image of authority and political power, the vision of death and sex, work and festivity. Mexico is the most Spanish country in Latin America; at the same time it is the most Indian. Mesoamerican civilization died a violent death, but Mexico is Mexico thanks to the Indian presence. Though the language and religion, the political institutions and the culture of the country are Western, there is one aspect of Mexico that faces in another direction—the Indian direction. Mexico is a nation between two civilizations and two pasts.

Above and beyond success and failure, Mexico is still asking itself the question that has occurred to most clear-thinking Mexicans since the end of the eighteenth century: the question about modernization. In the nineteenth century, it was believed that to adopt the new democratic and liberal principles was enough. Today, after almost two centuries of setbacks, we have realized that countries change very slowly, and that if such changes are to be fruitful they must be in harmony with the past and the traditions of each nation. And so Mexico has to find its own road to modernity. Our past must not be an obstacle but a starting point. This is extremely difficult, given the nature of our traditions—difficult but not impossible. To avoid new disasters, we Mexicans must reconcile ourselves with our past: only in this way shall we succeed in finding a route to modernity. The search for our own model of modernization is a theme directly linked with another: today we know that modernity, both the capitalist and the pseudo-socialist versions of the totalitarian bureaucracies, is mortally wounded in its very core—the idea of continuous, unlimited progress. The nations that inspired our nineteenth-century liberals—England, France, and especially the United States—are doubting, vacillating, and cannot find their way. They have ceased to be universal examples. The Mexicans of the nineteenth century turned their eyes toward the great Western democracies; we have nowhere to turn ours. . . .

The sickness of the West is moral rather than social and economic. . . . But the real, most profound discord lies in the soul. The future has become the realm of horror, and the present has turned into a desert. The liberal societies spin tirelessly, not forward but round and round. If they change, they are not transfigured. The hedonism of the West is the other face of desperation; its skepticism is not wisdom but renunciation. . . .

CHAPTER 33

WOMEN AND GLOBAL CHANGE

Women in virtually every part of the world encountered great changes during the twentieth and twenty-first centuries. Many gained new access to education and the right to vote. Many reduced their birth rate. It is possible to argue that some of the key features of traditional patriarchal society were beginning to yield, and this was a huge change in the human condition.

But there are complexities. Men sometimes retaliated. In certain areas, women's economic position worsened. High-sounding principles were often ignored. And there was great regional variety in all aspects of women's lives.

Documents in this section are organized into three sets. First, new international conventions for women, strongly reflecting feminist ideas about rights, played a genuine role in the process of change. Second, conditions of poor women in Mexico and Kenya help test ideas about change and indicate some of the variety that complicates the subject. Third, comments by educated women in India and Nigeria raise questions about the nature and direction of change, and about the validity of Western standards.

Some change is involved in all the materials presented; some of it even points in similar directions, for example, in the area of birth control and education. But great disparities show up as well, plus basic disputes about what directions change should take.

Questions

1. What are the key elements of the global human rights approach to gender issues?
2. According to peasant women's own statements, what aspects of village life and expectations have been changing most rapidly for them? What aspects have changed least?
3. What kinds of traditional values do women continue to express, even amid change?
4. What is the relationship between global standards and the lives and changing experiences of women in Kenya and Mexico? Were global rights statements meaningful reflections of civilizations and changes in women's lives?

5. What are the main differences, according to interview evidence, between the situations and attitudes of Mexican and of African women? Are there differences in relations with men in the two societies?

6. What are the problems surrounding birth control as an issue in rural society? Were conditions in this regard significantly different in Africa and Mexico during the 1970s?

7. Why does Madhu Kishwar praise arranged marriages?

8. What Nigerian traditions does Ifi Amadiume identify as particularly hard for Western scholars to understand? What are her criteria for judging women's conditions?

9. Do Amadiume and Kishwar agree on some aspects of women's goals in the West that they find objectionable?

10. Do Amadiume and Kishwar agree on the directions of recent change? Which one seems to have more confidence that things are still going well for women?

11. Do Amadiume and Kishwar share any attitudes with village women in Third World societies? Which one suggests a clearer affiliation with upper-class status? Which one emphasizes recent changes that might harm lower-class women?

For Further Discussion

1. What previous ideas and movements help explain the nature of the international women's rights agenda?

2. Judging by evidence from Mexico and Africa in the 1970s, have conditions for women on the whole been improving or deteriorating? Is there a similar process of "modernization" at work? How would a Western feminist judge the women's attitudes?

3. What are the advantages and limitations of interviewing as a source of evidence for contemporary history? Are interviewees likely to slant their remarks at all? What other evidence would help form a picture of women's views and conditions in late-twentieth-century Kenya and Mexico?

4. The evidence in Huston's interviews comes from the 1970s. How much change would you expect to have occurred, and in what directions, a quarter-century later? Would you expect the same kinds of change in Mexico and in Kenya?

5. Would Amadiume criticize Huston's approach as an example of Western bias about the Third World?

6. Why might upper-class Indian and African women differ about the directions of change in their societies in the twentieth century?

7. What is your evaluation of the relevance of Western feminist ideals to societies like India or Africa?

8. Will global human rights principles increasingly define women's lives?

FOURTH WORLD CONFERENCE ON WOMEN

The United Nations began developing special "years" for women in 1965; each year occasioned a major global conference and resounding proclamations of women's rights. These in turn helped spur changes in various national legislations and the creation of nongovernment organizations in many places, from Africa to Latin America, designed to further women's rights. The following document emanated from the major global conference of 1995, widely attended by women from all regions, but particularly from outside Western Europe and the United States

• • •

BEIJING DECLARATION (SEPTEMBER 1995)

We, the Governments participating in the Fourth World Conference on Women . . . recognizing that the status of women has advanced in some important respects in the past decade but that progress has been uneven, that inequalities between women and men have persisted and major obstacles remain, with serious consequences for the well-being of all people . . . and also recognizing that this situation is exacerbated by the increasing poverty that is affecting the lives of the majority of the world's people, in particular women and children, with origins in both the national and international domains, dedicate ourselves unreservedly to addressing these constraints and obstacles and thus enhancing further the advancement and empowerment of women all over the world, and agree that this requires urgent action in the spirit of determination, hope, cooperation and solidarity, now and to carry us forward into the next century. . . .

We are convinced that:
Women's empowerment and their full participation on the basis of equality in all spheres of society, including participation in the decision-making process and access to power, are fundamental for the achievement of equality, development and peace; Women's rights are human rights; Equal rights, opportunities and access to resources, equal sharing of responsibilities for the family by men and women, and a harmonious partnership between them are critical to their well-being and that of their families as well as to the consolidation of democracy; Eradication of poverty based on sustained economic growth, social development, environmental protection and social justice requires the involvement of women in economic and social development, equal opportunities and the full and equal participation of women and men as agents and beneficiaries of people-centered sustainable development; The explicit recognition and reaffirmation of the right of all women to control all aspects of their health, in particular their own fertility, is basic to their empowerment; Local, national, regional

and global peace is attainable and is inextricably linked with the advancement of women, who are a fundamental force for leadership, conflict resolution and the promotion of lasting peace at all levels; It is essential to design, implement and monitor, with the full participation of women, effective, efficient and mutually reinforcing gender-sensitive policies and programmes, including development policies and programmes, at all levels that will foster the empowerment and advancement of women. . . .

We are determined to:

Intensify efforts and actions to . . . ensure the full enjoyment by women and the girl child of all human rights and fundamental freedoms and take effective action against violations of these rights and freedoms; Take all necessary measures to eliminate all forms of discrimination against women and the girl child and remove all obstacles to gender equality and the advancement and empowerment of women; Encourage men to participate fully in all actions towards equality; Promote women's economic independence, including employment, and eradicate the persistent and increasing burden of poverty on women by addressing the structural causes of poverty through changes uneconomic, ensuring equal access for all women, including those in rural areas, as vital development agents, to productive resources, opportunities and public services; Promote people-centered sustainable development, including sustained economic growth, through the provision of basic education, life-long education, literacy and training, and primary health care for girls and women; Take positive steps to ensure peace for the advancement of women and, recognizing the leading role that women have played in the peace movement, work actively towards general and complete disarmament under strict and effective international control, and support negotiations on the conclusion, without delay, of a universal and multilaterally and effectively verifiable comprehensive nuclear-test-ban treaty which contributes to nuclear disarmament and the prevention of the proliferation of nuclear weapons in all its aspects; Prevent and eliminate all forms of violence against women and girls; Ensure equal access to and equal treatment of women and men in education and health care and enhance women's sexual and reproductive health as well as education; Promote and protect all human rights of women and girls; Intensify efforts to ensure equal enjoyment of all human rights and fundamental freedoms for all women and girls who face multiple barriers to their empowerment and advancement because of such factors as their race, age, language, ethnicity, culture, religion, or disability, or because they are indigenous people; Ensure respect for international law, including humanitarian law, in order to protect women and girls in particular; Develop the fullest potential of girls and women of all ages, ensure their full and equal participation in building a better world for all and enhance their role in the development process. . . .

VILLAGE WOMEN

INTERVIEWS WITH MEXICAN PEASANT WOMEN IN THE 1970S

These interviews were conducted by an American anthropologist, Perdita Huston. Huston was trained in ethnographic interview techniques, though in several cases she had to rely on interpreters. She was also inspired by a feminist concern for women's issues, including cases of clear mistreatment. The women who speak out here are from southern Mexico, many of them Indians.

• • •

Interview with a Zapotec Indian

Maria Luisa spoke to me about her sister's [Anna's] life:

"She is in the process of breaking up with her husband. They have four children, but they didn't get married until the third child was born. Then the priest said, 'If you don't get married, I'm not baptizing your children.'"

"Anna's husband wants to live like the old men used to live—having women right under his thumb—not the way it is today. Even our family is against it. They say, 'He has such old-fashioned ideas.' The woman has to be in the house. She has to confess everything to him. She can't have a thought of her own. Even that's okay. You can be jealous. You can even be a tyrant. *But you have to do your share.* You have to bring in money. The reason the family is so down on him is not because he's a tyrant, but because he doesn't fulfill his part of the marriage. She has to go out and look for food while he's gallivanting around. That's what doesn't make sense. You know—rules are rules."

"Now he's beating her even more than before because his mother is constantly filling his head with ideas. 'Anna doesn't cook good food,' she says—and things like that. He beats her up; she is black and blue on the thighs or on the back or wherever. He says he has the right to rule. You know, the male doesn't want to be made a fool of. He accuses other men of being weak. He says, 'I'm not like those men. I don't let women give orders in my house.'

"But Anna is a good wife. She works hard, and if he would let her out of the house, their family would have more money. She works hard in the field, but he doesn't even give her money for food. Granted, he doesn't really earn that much himself, but he *could.* He could take crops into town and sell them and bring back the money, but he doesn't. He feels she shouldn't have money. He works in the field, but he doesn't look for other work. So he gets very little. He doesn't want to sell

From Perdita Huston, *Third World Women Speak Out* (New York: Praeger Publishers, 1979), 41–42, 78–79, 82–83.

much, and there is not enough money to feed the family, so Anna has to sell things or borrow five pesos here and there. Then he gets enraged and blames her for not managing. . . .

[On education, asked what she would have wanted to learn at school]: "I don't know *what* exactly, but it would have been something that would earn money. We are very backward here and we don't know anything. . . . the problem is that we don't know how to *earn money*."

Interviews at a Birth Control Clinic

"They say terrible things about women who want to [practice birth control]. Some say, 'The only reason you want birth control is so you can go with other men.' Once the radio said, 'Father of the family, if you want to give your children a good up-bringing, take care of them well and remember that small families live better.' Well, my brother just laughed. You see, some people are very ignorant."

"The only thing I *don't* do is go to confession, because then I would have to confess that I take the pill, and the priest would say, 'Leave the church.' I could still go to mass, but he wouldn't give me holy communion if I told about the pill." . . .

"I went to school for a while, but the teacher didn't come to school very often, so we didn't learn much. I guess I taught myself to read."

"I have been married for four years. I have only these two children. The first is three, the other almost a year." . . .

"The main thing that makes the times different, I think, is the control women have over the number of children in a family. A family can be planned now; it can live a better life. Women have more facilities for everything because of this. I began to take contraceptives when this last child was eight months old. I take the pill."

"My husband wants a boy because these children are both girls; he doesn't know that I am taking the pill. He wants a boy and says that when I have one, then I can use contraceptives. I want to wait at least two years so that this little girl is older. Then I will try for the boy." . . .

"For me, family planning is very important because my husband does not earn big wages. For the moment, we just can't afford more than two children. . . .

"I told you we were very poor when I was a child. We were six children, and my father didn't earn much. That is why I want just two or three children. I don't want my children to grow up like me—without an education. I feel very ashamed and bad about not having any education. I want my children to go to school and learn many, many things. I don't want them to live by the rumors of the street. I want them to learn for themselves. I want them to be independent and proud of themselves."

INTERVIEWS WITH AFRICAN PEASANT WOMEN IN THE 1970S

In these selections, village women from Kenya provide most of the statements, discussing their goals in the context of changes and continuities they saw around them. Again, their statements can be compared with the judgments about rural life by Kenyan professionals such as a doctor and a social worker.

• • •

A Great-Grandmother

I don't really know my age, but I remember that I was married during the great war [World War I]. In those days we lived all right—happily. Things were quite different from what they are now. We got these clothes only recently. We used to wear something from banana fibers just to cover our lower parts. It was scratchy, but we were used to it. I think all the changes came when the churches came. We got our clothing, and then we said we should cover our bodies and go to school—maybe go to church.

"We had cows, goats, sheep, and hens. . . . Even the chickens didn't get sick in those days. These days, more people die than used to. We had no hospitals; we were just sick, and if you knew any medicines, any herbs, you used them. There were malaria, stomachaches, and backaches. But not many used to die. They lived to be very old men and women. When you heard so-and-so was dead, everyone used to go, because that was the only funeral in a long time.

"In those days, we also used to have old women who knew herbs and helped women in childbirth and with their babies' health. In the old days, even if you had ten children you could care for them. You were happy because you had many little girls and boys to be married, as well as many grandchildren. I had nine children; three died as babies. They had diarrhea and just died. I don't know why. Now children don't die as much any more because we have doctors and hospitals nearby." . . .

"What we need in this village is teachers to teach women handicrafts and sewing and agricultural skills. We have organized a women's group. I am one of the leaders. We are saving up for a building to meet in. All women are trying to earn money, and we want to have a building for our meetings. It will be called the 'adult education building'—with rooms for handicrafts, literacy, and other things."

"We also want our children to be educated—so we can have good leaders to keep our country good. I think now it is best to have only four children—so you can take care of them.

"It is better to educate a girl than a boy, although one should educate both. Girls are better. They help a lot. See this house? My daughters built it for me. If you don't

From Perdita Huston, *Third World Women Speak Out* (New York: Praeger Publishers, 1979), 12–13, 42–43, 72–73, 79–80.

have any daughters, who will build for you? The boys will marry and take care of their wives—that's all. They don't care about mothers. For example, if my son gets married, the daughter-in-law will say, 'Let's take our mothers to live with us.' The son will say, 'No, we will just have our own family and do our own things.' So you are left alone. What do you do?" . . .

"These days there is no trust. Men have defeated us. They don't listen: they have big heads. Before, we mixed with each other—men and women. There were no differences between us. We trusted one another, but now men are not straightforward. These are the changes taking place."

A Nineteen-Year-Old Student

"My mother has eleven children. She is my father's only wife. She works in the fields and grows the food we eat. She plants cabbage, spinach, and corn. She works very hard, but with so many children it is difficult to get enough food or money. All of my sisters and brothers go to school. One is already a teacher, and that is why I am trying to learn a profession. If I can get enough schooling, I can serve the country and my own family. I can also manage to have a life for myself. That is why I came to this school. We have a big family, and I have to help.

"My life is very different from my mother's. She just stayed in the family until she married. Life is much more difficult now because everybody is dependent on money. Long ago, money was unheard of. No one needed money. But now you can't even get food without cash. Times are very difficult. That is why the towns are creating daycare centers—so women can work and have their own lives. I have to work, for without it I will not have enough money for today's life.

"These are the problems I face and try to think about. How shall I manage to pick up this life so that I can live a better one? You know, we people of Kenya like to serve our parents when they are still alive—to help the family. But first, women have to get an education. Then if you get a large family and don't know how to feed it—if you don't have enough money for food—you can find work and get some cash. That's what I will teach my children: 'Get an education first.'" . . .

"If I had a chance to go to the university, I would learn more about health education. I could help women that way. If I were in a position of authority. I would really try to educate women. Right now, girls are left behind in education. It costs money, and parents think it is more important to educate boys. But I think that if people are intelligent, there is no difference. Girls and boys should be educated the same. . . . And I would change the laws so that men would understand women and their needs and not beat them as they do.

"I only hope that I will have a mature husband who will understand and discuss things with me."

A Leader of a Women's Cooperative

"Most women don't rely on their husbands now. If they get some money, well and good; and if they don't, they just try to get money for themselves—selling vegetables or making and selling handicrafts."

"Life is very difficult these days, and men are paying less attention to their wives. You see, men have wrongly just taken advantage of having more money. Instead of using money properly, to improve the lives of their families, they spend it on all the 'facilities' available at hotels. Instead of spending nights in their own homes, they fight at home and seek women outside—in the hotels. Many men cheat on their wives now because they are employed and have money. A husband can say, 'I have been sent as a driver to Nairobi' (or elsewhere), when he actually spends the money on girls."

"So women are fed up. They think now that relying on a man can be a problem. They say, 'We should try to do something ourselves. Then, whether we get something from our men or not, we still will be able to raise our children properly.' The problem that many women face is that they must become self-supporting. They either have no support from their husbands at all, or very little. And there is no law to protect them."

"But women *are* trying to do something for themselves, and if they had the capital they could establish businesses to help them make money. The main problem here is the money problem. Many women are alone. They need to earn for their families." . . .

"Women feel very hurt because they think their men don't recognize them as human beings. They are unhappy because of this inequality. I am lucky; my husband is good. He never took another wife. We are still together." . . .

Urban Family Planning Worker

"We get referrals from other workers. A nutritionist, for example, will come and tell us that she visited a home and feels that the home needs advice on family planning. So we go to the family and talk with them. We also go the child welfare clinic and talk with mothers there. We find that some do not feel free to talk about their problems there, so we go to their own homes and have further discussions. The woman might say, "I'm willing to practice family planning, but my husband is against it. I've tried to persuade him, but he has refused. So I don't know whether there is anything you can do for me.' " . . .

"Some say that they are able to care for their children—so they don't see why they should participate in family planning. Others say they don't see why they should plan their families, since the idea is not an African tradition but has been brought in by Westerners. Also, some men fear that when a woman starts using family planning, she is in that way exposed to the world and can go with any other man, since she knows she won't get pregnant. They don't trust their wives." . . .

. . . "Women fear medicines and they fear their husbands. There are a lot of fears, and it will take much time to catch on." . . .

"The men don't understand that family planning is good because it gives the woman time to rest between pregnancies. They don't care much about that, or about the condition of their children. You'll never see a man going to a family planning clinic. The men here believe: Let a woman be free of childbearing and she will go everywhere. They want a woman to have a child every year until she becomes old, while they are free to go gadding about. So if a woman doesn't keep on having children, her husband will get angry and take another wife."

A Female Midwife

The poor health here is not a poverty problem. There is plenty of land. The problem is the lack of knowledge about nutrition. That's one thing that has to be learned. If people knew how to utilize foods and what to plant to feed the children, it would be better. . . .

"The nutritional problem is also due to some of the superstitions and taboos. There are still many areas where people believe children should not eat eggs because, they say, the children will never talk. You just have to keep persuading people. When mothers realize that children who eat eggs *do* talk, they will convince other mothers that their children will not be harmed by eggs. But you can't *force* them to suddenly change what they do. First I ask them to try other things that give the same food nutrients as eggs. Women are not supposed to eat chicken either—although the men do. It's not fair."

UPPER-CLASS AND SCHOLARLY VIEWS

INDIA: MADHU KISHWAR ON LOVE AND MARRIAGE

Madhu Kishwar is an Indian scholar who has written widely on family issues; the next selection is from a magazine article by her on Indian and Western views of marriage. She reflects the influence of Western ideas, from her own education and from channels such as Hollywood films. But she relies more heavily on polling data and the evaluation of traditional practices, which she juxtaposes with Western models.

• • •

The recent Eye-witness-MARG opinion poll conducted with 1,715 adults in the five metropolitan cities reported in SUNDAY magazine's 9–15 January 1994 issue that 74

From Madhu Kishwar, "Love and Marriage," *Manushi: A Journal about Women and Society* 80 (1994): II, 13–14, 18. Reprinted by permission of the author.

percent of women and an almost equal proportion of men believe that arranged marriages are more likely to succeed than love marriages. Almost 80 percent of respondents felt that a young recently married couple—if they had a choice—should live with their parents. That these opinions are not a mindless hangover of "tradition" becomes evident as they report that over 90 percent of the same respondents believed that men should help with household chores, and eighty percent believed that, if they had one daughter and one son, they would leave an equal amount to each in any Will that they made. These poll results are supportive of some of my impressions gathered from talking to numerous young women, including my own students, as to why most young women are not very enamoured with "love" marriages.

Feminists, socialists and other radicals often project the system of arranged marriages as one of the key factors leading to women's oppression in India. This view derives from the West, which recognizes two supposedly polar opposite forms of marriage—"love marriage" versus arranged marriage. . . .

Self-Arranged Marriages

Critics of the family arranged marriage system in India have rightly focused on how prospective brides are humiliated by being endlessly displayed for approval when marriages are being negotiated by families. The ritual of *ladki dikhana,* with the inevitable rejections women (now even men) often undergo before being selected [is part of this process]. . . .

However, women do not really escape the pressures of displaying and parading themselves in cultures where they are expected to have self-arranged marriages. Witness the amount of effort a young woman in western societies has to put in to look attractive enough to hook eligible young men. One gets the feeling they are on constant self display as opposed to the periodic displays in family arranged marriages. Western women have to diet to stay trim since it is not fashionable nowadays to be fat, get artificial padding for their breasts (1.5 million American women are reported to have gone through silicon surgery to get their breasts reshaped or enlarged), try to get their complexion to glow, if not with real health, at least with a cosmetic blush. They must also learn how to be viewed as "attractive" and seductive to men, how to be a witty conversationalist as well as an ego booster—in short, to become the kind of appendage a man would feel proud to have around him. Needless to say, not all women manage to do all the above, though most drive themselves crazy trying. Western women have to compete hard with each other in order to hook a partner. And once having found him, they have to be alert to prevent other women from snatching him. . . .

The humiliations western women have to go through, having first to grab a man, and then to devise strategies to keep other women off him, is in many ways much worse than what a woman in parent-arranged marriages has to go through. She does not have to chase and hook men all by herself. Her father, her brother, her uncles and aunts and the entire *kunba* join together to hunt for a man. In that sense the woman concerned does not have to carry the burden of finding a husband all alone. And given the relative stability of marriage among communities where families take a lot of interest in keeping the marriage going, a woman is not so paranoid about her husband abandoning her in favour of a more attractive woman. Consequently, Indian women are not as desperate as their western counterparts to look for ever youthful, trim and sexually attractive marriage partners. . . .

NIGERIA: IFI AMADIUME

Ifi Amadiume, a Nigerian scholar here studying a village in the Ibo (Igbo) territory—the same part of Nigeria referred to by Chinua Achebe (ch. 28)—has published widely on African gender and family traditions. From a locally prominent family, she spent time as a student in the West, and from that experience she feels she gained knowledge that she can apply to comparisons with Africa.

• • •

When the 1960s and 1970s female academics and Western feminists began to attack social anthropology, riding on the crest of the new wave of women's studies, the issues they took on were androcentrism and sexism. . . . The methods they adopted indicated to Black women that White feminists were no less racist than the patriarchs of social anthropology whom they were busy condemning for male bias. They fantasized a measure of superiority over African and other Third World women. Black women's critique could not therefore be restricted to the male bias of social anthropology and not challenge White women. Drawing their data from the Third World, especially Africa, works on women produced in Europe and America have shown White women's unquestioning acceptance of anthropology's racist division of the world. In the debates in the West, the Third World supplied the 'raw data' for random sampling, citation and illustration of points. It baffles African women that Western academics and feminists feel no apprehension or disrespectful trivialization in taking on all of Africa or, indeed, all the Third World in one book. It is revealing that most such works have not been written by women from Third World nations; they, instead, tend to write about their particular ethnic group, their country or surrounding region. . . .

The flexibility of Igbo gender construction meant that gender was separate from biological sex. Daughters could become sons and consequently male. Daughters and women in general could be husbands to wives and consequently males in relation to their wives, etc. . . .

From Ifi Amadiume, *Male Daughters, Female Husbands. Gender and Sex in an African Society* (London: Zed Books, 1987), 3–4, 15, 89–90, 91, 132, 141. Reprinted by permission of the publisher.

An insight into this remarkable gender system is crucial to the understanding and appreciation of the political status women had in traditional Igbo societies and the political choices open to them. . . .

It can, therefore, be claimed that the Igbo language, in comparison with English, for example, has not built up rigid associations between certain adjectives or attributes and gender subjects, nor certain objects and gender possessive pronouns. The genderless word *mmadu*, humankind, applies to both sexes. There is no usage, as there is in English, of the word 'man' to represent both sexes, neither is there the cumbersome option of saying 'he or she,' 'his or her,' 'him or her.' In Igbo, O stands for he, she and even it, *a* stands for the impersonal one, and *nya* for the imperative, let him or her.

This linguistic system of few gender distinctions makes it possible to conceptualize certain social roles as separate from sex and gender, hence the possibility for either sex to fill the role. . . .

The use of these weapons of war must be understood in the context of polygynous marriage and compound structure. Of course it was possible for a man to turn to another wife when one wife refused to have sexual relations with him. The important point here is that women lived separately. The fact that a wife did not spend the night with her husband made it possible for her to use sexual refusal as a weapon of war without running the risk of marital rape. This is not the case for women in monogamous marriages who cling to the Christian idea of the sanctity and sexual exclusiveness of their matrimonial beds. Western feminists are still finding it difficult to have rape in marriage recognized as a legal offence.

Refusal of sexual compliance by a wife still proved effective even when a man had sexual access to other wives. Such refusal implied defiance and denial of rights, and was ultimately a challenge to a husband's authority over his wife. The customary solution was not for the man to take the law into his own hands; he had the option of calling in other members of the family or appealing to the formal patrilineage organizations. . . . Obviously the weapon of sexual denial was most effective when used collectively, either by all the wives of a man, all the wives of a patrilineage, or better still, all the women of Nnobi.

Indeed the earliest recorded mass protest movement by Igbo women was the Nwaobiala—the dancing women's movement of 1925. The basic demand of the movement, which was dominated by elderly women, was the rejection of Christianity and a return to traditional customs. Nnobi is mentioned as one of the three towns where a military escort was sent to restore order, as women there burnt the market, blocked the main road and piled refuse in the court house. Children were withdrawn from school and the market was boycotted. . . .

Overwhelming evidence shows that women in Nnobi and in Igboland in general were neither more comfortable nor more advantaged from an economic point of view under colonialism. They had lost their grip on the control of liquid cash; men had invaded the general market, and women were becoming helpless in their personal relations with husbands. But, most important of all, pro-female institutions were being eroded both by the church and the colonial administration. . . .

. . . [W]omen's centrality in the production and sale of palm-oil and kernels in traditional Nnobi society gave them a considerable advantage over their husbands. The introduction of pioneer oil mills mechanized the whole process of extracting the palm-oil and cracking the kernels. This, of course, meant a much higher oil yield which necessitated bulk buying by the agents of the mills and the channelling of most of the village's palm fruit to the mills. The main centre of production was therefore shifted from the family to the mills. At the same time, wives lost the near monopoly they enjoyed in the traditional method of production and the independent income they derived from it. . . . Instead of wives selling the palm-oil and keeping some of the profits, husbands now sold direct to the oil mills or their agents, and collected the money.

CHAPTER 34

GLOBAL CONSUMERISM AND ITS DISCONTENTS

One of the most striking developments of the past 120 years has been the emergence and growing importance of new forms of consumerism in literally every part of the world. Consumerism—an attachment to the process of acquiring and enjoying new material objects one does not strictly need—is hardly a new phenomenon, but until relatively recent times it was largely confined to the upper classes and sometimes shunned even there in favor of purely customary group styles and/or religious interests. Modern consumerism differs from past forms by becoming more important in the lives of many people and by spreading well beyond the upper classes.

From the first, modern consumerism has involved global products and global styles. Items like sugar, tea, and coffee were consumer pioneers as they spread to Western Europe—and all involved importation from other parts of the world. Chinese porcelain inspired a major consumer goods industry in eighteenth-century England. In the nineteenth century "oriental" rugs and furnishings, coming mainly from the Middle East, were all the rage in the West. In the twentieth century, Western and Japanese products gained growing global attention, from music to foods to toys to electronic gadgets. Consumer interests and "international" styles seemed to bridge across many cultural and political divides, creating some new types of comparisons in contemporary world history.

Despite its obvious importance, it is not easy to define what consumerism is or why it proves so attractive. This is one of the challenges in interpreting the following documents. At the same time, consumerism has long roused objections: it can be seen as shallow; as foreign; as disruptive of proper values; as negating appropriate social hierarchies. Global consumerism also remains quite uneven: more available by far to urban than to rural people, to industrialized than to developing economies, even to young as opposed to older. Analyzing documents and comparing their meanings can help identify not only why consumerism has become such a prominent force but also why it has not swept everyone along in its path.

Questions

1. **What are some of the major features of global consumerism? Do the Internet documents suggest the same kind of consumerism, or somewhat different approaches and interests?**
2. **Why does global consumerism find a greater audience among youth than among older people?**
3. **What is the relationship between global consumerism and Americanization?**
4. **What are some of the key objections to global consumerism, and from what kinds of people do they emanate?**
5. **How does consumerism figure into protests against "globalization"?**
6. **What issues are involved in interpreting the global role of a chain like McDonald's?**

For Further Discussion

1. **Does successful consumerism increase human happiness? If not, how can one explain why it attracts so much participation?**
2. **Are protests against global consumerism likely to gain ground?**
3. **Are some parts of the world more open to global consumerism than others?**
4. **How does the analysis of global consumerism relate to larger issues in world history?**

Consumerism on the Internet

The following documents come from 2004 sites on the Internet.

A MICHAEL JACKSON FAN IN SLOVENIA

TANJA KOVAC (A 23-YEAR-OLD FINANCIAL ASSISTANT): The first time I heard a Michael Jackson song was way back in 1987. It was the time when Michael was on his world tour for BAD. I was just 7 years old and I only knew Michael by the way he looks. When I first became his fan I didn't even know that he was a singer. I just came into my sister's room and saw a poster of him on the wall and my eyes immediately turned to him. I remember asking my sister who this man was and my mouth was just wide open. I just couldn't believe that one man could look so beautiful. A week after that I heard the whole BAD album when my sister brought it home so I could hear it. I guess my very first song by Michael was BAD since that's the first song on the

From: http://carniola.org/theglory/2004/04/tanja_kovac_mic.html.

album. When I heard it I fell in love with him even more. He just has it all: the looks, the voice and such a wonderful character. I remember being very much in shock over his whole image and music.

TGOC: *What's in your current Michael Jackson collection?*

TANJA: I have a large collection of Michael Jackson memorabilia. There are so many MJ things that people don't even know exist. I have all of his albums, singles, vinyls, picture discs, special edition discs, his rare mixes and tapes, Jackson 5 and The Jacksons albums . . . all about his music. Then I have so many of his books, magazines (from all over the world), song books, calendars, notebooks, PVC bags with MJ on it, puzzles, MJ perfumes, sculptures, badges, stickers, over 1500 of his original photos, over 100 videocassettes of rare footage of Michael Jackson, pillows, poster, promotional posters, tour books, flags, caps, Mystery drink cans, MJ dolls (which sing the Black or White song), T-shirts, Billie Jean glove, hats (one of them was touched by Michael himself), DVD's, concert tickets, original History tour bag. . . . My most special items are two Michael Jackson autographs that I got when I went to see Michael live (Berlin and London). I made a tattoo on my right arm of one of the autographs.

TGOC: *Tell me about the tattoo. Do you have any more—or are you planning on more?*

TANJA: I always wanted to have a MJ tattoo and this dream came true for me just two days after I met Micahel in Harrods, London. It was in June 2002. First I wanted to make a tattoo of Michael's face but since I didn't have enough money to do that, I decided it would be best to make a tattoo of a MJ autograph that my boyfriend got from Michael personally just a few days before. Everyone who saw it till this day has said it looks amazing, I've never heard anyone say anything bad about it. Yes, I plan to do more of them. I want a tattoo of Michael's face and I believe I will get it done soon.

TGOC: *Does your boyfriend ever get jealous of your love for Michael Jackson?*

TANJA: No. My boyfriend never gets jealous of my GIGANTIC love for Michael. He was even with me when I got the chance to meet Michael and didn't mind that I kissed Michael's hand. My boyfriend is a Michael Jackson fan as well.

TGOC: *Is it difficult, as a fan, to watch what's happening to MJ now? How do you know he is innocent? And what would you say to people who already think he's guilty?*

TANJA: Yes it is painful to see what is happening to him now. I cannot believe that people can be so mean and cruel to make such an injustice against him just because of money. It breaks my heart to see him in pain and I want this injustice to end very soon. I organized a vigil—support event here in Ljubljana to show all Slovenian people that Michael is being framed. Fans cam from all over Slovenia and even Croatia and Bosnia and together we talked to people about the truth of these allegations. We spread leaflets with information and gave Michael all our support. Everyone had a banner with them saying: "Michael is INNOCENT" and some MJ items like hats, gloves, T-shirts, posters; I made a webpage call JMSlo.com where I inform people about all the news that is happening with Micahel Jackson now. I translate the news from English to Slovenian so people can get the right information. I was sick and tired of reading false stories about Michael in our newspapers and that's why I decided to do MJSlo.com.

You ask me how I know that Michael is innocent? I have been a Michael Jackson fan for 17 years already and through the years I have lived and breathed Michael Jackson. I got to know him through his interviews, shows, rare footage that I have of him, private recordings, I got to meet him live six times and talk to him, and through all these years I have seen whatta man he is. He has a great heart and a brilliant mind and I tell you there is NO WAY Michael ever did what they accuse him of. Everyone who knows Michael personally says the same. That's just not in Michael's heart, he could not even think of that. It's people with sick minds that think like that. He is totally Innocent of any wrong doing.

To the people who already think he is guilty I would like to quote Michael's saying "Don't judge a man until you have walked in his moccasins for two weeks." Get the right information about these allegations, please visit MJSlo.com and read the truth about Michael Jackson and his life! If that's still not enough for you wait and hear the truth in court. Lies run sprints, truth runs marathons. The truth will win this marathon!!

MCDONALD'S AND LOVE IN CHINA

He ate so little, as the two of them say knees touching, eyes on each other, oblivious to those who shared their four-foot oval dining table. I sat uncomfortably on the child-sized seat directly across from the lovers, my knees banging against the table with each bit of my big Mac. The 30-something father with his three-year-old son munched noisily through a happy meal, slurping on their drinks, and playing with the Nemo toy. A voyeur, I watch the lovers eat and speak the language of love. A year in China has erased some of my initial discomfort when forced to invade personal space. Ten months ago my eyes would have remained on my food tray, attempting to decipher the symbols and Mandarin characters describing McDonald's newest advertising scheme. On this day, however, I sat transfixed by the scene a mere two feet before me. The university-aged lovers (a word the Chinese apply to boyfriend/girlfriend) shared a small hot tea, which remained capped and unopened, an order of spicy McWings, a

From: http://www.livinginchina.copm/archives/00690.html.

fish sandwich, and small fries. The woman was feasting on the chicken wing morsels; the man was feasting on the woman. He frequently stroked her long, dark hair, placing it behind her right shoulder. Both her hands were full of food, his remained free to assist her in opening cartons, peeling the paper from her sandwich. Leaning into each other, they were merely a burger distance apart as he fed her fries. I could have been on the moon. I don't understand Putonghua, literally common speech, however, I like to think I have slightly more success in people-watching than most. Attempting to match non-verbal communication with words I hear repeatedly, I manage life quite well in China. Besides, I was also once in love. The woman, abandoning the spicy wings and delicately picking up the fish sandwich (careful to keep it encased in its paper wrapper), spoke excitedly about some event. Gesture free, her rich voice, full of inflection, pauses, and excited, high tones caused the young man to maintain sustained eye contact, a thin mouth alternating between a shy smile and despairing frown. I watched him raise his eyebrows in amazement, and, finally, to laugh freely at her completed story. She took the last bite of a shared sandwich that he'd not touched. He picked up a nude French fry, offering it first to her before licking the salt. The tea, apparently forgotten and unattended, was getting cold. Chicken bones lay discarded in a tiny heap next to the crumpled fish wrapper and unused ketchup packages. I found myself part of a threesome. No longer aware of the little boy sitting on the fixed stool next to me making swimming noises with his cheeseburger and Nemo, I was swimming in love. The turquoise scarf she wore shimmered under the fluorescent light. The brown sweater he wore over layers of shirts added strength and maturity to his lean frame. Her petite cell phone hung from a red cord around her neck, resting halfway down her chest. His phone shared table space with their food tray. Neither stopped their look of love to send text messages to anyone. Western university students eat on-the-run at McDonald's. Their Chinese counterparts eat at McDonald's with special friends or lovers—a date place. Expensive, by Chinese standards, western-modern, and food for the soul—not one's health—is the draw. A safe, public place where diners are definitely still part of a crowd, yet easy for two people in love to carve a privacy zone just for their pleasure. Finishing the last of my ketchup dressed fires (yes, they taste the same as in the US), I gathered my trash, wiped my hands on a rare napkin, and picked up my backpack. No need to say good-by to my dining companions; tacit acknowledgement of my existence had never occurred. I could have stolen their last French fry.

Comments

I guess it's so romantic, though I can't completely understand the words and sentences in the article Cheers for love

Posted by zhaojy 03/05/04

Being a Chinese boy, I have read the lovely story for three times. I wish same story in my life.

Posted by Fuwei 03/31/04

A beautiful story. I see a bigger picture involved here. The much needed privacy for young lovers in an eating place. That's quite an achievement. I remember when I was still dating with my wife we had a tough time finding a private place for two young lovers. This was 5–6 years back in Hyderabad, India. Things have changed in India too now, the present crop of young lovers do not care much and there are more of them now so the number of places are increasing. Anyway, thanks for the lovely story. Suhit

Posted by Suhit Anatula 03/31/04

It's pathetic man, the whole article reflected how lonely you are!

Posted by 5600hp 04/04/04

GLOBAL WEB POSTINGS BY AMERICANS

I'm starting to think there are two kinds of "world cultural product." There's drive-by tourism stuff, that gets picked up from local scenes by global entrepreneurs, like, say the Tuareg singers at "Festival in the Desert."

Posted by Jamais Cascio at December 5, 2003 03:07 PM

Four CD's I listen to a lot (all a few years old now): Rachid Taha's *Medina*, Hedningarna's *Karelia Visa* (Finnish folk-inspired trance-y music), the Amores Perros soundtrack, *Mundial Muzique* (a sampler of new Brazillian lounge-y stuff)

Posted by Alex Steffen at December 5, 2003 03:23 PM

"Cibelle's mentor, Suba, was Servian. Cibelle sings in Portuguese and English, and currently lives and performs in London. Because Cibelle is a "Young World Diva." I didn't realize that "Young World Divas" existed until about 45 seconds ago, but you may rely upon it that I am intensely and persistently interested . . ."

And then there's product like Cibelle, which is originally made by a multinational globalized polyglot diaspora.

Number one is generally better art, but number two is a lot more interesting.

Posted by: Bruce Sterling at December 5, 2003 04:47 PM

A while back, a Turkish coworker lent me a CD by Turkish female singer songwriter name Nazan Ocel. I though it kicked serious ass. I have been trying to get a copy of this disk for 6 years now. It's been my hope that the shrinking world and increasing cultural cross-pollination would mean that I can get the rocking disks like this from other countries. I'd love to have some musical Marco Polo Leighton doing that with the Tuvan music, but I'd like to be able to get lots of the local music from around the world. Is anyone doing this now?

Posted by Dave Slusher at December 5, 2003 06:57 PM

I'm thinking there's a third kind of "world cultural product," somewhere between the first two: derivative of things from elsewhere than the place where it was made, constructed for a specifically local audience, but also effective in a more global way (sometimes with the aid of time). Example that comes to mind: the Ethiopiques series of CDs, compiling records that came out on the tiny Ethiopian label Amha in the early 70s—half their bloodline is from traditional pentatonic music, half is from American hard funk a la James Brown, and in 2003 they sound totally great. Try vol. 3, with hits by Mahmoud Ahmed, Alèmayèhu Eshèté, Hirut Bèqèlè, etc.

Posted by: Douglas Wolk at December 5, 2003 8:15 PM

ANTI-GLOBALIZATION PROTEST IN SEATTLE

In December 1999 a series of protests rocked Seattle on the occasion of a World Trade Organization meeting designed to discuss tariff reductions and the promotion of global trade. The following passage was written by Jeffrey St. Clair, a radical journalist and coeditor of the political newsletter *Counterpunch*. The Seattle protests foreshadowed a regular series of protests against the WTO, the World Bank, and other global organizations.

• • •

And the revolution will be started by: sea turtles. At noon about 2,000 people massed at the United Methodist Church, the HQ of the grassroots [organizations], for a march to convention center. It was Environment Day and the Earth Island Institute had prepared more than 500 sea turtle costumes for marchers to wear. The sea turtle became the prime symbol of the WTO's threats to environmental laws when a WTO tribunal ruled that the U.S. Endangered Species Act, which requires shrimp to be caught with turtle excluder devices, was an unfair trade barrier.

But the environmentalists weren't the only ones on the street Monday morning. In the first showing of a new solidarity, labor union members from the Steelworkers

From Alexander Cockburn, Jeffrey St. Clair, and Alan Sekula, *Five Days That Shook the World* (London: Verso, 2000), 16–21.

and the Longshoremen showed up to join the march. In fact, Steelworker Don Kegley led the march, alongside environmentalist Ben White. (White was later clubbed in the back of the head by a young man who was apparently angry that he couldn't do his Christmas shopping. The police pulled the youth away from White, but the man wasn't arrested. White played down the incident.) The throng of sea turtles and blue-jacketed union folk took off to the rhythm of a familiar chant that would echo down the streets of Seattle for days: "The people will never be divided!"

I walked next to Brad Spann, a Longshoreman from Tacoma, who hoisted up one of my favorite signs of the entire week: "Teamsters and Turtles Together at last!" Brad winked at me and said, "What the hell do you think old Hoffa [former Teamster leader] thinks of that?"

The march, which was too fast and courteous for my taste, was escorted by motorcycle police and ended essentially in a cage, a protest pen next to a construction site near the convention center. A large stage had been erected there hours earlier and Carl Pope, the director of the Sierra Club, was called forth to give the opening speech. The Club is the nation's most venerable environmental group. . . .

Standing near the stage I saw Brent Blackwelder, the head of Friends of the Earth. Behind his glasses and somewhat shambling manner, Blackwelder looks ever so professional. And he is by far the smartest of the environmenta CEOs. But he is also the most radical politically, the most willing to challenge the tired complacency of his fellow green executive. . . .

After the speechifying most of the marchers headed back to the church. But a contingent of about 200 ended up in front of McDonald's where a group of French farmers had mustered to denounce U.S. policy on biotech foods. Their leader was José Bove, a sheep farmer from Millau in southwest France and a leader of Confederation Paysanne, a French environmental group. In August, Bove had been jailed in France for leading a raid on a McDonald's restaurant under construction in Larzac. At the time, he was already awaiting charges that he destroyed a cache of Novartis' genetically engineered corn. Bove said his raid on the Larzac McDonald's was promoted by the U.S. decision to impose a heavy tariff on Roquefort cheese in retaliation for the European Union's refusal to import American hormone-treated beef. Bove's act of defiance earned him the praise of Jacques Chirac and Friends of the Earth. Bove said he was prepared to start a militant worldwide campaign against "Frankenstein" foods. "These actions will only stop when this mad logic comes to a halt," Bove said. "I don't demand clemency but justice."

Bove showed up at the Seattle McDonald's with rounds of Roquefort cheese, which he handed out to the crowd. After listening to a rousing speech against the evils of Monsanto, and its bovine growth hormone and RoundupReady Soybeans, the crowd stormed the McDonald's breaking its windows and urging customers and workers to join the marchers on the streets. This was the first shot in the battle for Seattle.

Who were these direct action warriors on the front lines? Earth First, the Alliance for Sustainable Jobs and the Environment (the new enviro-steelworker alliance), the Ruckus Society (a direct action training center), Jobs with Justice, Rainforest Action Network, Food Not Bombs, Global Exchange, and a small contingent of Anarchists, the dreaded Black Bloc.

There was also a robust international contingent on the streets Tuesday morning: French farmers, Korean greens [environmentalists], Canadian wheat growers, Mexican environmentalists, Chinese dissidents, Ecuadorian anti-dam organizers, U'wa tribes-people from the Columbian rainforest, and British campaigners against genetically modified foods. Indeed earlier, a group of Brits had cornered two Monsanto lobbyists behind an abandoned truck carrying an ad for the *Financial Times*. They detained the corporate flacks long enough to deliver a stern warning about the threat of franken-crops to wildlife, such as the Monarch butterfly. Then a wave of tear gas wafted over them and the Monsanto men fled, covering their eyes with their neckties.

Around 12:30 someone smashed the first storefront window. It could have been an anarchist. It could have been an agent provocateur or stray bullet or concussion grenade. What's clear, though, is that the vandalism—what there was of it—started more than two hours after the cops had attacked nonviolent protesters amassed at 6th and Union; protesters who had offered themselves up for arrest. At most, the dreaded Black Bloc, which was to become demonized by the press and some of the more staid leaders of labor and green groups, amounted to 50 people, many of them young women. Much of the so-called looting that took place was done not by the Anarchists, but by Seattle street gangs.

As the march turned up toward the Sheraton and was beaten back by cops on horses, I teamed up with Etienne Vernet and Ronnie Cumming. Cumming is the head of one of the feistiest groups in the U.S., the Pure Food Campaign, Monsanto's chief pain in the ass. Cumming hails from the oil town of Port Arthur, Texas. He went to Cambridge with another great foe of industrial agriculture, Prince Charles. Cumming was a civil rights organizer in Houston during the mid-sixties. "The energy here is incredible," Cumming said. "Black and white, labor and green, Americans, Europeans, Africans, and Asians arm in arm. It's the most hopeful I've felt since the height of the civil rights movement.

Vernet lives in Paris, where he is the leader of the radical green group EcoRopa. At that very moment the European delegates inside the convention were capitulating on a key issue: The EU, which had banned import of genetically engineered crops and hormone-treated beef, had agreed to a U.S. proposal to establish a scientific commit-tee to evaluate the health and environmental risks of biotech foods, a sure first step toward undermining the moratorium. Still Vernet was in a jolly mood, lively and in-vigorated, if a little bemused by the decorous nature of the crowd. "Americans seem to have been out of practice in these things," he told me. "Everyone's so polite. The only things on fire are dumpsters filled with refuse." He pointed to a shiny black

Lexus parked on Pine Street, which throngs of protesters had scrupulously avoided. In the windshield was a placard identifying it as belonging to a WTO delegate. "In Paris that car would be burning."

AMERICANISM AND CONSUMERISM

The following passage comes from *Adbusters Magazine*, in 2006. It reflects the decline of the United States in world opinion, after the invasion of Iraq and other developments, and offers an interesting opportunity to look at the relationship between world opinion and consumerism and to examine corporate strategies to deal with new complexities in the global market.

• • •

A marketing study released early this year puts a pretty savage point on the dilemma. Based on research conducted in the summer of 2005, Chicago branding agency Energy BBDO ranked the "likeability" of 54 globally-marketed brands amongst 13 to 18 years olds from a bakers dozen of countries, including the United States.

Of the big brands with roots in the USA, just five—Nike, Colgate, Coca-Cola, M&Ms and Kodak—made it into the top ten. Contrast this with ten years ago, when a comparable study conducted by D'Arcy Masius Benton & Bowles discovered near-total supremacy of US brands over the much-desired teen demographic, capturing eight of the top ten "likeability" slots.

It's clear that name recognition is not to blame for the decline. In the new study, McDonalds ranked second for name recognition, respectively, yet not even breaking the top twenty for likeability.

"An association with the US seemed to be a drag on the likeability of brands, despite high logo recognition," noted Chip Walker, executive vice president at Energy BBDO, in a January interview with *Women's Wear Daily*. "There seems to be a great ambivalence towards America among global teens."

While none of this spells out-and-out doom for US brands, being forced to stop drinking from the poisoned well has left marketers scrambling to uncover new formulas for generating teen cool.

Of the US entries in the current top ten, Nike has perhaps been the most aggressive in shedding its mantle of Americana in favor of "localizing" itself across the world. Hence the ongoing Joga Bonito (Play Beautiful) campaign, featuring the likes of Brazilian footballer Ronaldnho Gaúcho and the retired French icon Eric Cantona.

From Clayton Dach, "Global Teens Growing Indifferent to 'Brand America,'" Adbusters Magazine, http://www.adbusters.org/the_magazine/66/Global_Teens_Growing.

Hence, also, Nike's move to acquire other brands that already enjoy local cache—as with Canadian hockey-equipment manufacturer Bauer, now Nike Bauer—or its new, $43-million sponsorship deal with India's national cricket team.

In a roundabout way, then, it may be tempting to prophesy that the Brand America crisis could ultimately be a boon to those US brands that have been coasting on borrowed cool, obliging them to fabricate more resilient, bespoke identities that are better suited to emerging markets.

Tempting, yes, but likely also a tad hasty, given another major finding of the Energy BBDO study. "Marketers facing big trouble," note the study's authors, "62 percent of global teens are apathetic about marketing and advertising. That is, they are not anti-brand, but perhaps more dangerously, they just don't care—don't care about wearing brand logos, don't believe advertising, and feel there is too much advertising in the world."

This isn't a small matter of a few errant kids. The global teen market is huge and growing—in 2002, worth approximately $170 billion in the States alone. More trenchantly, adolescence is regarded as the ideal moment to begin cultivating "positive consideration" and brand loyalty, right at the moment when kids begin to make independent purchasing decisions. No wonder, then, that the specter of a disinterested, brand-apathetic teen is to a marketer what root rot is to a gardener: a sign of trouble, "dangerous" things to come.

Comments

I for one, speaking as a 17 year old, can understand being completely indifferent to brands. I work for minimum wage, and what I do with my money is strongly weighted on price as well as smart consumerism. I think that habit will only be solidified as I grow older. Why save my money for an overpriced piece of designer clothing made in a sweatshop when I can buy cheaper, higher quality goods from a local source?
Vance

I would love to think that US branding is on its way out, however, branding has proven to reinvent itself time and time again. Has anyone else ever heard of consumers being compared to roaches? Eventually, the consumer is so oversaturated with advertising that the cooperations will find more and more invasive ways to spray the consumer with their poison. If we are not careful, we will all end up living corporately sponsored lives. A gross exaggeration of what is slowly happening.
Hilde

I understand how teenage apathy could deteriorate the profits of various brand names. However, is not a move away from exasperated consumerism and American domination a positive thing? If teenagers are buying what they like and what is functional and

attracts them despite the brand name isn't market competition becoming more legitimate and less blind?
Sara

It is sad but true. After spending 17 years in the US, I came back to Pakistan. During my teen days, everyone wanted to go to the US for education but now 90% want to go to UK or Australia. If you ask them why, most of the time there is same answer. Culturally US has gone backwards and they have alienated themselves.
Usman

Many Americans already live branded lives: their clothing, personal grooming products, automobiles, and even speech habits (vocabulary, phrasing, etc.) and dietary practices are influenced heavily by what they see on television. How many times have I heard "talk to the hand," "take it to the next level," and "been there, done that, got the t-shirt," all of which appear to be the common tongue of talk show hosts like Oprah, etc?
Jon Koppenhoefer

I know things are different in China. Young people like big brands much more than others. Megalopolis culture holds that one lives better than other people through "excellence" brands.
Zhaisi

I find myself hating many of the brands on that list. I've found that brands with recognition, like Sony and the like, skimp on any kind of quality in their products. Liking a big brand doesn't set you apart from anyone and create individuality, but finding a little no-name with great products gives you identity.
Garrett

The truth is, even though American brands are falling out of favor, European and Asian consumerist brands will just pick up the slack. The news is an indicator of the decline in America's appeal—but it is not warming news about the reduction of consumerism.
E.J.

I bet I can guess why Colgate is high on the list. I think it's because of the tooth whitening stuff. But yea, I've always disliked wearing stuff with brandnames on display I just don't find it very stylish and the thinking that things are cooler just because what brand they are. I still don't have an Ipod, or a cell phone. But I don't really care! I get them when I need them, or have enough money. Also, ditto on the comment about how brands trying too hard is unattractive. I saw a commercial for Nike in the movies and it was about getting more air. Like I'm gonna fly if I wear those.
BLF

Some states in India just banned Coke and Pepsi products because they contain pesticides, 24x higher than the agreed limit. This will accelerate their brand deterioration outside of the US.
Chad

I completely agree on the strong anti-American trend with teens at the moment, but I think that most teens do not really think about which country the company they are buying is rooted. Although this does exclude some of the largest companies that are very well known for having US roots (e.g. Nike, McDonalds, Coca-Cola, etc.).

CHAPTER 35

TERRORISM AND ANTI-TERRORISM

The final decades of the twentieth century were filled with periodic encounters with terrorism. These spilled over, massively, to the twenty-first century when on September 11, 2001, nineteen terrorists commandeered four commercial airplanes in the United States and flew three of them into landmark buildings, the World Trade Center in New York and the Pentagon near Washington, DC. Approximately three thousand people died.

Along with globalization, terrorism becomes a central world history topic after the end of the Cold War. It raises huge questions about relationships among major civilizations, and it complicates any definition of globalization.

Terrorism is not easy to define or explain. It often involves violence by groups who believe their cause is just but who face opposition from a superior force. It often targets civilians, using modern technologies such as car bombs or hijacked airplanes. The most widespread terrorism in the early twenty-first century emanated from extremist Muslim groups protesting Western activities in the Middle East, including Israeli treatment of Palestinians. While some Western leaders simply condemned terrorism, others, while also condemning criminal tactics, urged an understanding of the motives involved as part of mounting opposition strategies.

The six passages that follow invite several kinds of comparison. The first is obvious: the huge differences in viewpoint between those who advocate terror and Western leaders who oppose it. What are the key premises in both camps? How do the assumptions of one group help explain those of the other? The second comparison, still involving the two camps, asks whether there are differences of approach within them—between British and American leaders or between self-styled terrorist leaders and those who carry out attacks directly. Finally, the third cluster of two documents explores positions of groups in the middle—opposed to terrorism but also concerned about excesses in response. Comparing this approach to the two more extreme camps raises the more subtle comparative question of whether any middle way is possible.

Questions

1. What was bin Laden's interpretation of Islam? How did he justify violence against the United States?
2. What were the emphases of the 9/11 terrorists? How do they compare to bin Laden's approach?
3. How can international terrorism best be defined? Why do some people find a definition difficult?
4. What were Tony Blair's main arguments against terrorism? What strategy does he suggest? How does his approach compare with that of President Bush?
5. How did the U.N. react to terrorism? What difficulties did it have in taking out a clear position?
6. How does Ramadan's argument compare to the definitions of Islam by bin Laden and the terrorists? To the arguments at Blair and Bush?
7. Is it possible to think of a settlement between the extremes where terrorism is involved?

For Further Discussion

1. Will terrorism and the struggle against it be the dominant issue of the twenty-first century?

OSAMA BIN LADEN'S DECREE AND THOUGHTS BY 9/11 TERRORISTS

The first document is a 1998 fatwa, or decree, by Osama bin Laden, the leader of the al Qaeda terrorist group; it was widely publicized. The second document is a letter left by several of the hijackers of the 9/11 flights, according to the U.S. Federal Bureau of Investigation; the *Los Angles Times* published a translation on September 29, 2001.

• • •

OSAMA BIN LADEN'S DECREE

The Arabian Peninsula has never—since God made it flat, created its desert, and encircled it with seas—been stormed by any forces like the crusader armies spreading in it like locusts, eating its riches and wiping out its plantations. All this is happening at a time in which nations are attacking Muslims like people fighting over a plate of food. In the light of the grave situation and the lack of support, we and you are obliged to discuss current events, and we should all agree on how to settle the matter.

No one argues today about facts that are known to everyone; we will list them, in order to remind everyone:

[For example], for over seven years the United States has been occupying the lands of Islam in the holiest places, the Arabian Peninsula, plundering its riches, dictating to its rulers, humiliating its people, terrorizing its neighbors, and turning its basis in the Peninsula into a spearhead through which to fight the neighboring Muslim peoples.

All these crimes and sins committed by the Americans are a clear declaration of war on God, his messenger, and Muslims. And ulema have throughout Islamic history unanimously agreed that the Jihad is an individual duty if the enemy destroys the Muslim countries. This was revealed by Imam Bin-Qadamah in "Al-Mughni," Imam al-Kisai in "Al-Badai," al-Qurtubi in his interpretation, and the shaykh of al-Islam in his books, where he said: "As for the fighting to repulse [an enemy], it is aimed at defending sanctity and religion, and it is a duty as agreed [by the ulema]. Nothing is more sacred than belief except repulsing an enemy who is attacking religion and life."

On that basis, and in compliance with God's order, we issue the following fatwa to all Muslims:

The ruling to kill the Americans and their allies—civilians and military—is an individual duty for every Muslim who can do it in any country in which it is possible to do it, in order to liberate the al-Aqsa Mosque and the holy mosque [Mecca] from their grip, and in order for their armies to move out of all the lands of Islam, defeated and unable to threaten any Muslim. This is in accordance with the words of Almighty God, "and fight the pagans all together as they fight you all together," and "fight them until there is no more tumult or oppression, and there prevail justice and faith in God."

Thoughts by 9/11 Terrorists

When you board the plane, remember that this is a battle in the sake of God, which is worth the whole world and all that is in it. As the Messenger (peace and blessings be upon him) has said.

When you sit in your seat, invoke the known supplications, and then be confident with the remembrance of God. "O you who believe, if you meet an army, then stand firm and invoke God much so that you may prosper."

And know that the Gardens of Paradise are beautified with its best ornaments, and its inhabitants are calling you. And if . . . do not let differences come between you, and listen and obey, and if you kill, then kill completely, because this is the way of the Chosen One.

On condition that . . . there is something greater than paying attention to the enemy or attacking him, because the harm in this is much greater. For the priority of the action of the group is much more important, since this is the duty of your mission. Don't take revenge for yourself only, but make your strike and everything on the basis of doing it for the sake of God.

PRIME MINISTER BLAIR'S SPEECH
AND PRESIDENT BUSH'S SPEECH

The first document below is from an October 2, 2001, speech by British Prime Minister Tony Blair, shortly before his nation joined the United States in an attack on Afghanistan as the center of terrorist activities. The second document is from the February 2002 State of the Union address by President George W. Bush, delivered shortly after the radical Islamic regime in Afghanistan had been defeated; this was the speech in which the president not only attacked terrorists but also condemned Iraq, Iran, and North Korea as an "axis of evil" because their weapons threatened the United States.

• • •

BLAIR'S SPEECH

So, what do we do?

Don't overreact some say. We aren't

We haven't lashed out. No missiles on the first night just for effect.

Don't kill innocent people. We are not the ones who waged war on the innocent. We seek the guilty.

Look for a diplomatic solution. There is no diplomacy with Bin Laden or the Taliban regime.

State an ultimatum and get their response. We stated the ultimatum; they haven't responded.

Understand the causes of terror. Yes, we should try, but let there be no moral ambiguity about this: nothing could ever justify the events of 11 September, and it is to turn justice on its head to pretend it could.

The action we take will be proportionate; targeted, we will do all we humanly can to avoid civilian casualties. But understand what we are dealing with. Listen to the calls of those passengers on the planes. Think of the children on them, told they were going to die.

There is no compromise possible with such people, no meeting of minds, no point of understanding with such terror.

Just a choice: defeat it or be defeated by it. And defeat it we must.

When we act to bring to account those that committed the atrocity of September 11, we do so, not out of bloodlust.

We do so because it is just. We do not act against Islam. The true followers of Islam are our brothers and sisters in this struggle. Bin Laden is no more obedient to the proper teaching of the Koran than those Crusaders of the 12th century who pillaged and murdered, represented the teaching of the Gospel.

It is time the west confronted its ignorance of Islam. Jews, Muslims and Christians are all children of Abraham.

This is the moment to bring the faiths closer together in understanding of our common values and heritage, a source of unity and strength.

So I believe this is a fight for freedom. And I want to make it a fight for justice too. Justice not only to punish the guilty. But justice to bring those same values of democracy and freedom to people round the world.

BUSH'S SPEECH

Our cause is just, and it continues. We have seen the depth of our enemies' hatred in videos, where they laugh about the loss of innocent life. And the depth of our enemies' hatred is equaled by the madness of the destruction they design. [In Afghanistan] we have found diagrams of American nuclear power plants and public water facilities, detailed instructions for making chemical weapons, surveillance maps of American cities, and thorough descriptions of landmarks in America and throughout the world What we have found confirms that, far from ending, our war against terror is only beginning. Most of the 19 men who hijacked planes on September the 11th were trained in Afghanistan's camps, and so were tens of thousands of others. Thousands of dangerous killers, schooled in the methods of murder, often supported by outlaw regimes, are now spread throughout the world like ticking time bombs, set to go off without warning.

Our nation will continue to be steadfast and patient and persistent in the pursuit of two great objectives. First, we will shut down terrorist camps, disrupt terrorist plans, and bring terrorists to justice. And, second, we must prevent the terrorists and regimes who seek chemical, biological or nuclear weapons from threatening the United States and the world.

We will work closely with our coalition to deny terrorists and their state sponsors the materials, technology, and expertise to make and deliver weapons of mass destruction. We will develop and deploy effective missile defenses to protect America and our allies from sudden attack. And all nations should know: America will do what is necessary to ensure our nation's security. We'll be deliberate, yet time is not on our side. I will not wait on events, while dangers gather. I will not stand by, as peril draws closer and closer. The United States of America will not permit the world's most dangerous regimes to threaten us with the world's most destructive weapons.

LESLIE PALTI AND TARIQ RAMADAN

The first document below, by an international relations expert, Leslie Palti, sums up United Nations discussions. Published in 2006, it is not an official U.N. statement. The second document is also from 2006, an article by the Swiss Muslim Tariq Ramadan, a leading European Muslim intellectual who earlier had been offered a faculty position by Notre Dame University that he had been unable to assume because the U.S. government would not allow him to enter the country.

• • •

LESLIE PALTI

The United Nations unequivocally condemns terrorism in all its forms as a violation of human rights. However, finding a rights-based approach to fighting it has been less obvious. The anti-terrorism debate hinges on finding the right balance between human rights protection and effective security measures. Are effective counter terrorism measures compatible with the full respect for fundamental freedoms? Is it necessary for States to make compromises and infringe on the rule of law in order to better protect their population from the threat of terrorism? In November 2002, Secretary-General Kofi Annan noted that the 11 September 2001 terrorist attacks have exacerbated the dilemma, "where an understandable focus on preventing still more terrible terrorist acts has increased concerns about the price we must pay in terms of cherished rights and liberties." He added: "We face a nearly unsolvable conflict between two imperatives of modern life protecting the traditional civil liberties of our citizens, and at the same time ensuring their safety from terrorist attacks with catastrophic consequences." Particular attention needed to be given to balancing anti-terrorism measures and the observance of human rights standards, Mr. Annan said, otherwise the fight against terrorism would be "self-defeating." For the United Nations, respect for human rights remains an integral part of any comprehensive counter-terrorism strategy. UN guidelines to help States strike a balance between human rights and combating terrorism have been established in a number of resolutions adopted by the General Assembly, Security Council and Commission on Human Rights. These resolutions stress that "States must ensure that any measures taken to combat terrorism comply with all their obligations under international law and should adopt such measure in accordance with international law."

The Challenge of Defining Terrorism

Fighting terrorism has been a long-standing concern of the General Assembly. Beginning in 1963, the United Nations has focused on building a legal framework to eliminate international terrorism and, to date, there are twelve major multilateral conventions about terrorism that constitute the main element of international law. However, despite this progress, one of the central challenges facing the Assembly has been the definition of terrorism itself. Each of the twelve conventions relies on an "operational" definition, based on specific terrorist "activities." Thus, separate treaties exist to address issues such as bombings, hijackings, hostage-taking and covert financing of terrorist activities, but a universal definition has yet to be adopted.

Since 1996, the Assembly's Sixth (Legal) Committee has worked on drafting a comprehensive convention on international terrorism, which will include a definition of terrorism. However, negotiations remain stalled due to disagreements between States on how to distinguish liberation movements from terrorist cells. Thus, until States resolve the adage that "one man's terrorist is another man's freedom fighter," the debate over a universal definition of terrorism will continue.

TARIQ RAMADAN, "THE GLOBAL IDEOLOGY OF FEAR"

When we examine the countries of the West or those of the South, particularly where the population is primarily Muslim, we can only conclude that fear is omnipresent and deeply ingrained. It is having an unmistakable impact on the way human beings perceive the world. We can observe at street level three principle effects:

First, fear, naturally and often unconsciously, breeds mistrust and potential conflict with the "Other." A binary vision of reality begins to impose the outlines of a protective "us" and of a threatening "them."

The second effect derives form the absolute domination of emotions in our relationships with the Other and of emotional responses to events. When fear rules, emotions undermine rational analysis. In such a state, we condemn the consequences of some actions and reject the individuals who commit it, but we don't seek to understand what led to such action. . . .

If we broaden our focus, we see a world that reflects these same considerations and postures. The "war" that has been unleashed to destroy terrorism is now founded on the same logical bases, but on a global scale.

Don't get me wrong. Terror is a fact, not an ideology, and the killing of innocent people must be condemned with no exception. It is the ideological use of its consequences that is problematic. The American neo-conservatives and their European imitators instigate and nurture a permanent sense of fear, which they wield as though it were an ideology. Their policies are based on a feeling of insecurity and a binary vision of the world. The imperative is one of self-protection, sometimes through draconian security policies that are hostile to freedom and, for some, openly unjust and discriminatory. After all, the West has become the "principal victim of terrorism."

We must break the bonds of our fear, master our impulse to see things only in black and white and recapture our critical spirit and our ability to listen. We must once more become thinking "subjects"—that and nothing else. And yet, to do so seems so difficult.

Muslims, whether they live in the West or in primarily Muslim countries, cannot under any circumstances endorse the ideology of fear, nor can they fall into the trap of a polarized, simplistic and caricatured reading of the world. By perpetuating the idea, which has now become an obsession, that they are either dominated (or members of a minority) and unappreciated or singled out and marginalized, they unconsciously accept the premises of those who propagate this emotion-based ideology, of those who seek to build walls and dig trenches, of those who promote prejudices, fuel insecurity and fan the fires of conflict. These propagandists of fear tirelessly spread the idea that Islam and Muslims are threatened by the future; by allowing themselves to be swept into a vicious circle of self-justification and defensiveness, Muslims confirm and lend credence to a debate whose terms have been deliberately skewed. . . .

We must make an effort to educate ourselves in order to bring together the search for meaning and for God and respect for the principles of justice, freedom and human fraternity. Against the temptation to close ourselves off, to see reality in black and white, we need an "intellectual jihad." We need to resist (jihad means, literally, effort and resistance), to strive for the universality of a message that transcends the particular and allows us to understand the common universal values that make up our horizon. . . .

The original spirit of the message of Islam is an invitation to us; it teaches us to open ourselves to the world, to make ours what is good (whatever its origin). It teaches us to understand that each of us has multiple, fluctuating identities, that diversity is a school for humility and respect, and that humanity is one, just as God is One.

CHAPTER 36

GLOBAL WARMING AND GLOBAL ENVIRONMENTALISM

Humans have affected the environment at least since the beginning of agriculture, sometimes with disastrous consequences. Industrialization in the nineteenth century accelerated the potential for environmental change, with deteriorations of air quality around factory centers and massive chemical spills running into rivers. Industrialization also indirectly prompted new environmental developments outside the industrial world, as planters scrambled to introduce crops like cotton or coffee in regions where they might worsen soil quality or encourage new erosion. With all this, it was only in the later twentieth century that humankind developed the indisputable capacity to affect global environmental conditions, and not just regional patterns. Efforts to distribute pollution through giant smokestacks, for example, produced acid rain that might damage forests in distant areas—thus Germany could affect Scandinavia and the American Midwest could touch Canada and New England.

Increased production of carbon dioxide and the reduction of tropical rain forests combined, in the judgment of most experts, to begin to raise the temperature of the earth, probably as early as the nineteenth century and certainly by the twentieth century. Concern mounted about possible increases in the levels of oceans, damage to a variety of species, and possibly more violent weather, all as a result of what became known as global warming.

Also in the later twentieth century, new kinds of global political efforts became possible to address climate issues. The United Nations and other agencies called conferences and encouraged new agreements to reduce air pollution. Nongovernmental organizations (NGOs) like Greenpeace arose to stimulate world opinion and policymakers to take a more constructive environmental role. (Greenpeace was founded in 1971, initially to resist nuclear testing; its environmental concerns shifted by 2000.) Key international initiatives included the Kyoto agreements, from 1997, setting limits on greenhouse gas emissions by the industrial nations; these agreements had been ratified by over 150 countries by 2006—including Japan, Russia, and the European Union—but the United States held back.

All this occurred amid ongoing debate and some striking differences in levels of concern. Scientists did not always agree with each other on the data involved. Politicians and general publics varied in their response. Among other things, an obvious gulf arose between the United States and other industrial societies that produced mutual bad feeling and prevented full international accord.

The following documents suggest some of the positions involved, ranging from environmental advocacy to official American resistance. There are three sets: first, two scholars, writing in the 1990s, set up obviously contrasting views of recent global experience and global prospects. Then more recent materials raise the policy issues associated with global warming directly. Comparison in this sense is straightforward, but it invites more subtle analysis about the extent of basic differences, about the reasons for the differences, and, possibly, about how the differences might be resolved. Finally, a third set provides recent data on pollutant emissions and opinion polls.

Questions

1. What are the main contrasts between the approaches of Simon and Myers? How can two presumably reasonable scholars disagree so completely?
2. How does current American environmental policy compare to the positions of Simon and of Myers?
3. What are the key reasons American policymakers have resisted global calls for international agreements to reduce pollutant emission?
4. What is the role of NGOs like Greenpeace in the environmental debate? How do Greenpeace's goals compare to those of the United States?
5. What is the relationship between policy and policy statements, on one hand, and actual levels of pollution, on the other?
6. How do international opinion polls relate to different national policies? Which comes first, the policy or the public attitude?

For Further Discussion

1. Why are Americans less concerned about global warming than people in most other parts of the world?
2. Are there ways to reconcile the American and the international approaches? Is the disagreement significant for United States's interests?
3. How does modern environmental history fit into world history more generally? How does it fit into a historical understanding of globalization?

A Basic Debate

Julian Simon is a professor of business administration in the United States who has written widely on issues of population growth. Norman Myers, British born but partly educated in the United States, works mainly on the preservation of animal species; he has served as advisor to the World Bank and the World Wildlife Association. The debate from which the following materials derive was held at Columbia University in 1992.

• • •

JULIAN SIMON

The gloom-and-doom about a "crisis" of our environment is all wrong on the scientific facts. Even the Environmental Protection Agency acknowledges that our air and water have been getting cleaner rather than dirtier in the past few decades. Every agricultural economist knows that the world's population has been eating ever better since World War II. Every resource economist knows that all natural resources have been getting more available rather than more scarce, as shown by their falling prices over the decades and centuries. And every demographer knows that the death rate has been falling all over the world—life expectancy almost tripling in the rich countries in the past two centuries, and almost doubling in the poor countries in just the past four decades.

The picture also is now clear that population growth does not hinder economic development. In the 1980s there was a complete reversal in the consensus of thinking of population economists about the effects of more people. In 1986, the National Research Council and the National Academy of Sciences completely overturned their "official" view away from the earlier worried view expressed in 1971. They noted the absence of any statistical evidence of a negative connection between population increase and economic growth. And they said that "The scarcity of exhaustible resources is at most a minor restraint on economic growth." . . .

The most important and amazing demographic fact—the greatest human achievement in history, in my view—is the decrease in the world's death rate. . . .

Let's put it differently. In the nineteenth century, the planet Earth could sustain only 1 billion people. Ten thousand years ago, only 4 million could keep themselves alive. Now, more than 5 billion people are living longer and more healthily than ever before, on average. The increase in the world's population represents our victory over death.

I would expect lovers of humanity to jump with joy at this triumph of human mind and organization over the killing forces of nature. Instead, many lament that

From Norman Myers and Julian L. Simon, *Scarcity or Abundance? A Debate on the Environment* (New York, W.W. Norton, 1994).

there are so many people alive to enjoy the gift of life. Some even express regret over the fall in the death rate. . . .

So by any measure, natural resources have been getting more available rather than more scarce.

When we take a long-run view, the picture is different, and considerably more complex, from the simple short run view of more people implying lower average income. In the very long run, more people almost surely imply more available resources and a higher income for everyone.

I suggest you test this proposition as follows:

Do you think that our standard of living would be as high as it is now if the population had never grown from about 4 million human beings perhaps 10,000 years ago? I don't think we'd now have electric light or gas heat or autos or penicillin or travel to the Moon or our present life expectancy of over seventy years at birth in rich countries—in comparison to the life expectancy of twenty to twenty-five years at birth in earlier eras—if population had not grown to its present numbers. If population had never grown, instead of the pleasant lunch you had, you would have been chasing rabbits and digging roots.

NORMAN MYERS

I believe that, by contrast with Julian Simon, we are at a watershed in human history because of the grand-scale environmental degradation that is overtaking our planet in conjunction with excessive population growth and consumerism. Unless we change these trends and patterns, we are going to have a tough time of it. And not only us, but dozens and hundreds of human generations into the future. In fact, in the case of mass extinction of species, as many as 200,000 generations to come will be impoverished because of what we are doing during the present few decades. . . .

What do I mean when I speak of prospective environmental ruin worldwide? Let me give you a few quick statistics, all of them supported by reports from the World Bank, United Nations agencies, the Rockefeller Foundation, and organizations of similar reputable sort. Soil erosion: during the past year we have lost 25 billion tons of topsoil around the world—and it's as severe in parts of Indiana as in India. This lost topsoil has cost us 9 million tons of grain, enough to make up the diets of well over 200 million people who are "undernourished" (the jargon term for people who are semi-starving). Also during the past year we have lost 150,000 square kilometers of tropical forest, taking with them a host of watershed services. The economic costs are sizeable: in the Ganges Valley alone in India, deforestation in the Himalayan foothills causes downstream flooding that imposes costs that, according to the Government of India, amount to well over $1 billion per year. During the past year, too, desertification has totaled 60,000 square kilometers, taking out agricultural lands with potential food output worth $42 billion.

Also during the past year, we have lost tens of thousands of species, again with an economic cost. When you visit your neighborhood pharmacy, there is one chance in two that the product on the counter before you would not be there if it were not for startpoint materials from wild plants and animals. The commercial value of these products is more than $40 billion a year. Think, then, of what we are losing when we hear of tens of thousands of species disappearing every year.

In the past year too, we have depleted the ozone layer still further. We have taken a solid step toward a greenhouse-affected world. And at the same time our Earth has taken on board another 93 million people, equivalent to more than a "new Mexico"—and this at a time when our Earth is straining under the burden of its present population of 5.5 billion people. . . .

Policy Views

UNITED STATES

The two documents in this section involve a statement by President George W. Bush in 2001 and a brief policy summary from the U.S. Environmental Protection Agency in 2002.

• • •

Text of a Letter from the President to Senators Hagel, Helms, Craig, and Roberts.

Thank you for your letter asking for the Administration's views on global climate change, in particular the Kyoto Protocol and efforts to regulate carbon dioxide under the Clean Air Act. My Administration takes the issue of global climate change very seriously.

As you know, I oppose the Kyoto Protocol because it exempts 80 percent of the world, including major population centers such as China and India, from compliance, and would cause serious harm to the U.S. economy. The Senate's vote, 95-0, shows that there is a clear consensus that the Kyoto Protocol is an unfair and ineffective means of addressing global climate change concerns.

As you also know, I support a comprehensive and balanced national energy policy that takes into account the importance of improving air quality. Consistent with this balanced approach, I intend to work with the Congress on a multipollutant strategy to

From: http://www.whitehouse.gov/news/releases/2001/03/20010314.html.

require power plants to reduce emissions of sulfur dioxide, nitrogen oxides, and mercury. Any such strategy would include phasing in reductions over a reasonable period of time, providing regulatory certainty, and offering market-based incentives to help industry meet the targets. I do not believe, however, that the government should impose on power plants mandatory emissions reductions for carbon dioxide, which is not a "pollutant" under the Clean Air Act.

A recently released Department of Energy Report, "Analysis of Strategies for Reducing Multiple Emissions from Power Plants," concluded that including caps on carbon dioxide emissions as part of a multiple emissions strategy would lead to an even more dramatic shift from coal to natural gas for electric power generation and significantly higher electricity prices compared to scenarios in which only sulfur dioxide and nitrogen oxides were reduced.

This is important new information that warrants a reevaluation, especially at a time of rising energy prices and a serious energy shortage. Coal generates more than half of America's electricity supply. At a time when California has already experienced energy shortages, and other Western states are worried about price and availability of energy this summer, we must be very careful not to take actions that could harm consumers. This is especially true given the incomplete state of scientific knowledge of the causes of, and solutions to, global climate change and the lack of commercially available technologies for removing and storing carbon dioxide.

Consistent with these concerns, we will continue to fully examine global climate change issues—including the science, technologies, market-based systems, and innovative options for addressing concentrations of greenhouse gases in the atmosphere. I am very optimistic that, with the proper focus and working with our friends and allies, we will be able to develop technologies, market incentives, and other creative ways to address global climate change.

I look forward to working with you and others to address global climate change issues in the context of a national energy policy that protects our environment, consumers, and economy.

Sincerely,
GEORGE W. BUSH

Environmental Protection Agency

THE BUSH ADMINISTRATION'S ENVIRONMENTAL PHILOSOPHY

The focus is on results—making our air, water, and land cleaner.

We need to employ the best science and data to inform our decision-making.

From http://www.whitehouse.gov/infocus/environment/key_bush_environmental_accomplishments.pdf.

Our policies should encourage innovation and the development of new, cleaner technologies.

We should continue to build on America's ethic of stewardship and personal responsibility through education and volunteer opportunies, and in our daily lives.

Opportunities for environmental improvements are not limited to Federal Government actions—states, tribes, local communities, and individuals must be included.

BUILDING ON OUR GREAT ENVIRONMENTAL PROGRESS

Over the last 30 years, our Nation has made great progress in providing for a better environment and improving public health. In that time, our economy grew 164 percent, population grew 39 percent, and our energy consumption increased 42 percent, yet air pollution from the six major pollutants decreased by 48 percent. In 2002, state data reported to EPA showed that approximately 251 million people (or 94 percent of the total population) were served by community water systems that met all health-based standards. This number is up from 79 percent in 1993.

JAPAN AND EUROPE

The Japanese Minister of Foreign Affairs, Nobutaka Machimura, provided remarks in October 2005. A European Union statement was issued in 2006. Both statements were addressed to international meetings on the environment.

MACHIMURA Nobutaka, Minister for Foreign Affairs of Japan
On the occasion of the Fourth Informal Meeting on
Further Actions against Climate Change

Climate change is a serious and long-term challenge that has the potential to affect every part of the globe, and human activities are contributing to the increases in greenhouse gases. We all know that concrete and urgent actions are required to arrest the rise of greenhouse gas emissions around the world. In February this year, the Kyoto Protocol entered into force. This means all Annex I ratifiers of the Protocol are now bound by the international law to meet their quantified greenhouse gas emissions reduction under the Protocol. For our part, the Government of Japan formulated the Kyoto Protocol Target Achievement Plan in April in order to firmly achieve its reduction target of 6%. The Plan pursues the balance between the environment and

From http://mofa.go.jp/policy/environment/warm/cop/message0510.html.

economic growth mainly through promoting technological innovations, improving energy efficiency, and collaboration by all stakeholders. Japan is strongly committed to meet its reduction goal.

The Kyoto Protocol is an important step to tackle the issue of climate change, but it is just a first step. We know further efforts have to be made for the long-term mitigation of greenhouse gases, in order to meet the ultimate objective, namely, the stabilization of greenhouse gas concentrations at a safer level. To achieve this goal, we must construct an encouraging and enabling framework, instead of a punitive one, so that both developing and developed countries will play active roles in intensive efforts to reduce greenhouse gases beyond the first commitment period of the Kyoto Protocol.

European Union

The World Meteorological Organization recently issued a report indicating that concentrations of carbon dioxide and other greenhouse gases in the atmosphere are at their highest levels ever. There are many concrete signs that this is already having consequences for climate and nature. The Artic ice is melting at an alarming rate. Last September, the ice cap had retreated a record 250 km north of Alaska. If this continues, there may be no ice at all during the summer of 2060. In this morning's edition of *Le Soir,* we can read of the Greenland ice disappearing much faster than expected. With glaciers moving 2500 metres per year instead of 300 there is a real possibility that the impact of climate change will be far worse than even our more radical models.

The economic impacts are also vast. The Association of British Insurers estimates that, by 2080, insured losses from hurricanes in the US alone could reach US$ 100–150 billion a year. And the changing climate will radically modify the basis for many of our core economic activities, such as agriculture, energy production and transport.

The scientific debate about the human causes of climate change is largely settled. Yet there remains an important gap between climate science and the global policy response. We cannot afford such gap. I believe there is now a window of opportunity to mobilize the world's key leaders in favour of an alliance agaist climate change. There is a high level of consensus on the need to act. Views still diverge on the adequate policy and approach, but few still doubt the need for a global response to climate change.

The EU is ready to engage in an open and constructive dialogue with all partners and major emitting countries. We must seize this opportunity and together provide a forward looking strategy for the future climate co-operation post-2012.

The EU will deliver on its climate policy and target of an 8% reduction in emissions of greenhouse gases. By 2004, the EU had cut its emission by 1%. With the additional measures planned in the second phase of the European Climate Change Programme, we should meet our 8% target, and maybe even overshoot it. This should be compared to significant emission increases in many parts of the world, including the US.

With a share of only 14% in global greenhouse gas emissions, the EU cannot resolve the problem on its own. But we are determined to demonstrate that pro-active climate policies give results, and that they do not endanger economic growth. . . .

Meeting the climate challenge requires efforts to reduce global emission by the widest possible group of industrialized countries and major developing nations. We of course expect the United States—as the world's main emitter of greenhouse gases with levels well above 1990—to take strong and resolute action on climate change, and I believe there are encouraging signs on the other side of the Atlantic.

GREENPEACE

The following announcement was provided to the international press in November 2005.

• • •

Time Is Running Out!

Greenpeace today unveiled a four metres tall hourglass outside the UN Climate Change Conference in Montreal to remind the arriving delegates that time is running out. The climate summit—the first since the Kyoto Protocol entered into force—opens today, beginning two weeks of crucial negotiations on climate protection.

"Time is running out for the climate. Climate change is not a distant problem to be dealt with sometime in the future. In fact we have very little time left to avoid the most catastrophic impacts. Without prompt, decisive action from governments here we will soon find ourselves riding a runaway train and it will be impossible to apply the brakes," said Stephanie Tunmore, Greenpeace International Climate Campaigner in Montreal. If climate change goes unchecked many of its effects will be irreversible. Glaciers in western China are expected to have largely disappeared by 2100; summer sea ice in the Arctic could be lost well before the end of the century according to some models, leaving polar bears, ice-dependent seals, walruses and certain sea-birds facing extinction; and over the next several decades there is a risk that regional climate changes combined with the effects of forest clearing could flip the ecosystems of the Amazon from forest to grassland or desert.

Greenpeace believes that the goal of climate policy should be to keep global average temperature rise to below 2°C above pre-industrial levels, a position also adopted by the European Union Heads of Government. It is still economically and scientifically possible to do this with known technological means. The decisions made in Montreal will determine whether or not those options remain viable.

From http://www.greenpeace.org/international/press/releases/time-is-running-out.

Greenpeace also believes that by strengthening and expanding the Kyoto Protocol for the next phase (2013–2017) a strong signal will be sent that will increase confidence in the carbon market and encourage business to invest in low carbon technology. The process for this should begin here in Montreal and be completed by 2008.

"The 156 Governments who have ratified the Kyoto Protocol now have the obligation to show that they mean it. They must get on with negotiating the next phase of Kyoto, with much stronger emission reduction targets for industrialised countries. We hold this planet in trust for our children and our children's children. Are we really prepared to look them in the eye and say 'Sorry, we just ran out of time'?" concluded Tunmore.

Greenpeace is an independent, campaigning organisation, which uses non-violent, creative confrontation to expose global environmental problems, and to force solutions essential to a green and peaceful future.

ENVIRONMENTAL DATA AND OPINION SURVEYS

The following tables, derived from United Nations data, show regional issues in the area of environmental pollution, and should be juxtaposed with policies and opinions stemming from different regions as well.

• • •

TABLE 36.1 GLOBAL EMISSIONS IN 2000

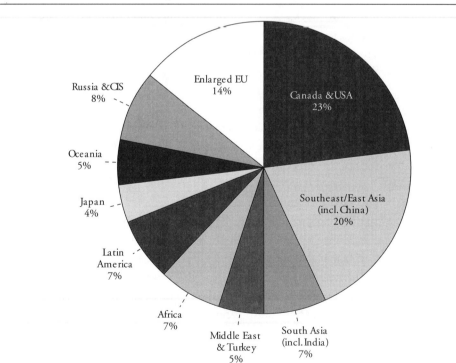

TABLE 36.2 GLOBAL GREENHOUSE GAS EMISSION PROJECTIONS*

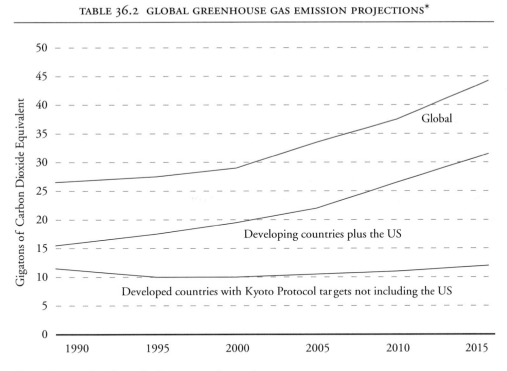

*Projections are based on a business-as-usual scenario.

TABLE 36.3 GLOBAL WARMING CONCERNS

	A Great Deal %	A Fair Amount %	Only a Little/Not At All %	DK %
United States	19	34	47	1
Great Britain	26	41	32	1
Spain	51	34	14	2
France	46	41	14	0
Germany	30	34	36	1
Russia	34	31	34	-
Indonesia	28	48	23	1
Egypt	24	51	23	1
Jordan	26	40	34	-
Turkey	41	29	23	8
Pakistan	31	25	39	5
Nigeria	45	33	20	2
Japan	66	27	7	0
India	65	20	13	2
China	20	41	37	2

Based on those who have heard about the "environmental problem of global warming."

TABLE 36.4 INTERNATIONAL NEWS STORIES PEOPLE HAVE—
AND HAVE NOT—HEARD ABOUT

	The Bird Flu Diseases	Global Warming
United States	92	91
Germany	100	95
France	100	97
Britain	97	100
Spain	99	93
Russia	98	80
Jordan	98	48
Egypt	96	47
Turkey	97	75
Indonesia	99	35
Pakistan	82	12
Nigeria	82	42
Japan	99	99
China	93	78
India	99	57

Percent who *have* heard of each news item.
Adapted from a United Nations survey, summer 2006.

ABOUT THE EDITOR

PETER N. STEARNS is Provost and Professor of History at George Mason University. He introduced a world history course in the mid-1980s, and has taught it every semester since. He has written a number of texts and essays in world history, and has contributed to world history projects for the College Board and other agencies. He is an active member of the World History Association. He is also past Vice President of the American Historical Association and its Teaching Division. A social historian by training, he has written over fifty books on topics in U.S. and European social history as well as world history. At Carnegie Mellon, he has won the university's major teaching prize and has been active in various aspects of curriculum planning. He is also increasingly interested in approaches to training students in the skills of historical analysis, including comparison, and has participated in a number of innovative exercises and assessments.